HIGH

Also by Erika Fatland in English translation

Sovietistan (2019)

The Border (2020)

Erika Fatland

HIGH

A journey across the Himalayas
through Pakistan, India, Bhutan, Nepal and China

Translated from the Norwegian by
Kari Dickson

MACLEHOSE PRESS
QUERCUS · LONDON

First published in the Norwegian language as *Høyt: En Reise i Himalaya* by
Kagge Forlag, Oslo, in 2020

First published in Great Britain in 2022 by

MacLehose Press
An imprint of Quercus Editions Limited
Carmelite House
50 Victoria Embankment
London EC4Y 0DZ

An Hachette UK company

This translation has been published with the financial support of NORLA

The moral right of Erika Fatland to be identified as the author of this work has been
asserted in accordance with the Copyright, Designs and Patents Act, 1988.

Kari Dickson asserts her moral right to be identified as
the translator of the work.

A CIP catalogue record for this book is available from the British Library.

ISBN (HB) 978 1 52941 687 9
ISBN (TPB) 978 1 52941 688 6
ISBN (Ebook) 978 1 52941 690 9

10 9 8 7 6 5 4 3 2 1

Designed and typeset in Albertina by Libanus Press, Marlborough
Printed and bound in Great Britain by Clays Ltd, Elcograf S.p.A.

Papers used by Quercus Books are from well-managed forests and
other responsible sources.

For my adventurous grandparents:

Solfrid Grønnestad
Erik "Bessen" Grønnestad (died 2019)
&
Ragnhild Fatland
Ole Fatland (died 2020)

CONTENTS

SECOND STAGE

LIST OF ILLUSTRATIONS

India

1. Kashmir: the floating vegetable market in Srinagar
2. Kashmir: "If there is a paradise on earth, it is this, it is this, it is this."
3. The Golden Temple in Amritsar.
4. Haji Hassan has stayed in the same place, despite the wars that have come and gone and the borders that have moved back and forth.
5. Regimented in death: the Indian military cemetery in Drass, a memorial to the first war between two nuclear powers in the history of the world.
6. The Spiti Valley in India, "Little Tibet": the road into the valley is, if possible, even more dramatic than the scenery.
7. Altitude with attitude: all the roads were closed and the valley was cut off by unexpected extreme weather in the region.
8. A young boy on the threshold of monastery life.
9. The author chose not to share this photograph with her family until she had returned from the Spiti Valley.
10. Mini nuns reading diligently during morning prayers.
11. The Fab Four: spiritual tourism in Rishikesh. The maharishi was not there when the mural was painted.
12. The young Ganges flows down to the lowlands: sunset ceremony in Hardiwar.
13. A pilgrim washes himself in the clean, ice-cold water.
14. Royal hospitality: Semla, the former princess of Sikkim.

Bhutan

1. During the day, the dances are performed by monks – in clothes. At night, things get wilder.
2. Universal characters: the Clown . . .
3. . . . and Death.
4. Loneliness in ambient lighting: young men in Mongar sing karaoke for absent women.
5. Darts as an action sport: archery is Bhutan's national sport, but darts is not far behind, at number two.
6. Double hospitality: Two happy sisters in Merak.
7. The enormous Buddha outside Thimpu welcomes visitors to the city with huge serenity.
8. The phallus is a remarkably common symbol in Bhutan.
9. On the edge between beauty and destruction: the Tiger's Nest, one of the most sacred temples in the Himalayas, clings to the mountainside.

10. The peculiar takin, Bhutan's national animal, is a goat antelope, or gnu goat. The outside world thought for a long time that it was a mythical beast, like the yeti.

India
1. King for a new era: Towei Phawang, angh of the Konyak people, in his house that straddles the India–Myanmar border.
2. Apatani women from the Ziro Valley, Arunachal Pradesh.

SECOND STAGE

Nepal
1. Kathmandu Valley: the goddess inhabits them. Matina (above left), royal kumari 2008–2017; Chanira (below), kumari 2000–2010, and Dhana (above right), who never stopped being a living goddess.
2. Death machine: Everest Base Camp, 5,364 MSL. The treacherous Khumbu Icefall, which all the climbers have to navigate on their way up to the Holy Mother, can be seen behind the enormous camp on a black glacier.
3. Necessary companions: everything has to be carried up on tired backs.
4. Living military legends: the Brigade of Gurkhas. Hopeful aspirants.
5. More than seven hundred temples and historical monuments were damaged by the earthquake in 2015. The extensive restoration work will take many years yet.
6. Angel Lama – proud winner of Nepal's first trans beauty contest.
7. This goat kid will have a short life.
8. In another world: possessed by the gods, shamans dance for the people of Turmakhad.
9. Local reformer: Shoudana, the shaman in Simikot, has reduced the number of days that women have to sleep in a menstruation hut from nine to five.

China
1. The border: Upper Mustang to the left and Tibet to the right of the barbed-wire fence.
2. Tibet: high-altitude and barren, with one of the driest climates in Asia. The photograph is from the area that was once the Guge kingdom.

3. Reverent prayer at the journey's end: two Indian pilgrims arrive at Lake Manasarovar, which is so holy that its water can wash away the sins of a hundred lives.
4. Thousands of pilgrims from all over Tibet meet at the holy Mount Kailash to see the flag pole being raised during Saga Dawa, in the holiest of all months. These women have with them prayer flags and prayer wheels.
5. Thousands of pilgrims walk around the holy mountain. Every Tibetan should make a pilgrimage to Kailash at least twice in their lives. Bad weather is no obstacle.
6. Above the tree line: a few blades of grass among the stones. Mount Everest can be seen in the background.
7. Lhasa today: a modern, Chinese provincial city on Tibetan soil.
8. The mighty Potala Palace, which no longer houses the Dalai Lama.
9. There are prayer flags and butter lamps everywhere, as countless as the prayers and hopes of the devout Tibetans.
10. Tiger Leaping Gorge: China's mass tourism at home.
11. In the Kingdom of Women, the maternal grandmother is boss. Kumu welcomes me to her grandmother room. She loves having visitors.

A Bad Omen

It was early in the morning and the **mountain plain** was already teem- 4750 MSL
ing with joyful Tibetans. Delicate snowflakes pirouetted in the thin air.
In the middle of the plain, a long pole, wrapped in yak hide and colourful prayer flags, lay propped at a gentle angle on a structure of staves.
At twenty-five metres, it is the tallest flagpole in Tibet. Long, thick
ropes had been tethered to the solid wooden pole and laid out neatly
along the ground, ready for the pole setters. Two trucks, which looked
absurdly out of place among all the festivities, were there to help.

Several thousand people had gathered, many having travelled for
days, crossing the mountain range to reach this holiest of holy mountains in the middle of this holy month, Saga Dawa. Buddhists believe
that the effects of everything they do in this month, both good and
bad, will be amplified tenfold. And on this day, the fifteenth day of Saga
Dawa, the most sacred day of all, the day when the Buddha was born
and also the day he entered Nirvana, their actions are multiplied a
hundred times over.

The women wore handwoven woollen dresses and silk shirts, with
heavy silver jewellery, and the men wore knee-length fur or silk coats,
and big hats. Their painstaking hairstyles and colourful costumes
indicated where they were from in Tibet – how far they had travelled.
But even more impressive than the lengths of their journeys was
the fact that they had managed to collect all the papers, stamps and
signatures necessary to cross the many invisible district boundaries
and get through all the checks in order to be here, now, this very
morning, as the delicate snowflakes danced in the air. The Chinese

authorities fear the Tibetans' deep, religious faith because they cannot control it, and they are particularly afraid of events like this, when thousands of believers from even the most isolated villages gather.

The authorities were present in force. Groups of riot police, in heavy knee pads, helmets and bullet-proof vests, equipped with batons and shields, marched back and forth past the children and prayer flags. Grim-faced policemen watched over the pilgrims queuing to be blessed by the monks at the small temple that stood on a slope above the plateau. They were there to make sure that everything was orderly, that no-one jumped the queue, or stood talking to a monk for too long; that things kept moving and progressed at a satisfactory pace. The monks sat in a long line, dressed in their red and saffron robes and large hats, beating their drums, blowing their horns or bowed over handwritten manuscripts as they chanted quietly.

Down on the plain, the crowd moved slowly around the flagpole, with prayer wheels and beads in their hands as they mumbled the sacred mantra: *Om mani padme hum, om mani padme hum.* The young and old prostrated themselves, arms above their heads in prayer, then stood up and walked a few steps before prostrating themselves again. *Om mani padme hum.* I let myself be pulled along by the current, by the flow, and circled the pole with the pilgrims, enveloped in colour and prayer. *Om mani padme hum.* Time ceased, time drifted, time was the snowflakes that swirled in the air.

The pole setters took up their positions, each by their given rope. The crowd stood still and watched the men in anticipation, as they pulled and tested the ropes.

Ki-ki-so-so! the onlookers murmured in encouragement, softly at first, then louder and louder. *Ki-ki-so-so! Ki-ki-so-so-lha-Gyalo!* Victory to the gods! Slowly the pole rose up to the sky, helped by the pole setters and two trucks. *So-so-so!* When, a few minutes later, the flagpole had been raised upright, the pilgrims exploded with ecstatic cries: *Ki-ki-so-so!* Paper prayer flags were thrown up into the air together with the toasted barley flour known as tsampa. Soon I was covered in flour; we were all covered in flour. The crowd started to move again in a wide circle round the pole, thousands of open, beaming faces. They started to move faster and faster. *Ki-ki-so-so!* The atmosphere was electric. Once again, I allowed myself to be pulled along by the throng, round the pole, enveloped in joy and finely ground tsampa.

I stopped to take one last picture before I went back to Jinpa, my guide, who was waiting up by the prayer flags at the temple. Technically, I wasn't allowed to be more than five metres from him, as the police had told me at an information meeting the day before; foreigners had to be controlled. But Jinpa was quite relaxed and generally let me do as I pleased.

I got out my camera, pressed the shutter button and managed to capture the flagpole in free fall for ever.

There was complete silence. Everyone stopped, and stood staring at the fallen flagpole, which lay at an awkward angle on the ground, presumably broken. No-one called *ki-ki-so-so*, no-one threw tsampa or prayer flags into the air. Some were weeping. Others merely stared, paralysed by shock.

I found Jinpa, who had fallen to his knees.

"This has never happened before," he said gravely. "Never, in three hundred years. The flagpole has occasionally been crooked, not entirely upright, and that was always interpreted as a bad omen for the coming year. But this . . . This is a very bad omen. *Very* bad. For those of us who are here, for the whole of Tibet."

The monks by the temple continued to recite mantras in deep, penetrating voices, but now with knitted brows. The men who only minutes before had raised the flagpole and been lauded as heroes now wandered around in a daze, glancing over at the broken wood in dismay.

Jinpa stood up and looked at me. His eyes were glassy.

"Come," he said, his eyes wet. "We have to start walking. We have a long way to go."

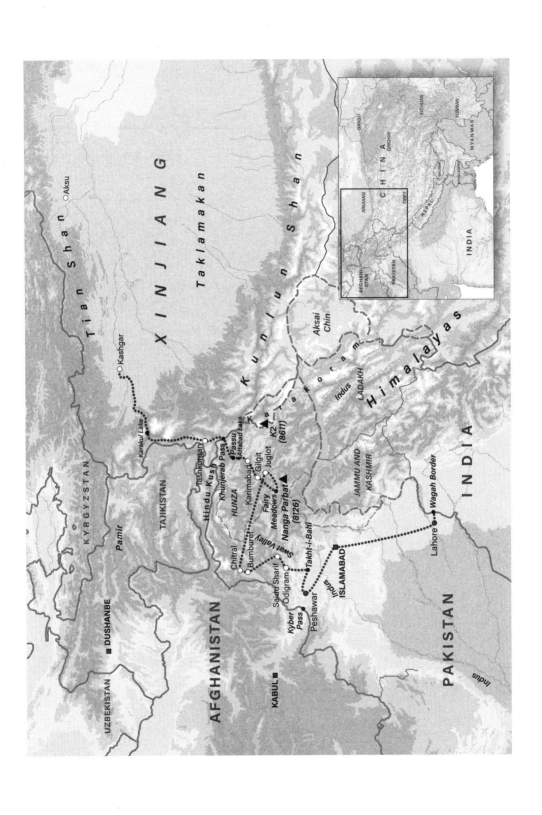

FIRST STAGE

July–December 2018

"If there is a paradise on earth,
it is this, it is this, it is this."
Ascribed to the poet Hazrat Amir Khusrau

The New Silk Road

Where does a mountain start and finish, or a mountain range, or a journey?

If one looks at the mountains in Asia on a physical map – a topographical map without names – one sees the surface of the earth, frozen movements and waves in the geology, geometric patterns and fractals. But no beginning and no end, no clear delimitation.

The mountains we know as the Himalayas, which in Sanskrit means "abode of the snow", lie like an enormous, curved barrier of rock massifs, glaciers and deep valleys between the Eurasian continent to the north, where Siberia's undulating, forested wilderness slips into the steppes and deserts of Kazakhstan, Mongolia and China, and the Indian subcontinent to the south, stretching from Pakistan in the west to Myanmar in the east. At the northern end of the Himalayas lies the Tibetan mountain plateau; at the southern end, towards India and Pakistan, the range ends more abruptly, like a shield of towering peaks. Less than a century ago, the steep mountainsides were home to a patchwork of small mountain kingdoms, most of which have now been swallowed by the large, powerful states. The only one that remains is the kingdom of Bhutan.

On the ground, as well as on the map, the mountain massif has no defined start or finish. To the west, the Himalayas are linked to the Pamir, Karakoram and Hindu Kush mountain ranges. Would it then be more correct to say that the mountain chain starts at the Shibar Pass in Afghanistan, where the Hindu Kush perhaps ends, or at Nanga Parbat in Pakistan, the highest mountain to the west before the range ceases to be called the Himalayas? In Kyrgyzstan, the Pamir Mountains meet Tian Shan, the Celestial Mountains, which to the north become the Altai Mountains and to the east seamlessly become a mountain range called Sayan that ends at the Sea of Okhotsk in the east. Could one then say that the Himalayas actually end, or perhaps start, by the Pacific Ocean?

And if one was to widen the picture even more, it could be argued that the Himalayas are part of the Alpine orogeny, which started some sixty to eighty million years ago when the African and Indo-Australian tectonic plates collided with Eurasia to the north, and initially gave rise to the Caucasus Mountains, the Taurus Mountains, the Alps, the Pyrenees and the Atlas Mountains, and later to the Pamir Mountains, the Hindu Kush, the Karakoram – and the Himalayas. If one includes the extended family of Alpine mountain ranges, the Himalayas and its relatives, close and distant, stretch from the Atlantic Ocean in the west to the Pacific Ocean in the east.

Whichever definition one chooses, no-one would say that the 1270 MSL Himalayas start in the old Silk Road city of **Kashgar** in China's Xinjiang Province, in the middle of the dry Tarim Basin, about as far west in China as it is possible to go. But that is where *my* journey to the Himalayas began, and the prologue was rather longer than planned. I could not follow the Silk Road south to the Himalayas until I had a piece of paper that would allow me to travel freely over the pass into Pakistan. The Indians were primarily to blame for the delay, and all I could do was wait, patiently.

I had applied for an Indian visa well in advance of my departure date, but the process was never-ending, as the embassy kept asking for more and more information: where was I going to stay, where was I going to go, how was I going to travel, who was I travelling with, why was I going to India in the first place? This continued until, eventually, I no longer had plenty of time; in fact, time was running out. I gave up on the Indian embassy and concentrated on the Pakistan embassy instead, but they were slow as well. Some of the staff were on holiday, apparently. They might be able to issue a visa the following week, or the week after. Then, suddenly, it was time to go and I boarded the plane for China as planned, and was given entry with my emergency passport. My main passport was still at the Pakistan embassy in Oslo. Unlike their colleagues from south of the mountains, the Chinese bureaucrats were a brilliant example of efficiency and my visa application had been fast-tracked, as ordered. So there I was, stuck in Kashgar, waiting for the Pakistan consular section in Oslo to return from their holidays and for my real passport with the magic piece of paper to arrive so that I could start my journey to the mountains.

Such are the prosaic problems of the modern traveller. The transport part takes no time at all these days; it is the bureaucracy that is interminable. We are constantly being told that we live in a world without borders, in a globalised age, but only if you have the right passport and the right papers. What do adventurous globetrotters talk about when they meet? They talk about bureaucracy, about consulates, about visa extensions and application procedures.

While I waited to continue my journey, I walked around the quiet streets of Kashgar. At the entrance to the city's most important landmark, the pale-yellow Id Kah Mosque, I was stopped by a stern policeman.

"Passport!" he barked. The right papers are also needed to enter God's house these days.

"It's back at the hotel," I said.

"Then I can't let you in," he said. "And you're not allowed to take photographs inside the mosque," he added, gruffly. "Photography is strictly forbidden."

I wandered back out onto the large, newly renovated square. A handful of grey-haired men were sitting in the shade of some trees, listening to the call to prayer on a mobile phone. Down by the road, three Chinese children were clinging onto the humps of a scabby camel while their parents eagerly documented the occasion. Otherwise, the place was deserted.

There was a subway to the other side of the busy road. There in the half-dark was another ID checkpoint. The Chinese tourists and I were waved on past the metal detector; only the native Uighurs were made to queue for a full check. As a matter of course, they put their bags on the conveyor belt, scanned their ID cards and looked into the camera. Back out in the daylight, by the entrance to the famous old town, there was yet another ID check. Once again, I was waved in past a queue of local women and children.

At the market inside the old town, one of the stalls sold pomegranate juice, another had round flatbreads on display, some offered noodles, skewers of meat and steamed mutton, while others again tempted with juicy honeydew melons, sun-ripened apricots and large bunches of grapes. The smell of food hung heavy over the market, and eager Chinese tourists thronged around the monumental pots of meat. Kashgar is known far and wide for its lively markets – in many ways, the entire city is one great bazaar. On every street corner was someone selling something edible from a stall. The women traders were dressed in big, flowery dresses, the older men in colourful, round hats. Flocks of Chinese tourists photographed the exotic locals with semi-professional, half-metre lenses. As Kashgar is one of China's western outposts, and the city is closer to Baghdad than Beijing, many of them were a long way from home.

I navigated my way through all the food stalls and slipped into one of the narrow alleyways. The old town did not look big on the map, but I immediately got lost in the winding, labyrinthine streets. Everywhere I looked there were traditional, light-brown adobe buildings. Small girls in princess dresses ran up to me to touch my hair, calling *ni hao*; a couple were even brave enough to say a shy *hello*. Old women sat in the doorways drinking tea. They smiled and said *salaam* as I passed.

The tourist authorities had posted signs and maps everywhere, but they were of little help, as they gave no names, they simply showed the various routes that could be followed through the labyrinth. Route 1, route 2, route 3. Every now and then I came across Chinese tourists with selfie sticks and headwear to protect them from the sun, but for the most part I was alone with gaggles of laughing children and wrinkled grandmothers. The dusty streets twisted hither and thither; the quaint alleyways all looked like something from *A Thousand and One Nights*. This, I thought, this – minus the maps and selfie sticks, and with more camels and donkeys – must be what Kashgar was like almost two thousand years ago, when merchants had just started to transport silk, paper, spices and other lucrative goods along the caravan routes from east to west.

When, at the turn of the century, the film crew behind *The Kite Runner* was looking for somewhere to film that was safer than Kabul, they chose Kashgar, the best-preserved and largest Islamic old town in Central Asia. Nearly two decades later they would probably have had to look for something more authentic. Had I not known, I might not have noticed, because the work was so well done, with such apparent respect for tradition. But all the angles and corners were straight. All the adobe walls were perfect, without a single blemish, without any unevenness. Every now and then I came across steps that led nowhere, or streets that stopped dead at the city wall, as the street grid had been drastically altered. And apart from the laughing children who followed me, the streets were largely empty.

Kashgar's famous old town is nothing more than a decorative stage set now. Beautiful and atmospheric, but in reality brand new.

The evacuation and demolition of the old town started in 2009. According to the Chinese authorities, the buildings were not safe in the event of an earthquake, and they were in desperate need of an upgrade and modernisation. But instead of renovating the old buildings that had stood for centuries, the Chinese, true to style, set to with bulldozers. And they were thorough. More than sixty-five thousand houses were pulled down and more than two hundred thousand people lost their homes. Many of them now live in small, modern flats in characterless tower blocks on the outskirts of the city.

When I had been wandering around for a bit more than an hour, I found myself back at the massive entrance to the old town, which was also brand new. A sign in Uighur, Chinese and English said that it was the gateway to Kashgar Old City. The five As to the left of the gateway meant this was a five-star attraction, an honour bestowed in 2014 when the brand-new old town was finished.

On the other side of the street, a tiny part of the original old town had been left untouched. There was no sense of orderliness here. Most of the buildings were built higgledy-piggledy on top of each other and were in a state of ruin. The remains of the city wall looked more like a dried mudslide than a wall, and any space between the buildings was full of rubbish. I was prevented from entering by four policemen. They were sitting smoking in the shade of a parasol and it was obvious that their only task was to stop tourists from going into the old old town. I tried to tease out of them why there was no access, but to no avail: the policemen spoke only Chinese. A large sign by the table said in three languages, one of which was a kind of English, that entry was forbidden: REMINDER: DEAR VISITOR, DUE TO THE HATHPACE FOLK HOUSE IS DRESSING UP, CAN NOT ENTER INSIDE, PLEASE FORGIVE ME. The Chinese have complete confidence in automatic computer translations. Chinese tourists were also stopped, but Uighur women with young children at their heels were allowed to pass.

However, no-one stopped me from walking *around* the remains of Kashgar's crumbling old town. To begin with, I harboured a hope that I might find another, less official way in, but there was a policeman at every entrance, no matter how narrow and wretched.

Occasionally I caught a glimpse in through the windows of the crooked, tumbledown buildings. The people inside were drinking tea or watching television. *State* television, I presume. Only recently, not watching the state television channel had been identified as a sign of extremism, as had fasting during Ramadan and giving a newborn baby an Islamic name. In terms of statistics, there was a considerable chance that some of the TV viewers lounging on the sofas in these slums were Han Chinese, parachuted in from more central parts of China to teach the Muslim population of the Wild West how to live modern lives that followed the party line.

George Orwell's dystopia from 1948 pales in comparison with Xinjiang Province in 2018.

It was Donald Duck who first introduced me to the Himalayas. Just as my travels to Central Asia and all the countries ending in "stan" were perhaps inspired by Donald's many escapades in Farawaystan, the seeds for my current expedition had been sown by Carl Barks. As a child, I fell asleep with Donald Duck and I woke up with Donald Duck – in fact, I actually learned to read with Donald Duck. My father only ever read Donald Duck magazines to me in bed, and when he fell asleep, which he often did, I would have to carry on reading by myself.

When I got older, I of course read other things, and I was fascinated by the home atlas. We did not have a globe, but we had several thick atlases. In my imagination, I travelled all over these maps, and nowhere were the names more magical than in the brown and white mountain range between India and China: *Hindu Kush. Thimpu. Lhasa. Hunza. Kathmandu. Sikkim. Karakoram. Annapurna.* And the most beautiful name of all: *Himalaya.* I never tired of repeating the sounds to myself: *Hi-ma-la-ya.*

In one of my favourite stories from Duckburg, Carl Barks allows Uncle Scrooge to have a breakdown. His condition is serious: he can no longer bear to look at or hear about money. In the end, Donald and his nephews take Scrooge to the hidden valley of Tralla La high up in the Himalayas, where apparently money does not exist. The valley is so isolated that they can only parachute in, but all their efforts pay off: they find an earthly paradise, where the people are joyful, happy and harmonious.

There are not many places in the world that are as shrouded in myth as the Himalayas. The mountains were a final frontier for many explorers. Even at the start of the twentieth century, Western adventurers continued to dress up as local merchants and pilgrims in the hope of getting to Lhasa, Tibet's legendary capital, and for several decades after flags had been staked in both the South and the North Pole, the highest peaks of the Himalayas remained unconquered. Then there were all the stories and mysticism. Books about hidden valleys where no-one got old and no-one died, where everyone lived in enlightened harmony and possessed deep insight and great wisdom, flew off the shelves of bookshops in Paris, London and New York.

Uncle Scrooge did not stay long in Tralla La. He had taken with him some bottles of medication in case he had a relapse, and the locals became obsessed with the bottle tops, which they considered to be rare treasures, so they started to barter with them. In order to solve this problem, Uncle Scrooge had planes drop a billion bottle tops in the valley. The fields were covered in bottle tops, and this proved to be too much of a good thing. The inhabitants were furious, and the ducks had no choice but to flee from the valley.

When I started travelling at nineteen, my first choice was obvious: I had to see the Himalayas. My meeting with the chaotic streets of Kathmandu, where the tourist shops jostle for space, and the Tibetan villages in Annapurna, where pizza and spaghetti are on the menu, left me disgusted but wanting more. Many years later, I went to Bhutan, and discovered a very different Himalayan reality, but this too had been modified and cushioned to suit the modern, Western explorer.

I sensed and had read that the Himalayas were so much more than this, much more than the dream of paradise for spiritual tourists or mountaineers. The cultural and linguistic diversity is enormous, as large and small ethnic groups have sought refuge over the centuries in the remote, inaccessible valleys, where many of them have remained more or less undisturbed to the present day. Mountaineers write about the mountains they climb and their own exertions; explorers more often than not write more about themselves than the societies they "discover". The Himalayas are not only high, they are also long; the range crosses five countries, from China and India in the north, through Bhutan and Nepal, to Pakistan in the north-west. I wanted to discover what life stories and cultures were to be found there, beyond the well-trodden paths, high up in the valleys and villages of the mountains with the beautiful name.

Soon I would travel both far and high.

But first, I had to get the holy grail that was my visa. The people at the Pakistani embassy in Oslo were still on holiday, and the week rolled into the weekend and on to Sunday, the day of the legendary livestock market in Kashgar. I took a taxi from the centre and followed the pungent smell of cattle past the melon sellers and butchers, until I came to the livestock. At the entrance to this part of the market, I was stopped by three policemen, who all pointed sternly at my camera.

"No photos!" they shouted in unison.

"Why?" I asked, but got no answer other than being told again, "No photos!" It made no sense. The livestock market in Kashgar is famous for being one of the best and most interesting in the world. People travelled from afar with suitcases full of expensive camera equipment to experience it for themselves.

The market area itself reeked of fur, faeces and fear. The place was heaving with sheep and fine oxen and the odd obstreperous donkey. The animals stood cheek by jowl, tied to the temporary fences or squashed together on truck beds. People were shouting and bartering everywhere, fistfuls of banknotes were counted and exchanged. The men had calloused hands and were dressed in dirty work clothes. The women wore long dresses covered in shit. Here and there I came across Chinese tourists wearing face masks. None of them paid any heed to the fact that photography was not allowed, and the farmers did not seem to mind being photographed – they were too busy for that. The police tended to stay in their guardhouse by the entrance, at a safe distance from the cowpats, sheep droppings – and tourists.

Kashgar and trade are more or less synonymous. The city's strategic location at the base of the Pamir Mountains meant that whoever controlled Kashgar also controlled the trade routes west to Persia and south to Kashmir. There were caravan routes from Kashgar to Xian in the north-east and Kazakhstan in the north. Marco Polo, who passed through the city on his expedition to China in the thirteenth century, described Kashgar as "the finest and largest"[1] city in the region.

Kashgar's history is long and turbulent. Over the centuries, the city has been ruled by the Greco-Bactrian Kushan dynasty, Tibetan kings, Chinese emperors, Arabic caliphates, Mongolian khanates and Turkish dynasties. The Chinese did not dominate until the eighteenth century: Xinjiang Province, and therefore also the city of Kashgar, was not permanently incorporated into the Chinese empire until 1757. Xinjiang means "new frontier".

Xinjiang is the most westerly province in China, and the biggest by far: it covers an area that is larger than Spain, France, Germany and the UK combined. The province has borders with eight countries – Russia, Mongolia, Kazakhstan, Kyrgyzstan, Tajikistan, Afghanistan, Pakistan and India – and is crucial to the development of the New Silk Road, or the Belt and Road Initiative (the BRI), as the Chinese authorities' new pet project is officially called. The plan is to connect China with the other countries in Asia, as well as with Europe and Africa, via an enormous network of new roads, railway systems and shipping routes – a modern Silk Road, with China as the world's main supplier of labour, big loans, cheap electronics and mass-produced clothes. China has cracked the code: in the age of hyper capitalism, when anything can be sold and free competition is god, empire building takes on a different form. Why occupy when you can buy? Why subjugate a country with force when you can be the cheapest supplier to their markets?

Even though Xinjiang is half the size of India in terms of area, the population is the same as that of Beijing – around twenty million. The central Asian terrain is inhospitable, and enormous areas, such as the Tian Shan Mountains and Taklamakan Desert, are uninhabitable. In the past few decades, the number of Han Chinese in Xinjiang has increased dramatically, but still is no more than half the population of Uighurs. More than ninety per cent of the population in the rest of China is Han Chinese; Xinjiang and Tibet are the only provinces where they are not yet the majority.

The Uighurs are a Turkic people with roots in Mongolia and the area south of Lake Baikal in Russia. When they were driven out of Mongolia by the Yensei Kyrgyz in the ninth century, they settled in the area that now includes Xinjiang. Here they established the kingdom of Qocho, also known as Uighuristan. In the thirteenth century, the Uighurs surrendered to Genghis Khan's cruel army and for centuries were ruled by various Mongolian khanates. The Uighurs were originally Buddhists and Manichaeists, but converted to Islam under the Mongols.

The Chinese have had to work hard to maintain their rule over the new territory. Towards the end of the 1860s, Yaqub Beg, a brutal warlord from what is now Uzbekistan, took control of large parts of Xinjiang. Beg tyrannised the region for almost a decade before the

Chinese eventually managed to force him out. In the meantime, the Russians had taken the opportunity to occupy the Ili Valley in the north, but gave it back to the Chinese ten years later – for a handsome sum of money. When the Qing dynasty collapsed in 1912, and the first Chinese republic was announced, Xinjiang was more or less left to itself. Once again, Russia seized their chance, and by the 1930s Xinjiang was a Soviet colony in all but name. The Russians controlled everything from the oil wells to the tin mines, Russian was the most popular foreign language, and in good communist style, many of the mosques were converted into community centres and theatres. The old Soviet consulate in the centre of Kashgar still stands as a monument to this Russian influence. It is now a cheap hotel, but the extravagant gardens, complete with Greek-inspired statues, pavilions and fountains, bear witness to past grandeur.

At the same time that the Soviet Russians dominated the region, the local population had a national awakening. The Turkic-speaking Muslims once again started to call themselves Uighurs, heirs to the kingdom of Uighuristan, a name that had lain dormant for centuries. There were those who dreamed of creating Turkestan, an independent republic for the Turkic peoples of Central Asia, and at the start of the 1930s, East Turkestan emerged. With the support of the Chinese nationalist party, the Kuomintang, a Muslim army attacked Kashgar in 1934. Several thousand Uighurs were killed in the ensuing battles, and the East Turkestan republic died with them. It was resurrected again for a short period ten years later, in the Ili Valley, in the north of Xinjiang, with considerable support from the Soviet Union. The second East Turkestan Republic, which had its own monetary system and army, relinquished its independence for good when Mao came to power in 1949.

More recently, there have again been rumblings in China's Wild West, which have resulted in numerous terrorist attacks. In March 2014, for example, a group of Uighur terrorists attacked random passengers with knives at the train station in Kunming in Yunnan Province, more than two thousand kilometres from Xinjiang. Thirteen people were killed and more than a hundred and forty wounded. Some weeks later, forty-three people were killed by a car bomb in the vegetable market in Urumqi, the largest city in Xinjiang. In September the following year, more than fifty people were killed in a knife attack at a coal mine in Aksu, in western Xinjiang, and again Uighurs were responsible for the attack.

The Chinese authorities have now implemented draconian measures to crush the Uighur separatist movement. Since 2017, more than one million Uighurs have been held in state internment camps. The Chinese authorities prefer to call them "re-education camps", but in reality, they are like modern-day concentration camps, with watch towers and surrounded by high walls and barbed wire. Former prisoners have told how they were forced to sing songs in praise of the Communist Party, and that difficult prisoners were beaten, raped, denied food and held in isolation. In many cases, Han Chinese have moved in with the families of prisoners in order to supervise the relatives and teach them about Chinese values.

The detention camps have been hailed as a great success: there have been no terrorist attacks in Xinjiang since 2016.

On my way back from the livestock market, I tried to visit the Id Kah Mosque again. I had come prepared, with my emergency passport in my bag, but the door was locked. There was a sign that said the mosque closed at seven in the evening, which in practice meant five. As Xinjiang lies so far west, the people here operate according to their own time, Xinjiang time, which is about two hours behind Beijing time. Officially, however, the whole of China is run on Beijing time, so the mosque was now closed.

There was still no news from the Pakistani embassy the next day. My visa would possibly be ready by the end of the week, or the following week. It began to dawn on me that my stay in Kashgar might be longer than expected, so I changed tactic. I remembered that someone I knew was an acquaintance of the former Pakistani ambassador. I contacted her and she immediately sent an email to the embassy. It worked like magic: within a few hours, the visa was on its way to Kashgar by express post. Soon, very soon, my journey to the many kingdoms and communities of the Himalayas could begin.

In the meantime, I visited the Afaq Khoja Mausoleum, the most sacred place in Xinjiang. The mausoleum lies a few kilometres from the centre of Kashgar, and with its large dome and majestic arched entrance, covered in green and white ceramic tiles, it is reminiscent of so many other buildings in other cities along the Silk Road, such as Samarkand and Bukhara. The mausoleum was built in 1640 as the tomb of the Sufi master Muhammad Yusef by his son, Afaq Khoja, after whom the mausoleum is named. He is also buried there. However, the mausoleum is now best known as the tomb of the Fragrant Concubine.

According to myth, Afaq Khoja's granddaughter Iparhan, or Xiang Fei, as she was called in Chinese, was so beautiful and fragrant that when Emperor Qianlong heard about her, he asked for her to be sent to him as a concubine. If Chinese legend is to be believed, the beauty from the west was given a delightful room with her own garden, but the luxury of the imperial palace was not enough to dull her longing for home. The emperor was desperate and did whatever he could to make her happy; he built a mosque for her and recreated a Uighur village and a Muslim bazaar outside her window. In the end he sent his servants to Kashgar to bring back a Chinese jujube tree that bore golden fruit. Xiang Fei finally understood how much he loved her and in return was loyal to him until she died. After her death, her body was brought back to Kashgar as a symbol of national unity and the emperor's love. It is said that Xiang Fei's final journey took three years.

The Uighur version, on the other hand, ends in tragedy. Xiang Fei's heart was bursting with hate and thoughts of revenge, and she defended herself against the emperor's advances with small knives that she kept hidden in her sleeves. The emperor's mother was concerned for her son's security, and one day when she was alone with Xiang Fei she gave her an ultimatum: behave like a proper concubine or commit suicide. In one version, Xiang Fei is then poisoned; in another, she does as her mother-in-law advises and hangs herself with a silk scarf.

These days, however, it is the romantic Chinese version that dominates. Xiang Fei has had restaurants and perfumes named after her, TV series, films and ballets have been made about her, and one can also take a guided tour of her tomb. It is likely that the myth is based on a concubine who did actually exist, namely Concubine Rong, who came to the imperial palace in Beijing from west China in the 1760s. Concubine Rong died from an illness at the age of fifty-three, but is buried in Beijing, more than four thousand kilometres from the Fragrant Concubine's famous grave in Kashgar. No-one knows who actually lies in the grave.

To the right of the mausoleum were rows of rough, dry clay graves. In the past, there were graves in front of the mausoleum as well, as Muslims believe it is auspicious to be buried close to shrines. When the mausoleum became a popular tourist attraction, the Chinese authorities removed these graves and planted a rose garden instead. In one corner of the rose garden is a sign that says: BEST SPOT FOR TAKING PHOTOS. They want tourists travelling to Xinjiang to return home with photographs of roses, not of old graves or mistreated livestock.

And certainly not of mosque interiors.

I did eventually manage to get past the yellow walls of the Id Kah Mosque. An attendant scanned my pass, while another took my forty-five yuan entrance fee.

"You're not allowed to take pictures," the attendant said, as she handed me my ticket and change.

"Photography is not permitted," the other attendant said, before giving me my passport.

"Photography is forbidden," a third attendant said, then checked my bag before allowing me through into the mosque courtyard.

There is room for more than twenty thousand people inside the walls, which makes Id Kah not only the biggest mosque in Kashgar, but also in China. The mosque building itself is, however, small and wooden, and more than six hundred years old. I normally cover my head when I visit mosques, as one should, but in Xinjiang headscarves are forbidden. As are long beards and Muslim clothes. Any outward sign of being a Muslim is an open invitation to "re-education".

"Thousands of Muslims come here to pray every day," it said on the website of the Chinese travel bureau, Travel China Guide, but apart from a dozen or so Chinese tourists, the mosque was empty. There were several big surveillance cameras in the trees outside, and a guard stood by every street light keeping watch.

"No pictures," one of them barked as I passed him on my way out of the mosque. On the benches outside, in the shade of some leafy trees, a handful of old men sat with their hands shaped like a bowl in front of their faces, whispering under their breath. Perhaps they were praying for better times.

I could track the progress of my passport as it travelled from Oslo to Kashgar. The day after it was sent, it reached Hong Kong, and I started to get ready to travel south, to the mountains. From Hong Kong, it travelled to Guangzhou, but there it stopped. My passport was stranded in Guangzhou. I contacted the shipping agent's customer services, and was told that the passport was in Guangzhou, which I already knew. The days passed, and nothing happened. I googled Guangzhou and discovered that fifteen million people live there, nearly three times more than the entire population of Norway. Why had I never heard of Guangzhou before? I carried on reading and learned that Guangzhou was the Chinese name for Canton, and that it had not only played a key role in the Opium Wars, but had also been an important stopping point on the Silk Road. While Kashgar had been a hub for camel caravans, Guangzhou was the terminal for maritime trade.

And I was about as far from the sea as it was possible to be.

On one of the days that I spent waiting for my passport to leave Guangzhou, I headed north from Kashgar, towards the border with Kyrgyzstan. The flat, barren landscape ended abruptly in dramatic limestone formations, up to several metres high, with the odd cactus or patch of scrub adding a splash of green to the brown. Deep gorges ran through the terrain, carved by water and rivers that had once run down from the Tibetan Plateau to the lowlands.

The last British consul-general, Eric Shipton, undertook several strenuous explorations of the area in 1947. Shipton was an excellent mountaineer and had already taken part in several relatively success-ful Mount Everest expeditions, although no-one had yet managed to reach the peak. He was looking for an enormous archway in the desert mountains he had once seen from a distance outside Kashgar. He finally found it on the third attempt. The Uighur name for the arch is Tushuk Tash, the mountain with a hole in it, but it is now better known internationally as Shipton's Arch. Until relatively recently, an island, a sea or a continent was not properly discovered until a European man had written about it and left his mark there.

Shipton's Arch was recorded in the Guinness Book of Records as the largest natural arch in the world, but was then taken out again, as no-one could find the way back to it. Only half a century later, in the year 2000, did an expedition party sent by *National Geographic* manage to find the hidden but never forgotten rock formation.

Once it had been rediscovered, a road was built almost all the way to the arch. This was then joined by a car park and visitors' centre with toilets and a shop. The police are also there to check every visitor's papers. It takes about an hour to walk from here to the arch, and benches and tables have been set up along the way so people can rest.

The path ran along the bottom of the gorges where once rivers had flowed, flanked by limestone cliffs so full of holes, circles and lines that they almost resembled art. I had to imagine the overwhelming, majestic silence, however, since I was surrounded by chattering masses, as is the case almost everywhere in China. Some tourists were equipped for a strenuous hike in the mountains, others tottered along the gravel path in short, tight dresses and high heels, with atmospheric music blasting from their mobile phones.

Some broad wooden steps led up to the viewing platform. It was only once I was standing there that I could appreciate the full size of the arch: it reached down into the valley and was so geometric, so perfect in form, it could have been carved by a master. Some black birds were gliding on the air streams inside the actual arch – they flew up and down in playful spirals, as though they were doing gymnastics.

Suddenly, one day, the blessed visa was waiting for me at the reception desk. I had almost given up; the mountains felt like a distant, unrealistic dream. I had got used to being settled in one place and had started to feel at home in Kashgar.

I walked through the newly renovated, organised chaos of the old town for the last time. Once again I got lost and ended up by the gigantic statue of Mao in the People's Square. It had been erected during the Cultural Revolution and at more than twenty-four metres was one of the four largest Mao statues in China. Obviously, it was not cheap to install such an enormous statue, but the city council knew how to solve the issue and had encouraged the inhabitants to donate money voluntarily. Those who didn't have money could donate their ration cards. And people opened their purses, of course, whether they could afford it or not. Once the finances were in place, another problem arose: how on earth were they going to find enough building materials in the desert? In the end, the statue had to be transported in pieces, on sixteen lorries, from central China to Kashgar. Craftsmen then spent months putting the pieces together and raising the statue, which was unveiled in 1969.

There was not a soul to be seen in the concrete square around the statue. A lone guard sat in a tiny security hut and watched over the founding father of the People's Republic.

How many people are employed by the police and security services in China? It must be millions. In recent times, the country has spent more money on domestic security than on the military – and China's defence budget is the second largest in the world. It is estimated that in 2020 the Chinese state spent USD 252.3 billion on defence annually.* That is still outstripped by the budget for domestic security.

That evening, my last in Kashgar, I went for a walk around the hotel, which was a few kilometres from the old town and surrounded by low blocks of flats. The neighbourhood was well organised and well looked after, with wide six-lane highways, and a separate road for motorbikes and scooters, of which there are so many. Bicycles, which only a few years ago were the very symbol of Chinese urban life, were now conspicuous by their absence, as were the Uighurs. There were only Han Chinese as far as the eye could see, and most of them had moved here recently, it was safe to assume. Trees and colourful flowers had been planted in straight, orderly lines by the edge of the road. The broad pavements were full of families out for an

---

* https://www.statista.com/statistics/267035/china-military-spending/#:~:text =In%202020%2C%20China's%20military%20spending,estimated%20252.3%20 billion%20U.S.%20dollars

evening stroll. Some girls had taken up position outside one of the blocks of flats and were doing aerobics; they followed the instructions of a happy voice coming from a portable loudspeaker. Unlike in the old town, which was full of children, each couple here only had one child.

No-one knows exactly how many Uighurs are being held in the state re-education camps, but estimates vary from one to one and a half million. If the estimates are right, this means that at least one in every ten Uighurs is currently being held against their will in a detention camp. In other words, all the Uighurs I saw on the street, in the livestock market, in the old town, all the Uighurs who worked in the hotel where I was staying, and in the restaurants where I ate, absolutely all the Uighurs I came into contact with, in one way or another, knew someone who was imprisoned.

But I could not ask. The surveillance was absolute. If someone talked to a foreigner, it would not go unnoticed.

How do you recognise suppression? What would I have picked up if I had not known what I knew? And what did I actually pick up?

An avenue of green trees had been planted alongside a narrow, dirty river that reeked of sewage, and small footbridges had been built across the river. The restaurants and shops were still open, even though it was getting on for midnight, Beijing time, and there were small families, couples and groups of friends sitting everywhere, eating, chatting and enjoying themselves. If one ignored all the Uighurs who were selling meat skewers and round flatbreads, and the strong police presence, the atmosphere was much like that in any other provincial Chinese town.

But one also has to include in the equation all that one does not see or hear. The last time that I had been in Xinjiang, three years before, many of the women wore colourful headscarves; now all the women had bare heads. None of the men I saw had long beards, the muezzin's insistent call to prayer no longer boomed across the city from loudspeakers five times a day, and the only people in the mosque were Chinese tourists.

And then there are all the things one does not want to see or dare see. When I got back to the hotel that evening, four policemen stood bent over the reception desk studying a list of names. It was clear that they were looking for someone; judging by the reception-ist's distressed face, they would soon find whoever it was they were looking for.

I scurried past and locked the door to my room.

No-one leaves Kashgar unnoticed. On the way out of the city, I was stopped at three checkpoints, and each time I had to send my luggage through an X-ray machine, have my passport scanned and give my fingerprints. The other passengers in the car, a family from Beijing, were generally allowed to stay in the car, while I and busloads of Uighurs filed in long queues through the security check.

The road itself was in perfect condition and frequent radar checks meant that the driver stuck rigorously to the strict speed limit. Finally, finally I was on my way out towards Pakistan, to the Himalayas. My fellow Chinese passengers were fast asleep, and I also nodded off. When I woke up, there were rusty-coloured mountains all around, and the Chinese family asked for a stop to stretch their legs. The wife's hair was as red as the mountains, and her husband took photo-graphs of her from every angle. When he refused to take any more pictures, she asked me to step in.

The mountains got higher and steeper with every bend in the road, and soon we could see snowy peaks. The woman with the red hair wanted another photo stop. The landscape was wilder, the air was thinner. I thought about Wilfred Skrede, a young Norwegian who travelled the same route a little under eighty years earlier, in 1941. Norway was occupied by the Nazis and at war, and Skrede was on his way to Canada to the Norwegian air force training camp,

Little Norway. As crossing the North Sea was dangerous, to get to Canada he went through Sweden, Finland, the Soviet Union and Xinjiang, over the mountains to what is now Pakistan and Kashmir, and then on to the port in Singapore. The journey took over a year, and Skrede was arrested several times along the way. He broke his back in a car accident in Xinjiang, and convalesced in Kashgar, thanks to the generous hospitality of the British consul-general Shipton, him of the arch. The young Norwegian stayed with the mountaineering consul for a month, "and I look back on those days as some of the happiest in my life," Skrede writes in his memoirs. When his back was more or less healed, he carried on south towards the mountains. The journey from Kashgar to Tashkurgan took eleven days on horseback and he was accompanied by armed guards, as the local warlord feared that the Norwegian might be a spy. When the horses were too tired to go any further, due to the thin mountain air, they were stabbed in the muzzle so they bled, and could then manage to go a little further. Bleached bones on the mountainside bore witness to all the others that had given up for good.

"For centuries, caravans have travelled between Kashmir and Kashgar," Skrede writes. "Many think it sounds so romantic and beautiful, but anyone who has crossed the Chichiklik Pass has seen for himself the hell that this trade route has been for thousands of tortured nags, driven to exhaustion and a painful death, with no Allah to call on."[2]

Providing that all your papers are in order, the journey from Kashgar to Tashkurgan now takes no more than a day, with time for lunch and photo stops. The Karakoram Highway, an important part of the New Silk Road, undulates like a black asphalt snake along the mountainside all the way from Kashgar to Gilgit in Pakistan. We 3645 MSL were given a new photo opportunity by **Karakul Lake**, where the snow-capped blue mountains were reflected in the water. Hundreds of Chinese tourists were already there, eternalising the stunning scenery. Kyrgyz with broad faces and narrow eyes offered horse rides, meat skewers, ethnic jewellery, and opportunities to be photographed in typical nomad clothes, but we had to press on. We still had a long way to go. Until only a few years ago, it was possible to spend the night in traditional Kyrgyz yurts by the lake, as Skrede had done in the 1940s, but the authorities have put a stop to that kind of freedom, and now it is only possible to stay in regulated conditions, in approved hotels. Exceptions can be made, of course, but will cost you in excess of about six hundred pounds.

We ate our lunch, which consisted of noodles with big chunks of meat, in a small parking space in a huge car park. None of the other passengers could speak English, but the driver downloaded a translation app on his telephone so he could give me practical information. The woman with the red hair borrowed his phone and asked in quick succession where I came from, how old I was, if I was married, if I had children, if I did not want children, and, finally, the question she was clearly dying to ask. She looked at me in anticipation as the mechanical app-voice translated into English: "Does your skin not get sunburnt?"

I shook my head. The woman looked at me in disbelief. She never left the car without a hat, scarf and thin jacket to protect herself from the sun. I took the suncream out of my bag and showed it to her. She smiled, and produced exactly the same cream from her own bag, also factor fifty.

Tashkurgan means "stone fort", which is a suitable name for the 3094 MSL only tourist attraction in the town, a 2,200-year-old stone fort. Once upon a time there had been a whole town here, but all that remained of the ancient inhabitants were some messy piles of stones. There was not much left of the old fort either. Some brand-new wooden steps, with accompanying warning signs, led up to the top of the ruins. From here there was a view to the river and grassy plain, where a herd of small cows was grazing peacefully. A couple of white yurts stood out from all the green. Whereas the Uighurs dominate in Kashgar, and the Kyrgyz around Karakul Lake, the ethnic Tajiks are the majority in Tashkurgan. Most of the women wore the traditional flat hats covered by a veil that was loosely tied under the chin, or on the chest.

It was thirty degrees centigrade in the shade, and I regretted not following the receptionist's advice to take a parasol for protection. The town was quiet and sleepy. Small shops opened out onto the street and children ran around, while old men and stooped women passed the time together. If it was like this now in the middle of the high season, what on earth was it like in winter, when the snow fell thick and heavy and the road was shut for months at a time?

The town's extreme location, more than three thousand metres above sea level, surrounded by mountains that are almost twice as high, is also the reason for its existence. For more than two thousand years, the fort was an important stop on the southern Silk Road from China over the Karakoram Mountains to Srinagar and Leh in India.

And now, Tashkurgan is about to become an important hub once again.

My initial impression of Tashkurgan was of a typical Asian border town, square and windswept. But the roads were remarkably well maintained and wide, with impressive roundabouts and excellent lighting, and many of the administration buildings were showy and brand new. The new, bright-pink fire station, for example, was bigger than any of the hotels. There are plans for an international airport, and soon the road may no longer be closed for months on end in winter. A future ambition is to keep the border with Pakistan open all year round, and the future is closer than ever.

The stated goal of the ambitious and expensive China–Pakistan Economic Corridor (CPEC), a joint project, is to have high-standard road connections from Kashgar all the way to the Pakistani port of Karachi, and, in time, a rail connection too. Work is already well under way and nowhere has China invested more in infrastructure than in its neighbour, Pakistan. When the road is finished, trailers will be able to take this short cut from western China, through Pakistan, to waiting ships on the Arabian Sea, instead of driving through central China to reach the Chinese ports. Tashkurgan will then be the single most important border town in the Himalayas. The possibilities and opportunities are incredible, and in the past few years businessmen from all over China have flocked to this tiny outpost in the hope of making a good deal, and an imminently brighter future.

"Are you not going to watch the dancing?" the astonished receptionist asked me when I got back to the hotel, hot and sweaty after a long day in the sun. "The other tourists have all gone to the ethno village to watch the dancing. I thought you were there too."

"What dancing?" I asked.

"The cultural dance show. Did no-one tell you about it? There's one every evening and it's very popular with our guests."

I did not want to be known as the one who missed the cultural dance show, so I trudged over to the ethno village, which was just outside the centre of town. On my way, I met a woman who was obviously going the same way, as she was all dressed up in a long, red dress and heavy necklace. I started to chat to her and asked if she had ever been in Tajikistan. The answer was no.

"I am a *Chinese* Tajik," she explained.

Half a dozen policemen and four heavily armed soldiers were in charge of the dance show security. The woman in the red dress invited me into a typical Tajik house that stood nearby. As in every Tajik home, there were benches along the wall and an intricately carved wooden pillar in the middle of the room. I admired the beautiful, embroidered cushions.

"They're for sale," the woman said. "Would you like to buy one? You can get a discount if you buy two."

The Chinese Tajiks, like their brothers and sisters in Pamir, are Ismailis, so I had expected to see a framed picture of the Aga Khan, their religious leader. But the walls were full of China's communist leaders instead, from Mao to Xi. Suddenly we heard drums and cheers from outside. The show had started, and the "bride" and "groom" were led into the square. There were around a hundred Chinese tourists there, who all tried to capture the show as best they could with their advanced camera lenses. Someone lit the fire that had been prepared to represent the Tajiks' Zoroastrian roots, and then they started to dance in a circle round the flickering flames, further illuminated by an explosion of flashbulbs.

Many of the locals also came to see the show. There was precious little else to do in the evenings in Tashkurgan. I left the cultural party and wandered back to the hotel long before the fraternisation started. The receptionist had warned that the show always ended with the Chinese and the Tajiks dancing together.

That is what the authorities want the ethnic groups to be, I mused as I walked along the dark, empty streets. Dance, colourful folk costumes, a fun tourist attraction, pure folklore.

The hotel was also quiet and empty. I found my way out to the veranda, and sat down under a clear, star-filled border-town sky. I ordered a beer.

My last for a long time.

High Stakes

Outside the Customs and Immigration Office in the centre of Tashkurgan, a handful of men were waiting in the shade. A man in his late twenties came towards me and introduced himself as Umair. His pale skin was acned and his jet-black hair was slick with wax.

"Do you believe everything you read in the news?" he asked, once we were done with the usual courtesies.

"Well—" I said.

"What about 9/11?" he interrupted. "Do you really think the son of a Saudi billionaire was behind it? I'm an engineer, and I have to tell you – and you can check it yourself, by all means, American engineers say the same, in fact engineers all over the world say the same as me: *the towers could not have collapsed in the way they did because of an airplane!* The crash could never have generated enough heat to melt the iron and steel structures. Do you realise how much heat is needed to make constructions like that melt?"

"No idea," I said. "But the Taliban have also been behind a number of terrorist attacks in Pakistan as well and—"

"Yes, we've had terrorist attacks in Pakistan as well," Umair interrupted again. "And yes, we've got problems with the Taliban, but tell me, where do the Taliban come from?" He did not wait for an answer, as he already had one: "You see, the Taliban were created by the Russians and the Americans." His look was intense. "Almost none of the terrorists who've been caught have been circumcised, and their weapons don't come from here. I mean, I don't know if it's true or not," his voice was less certain now, "I'm just telling you the plain facts so you can make up your own mind."

More and more men came over. One of the newer arrivals heard that I was from Norway.

"I'm engaged to a Norwegian-Pakistani girl," he said. "We met when she was studying in Islamabad."

"Do you plan to live in Norway or Pakistan?"

"Norway, of course."

"Whereabouts in Norway?"

"I don't know yet, because I've never been to Norway," he said. "But I'll find a good place for us, somewhere that's good for Pakistanis to live, where there are other Pakistanis."

"I don't understand that," Umair said. "Why move abroad if you only want to be with Pakistanis?"

We had to wait outside for more than an hour before we were allowed through the sluices by the security guards who were there to make sure everything was done in an orderly manner. We had to stand upright in a straight line, and talking was forbidden. Our luggage was passed through an enormous scanner, and then we were given our exit stamps from China.

About forty people were travelling to Pakistan that day: Pakistani men weighed down with luggage, a dozen Chinese tourists on a group tour, dressed in Gore-tex from top to toe – and me. We were escorted onto the waiting minibuses. I found an empty seat by the window, and ended up sitting next to Abdul, a medical student from Lahore. His thick beard and glasses made it difficult to guess how old he was, but I soon found out he was twenty-four, and unmarried. He had just finished a five-year medical course somewhere in central China and was now on his way home to do a year's clinical work in a hospital where he understood the language.

"Why do you want to be a doctor?" I asked. After more than two weeks in China it felt almost exhilarating to be able to have an easy conversation in English, and I could not stop asking questions.

"My parents wanted me to be a doctor," Abdul said. "I respect them and trust that they know what's best for me."

"Do you trust them to find you a wife as well?" I probed.

"Yes, I trust them, but naturally they will have to take my own wishes into consideration as well." He looked down. "There was a girl I wanted to marry, a few years ago. I told my parents, and they gave their permission. But we didn't live happily ever after."

"You didn't get married?"

"No." Abdul let out an almost inaudible sigh, and changed the subject. "It's not always easy to know what's true when it comes to history," he said. "There are always so many interpretations, opinions and theories. Take the Jews, for example. Everyone says that Hitler killed masses of people, I mean, a lot . . ."

"Six million," I said.

"Yes, like I said, a lot. But perhaps he didn't kill as many as that, just quite a lot, and it was a deal that the Jews made with the USA so they could settle in Palestine? In the Ottoman empire, no Jews were allowed to live in Palestine. I'm not saying that that's what *actually* happened, just that it's a possibility."

"Have you ever visited the concentration camps in Poland?" I asked.

"No, I've only read about them on the internet. Anyway, my point is that there are always multiple versions of history. And it's not always easy to know which one is right."

"Exactly!" a tall man in his thirties shouted from a window seat on the other side of the aisle. I found out later that his name was Muhammed and he was in the final stages of a PhD in pharmacology in China.

"These days, there's only two narratives about what's going on in Pakistan," Muhammed said. "The Americans did everything right, or the Americans did everything wrong. But what will people think in a hundred years' time? What is in fact right and what is wrong?"

I didn't manage to eat the little snack that I'd bought for the journey, as Abdul and Muhammed were constantly sharing their generous food packs while they philosophised about the inherent relativity of truth.

"I don't like Chinese food," Abdul said.

"No, Chinese food is disgusting," the pharmacologist said in agreement.

"Don't you even like noodles?" I asked.

"Noodles? They're for children!" Muhammed mimed how they slurp up the long strings, then laughed scornfully.

"I make pretty good Pakistani food now, after all the years in China," Abdul said and handed me a pile of home-made chapattis, a flat, round bread made from flour, water and salt.

"Did you know that the Chinese eat snakes?" Muhammed asked. "And dogs and frogs and insects? They eat *everything!*"

Fortunately, the two young Chinese men sitting in front of us did not understand a word of English. And even if they did, they had dropped off as soon as the driver started the engine, and were still sound asleep.

"I'd like to give this one here a piece of my mind!" Muhammed said, and gave the thin Pakistani boy beside him a gentle shake. "He's left school so he can travel back and forth between Pakistan and China to sell precious stones. But he's young, he should be at school."

As the boy understood no English, Muhammed translated his tirade. The boy gave a shy smile and pulled up a photograph on his phone of a beautiful girl wrapped in a large, brightly coloured shawl.

"I'm in love with her, and my parents have now arranged our engagement," he said proudly. "We're soon to be married."

Muhammed shook his head in despair.

"He's throwing away his life and is too stupid to realise it himself!"

The road stretched out in a straight line ahead of us over the grey plateau, ringed by gently sloping, snowy peaks. I could tell from the gentle but increasing pressure on my temples that we were climbing. Every so often we passed small flocks of goats, the odd donkey, a herd of yaks, two or three yurts out on the plain, a lonely herdsman – but for the most part, we had the road and the landscape to ourselves. The signs advised a maximum speed of forty kilometres per hour, but it was obvious there were no speed cameras here. At the final Chinese border post, two young soldiers dressed in thick fur-lined coats checked that we all had the day's date stamped in our passports, then waved us on.

The final ascent was steep. The pressure on my temples was intense and my ears were full of air bubbles. A few minutes later we reached **the highest border crossing in the world.** The Pakistanis burst into   4693 MSL wild applause as we drove out of China and through the grandiose concrete gateway into Pakistan.

The driver graciously allowed us a two-minute photo stop. As soon as I stepped out of the minibus, I was surrounded by stout men with bushy beards wearing long, white tunics and sandals, who all wanted a selfie with the pale foreigner. In contrast to the Chinese side, people can go right up to the border in Pakistan, and it has become a popular tourist attraction. The bearded men waved their mobile phones around like excited children and I smiled in every direction with new faces popping up beside me all the time until the driver grew impatient and tooted the horn. I broke away from the camera flashes with a feeling of relief.

"Are you not happy?" Abdul asked. He beamed as we drove towards the Pakistani border checkpoint, which was about a hundred kilometres down in the valley.

"Yes, of course I'm happy," I said, politely.

"We are *extremely* happy to be in our own country again," Muhammed said. "At last we can breathe freely. You're constantly being watched in China. Now we're free."

The road wound sharply down the Khunjerab Pass, following a

fast-flowing river, flanked by rugged, brown mountains that were so high I couldn't see the peaks from the minibus window. Khunjerab means "blood valley" in Wakhi, the Persian language spoken by the Wakhi people who live in Upper Hunza, in Tashkurgan and on the Tajik and Afghan sides of the border. Political borders seldom follow linguistic borders in these mountains. The name was apparently inspired by the frequent bloody ambushes on passing caravans in the heyday of the Silk Road.

The valley has also lived up to its name in modern times: more than a thousand labourers died in landslides and other accidents while building the road we were driving on. It was constructed in the 1960s, after Pakistan and China had agreed on the border. The negotiations ended with China ceding grazing grounds to Pakistan in exchange for an area measuring some five thousand square kilometres to the north-east. The area that was ceded to China is part of the disputed Kashmir region. India has never recognised either the agreement or the border, and the border between China and India has not been ratified. In more remote corners of the Himalayas, the borders dissolve into disputed dotted lines that are guarded by heavily armed soldiers and nuclear warheads. There have been many conflicts and the potential for more is ever present, but all is peace and harmony between Pakistan and China, which both see India as the enemy. The fact that the two countries were able to agree on the border at such an early stage of Pakistan's existence provided fertile ground for a bilateral friendship, which is regularly nourished by generous loans from China.

"Pakistan gave away its territory to China because the authorities were scared that the Soviet Union would attack us," Abdul said. "The war in Afghanistan was actually about the Pakistani ports in the south."

"Oh, right," I said.

"Everyone knows that," Abdul said, with a shrug.

Down and down we went; the pressure on my temples eased, then disappeared altogether. The mountains appeared to be empty and barren, but according to my guidebook they are home to several threatened species such as the Marco Polo sheep, the Siberian musk deer and the snow leopard. I was by now used to sitting in the minibus and driving on and on and on, so I was caught by surprise when Muhammed told me that we had reached the Pakistani border check in **Sost**.   2800 MSL

"Promise that you'll come and visit me and my family in Swat!" he called, before he disappeared out of the small, tired border building.

As I stood waiting in the short but chaotic queue to have my passport stamped, a lean, energetic man came over to me. He was dressed from head to toe in denim, his hair was dark blond and his skin golden brown; he looked more like a spaghetti western hero than a typical Pakistani.

"I'm Akhtar, your guide," he said. "I've been waiting for you for five hours already. You never know when the bus from China is going to arrive."

Outside, there was a large queue of colourful trucks decorated with dragons, film stars and quotes from the Koran. They were waiting for goods from China that they would then transport to the ports. Fortunately, we were not going that far, and after only thirty minutes or so arrived in Akhtar's village, **Passu**.   2450 MSL

"All the guides I worked with in the 1990s now have foreign wives," he said. "One lives in Australia, another in Canada, and another in France."

"And no-one wanted to marry you?" I asked.

"Yes, sure, but I was already married," he said, with a grin. "And in any case, I can't imagine living anywhere other than Passu. It's my paradise."

About four hundred people live in Passu, but in the summer this number more than doubles. The village spreads over a plain close to the river. It is remarkably lush, thanks to an intricate watering system. People grow potatoes and vegetables in their small gardens. The apple trees and plum trees were in full bloom, and the flat roofs of the houses were covered in apricots that had been laid out to dry.

Akhtar knew everyone in the little village and greeted everyone we met with joy. Most of the women here choose to be bare-headed unlike the women in Kashgar, who have no choice. Many of them were fair-skinned and some even had blue eyes, and most had dark-blonde, sun-bleached hair like Akhtar. They reminded me of the people I had met in Pamir a few years before, which is perhaps not so strange, as we were not far from the border with Tajikistan. The Wakhi people of Hunza are closely related to the people who live in Pamir in Tajikistan, in Tashkurgan in China and the Wakhan Corridor in Afghanistan. Once upon a time they could visit each other freely and lived as one people, but now they are separated by red lines on the map and strict visa regulations.

Towering mountains that were six to seven thousand metres high surrounded the village like a film set. In terms of geology, I could argue that I was already in the Himalayas – many experts see the Karakoram Mountains as part of the Himalayas – but in terms of language and semantics, I was in Karakoram, the mountain range that stretches about five hundred kilometres from the borders of India, Pakistan and China a little way into Afghanistan and Tajikistan. Karakoram means "black gravel" in Turkic, but the name does not do the mountains justice: no range in the world can boast a greater number of peaks over seven thousand metres.

"We don't normally give names to mountains under seven thousand metres," Akhtar told me with a shrug. "There are too many of them."

The Karakoram Mountains are known for being steep and impassable. K2, for example, the second highest mountain in the world, is far harder to climb than Mount Everest. For the longest time, Hunza was one of the most inaccessible parts of Karakoram, and myths about the place and its people abound. The paths that led here were legendary.

"Soon we could see glimpses of the Hunza River, white against the black gorge below us," wrote the young Wilfred Skrede about his journey through the Hunza Valley in 1941. "It was a thousand feet down and the mountainside was nearly vertical. On both sides of the valley, the mountains rose up several thousand feet. Shrukker and the boy had to heave and haul to get the horses to move. Riding them was out of the question. The steep mountainsides were full of loose stone and poor rock. Bursting with pride, Shrukker told us about all the fatal accidents that had happened here."

These hazardous paths have been the tiny principality's greatest defence through the centuries. Hunza lies tucked between Tibet to the north, Kashmir to the east and Afghanistan to the west, but as it was so difficult to get there, the local emir was generally left to rule in peace. The few Western explorers who managed to reach Hunza in one piece, before the road was completed in the 1970s, described Hunza as a Garden of Eden, an earthly paradise (presumably as a result of the adrenaline and endorphins released by their efforts), a Shangri-La, a secret mountain kingdom peopled by descendants of Alexander the Great; a place where people were so healthy, harmonious and democratic that they lived to an exceptional age, sometimes even to one hundred and fifty.

"The oldest ever person in the village lived to be one hundred and twelve," Akhtar said. "He died last year. My grandmother will soon be a hundred and is healthy and well. People here live to a ripe old age, but our generation are not likely to live as long," he said with a sigh, and lit a cigarette. "We're not as healthy. I managed to stop smoking for six months, but then I put on so much weight that I started again."

There was no electricity or internet in the simple hotel where I was staying. But the place was lively enough, thanks to a large, jolly family from Lahore.

"What brings a foreigner to these parts?" the matriarch in the family asked. "And what is your impression of the Pakistanis? Be honest! What do you think of Pakistan? Be even more honest!"

The entire family looked at me in anticipation.

"I've just arrived, so it's a little early to say, really," I said. They seemed so disappointed by my answer that I promptly added that it was very, very beautiful here, and that Pakistanis were very, very friendly people and that Pakistan was a very, very interesting country.

I fell asleep early, despite the heated discussions between family members in the room next door, and I was woken early by an equally heated discussion among a herd of small mountain cattle in the garden outside my window.

During breakfast, Akhtar kept glancing furtively over at the tourists from Lahore.

"I can't understand why Pakistanis come here," he said, bitterly. Strictly speaking, he was a Pakistani himself, but he consistently called himself a Wakhi from Hunza. For Akhtar, the term "Pakistani" was derogatory, and reserved for people from the densely populated Punjab Province in the south.

"City folk just sit in cars all day long," he said. "Passu has to be experienced on foot."

So as not to be pigeon-holed as a city person, I suggested that we walk to the Passu Glacier after breakfast. The path was rocky and partially overgrown, but Akhtar, who was the son of a mountaineer, raced up the valley, so light on his feet that you might think he had springs in his shoes. We had to scramble and climb over scree for the final stretch; I made sure to look down as a little as possible.

"Is there much further to go?" I asked, out of breath.

"No, we're there now," Akhtar said.

"But where is the glacier?" I asked, bewildered.

"Right in front of your nose," Akhtar said and pointed at an enormous pile of black gravel about a hundred metres in front of us. I had been looking for ice and snow, but Passu Glacier was completely black, covered in tiny stones and sand. Karakoram lived up to its name after all.

"There," Akhtar said, and pointed at the lake that had formed at the mouth of the glacier. "The glacier was there when I was a boy. There wasn't a lake. And that's how far it came ten years ago," he said, indicating a point about halfway up the mountainside. "Only three years ago, we used to take tourists to where we are now. We could walk out onto the glacier from here."

Torrents of meltwater ran off the glacier and into the new lake. Passu Glacier is shrinking by about four metres a month, and is melting with ever increasing speed. The glaciers of Karakoram, the Himalayas and the Hindu Kush are often called "the world's third pole". There are, in all, fifty-four thousand glaciers in this mountain region and nowhere does the ice lie as packed as Karakoram; with the exception of the poles, Karakoram has the highest density of glaciers in the world. In Pakistan alone, there are more than seven thousand glaciers, and about three-quarters of the country's water reserves are stored in the ice. The Himalayas, "abode of the snow", are also the home of ice.

Or rather, once were. Most of the glaciers are now melting at record speed. An average of eight billion tons of ice melts every year, and that does not include all the tons that are replaced by new snow. The process is self-reinforcing and therefore speeds up each year. It is highly likely that two-thirds of the glaciers will have melted by the end of the century. These glaciers supply the biggest and most important rivers in Asia with water, including the Indus, Ganges and Mekong, so the consequences of this will be catastrophic. Not only will anyone who lives in the mountain region – about a quarter of a billion people – run out of water, but anyone who relies on water from these rivers will suffer as a result: in other words, more than one and a half billion people. But the water shortage will not be the only consequence of these drastic changes to the eco system; there will also be an increased risk of landslides and flooding. Even though the volume of water may remain constant, the water supply will be more erratic: drought followed by flooding, which is then followed by drought again.

In short, it will be even more dangerous than it already is to live in the mountains and on the banks of these great waterways.

*

2559 MSL **Attabad Lake** is given 4.8 out of five stars on Google, and is one of the most popular tourist attractions in the region. Many of the reviews extol its beauty and describe the lake as "one of the most beautiful in Pakistan". Others rhapsodise about the waterskiing opportunities, the boats and fish. The turquoise lake is known for its astonishing beauty, surrounded as it is by photogenic mountains, and indeed, thanks to canny businessmen, there are boat trips and jet ski rentals to suit everyone. A panoramic restaurant is also under construction.

But beneath this idyllic surface lie roads, schools, mosques, shops and restaurants, entire villages. Because Attabad Lake is, in fact, brand new.

On January 4, 2010, the village of Attabad was hit by an enormous landslide. The entire village was swallowed up and about twenty people were reported dead. The landslide was so substantial that it completely blocked the Hunza River, and the lake grew as a result. The authorities were not able to start the clean-up before June, by which time the lake was twenty-two kilometres long and up to a hundred metres deep. More than four hundred houses were submerged by the rising water and six thousand people had to be evacuated. All the villages north of this natural dam were without road access for years; all the bridges and roads were under water, and more or less all trade with China ground to a halt.

"A lot of the houses in Passu were also under water," Akhtar told me. "For five years, it took three hours by boat to reach the road."

Akhtar was full of stories about villages that had been swallowed by landslides or flooded. Once upon a time, Passu had actually been on the other side of the river, but in 1964 the whole village was buried by a landslide. No-one died, but the inhabitants were forced to move to the other side of the river.

The Attabad catastrophe had been predicted. In August 2009, the Geological Survey of Pakistan had done some studies in the area, and the scientists concluded that Attabad lay in a high-risk zone. A number of recent earthquakes had destabilised the rock mass and it was only a matter of time before it started to break up. The geologists recommended that the local authorities evacuate people living in the most dangerous areas, but nothing was done, and only months later, the predicted landslide occurred.

As the original road had been submerged, the new road to **Karimabad**, our next stop, passed through four tunnels built by the 2500 MSL Chinese, which are known as the Pakistan–China friendship tunnels. The town was once called Baltit, but in 1976, after all the principalities were dissolved by the then prime minister Ali Bhutto, the name was changed to Karimabad in honour of His Highness Karim Aga Khan, the religious leader of the Ismaili community. The majority of people in Hunza are Ismaili Muslims, a branch of Shia Islam that places great importance on education and science. The Ismailis only pray three times a day, many do not fast during Ramadan, and only a small number of women cover their heads.

"The Aga Khan says that if you have two children, a son and a daughter, and you can only afford to give one of them schooling, then you should prioritise the girl," Akhtar said.

More than forty per cent of the adult population in Pakistan is illiterate, but in Hunza this figure is lower than twenty per cent. More or less all young people can read and write, including the girls. And, as if to underline this, there was a girls' high school close to the hotel where I stayed. The school was financed by the Aga Khan Foundation, and was attractive and well maintained, with green spaces, modern buildings, table tennis tables and badminton courts. Three girls were sitting on the steps up to the dormitory building, doing their home-work. They were all in their final year and only had one and a half semesters to go.

"What are you going to do when you finish?" I asked.

"I'm going to be an engineer," one said.

"I'm going to study business and finance," said another.

"And I'm going to do medicine in Lahore," said the third.

On the other side of town was Pakistan's only carpentry work-shop run by women. The head of the workshop, Bibi Amina, a forceful lady with short brown hair and keen eyes, showed me around. She was thirty-three and had worked there for ten years. The workshop was established with support from foreign embassies and charities, but had now been operating as a profitable business for many years.

"Why did you want to become a carpenter?" I asked.

"To get out of the poverty trap," she said, pragmatically. "And to do something different."

The workshop was spacious, and we picked our way around large saws, work benches, thick planks and angle grinders.

"Is it difficult?" I asked.

"Not for me, no," Bibi said. "I can make anything: furniture, doors, entire houses – I can do it all."

"Do you have a family?"

"I'm married and have a three-year-old son. My husband works as a chef in Abu Dhabi and comes home in the holidays."

"It can't be easy having a husband who's away so much," I said, with sympathy. "Do you miss him?"

"Not at all," Bibi said, "it's fine. There's nothing but problems whenever he's home!"

"Have there been any negative reactions to your choice of such an untraditional profession for women?" I asked. Even though Hunza is one of the most liberal places in Pakistan, I had noticed that only men worked in the hotels, restaurants and shops.

"It wasn't easy to begin with, and lots of men told us it was men's work and women shouldn't be doing it, it was against our religion and our culture," Bibi said. "But now that we're successful, it's fine."

"Would you like your son to follow you and become a carpenter?" I asked, in parting.

"Oh no, I've got greater plans for him than that! He's going to be an architect. Now that's a good profession. It's better to design houses than to build them!"

The mir's old summer palace towered over the houses and hotels in Karimabad. Though perhaps towered is not the right word, as the palace was neither particularly big nor impressive, and was made from simple materials such as wood and stone. The thick, solid walls were covered in clay, and in the small, primitively decorated rooms, the seats were on the floor along the walls. Before the principalities were dissolved, north Pakistan had been divided between seven absolute monarchs, of which the mir of Hunza was one. The oldest parts of the palace were more than seven hundred years old, whereas the most recent additions, including some colourful glass windows and a dial telephone, were from the time of the British Raj. A dusty Russian pistol hung on the wall, a reminder of the international tensions that played out in the region towards the end of the nineteenth century, when the British and Russian empires wrangled for influence in Central Asia. This power struggle has gone down in history as the Great Game, an expression that was immortalised in Rudyard Kipling's famous novel, *Kim*.

Hunza only became an important pawn towards the end of the game, after Russia had conquered the greater part of Central Asia, including what is now Uzbekistan and Turkmenistan. In the summer of 1889, there were rumours that the Russian captain Bronislav Grombchevsky had paid the mir of Hunza a visit and been well received, and so was planning further visits. The British deemed Hunza to be within their sphere of interest – though that had never stopped the Russians before – and decided to take the matter in hand. The British had long feared a Russian attack: if they got hold of Hunza, it was not far to India, the jewel in the crown. In August the same year, the British agent Francis Younghusband was sent to Hunza to have a serious talk with the mir. Not only was the mir in the process of allying himself with the enemy, he had also been behind the systematic plundering of caravans travelling along the trade route from Leh in North India to Yarkand in China.

Younghusband was only twenty-six, but already a weathered explorer. Some years before he had travelled alone from Beijing to Kashmir, crossing Manchuria, the Gobi Desert and the more or less impassable Mustagh Pass in the Karakoram Mountains. The pass has only been crossed twice since. As a reward for this feat, Younghusband was invited to join the Royal Geographical Society, and became the youngest member ever. By the time he set off for Hunza, he had risen through the military ranks to captain. Younghusband was an old-school explorer, fearless and dedicated. He maintained British etiquette at all times and took a cold bath every day if possible, even if this meant his servants had to make a hole in the ice.

Some days after Younghusband and his party had arrived in Hunza, a messenger appeared with a rather unexpected invitation: would he join Captain Grombchevsky for dinner! The two gentlemen met the next day for soup, stew and substantial amounts of vodka in the Russian camp in the Karakoram Mountains. The meeting was historic: it was the first time that two of the players had met in the field while both on a mission on behalf of their empires. The tone was surprisingly open and Grombchevsky was more than happy to confirm the nagging fear of the British: there was nothing Russia desired more than to invade India, he all but bragged. Younghusband could not fail to notice that Pamir, one of the few areas in Central Asia that was not yet occupied by Russia, was marked in red on Grombchevsky's map.

When they had drunk together and exchanged stories of wild adventures for two days, the two men went their separate ways.

"We and the Russians are rivals, but I am sure that individual Russian and English officers like each other a great deal better than they do the individuals of nations with which they are not in rivalry," Younghusband wrote in his bestselling book *The Heart of a Continent*. He continued: "We are both playing at a big game, and we should not be one jot better off for trying to conceal the fact."[3]

However, Younghusband fails to mention that he nearly sent Grombchevsky and his men to their deaths, shortly after this pleasant interlude. The Russians wished to carry on to Ladakh, which was under British control. Younghusband persuaded the local Kyrgyz to direct them to a treacherous and impossible route which led to nowhere other than the high plateaux and mountains without pastures. The horses died on the way, and all the Cossacks suffered from frostbite as a result, but managed to find their way to safety in the nick of time. Captain Grombchevsky was still hobbling around on crutches almost twelve months later. He never found out that it was his dinner guest who had led them astray. Several decades later, as he lay on his deathbed, he sent his old rival a letter and a book that he had written about his adventures in Central Asia. Younghusband was then at the peak of his career – he was president of the Royal Geographical Society and laden with medals and orders.

Grombchevsky had also risen through the ranks to become a lieutenant general. In the revolution that started in 1917, he sided with the Whites and was sent to the Far East, where he fought against the Bolsheviks for three years. When defeat became fact, he miraculously managed to make his way back to Poland via Japan. He died in Warsaw in 1926 at the age of seventy-one.

Younghusband's meetings with Safdar Ali, the mir of Hunza, were not quite so pleasant. Younghusband was struck by how fair-skinned the mir was, with reddish hair, but had little else favourable to say of him. The more often they met, the more he was irritated by the mir's uncouthness. Safdar Ali immediately confessed that he was behind the ambushes on the caravans, and said he would be willing to put a stop to them on condition that the British gave him financial recompense – after all, the plundered riches were his main source of income. It gradually dawned on Younghusband that the mir's bluntness in making this demand was neither down to courage nor strength of character, but, rather, a complete ignorance of the world. "He was under the impression that the Empress of India, the Czar of Russia and the Emperor of China were chiefs of neighbouring tribes. [. . .] He and Alexander the Great were on a par. When I asked him if he had ever been to India, he said that 'great kings' like himself and Alexander never left their own country!" [4]

The mir was so boorish that in the end Younghusband refused to meet him. This did not stop the mir from sending a steady stream of messengers to the British queen's envoy to ask for more presents, such as nose bags and soap; he even asked for the tent where Younghusband was quartered. The fact that Safdar Ali had murdered his own father a couple of years earlier and thrown two of his brothers over a cliff in order to gain power did nothing to enhance Younghusband's impression of him.

He was not in the best of humour when he left Hunza just before Christmas, having failed to secure any firm promises from the mir.

Two years later, in 1891, the Russians occupied Pamir. Young-husband, who was in the area on a reconnaissance mission that summer, was woken one morning by twenty Cossacks and Russian officers riding up to his tent. Only three days before, he had had dinner with them and toasted Queen Victoria and Tsar Alexander, but the mood was very different now. The Russians informed him that he was on Russian territory and asked him to leave the area. The situation was not improved by the fact that Safdar Ali had contin-ued to ambush caravans travelling to and from India. So the British decided to "close the door" to India once and for all. They gathered an army of more than a thousand men, conquered the neighbouring princely state of Nagar and from there marched into Hunza. Safdar Ali realised that the Russians would not come to his aid, as he had hoped for so long, and fled to Kashgar with his wives and children, and all the treasures he had stolen.

The British then installed his half-brother, Muhammad Nazim Khan, on the throne and maintained their supremacy in Hunza until India was lost to them in 1947.

"The guide at the summer palace said that political prisoners were never held for more than a week, but that's not true," Akhtar said, as we walked back down to the centre of Karimabad. "In 1974, the year before all kingdoms in Pakistan were disbanded, a man from Passu was held in the mir's dungeon for six months. And by the way, did you notice how big the corn silos were?"

I nodded.

"The people of Upper Hunza had to pay high taxes to the mir," Akhtar said. "If we came with a small goat, we'd be told to come back with a bigger one. He was never satisfied. But not only did we have to pay taxes to the mir, we also had to pay his bodyguards and other people in the south. No-one could leave the mir's territory without permission, especially not those of us from the north."

We stopped by the first café for a coffee. Akhtar was a good friend of the owner, Didar Ali, a good-natured man in his sixties.

"Wow, an Italian coffee machine!" I exclaimed, pointing at the impressive machine that took up half the bar area.

"Yes, but we don't have enough electricity to use it!" Didar Ali said, laughing. "We've got a hydro-power station here that was built by the Norwegians in the nineties."

"Is it still operating?" I asked.

"Oh yes," Didar said, shaking with laughter. "Well, ten per cent of it, at least!"

"What was the last mir like?" I asked, once I had my cappuccino, made with an espresso pot and hand-frothed milk.

"When I was young, I used to go around shouting anti-mir slogans," Didar said. "I would shout: 'We want freedom!' But the elders wanted to keep the system as it was, they thought democracy wasn't real. The Great Game hasn't finished, you see, it's still going on, only the players have changed. We now have the Americans instead of the British, and the Chinese have taken over from the Russians."

"In Passu, we're talking about moving the whole village away from the road," Akhtar interrupted. "The traffic and Pakistanis are bad enough as it is, and it will only get worse."

"Personally, I'm grateful for China's investment in the region," Didar said. "When I was in Kashgar in the 1990s, there were more camels than cars. The place is unrecognisable now. It's incredible what the Chinese have done! After 9/11, tourists stopped coming here and lots of the hotels went bust. Now at least there are Pakistani tourists, thanks to the road that the Chinese built."

"Far too many, if you ask me," Akhtar said, resentfully. "I ran a hotel in Passu for a while, and our guests were almost exclusively Pakistani. They were always complaining about the food, there was always something wrong. We had to stop giving them towels as well, because they always took them when they left, or polished their shoes with them. Sometimes they used the sheets as well. I don't understand why they come here, they just sit in their cars and complain that there are mountains everywhere."

"I admire the EU!" Didar said, unperturbed. "Imagine what we could achieve here in this region if only we worked together! Pakistan, India, Iran, Afghanistan – just think of the potential!"

"Perhaps you should agree on your borders first of all?" I said.

"As India thinks that Hunza and Gilgit-Baltistan, in other words, the whole of north Pakistan is part of Kashmir, we're not even properly a part of Pakistan, we just happen to fall under Pakistani rule," Didar complained. "We can only vote in local elections, not general elections."

"On the bright side, we don't need to pay tax," Akhtar said.

"But practically no-one pays tax anyway," Didar said, with a sigh.

On my last evening in Hunza, we drove up to Duikar, a famous viewing point, from where you could see the whole of Karimabad. The clouds that had hidden the mountains like a curtain had just parted. Behind us there was a clear view to Hunza peak and Lady Finger, and in front of us we could see Golden Peak and Rakaposhi, which is the highest mountain in Hunza at 7788 MSL. The view was unsurpassable, so sublime, so awe-inspiring that even the thesaurus does not have words to describe it. As the sun was setting, the light and colours were constantly changing; one moment the sky was salmon pink, the next like molten gold. The Japanese lady standing beside me could not get enough either; she must have taken at least a thousand photographs. Every so often, she let out an almost feral *Oooooh!*

There are two things I still regret from my travels in the Himalayas. And one is that I did not stay longer in Hunza.

Family Planning in Fairyland

3300 MSL The road up to the **Fairy Meadows** is reckoned to be one of the most dangerous in the world, and with good reason. Local farmers carved out the road that twists and turns like a thread up the steep mountainside, which is unstable and prone to rockfalls and avalanches. The road was barely wide enough for one jeep, with only the tiniest margin, and every bend was a hairpin. If we met another jeep coming down, the driver had to reverse and balance on the edge of the road, with half the wheel hanging over the drop.

At one point, the driver got out and poured cold water on the engine, which gave my nerves some respite.

"What's the hardest thing about this job?" I asked the driver. His name was Alfidin and he looked about fifteen, but he had been driving up and down the mountainside five or six times a day for the past ten years.

"Nothing," Alfidin assured me, and got back in behind the wheel. I closed my eyes.

The journey up took an hour and a half, but it felt more like a week and a half. When I got out of the jeep, I was soaked in sweat, even though we had not yet started walking. The final stretch up to the Fairy Meadows had to be done on foot, not because it was not possible to build a road, but rather because the local farmers wanted to keep their livelihood. A porter took my rucksack and disappeared with a smile, and Akhtar went off to sort out our escort. In the far distance, I could make out the snow-covered peaks of Nanga Parbat, the western anchor of the Himalayas.

The first European to write about Nanga Parbat was the German botanist and explorer Adolf Schlagintweit. He travelled in the Himalayas and Karakoram in the mid-nineteenth century, in order to study the mountains and the earth's magnetic field. He was told by the locals that the M-shaped mountain, which was actually part of a twenty-kilometre-long range, was known by two names: Nanga Parbat, which means "Naked Mountain" in Urdu, and Diamir, which means "King of the Mountains" in the local language. Schlagintweit continued north through Hunza and the Khunjerab Pass. The original plan was that he would travel back to Germany via Turkestan and Russia, but he got no further than Kashgar. Here he was accused of being a Chinese spy and was executed by the brutal emir. Schlagintweit was only twenty-eight years old.

Nanga Parbat has claimed many German lives since then. Even though no formal agreements were signed, the highest mountains in the Himalayas and Karakoram were divided more or less equally between various European countries: the British claimed Mount Everest, the Italians focused on K2, the French on Annapurna, and the Germans set their sights on Nanga Parbat, the naked mountain.

The peak is 8125 MSL, making it the ninth highest in the world. During the rise of national socialism in Germany in the 1930s, climbing Nanga Parbat became an obsession, the ultimate test of manhood, the very symbol of Arian superiority and *Kameradschaft*. The first six attempts to reach the top were unsuccessful and more than thirty lives were lost. It was not until 1953, some weeks after Edmund Hillary and Tenzing Norgay had conquered Mount Everest, that a person stood on the summit of Nanga Parbat for the first time. The expedition party had decided to retreat because of the bad weather, but the 29-year-old Austrian Hermann Buhl carried on regardless and made a solo ascent without oxygen. He reached the peak at seven o'clock in the evening of July 3. As it was too late to go back down, and he had no sleeping bag or tent, he was forced to stand through the night in clothing that was unsuitable for such heights. He had the face of an old man when he returned to the camp the following morning suffering from frostbite, dehydration and exhaustion. Four years later, Buhl was caught in an avalanche at 7,300 metres, having nearly reached the top of Chogolisa in Karakoram. His body was never found.

Nanga Parbat has since been climbed many times, but is still reckoned to be one of the most dangerous mountains in the world. For every third mountaineer who succeeds in reaching the top, there is one who dies – only Annapurna in Nepal has a higher death rate in terms of the Himalayas. Nanga Parbat has therefore earned itself the nickname Killer Mountain. The local authorities have tried to curb the use of this morbid moniker, as after the terrible events in summer 2013 it was a little too apt.

In the evening of June 22, 2013, sixteen armed men stormed into Nanga Parbat Base Camp, having walked for two days to get there. They screamed that they were from the Taliban, from Al-Qaeda, and forced the mountaineers, guides, porters and cooks out of their tents. Ten foreign mountaineers were executed on the spot that evening.

We had no ambitions of conquering Nanga Parbat. Our destination was far less strenuous: we were heading for Märchenwiese or Fairy Meadows. It is said that the place was given this name by a group of German climbers in the 1950s, who were charmed by the green slopes and spectacular view to Nanga Parbat. As I was a foreigner, I had to be escorted up to the meadows by an armed policeman. The authorities were not taking any more chances – the service was free of charge, but there was no choice in the matter. My guard was called Bartak and was a tall, thin man in his late forties, with a long, brown beard, friendly eyes and a well-oiled Kalashnikov.

I was the only foreign tourist on the path, and, for once, I outstripped everyone. I passed one panting city youth after another, who all, without exception, were playing music at full volume on their mobile phones to drown out the silence of the mountain. Young men from the village went around offering horses to any hikers of girth. The horses were not left idle for long. An unbroken line of juice cartons, chewing gum paper, empty crisp packets and chocolate wrappers ran parallel to the path.

"They live in rubbish and they die in rubbish," Akhtar said scornfully.

The meadows lived up to their name. They were covered in bright green grass, surrounded by poplars and did indeed have a superb view of Killer Mountain. Several dozen tents and primitive cabins were there to welcome the tourists. As we ate some steaming hot lentil soup in one of the simple cafés, we heard yelling and shouting from the other end of the Fairy Meadows.

"You're in luck," Akhtar said, pushing his soup plate to one side. "Come on!"

I ran after him and found myself in a frenzy of horse hooves and mallets. The men of the village watched the polo match from the roofs and boulders, cheering and shouting. Akhtar and I found a quieter spot on the slope and sat down to watch. The players did not appear to follow any rules, taking aim with their mallets at their opponents as well as the ball. They pulled and pushed and then suddenly, without warning, someone hit the ball in our direction. The horses thundered towards us. Akhtar and I jumped up and ran uphill as fast as our legs could carry us, but the horses were faster, and soon we were surrounded by hooves and tails. The other spectators laughed so much they were in danger of falling off the roofs.

That evening, I was joined by three men in their thirties from Islamabad. They made a fire and we sat and talked Pakistani politics under the stars.

"The new prime minister, Imran Khan, is a good man," one of them said. He had shoulder-length hair and was wearing a leather jacket.

Khan had been sworn in as prime minister only a few days before. As a young man, he was one of the best cricketers in the world, and as captain of Pakistan's national cricket team he led them to victory in the World Cup in 1992. Four years later he established the Pakistan Tehreek-e-Insaf (Pakistan Movement for Justice) party, and over the years became a prominent opposition politician. In 2018, he was successful in the general election, with his party winning 110 of the 269 seats in parliament.

"Unlike other politicians, Imran Khan is not interested in money," the man in the leather jacket said. "He could have got millions of dollars when he divorced his first wife, who was loaded, but he didn't want it. They got divorced because she couldn't bear to live in Pakistan any longer, whereas he wanted to do something for his country. There's an honesty about it. But his second ex-wife . . . well, she's still writing books."

"What kind of books does she write?" I asked.

The men chuckled.

"Books that aren't suitable for children," said his friend, who sported a thick, short beard. "She started to write them after she met Imran Khan, if you see what I mean. He's a playboy, that's his one great weakness."

He did not seem to think it was much of a weakness though.

"Have you tasted Hunza water?" the first one asked. "They're known for it here. It's really good, better than brandy."

"I haven't drunk a drop since I came to Pakistan," I said.

"What? You haven't?" The third man looked at me astounded. "Poor you! We would gladly give you some, but unfortunately we've only got marijuana."

"What kind of Muslims are you?" I asked, jokingly.

"There are strong Muslims and there are weak Muslims," the bearded man answered. "We're relatively weak. In Pakistan, you can get anything you want, if you know the right people."

"I hope Imran Khan will liberalise the country and make it less strict," his friend said.

"Hasn't he got a very religious wife now?" I asked. "Doesn't she wear a burka?"

"*She* is very religious, yes. But he isn't. Luckily."

The fresh mountain air had made me sleepy, so I decided to have an early night. After I had crept into my sleeping bag, a disco started by the fire. The three friends must have brought loudspeakers with them all the way from Islamabad.

The following day, Akhtar introduced me to a friend, Mursalin Khan.

"Mursalin wants to show you the village," he said. "I'm a man and I have no relatives here, so I can't go in."

"But I can?"

"Yes, of course. You're a woman."

Mursalin had a narrow face, a pointed nose, a furrowed brow and a full beard. He looked as though he was well over fifty, but was actually only thirty-four, the same age as me, or so he said. He spoke good English and, like most people up here, was dressed in a down jacket and shalwar kameez, the traditional South-east Asian outfit that is worn by both women and men and comprises a long, loose shirt or tunic and wide, baggy trousers.

The village was behind a fence just above the polo pitch, and everything behind the fence belonged to a hidden world.

"Once they're ten or eleven, the women are not allowed out of the village anymore," Mursalin explained. "They have to follow special routes when they go down to work in the fields, so as few people as possible see them."

Mursalin took me to his house, a simple wooden hut with an earthen floor. His wife, sister-in-law and a handful of children of different ages sat leaning against the wall inside. They greeted us with a smile, but said nothing. None of them could speak English.

"My wife works with family planning," Mursalin said. "It's something new that the authorities have introduced. The women here don't normally work, but I'm happy for her to have the job. I trust her and she trusts me."

"How many children do you have?" I asked.

He thought for a moment.

"About eight. You see, *we* don't use family planning, we welcome all the children we are given."

On Mursalin's orders, his oldest daughter served us homemade lassi, first salty, then sweet. According to Mursalin, his wife was thirty-five or thirty-six and already had grey hair under her headscarf. She turned towards us and spoke quietly to her husband.

"She wants to know if you're married," Mursalin said.

I nodded and his wife then asked how long I had been married, and if I had any children.

"My wife has given me permission to take another wife, a foreigner," Mursalin said suddenly.

"Does she have to be a foreigner?" I retorted.

"Yes, I don't want to marry another local woman. My plan is to move abroad and work hard and earn lots of money to help my family back here."

"Do you have any preferences when it comes to the country?" I asked.

"No, she can be from anywhere. Japan, France, Germany, Korea ... It doesn't really matter, as long as we get on and respect each other."

"How do you think your foreign wife will feel about the fact that you've got a wife and eight children in Pakistan?"

"I'll have to find someone who is tolerant," Mursalin said. "Mutual understanding is so important. I guided for a German woman yesterday, showed her around the mountains here. As we walked, I told her about my plans, as I'm telling you now, and she got really angry and said she had a boyfriend at home. She refused to talk to me afterwards. It's such a shame it had to end like that. I don't understand why she got so angry." He shook his head, then looked straight at me. "Ask her! Please, just ask her yourself."

"I'm sorry?" I looked at him, bewildered.

"Ask her, ask my wife if she's happy for me to take another wife."

"Are you happy for your husband to take another wife?" I asked, obediently. Mursalin was pleased to translate my question.

His wife smiled and nodded.

"Why do you allow it?" I asked, and Mursalin translated.

"That's the way in Islam," she said. "A man can have four wives."

"She has far stronger faith than me," Mursalin said. "She prays and fasts and follows the rules. I try to be as good as I can, but I'm not as strong. And anyway, I think the most important thing is to be a good person. Are you a Christian?"

I shook my head.

"What religion are you then?"

"I don't have a religion," I said.

Mursalin looked at me, dumbfounded, and explained the situation to the women. A fast conversation ensued.

"They say that you're free to become a Muslim then," Mursalin said. "Because you do believe in God, don't you?"

"No, I'm afraid I don't," I said.

"How do you explain all this then?" Mursalin asked, throwing open his arms. "The sun, the moon, a day like today? Why are we alive? Why do we die? Can you answer me that?"

I had no quick answer.

"There you go!" Mursalin said, triumphant. "Science isn't enough. The only logical explanation is that there is a god. And it's obvious that Islam is the best religion, because it's the last. The correct religion. It's all in the Koran, even the Bible and Jesus and other religions are mentioned. You don't seriously believe that humans have evolved from apes? What nonsense! In the Koran it says that man was created by God, and woman was created from man's rib. It's the only logical explanation."

He proceeded to tell me about the prayer rituals and which prayers should be said when.

"Is it long until the next prayers?" I asked hopefully.

Mursalin look at his watch.

"Twenty-five minutes," he said, but did not seem in any rush. Instead, he showed me around the upper part of the village, taking pains to point out which fields he owned, which animals belonged to him and which people worked for him.

"They're from the north," he explained. "I have paid them lots of money, several hundred thousand rupees, to work for me. If they want to stop working for me, they have to pay me back the entire sum. I also give them around two thousand rupees a year."

Some quick mental arithmetic told me that two thousand rupees was about eight pounds.

"That's not much," I said.

"No, but they get food and lodgings as well. And I'm not only responsible for my workers, but also for their families. When one of them marries off a daughter, for example, I normally give ten thousand rupees for the dowry. I also pay the medical expenses if any of them get ill."

The houses we passed were small and simple, and almost entirely without furniture. Wherever we went, there were hens, cattle, goats and small children. Outside one of the houses, a half-naked boy of about five or six lay on the ground, staring into the air with empty eyes. The flies hovered like clouds above him.

"He was born like that," Mursalin said. "He just lies there."

As we walked out of the village, the imam called people to prayer from the mosque, but Mursalin still appeared to be in no rush. Instead, he took me out onto a plateau at the end of the village, where there was a panoramic view to the west and the Karakoram and Hindu

Kush. The Indus River twisted like a brown intestine between the two great mountain ranges. From the other end of the village, there was a panoramic view to Nanga Parbat and the Himalayas, which stretched east through India, Nepal and Bhutan, all the way to Namcha Barwa in Tibet, the eastern anchor of the Himalayas, more than two thousand kilometres away. And the Fairy Meadows lie nestled in the middle of these three massifs, the highest mountains in the world, like an exceptionally conservative, fossilised magic realm.

Four or five bearded men were standing spread out across the plateau when we arrived. They were all staring intently at their phones. No modern signals have managed to penetrate the fences that enclose the Fairy Meadows, and this was the only place where they could reach the world outside.

Mursalin insisted on accompanying me back to the cabins, and Akhtar did not need to ask him twice to have supper with us. While we waited for the food, Mursalin disappeared. The lentils had been put on the table and had time to cool before he came back. With a secretive smile, he produced a Coke bottle full of cloudy, light-brown liquid from his jacket, and then with ceremonial discretion poured a glass for each of us. It tasted like diluted, cheap grappa.

"Hunza water," Mursalin whispered, casting a furtive look around the room. "I bought it a couple of days ago, but haven't had any reason to drink until now. Cheers!" He lifted the glass and downed the light-brown substance. "Wonderful, isn't it?"

Akhtar wrinkled his nose but said nothing. I nodded politely.

"Let's raise a glass to Pakistan," Mursalin said, and charged our glasses. "And to Imran Khan! Pakistan needs new energy. We need a new Pakistan. Cheers!"

Feast and Fast

From the Fairy Meadows and Nanga Parbat, the Himalayas run east towards India, but there are only two border crossings between Pakistan and India, and the closest one was a good deal further south, near Lahore. The days when caravans could freely cross mountain passes and national borders are long gone. While it is constantly said that the world is getting smaller and there are fewer and fewer boundaries, never before have borders been more rigid than they are now. There can be no doubt that the map takes precedence over terrain: the abstract red lines of the map are fiercely guarded on the ground by cameras, motion sensors, armed guards, and often also by physical barriers such as barbed wire, fences and walls. Even in this relatively forgotten corner of the world, high above the tree line, where the red lines are replaced by dotted lines – disputed, controversial and non-ratified – the nearly-borders of maps are carved in granite, locked in a frozen conflict between two countries that once were united.

As it was not possible to follow the mountains east, I headed west, towards Afghanistan and the Hindu Kush, an elaborate detour on my journey towards the official border crossing at Lahore.

At the village of **Juglot**, forty kilometres south of Gilgit, the Gilgit and Indus rivers merge, and the Hindu Kush, Himalaya and Karakoram mountain ranges meet, or separate. A weathered sign gave information about the local geography: we were standing with our backs to the Hindu Kush; to the left of the Gilgit River we could see the Karakoram, and the mountains to the right of the Indus and the Gilgit were part of the Himalayas. The water in the rivers was a turgid dirty brown, while the mountains were a lighter brown, steep and barren; the black of the asphalt road, paid for with Chinese loans and subsidies, was the only thing that broke up the shades of brown.

I could not differentiate between the three ranges. One mountainside looked much like the other, but Akhtar insisted that *his* mountains, the Karakoram, stood out as the most beautiful.

Later that afternoon, the brown peaks of all the ranges that towered up on each side of the Gilgit River were hidden by dark-grey clouds. The wind blew up and within minutes a heavy shower had turned the gravel track to mud. We soon came to a halt behind a long queue of stranded cars. There had been a landslide a few hundred metres ahead, and the road was blocked by boulders and piles of scree and earth. A couple of dozen men had got out of their cars to take a closer look at the landslide, and stood with crossed arms examining the mass of stones. The women stayed in the cars, covered and invisible. After about an hour, a single bulldozer came to our aid, and after a couple of hours more, as darkness fell, the road was finally cleared.

When I think back on my travels in the Himalayas, it feels as though I spent most of my time in vehicles of some sort on bumpy, dusty, narrow roads that were prone to landslides. In many places the speed limit was fifteen or twenty kilometres an hour, and we travelled at a snail's pace while the sun slowly descended in the sky. The next day was the same, and so the weeks and months – life, in fact – passed, as the drivers and I were coated in a layer of fine dust and the mountains slid past outside the dirty car window, ever higher, steeper and browner, the Hindu Kush to our left and Karakoram to our right.

The police and military road blocks became a welcome distraction. On our way to Chitral, the next destination, we were stopped sixteen times, and each time the same questions had to be answered:

nationality, passport number, visa number and telephone number.

3700 MSL   The next day, in the afternoon, we went through the **Shandur Pass**, which is home to the world's highest polo pitch. For a week in July every year, the grassy slopes are covered by a colourful patchwork of tents, and teem with horses, riders and spectators, but now, in August, the pitch was bare and deserted – the only life to be seen was a handful of grazing yaks and two young soldiers who were there to ensure that all foreigners who went through the pass were duly registered.

1494 MSL   Hours later, we eventually reached **Chitral**, where I once again had to register, this time at the police station in a small office designated FOREIGNERS REGISTRATION. A short, bespectacled bureaucrat sat behind a tower of forms that he filled out by hand. The shelves were full of dusty sheaves of paper held together by rubber bands. On the wall behind him hung a huge poster with neat columns recording all the foreigners who had visited Chitral since the 1990s. Tourist numbers plummeted following the terrorist attack on the Twin Towers, and have still not returned to previous levels.

Once I had my pass and a new, armed guard had arrived, we carried on south towards the border with Afghanistan and Kafiristan, Land of the Infidels. The road that led there, to one of the most isolated and inaccessible places in Pakistan, was even narrower than normal, with a steep drop down to the river on one side. Kafiristan originally covered an area that included north-west Pakistan and east Afghanistan, and was inhabited by about sixty thousand fair, blue-eyed people, who worshipped various gods. According to legend, they were descendants of Alexander the Great and his army, who conquered Poros, the king of Punjab, in 326 BCE. A number of linguists believe that the various peoples of Kafiristan are actually older than that, and possibly have their origins in one of the earliest Indo-Aryan immigration waves, before the main influx from the west around three and a half thousand years ago.

In 1893, these people found themselves on either side of the roughly 2,500-kilometre border that was drawn up by Henry Mortimer Durand, the Foreign Secretary of India at the time, which is now the porous border between Afghanistan and Pakistan. The Durand Line cut through ethnic groups, tribes and families without mercy or consideration: those who found themselves to the west of the invisible line were under the rule of the Afghan emir, while those who lived to the east became subjects of Queen Victoria. A couple of years after the line had been drawn, the emir of Afghanistan, Abdur Rhaman Khan, launched an attack on the infidels on his side of the border to force them to convert to Islam, possibly the last forced conversion in history. And to mark the success of his mission, the emir decided to change the name of the region from Kafiristan to Nuristan, Land of Light.

The Kalash people escaped this mass conversion, as they lived on the British side of the border, in what is now Pakistan, in the three remote valleys of Birir, Rumbur and Bumburet. Today, there are only about four thousand Kalash people, making them the smallest ethnic minority in Pakistan, and the only surviving people from Kafiristan.

Coming to **Bumburet** was a bit like arriving in a different country. 1100 MSL Even the houses were different, built of timber with decorated window and door frames. Most buildings had an open veranda on the top floor, covered by a slanting, metal roof. The men wore baggy trousers and light, loose tunics as they do everywhere in the villages of Pakistan, but the Kalash women's traditional dress was unlike anything I had seen. They wore long black dresses, with large, intricate patterns in bright colours such as turquoise and gold, drawn in at the waist by wide, embroidered belts. Under the dresses, they wore baggy, black trousers, which were also embroidered with intricate patterns. They gathered their hair in two thick plaits, with a thinner plait over the forehead. This was then pulled back carefully under a beaded headdress, which was round, like a crown. A tail of colourful beads and cowrie shells hung down their backs, stopping about halfway, and their necks were adorned with heavy bead necklaces. They walked with straight backs, alone or in small groups, so startlingly visible in their bright dresses and jewellery that it seemed to be a protest against the general attitude to women in the country in which they lived.

When we got to the simple guest house it was already dark, and too late to get hold of any of the Kalash's famous home-made wine, much to Akhtar's disappointment. I brushed the mouse droppings off the sheet and immediately fell asleep.

The next day, we followed the sounds of a crowd to a house that was teeming with people. Akhtar asked if we could come in. We were welcomed warmly and immediately offered two low chairs, freshly prepared thick pancakes and home-made crumbly cheese. A young woman wearing a traditional Kalash dress with green embroidery sat down beside us. Her name was Zaina Bibi and she was twenty-seven years old, with a round, friendly face and bright smile.

"Ask me anything you want to know. Anything at all, and I will do my best to answer," she said in good English. "You've come all this way to visit us, so it would be a shame not to get answers to all your questions."

She did not need to ask me twice.

"Why are there so many people here?" was my first question.

"My cousin died in Karachi a couple of weeks ago. It was completely unexpected, and no-one knows why he died. He's laid out in the temple over there." Zaina pointed to the large wooden house opposite. "For the past two weeks, people have been coming from the other villages to dance for the deceased. His close family and friends are weeping all the time, and the elders sing laments. The family has to slaughter goats and cows to feed all the visitors from neighbouring villages. Funerals are really expensive. You have to sacrifice a hundred goats, or more. There are so many people to feed! In the old days, we used to make *gandaoer* – large wooden statues to symbolise the deceased, which would be buried alongside the body – a year after the death, but practically no-one can afford it anymore."

"To make the statue?"

"No, not the statue, the celebration! On the first anniversary of the death, the deceased's family had to invite the whole village for a huge meal. Oh, but when a girl dies, there's no dancing, everyone just cries. And the wake is only one day for girls."

"Why do you dance for men who have died?" I asked.

"Hmm, I don't actually know." Zaina scratched her head and thought about it. "The elders say that it's an old tradition, and we have to respect traditions, we can't change them, as then our culture would disappear. We'll be celebrating the harvest festival soon, and then we all dance," she added. "After the celebration, we're allowed to eat walnuts, grapes and corn, but never before. In summer we often dance every evening, but since my cousin's death we haven't danced. Maybe we'll be allowed to dance again this evening. I hope so!"

She smiled, poured me another cup of tea and put out more cheese on the plate.

"We have a lot of trouble with our neighbours and the Taliban," she said, serious once again. "A few years ago, people came here and killed our goatherds and stole our goats. The authorities say that they can't protect us, and that it would be best if we didn't keep livestock. Lots of people have sold their animals. I personally studied in Peshawar, and have a master's degree in nutrition. I was advised not to say that I was a Kalash in Peshawar, so I said that I came from somewhere far away and wore ordinary Pakistani clothes. Life in Peshawar was very lonely. It's better here, with my people. I'm going to stay here now."

"Have many Kalash people converted to Islam?" I asked.

"Yes, lots of my friends have become Muslims, and live elsewhere now, in Islamabad, Karachi, Lahore," Zaina said. "Their poor parents. Mine would be so sad if I converted. We're not rich, and my parents had to sell goats and cows to pay for our education. So I owed it to them to come back. Every now and then Muslims come and tell us that we'll go to hell when we die, that we're kafirs, disbelievers, and that paradise is only for Muslims. I've asked them a couple of times if anyone has ever come back from paradise to tell them that, but they just get angry and say that I'm making fun of their religion, and that they will kill me. I think what is most important is that we do good things while we're alive. We also believe that the soul lives on after death. If you've done lots of good deeds, your soul will find peace. But if you haven't done many good things, your soul will be restless and without peace."

When we left the house, there was enormous activity outside. A group of men were busy decorating the square for the harvest festival, with glitter and colourful streamers, and hordes of children danced around happily. Two young women stood at the edge of the square watching the preparations.

"She's only eighteen, but she just got married," said the older girl, nodding at the younger, who burst out laughing when her civil status became the topic of conversation.

"Was it an arranged marriage?" I asked.

"We don't do that here," the older woman laughed. "They eloped!"

"How did you meet?" I asked the newly married eighteen-year-old. The girl burst out laughing again when Akhtar translated the question. It took a long time before she was able to answer, but then between bouts of laughter and giggles she managed to tell us that he was a policeman and had worked in her village. They had been a couple and sent each other messages in secret for two years, and eventually eloped. That is to say, *she* ran away to his parents, as was the custom, and later they got married.

"My life was good before as well, but now it's even better." She blushed, then burst out laughing again. "I miss my family, of course, but basically my in-laws are just like my parents."

In the evening, the women gathered together for a dance. The small square was dark and dusty, and I could only just see their swinging dresses. A drum was the only accompaniment and the rhythm was simple but fast. More and more women arrived, and they danced in circles around the square in groups of three, spinning on their own axis as they part sang, part shouted *AAAaaaah!* again and again. At regular intervals, the small groups grew into long chains of women that moved sideways in the dark, one body, one voice, one long vowel.

The following morning, I went for a wander through the village. Bumburet lay between steep, green hills, making for a dramatic location. At one point, the road once ran closer to the river; the old road was destroyed in an earthquake in 2015, which also toppled scores of houses and shops. Everywhere, I could see the women sewing or washing dresses for the harvest festival, and happy children skipped and danced around, giddy with excitement.

After visiting the local museum I bumped into Zaina again. She held a small bag with shampoo and a hairbrush, and her two long plaits were dripping.

"I've just been to the bathhouse down by the river to wash my hair," she said. "Only men and children are allowed to wash at home. The women have to go down to the river."

"Why is that?" I asked.

Zaina shrugged. "It's an old rule. Probably something to do with our religion. It's fine in summer, but in winter we have to carry the warm water from here down to the bathhouse."

She smiled, and invited me into her house.

"It's not very clean, I'm afraid." She motioned apologetically at the spotlessly clean wooden floor. "I normally scrub the floor every second week, but there have been problems with the water supply recently."

There were two single beds in the corners, and the shelves on the wall were full of food and kitchen utensils.

"Most people seem to get married early here, but not you," I said.

"No, not me . . . I had lots of offers when I was younger, but said they would have to wait. I wanted to get an education first, take a master's degree. But my suitors didn't wait, none of them waited. Now they all have three or four children."

A slight, hunchbacked woman in an old, patched dress came into the room. She had big ears and a big nose, sunken cheeks and lips so thin they were almost invisible. Her shiny hair was still dark and in narrow plaits. She wore the traditional colourful headpiece.

"This is my grandmother, Jamki," Zaina explained.

I smiled politely at the old lady, who squeezed my hand with a smile.

"How old are you?" I said.

Zaina translated my question for the old woman and then her answer for me: "She doesn't know how old she is. She might be eighty, she might be a hundred."

"Was life here very different when you were young?" I asked. The old woman burst out laughing, a hoarse and dry laughter. Then she started to talk in a tremulous, high voice. "When I was young, we wore woollen clothes. They were very heavy and it took a year to make them. We had leather shoes and we didn't have chapattis, like we do now. We made walnut bread and walnut curry. Everyone was enormously strong, and there were no schools. I got married when I was twelve or fourteen. The elders in the village came to speak to my parents and said that I should get married. My parents didn't have much say, really. Everyone was poor in those days, and Pakistan was not independent. We were ruled by local royalty, who came from Afghanistan. They were Muslims and took our crops, they killed people whenever they had a mind, and did terrible things to our young girls. They forced us to work for them as slaves, and tried to convert us to Islam. At the time, we had to celebrate all our festivals in secret, up in the mountains. We didn't have much food, and we gave our children dry, crushed pears and pumpkin. We took our animals to the fields early in the morning and stayed until evening. These days, young girls stay at home all the time. And yet I think there was more love back then. What little people had, they shared with each other. Nowadays, people just think of themselves, and the young people don't dance anymore, not like we used too."

"How many gods do you have?" I asked. I had learned in the museum that the Kalash people worship twelve gods.

"We have only one god," Zaina's grandmother said. "But we have special songs for the walnut, the grape, the apricot, the snow, and so forth. We have lots of songs!"

"Why can't women wash at home?"

"Women have so much hair!" said the old woman, with a hoarse laugh. "If we were to wash at home, there would be hair everywhere! And hygiene is important. The same is true of birth and menstruation. We have special houses for that, houses are kept very clean. It's better for women that way. Men are not allowed into the women's houses; they don't know what goes on there. It's our secret world."

Some of the people I met there had fair hair and blue eyes, like the inhabitants of Hunza, but the vast majority had jet-black hair and brown eyes. DNA analyses are yet to prove any relationship between the Kalash people and the Greek. However, the myth that the Kalash are descendants of Alexander the Great has endured; there are dozens of articles with romantic titles such as "The Lost Children of Alexander the Great". Perhaps inspired by this, the Greek authorities have made great efforts to support this small, pagan people in the Hindu Kush. And thanks to the investment from Greece, Kalash women now have large, comfortable houses to stay in when they are not able to be at home. The Greeks have also paid for libraries, schools and museums in the Kalash valleys. A teacher, Athanasios Lerounis, was the driving force behind the Greek commitment. He had been visiting the Kalash people regularly for fifteen years, and had learned the language so well that he had developed a written form when he was kidnapped by the Taliban in 2009. One of his two guards was killed during his abduction. Lerounis was released seven months later for a large sum of money, and, for his own safety, has not been back to visit the three Kalash valleys since.

No-one knew when the harvest festival, *uchaw*, would begin. Some said the dancing would start at eight, but others thought it would be ten, and still others insisted it would be twelve on the dot. There was a small ceremony early in the morning, with prayers and cheese, for the goatherds, but only men were allowed.

To be sure I did not miss it, I went up to the square soon after breakfast. Even this, the concrete dance floor, was a gift from the Greek authorities. The square was full of children running around with sweets in their mouth. Animated Italian tourists took photographs of the children from every angle, but no-one was dancing. A dozen heavily armed Pakistani policemen were spread around the square and surrounding hills to frighten off any would-be terrorists.

Through the morning, people arrived at the square dressed in their finest clothes. The men had decorated their felt hats with feathers and flowers, and the women had got out their *kupas*, the party headpiece, decorated with beads and beautiful small shells, even though we were far from the sea.

"They're waiting for a politician," Akhtar said. "Once he's arrived, the celebrations will start."

Wazir Zada, the first Kalash minority representative in the Khyber Pakhtunkhwa parliament, eventually turned up in the afternoon. The Kalash had only been recognised as a separate ethnic group the year before, which was why they had never had a representative in the regional parliament.

Zada posed for photographs with a handful of tourists, gave a short speech, took part in one dance with great pomp and ceremony, then hurried on his way. I managed to catch him just as he was about to leave the village, so I got straight to the point.

"What are the main challenges that the Kalash people face today?"

"For the first time in history, there's a Kalash representative in the parliament," he said. "I am going to fight to protect our culture, because if we don't, it will probably disappear. As I'm sure you noticed, the road here is not particularly good, it's challenging. But, at the same time, it's perhaps a blessing, as more people would come here if it were better, and we don't have the capacity to welcome many more. Where are you from?"

"Norway," I said.

"Oh, wonderful!" Zada exclaimed. "We have had so much help from our friends in Italy. Let's take a photograph together." He got out his mobile, took a selfie, then rushed off, in the way of politicians.

The dance floor was now heaving with joyful dancers. The dance was the same as the previous evening, only there were many, many more people and drums. The women moved slowly round in their circles, linked together, as they sang: *AAAaaaah!* And the men made up lines of three or five, the younger ones running and crashing into the rows of women, cheering and laughing. The village was transformed into a disorganised, chaotic body, a mass of energy, song and colour.

Akhtar and I were leaving for Swat Valley that afternoon and had a seven-hour drive ahead of us, so I reluctantly pulled myself away from the dance, the laughter, the drums, the embroidered dresses and the happy smiles.

*

We officially left the Kalash valleys at the police checkpoint by the bridge, and bade farewell to our armed guard, who would soon have new foreigners to look after. The women we passed on the road turned away as we approached, so we only saw their backs and long headscarves. A few hours later, further south, the headscarves were replaced by burkas. The women walking by the side of the road, always accompanied by a man or a boy, had lost any shape or form, their eyes looking straight ahead through the cotton netting that acted as a filter between them and the world.

My memory of the happy, colourful Kalash people, the drums and the dancing was already beginning to fade. It was as though, for a short while, I had been in another country, a pagan Shangri-La. Gradually the roads become flatter, wider, better; we sped through two tunnels, which it had taken more than thirty years to build, and suddenly we were in Swat. The countryside was green and lush, hazy – but the streets were eerily empty, and all the shops and restaurants were closed. There were piles of goats' heads and loose sheepskins on the street corners, the remains of the day's mass slaughter. The blood was still trickling in streams on the pavements. The Muslims were also celebrating: the first day of *id al-adha*, and everyone who could afford to had slaughtered a sheep or a goat in honour of Ibrahim, or Abraham, as he is known to the Jews and Christians, to celebrate the fact that he did not have to sacrifice his son, Ismail (in the Jewish and Christian teachings, he is asked to sacrifice his son, Isaac). Even though the names differ, the story ends well in all three world religions: God was testing the loyalty of his servant, and a lamb was sacrificed in place of the boy. Human sacrifice was no longer necessary.

Presumably, everyone was at home, even restaurant chefs, hotel chefs and street vendors, gathered with relatives, close and distant, around a feast of steaming lamb stew. Dark was falling. We had still not found anywhere to eat and had a long way to go. There were a few men out walking, in the middle of the road and by the side, all wearing long, light-coloured tunics, but there were no women to be seen, only mounds of fleeces, open-mouthed goats' heads, streams of blood and headlights that danced as they blinded us in passing.

Love in the Time of the Taliban

Muhammed, the pharmacologist I met on the minibus from China to Pakistan, had been sending messages and calling me every day to find out when I would visit him and his family. He lived in the village of **Odigram**, a few kilometres west of Saidu Sharif, the capital city of the district of Swat, but I did not even notice where Saidu Sharif ended and Odigram began. We followed a long street of dilapidated buildings, rubbish, chaotic traffic and even more chaotic wiring, and at some point the street changed name, and we slipped out from the city into the village. Odigram was called Ora by the Greeks, and is best known for being conquered by Alexander the Great in 326 BCE.

Muhammed welcomed us with delight. On the bus, he had been wearing jeans and a leather jacket, but now he was wearing a light-brown tunic and baggy trousers. Akhtar and the driver were taken to a guest room outside the house, towards the street, whereas I was allowed in behind the closed gate. The bedrooms were arranged around a large, airy atrium that was furnished with low benches and a small table. In one corner, there was a simple kitchen that had a roof but no walls. Muhammed's father was lying on one of the benches with a blanket over him; he was so small and frail that he was surely in danger of disappearing into the folds in the blanket at any moment. Muhammed's mother wished me welcome with a kiss on each cheek, and I also met Muhammed's young wife and sister and brother. The atrium was full of children, but none of them bothered to introduce themselves. Muhammed's sister-in-law, who was on her way out, groaned as she took out her burka.

"It's so hot," she grumbled. "It's so tight around my head, and difficult to see."

"It's our culture," Muhammed interrupted. "Women here dress like that. They always have done."

"Are you hungry, would you like some food?" his mother asked, with a smile. Muhammed translated. I politely declined, but the women started to busy themselves in the kitchen, nevertheless, and soon came back with freshly pressed mango juice, cakes, fruit salad and sweet, milky tea.

"She doesn't eat enough, you have to give her more food," the old father said, from the blanket folds.

Muhammed's younger brother was called Ahmed. He was thirty, with spectacles, a narrow, oval face and a trimmed beard, and was dressed in jeans and a T-shirt. He smiled at me.

"So, you're Norwegian?" It was more of a statement than a question.

I nodded.

"Fantastic!" Ahmed clapped his hands in delight. "I'm working on a PhD about the Norwegian anthropologist Fredrik Barth!"

"Are you really?" I exclaimed. "I'm a social anthropologist, and Fredrik Barth was my great hero. I was actually lucky enough to meet him a few times, and it was like meeting God! What are you writing about?"

"I'm comparing what Barth wrote about the Swat Valley in the 1950s with what it's like now," Ahmed said enthusiastically. "Everything he wrote about has changed! Not only was Swat an independent princely state back then, and we weren't part of either Pakistan or Afghanistan, the culture was completely different from what it is now. Barth describes customs that I've never even heard of. The social institutions, how married couples should behave together, everything is different. For example, Barth describes something called *hujra*, a place where the leading figures in the community met in the evenings. It was a tradition unique to Swat, but no longer exists. The women had their *gudar*, but that doesn't exist anymore either. I didn't know about any of it until I read Barth!"

We sat and talked about Barth and his travels for a long time, and the fact that his best-known theory – that identity and awareness of one's own culture is created only in meeting another, unknown group, in other words, in crossing boundaries – was inspired by his fieldwork in Swat. Muhammed had gone out to entertain Akhtar and the driver in the guest room. The rest of the family, including the children, sat closely around us and watched with silent curiosity. The women made sure that our cups were always full of tea.

"Swat is still a very conservative society," Ahmed said. "Our women don't have it easy."

"Do they never protest?" I asked.

"Protest?" He gave a dry laugh. "No, they would never even dream of protesting."

A girl of about five, his niece, crept up into his lap and whispered something in his ear.

"She thinks you're very beautiful," Ahmed said. "She wants to know how you got such lovely fair hair."

"Tell her that she's beautiful too," I said.

"The same sad fate awaits this little girl," he said, with a sigh. "She'll get married and be chained to the home. She will have no opportunities."

"Only if everyone tells her that's the case," I said.

"That's true," Ahmed nodded. "I'll tell her she has to get an education and a job! You must meet my wife, by the way, she also speaks English." He waved to a young woman who was sitting on one of the benches by the wall, a couple of metres away from the rest of the family. She had beautiful, dark eyes and was dressed in light, traditional clothes. A delicate, cream-coloured scarf hung loosely over her long hair.

"Come over here, Sara, sit closer to us. You can speak English with her, no-one else will understand what you're saying."

"Yes, come and sit with us," I repeated. She was eventually persuaded and came closer.

"We've been married for fifty days," Ahmed said, with a smile. His eyes were sparkling.

"How did you meet?" I asked.

"That's a very good question!" Ahmed laughed merrily. "We'd barely met before we got married."

"So it was an arranged marriage?"

"No, no, it was a love marriage, the first in the family."

"But you hadn't met before?" I said, confused.

"No!"

"How did you communicate then? By mobile phone?"

"Okay, okay, let me explain," Ahmed said. "We have to go back to 2009. To escape the Taliban who controlled Swat Valley at the time, the whole family lived in a camp for internally displaced people. It was there that I met Sara's older sister, who was a student and helped refugees in her spare time. She faced many challenges, but never gave up, and I was fascinated by her courage. As I was also a student, I did something unimaginable: I asked for her telephone number – and got it! We started to chat a lot after that. We discussed everything. Education, life, everything. When I started to look around for a partner, her little sister was also looking for a husband, and we realised that we were meant to be."

"So you met Sara through her older sister?"

"Yes, yes, that's how it happened," Ahmed shouted with glee. "But she was very young when I first got to know her, only a child, really."

"I don't quite follow," I said. "How did you actually get to know Sara? It was her big sister you were chatting with."

"Sara shared a bed with her sister, so I got to know them both at the same time! I was really impressed by Sara from the start.

She seemed so sensitive and wise. No matter what I asked, she always had a good answer. She wanted to do something with her life. Her greatest dream was to serve humanity."

"And how do you hope to serve humanity, Sara?" I asked.

"Through him," Sara said, smiling, and nodded at Ahmed.

"I'm so proud of her," Ahmed said. "She's a pioneer! She's the first one in her family to marry for love. She had to fight for two years to be allowed to marry me."

"In our family, it's normal to marry a relative," Sara said. "I practically had to fight with my cousin in order not to marry him."

"And I had to fight too," Ahmed said. "Nearly every day for six months, I had to fight. My father was the only one who supported me. He said that I should marry the one I wanted to marry."

"When did you meet face to face for the first time?" I asked out of curiosity.

"In 2016," Ahmed replied. "On Valentine's Day. She had a veil in front of her face, so I could only see her eyes, but I was besotted all the same. We met in an ice-cream bar. She came with her sister, because a woman can't go anywhere alone in these parts. One year later, to the day, on Valentine's Day, I proposed. I rang her and asked if she would marry me, and she just cried and cried. She didn't give me an answer for a whole month. And I tell you, it was a very long month! I was so scared she would say no! I actually thought she wouldn't reply at all. Her cousin was pestering her and wanted to marry her. But she said yes! And I jumped up and down, up and down, up and down, I was so happy!"

"Did the cousin come to your wedding?" I asked. I imagined that the atmosphere might have been a bit tense if he had.

"No, are you crazy?" Ahmed looked at me in dismay. "Once we're married, men have no contact whatsoever with their female cousins, and women have no contact with their male cousins. I don't even have my cousins' telephone numbers. Men are only allowed to be with their sisters, sisters-in-law, mothers and mothers-in-law. And their daughters and granddaughters, of course. That's it. That's how strict things are here."

He looked round. Muhammed was still with Akhtar and the driver.

"No-one in the family knows what we've just told you," he whispered, with a wink. "And as we're speaking English, none of them here will understand what we're saying."

"What did you tell the family?" I asked.

"We said that we'd met at college and that we'd studied together," Sara said and laughed.

"She was just a child when I was a student, but they don't know that," Ahmed said. "They've never studied. Sara is the first person in the family to have a master's degree, in sociology. I'm so proud of her!"

"What was it like for you, moving in with Ahmed's family?" I asked Sara.

"It was hard," she said, quietly. "The culture, the people, the family, it was all so hard. And still is."

"What is it that's difficult?"

She looked down at the floor and said nothing.

"You can speak openly," her enamoured new husband said. "I can leave, if you like, so you can talk honestly. Tell her, don't hide anything!"

But Sara did not want to talk and looked the other way in silence.

"You've got a master's degree, but you're not working," I said. "Is it not boring just to stay at home?"

"Yes, it's incredibly boring," Sara said, and looked at me.

"I know she's bored," said Ahmed, who himself taught sociology at the same time as doing his PhD. "We talk a lot about it when we're alone. It's not easy for women in our society to get a job. It's our culture, unfortunately. Our culture forces us to do lots of things that we don't want to. This morning, for example, I had to wake

Sara early, even though she was tired after serving guests until late into the night yesterday. I just wanted to let her sleep, but my parents insisted, they were having more guests. So what did I do? I woke her, even though I didn't want to."

"Would you like to work, Sara?" I asked.

"Yes," was her immediate reply. "I want to work as a teacher at the university."

"There are a handful of women who are teachers in our field," Ahmed said. "Maybe three or four. But it's unusual. I would be happy for her to work, but it's not that easy."

"You've already got a master's degree," I said to Sara. "Would you like to take a PhD?"

"Oh yes!" She smiled broadly, and glanced over at her husband.

"There are lots of women in Pakistan who do PhDs," Ahmed said. "But in these parts . . . it's not so easy."

"Couldn't you just move to Islamabad, for example?" I said.

He shook his head, sadly.

"No, that's not possible. Our culture is too strong. To move from here is unthinkable."

"But surely she can be allowed to work, so she doesn't need to be bored and alone all day," I said. "That's not a life."

Sara looked at her husband with hope.

"Fine," Ahmed smiled, full of love. "She'll be allowed to work. I promise."

Sara beamed.

"You know, this is the first time that Sara and I are sitting at this table having a nice chat. Normally we just eat here. There's not a good atmosphere in the house; they order her around all the time. 'Get this, get that, go to the market, do this, do that.' My wife is not happy here, but Muhammed's wife is even more unhappy. She gets mistreated, especially by Muhammed. He hits her."

Just then, Muhammed came through the door, and as though

to demonstrate what his younger brother had just said, he marched over to his wife and slapped her around the head before sitting down beside me.

"You mustn't hit her," I said.

"Why not?" Muhammed forced a smile. "It's our culture. Wives should be beaten, they have to be held down, like springs. Otherwise they jump up and get out of control. Like that," he said and pointed at a child's bike that was propped up against the wall. "The springs have to be kept in place for it to work, all the parts have to be held tightly together."

"Your wife is not a bicycle," I said.

Ahmed squealed with delight and took my hand. "Exactly, exactly!"

"It's our culture," Muhammed said, curtly.

"Culture is a poor excuse for being horrible to your wife," I said, and Ahmed jumped up and shouted eagerly: "Yes, yes, that's it! Culture is a poor excuse!"

Before I left, I promised Ahmed and Sara that I would contact them again to find out if Ahmed had kept his promise and let Sara get a job.

I never got an answer.

The Pakistani Taliban, Tehrik-e-Taliban, was established in 2007 and the same year took control of the conservative Swat Valley. The Taliban rule lasted two years, and during this time it was forbidden for girls to go to school. Sharia law was introduced everywhere and anyone who broke the law risked being hanged in the market square. Long after the Pakistani military had driven the Taliban out of Swat, there were sympathisers and live cells in Pakistan, in the north-west and along the border with Afghanistan, in particular. In 2012, the later-to-be Nobel prizewinner Malala Yousafzai was shot in the head by a Taliban supporter in Swat Valley because she had publicly defended the right to education for girls.

The Taliban fought against not only what they perceived to be Western, anti-Islamic culture, but also against their own cultural heritage. In autumn 2007, the Tehrik-e-Taliban decided to destroy the enormous 1,500-year-old Buddha in Swat. The face in particular was badly damaged; fortunately not all the explosives went off. The relief, which was once an important place of pilgrimage, was the second largest Buddha in Central Asia, after the one in Bamiyan Valley in Afghanistan, which the Taliban had already blown up in 2001.

There was no road up to the enormous relief, so Ahktar and I had to scramble over boulders and follow overgrown paths to get there. On the way, we passed a small farm with donkeys and bleating goats. The farmer, a sinewy old man with a wrinkled face like leather, accompanied us in silence for the last stretch. He did not speak Urdu, and Akhtar could not speak the local language, but without the farmer's help we would probably never have found the statue, even though it was enormous. Dignified, with his legs in the lotus position, and a distant, peaceful expression on his face, the Buddha was carved into the rock face at the start of the seventh century. It was barely possible to see where the Italian archaeologists had restored the 1,500-year-old forms. The restoration work had taken many years and had only been completed a few weeks earlier.

Despite the Taliban's attempts to delete the past, there were physical traces of Buddhism's former glory everywhere in Swat. I met the archaeologist Muhammad Usman Mardavi in the ruins of the Takht-i-Bahi Buddhist monastery, one of the most important sites in Pakistan, and together we climbed the steep hills in the baking sun. There were people everywhere, many of them carrying huge loudspeakers, propane gas bottles and picnic baskets. In the court-yard in front of what must have been the main building, groups of young men danced happily, shouting and cheering in the suffocating heat. The ruins were awash with rubbish; it was obviously a popular place to celebrate Eid.

"Only around thirty per cent of the site has been excavated," Mardavi told me, and pointed to the jagged mountains around us. "We don't know how much lies underneath these mountains, as we haven't got that far yet. The entire Takht-i-Bahi site measured some sixty hectares, and included monasteries, stupas – Buddhist shrines, that is – and underground meditation cells as well as secular buildings. Some of the structures were three storeys high, and if you study them carefully you will see that they are earthquake-proof. The people who built all of this must have been excellent engineers, because there are constantly earthquakes in this part of the Hindu Kush. The monastery was in use until the seventh century, when the Gandhara kingdom started to decline."

"Pakistan has an incredibly rich history," I said.

"Yes, of course. After all, people have lived here for more than twelve thousand years," the archaeologist said. "More than eighty-seven thousand archaeological sites have been registered in Pakistan. Very few of them have been excavated, because it would cost billions to excavate them all, not to mention the maintenance costs . . ."

He looked sadly around at the barbecue parties and dance orgies.

"All of the ancient civilisations flourished on the banks of a river," Mardavi said. "The Egyptians had the Nile, the Sumerians had the Tigris. And the Indus civilisation grew on the banks of the Indus. Of the four hundred ancient cities and towns that were known to lie on the banks of the Indus, only Harappa and Mohenjo-Daro have been excavated. The people who lived there had standard weights and a writing system that was not pictographic. They built with stones and bricks and had advanced drainage systems. One might wonder if the people then were more intelligent than us . . ."

"When was Islam introduced?" I asked, as loudly as I could to be heard over the different Pakistani pop songs that were blaring out of the many portable loudspeakers.

"In 1023, when Mahmud of Ghazni attacked the Swat Valley,"

he replied. "Before that time, the people here were Buddhists and Hindus. Buddhism found its way here very early on, more than two thousand years ago, and Swat was, for a long time, one of the most important pilgrimages for Buddhists in the region. People travelled from far and wide to learn from the teachers who lived here – some even came from China. Many people, myself included, believe that Padmasambhava, also known as Guru Rinpoche, was born here in Swat in the eighth century. It has not yet been discovered where exactly he was born, so that remains a bit of a mystery. Padmasambhava spread tantric Buddhism to the Himalayas, including Tibet and Bhutan. You'll find he crops up wherever you go on your travels here in the mountains."

I already longed for high altitudes, away from the road checks, traffic chaos, silent ghost women, armed guards and staring men. The mountains were not far away, I could see the white peaks in the distance, but the mountains also included the valleys and passes, and rivers that flowed from them, and the cities and towns that lay at their feet.

331 MSL **Peshawar** lies just south of Takht-i-Bahi and is one of the oldest cities in South Asia. Its history is a textbook in Central Asian dynasties: the Persians, Greeks, Indians, Turks and Afghans have all passed through, and Buddhists, Hindus, Muslims, Sikhs and Christians have ruled here. Because of its location just east of the strategic Khyber Pass, one of the few places where it is possible to cross the inhospitable Hindu Kush mountains, Peshawar was an important stopping point on the trade route between the Indian subcontinent and Central Asia, and thus also a natural target for invading armies. For example, Mahmud of Ghazni, who introduced Islam to the Swat Valley, travelled along the trade route, and was followed by Genghis Khan's Mongol army a couple of centuries later. Alexander the Great and his army also rode through the Khyber Pass, and even though

Alexander's vast empire did not survive the mighty general's death, Greek continued to be the language of administration in Peshawar for several hundred years. Many of the Buddhist statues that were made during this period are remarkably similar to the statues of the gods on the Acropolis.

The notoriously bad-tempered American writer, Paul Theroux, describes Peshawar with surprising warmth in his travel classic *The Great Railway Bazaar*. "I could happily have moved here," he writes, "settled down on a veranda and got old watching the sunsets over the Khyber Pass." Powerful words indeed, coming from Theroux.

Obviously, a fair amount has happened in Peshawar since the American travel writer visited the city in the 1970s. Or perhaps it would be more correct to say that remarkably little has happened. The old colonial buildings are even more dilapidated than the houses in old Havana, but unlike the Cuban capital, where time has famously stood still, certainly in terms of architecture, ugly, new concrete buildings have sprung up between the wooden houses in Peshawar. People no longer live in the ramshackle old buildings, and many use them for storage instead. Once upon a time, perhaps even as recently as the 1970s when Paul Theroux was wandering through the bazaars, dreaming of growing old here, the city must have been beautiful and full of colour, with airy wooden verandas decorated with carvings and intricate facades. Today it is full of rubbish, a sense of decay and fascinating, anarchic power line systems. The lines are wrapped around each other in chaotic bundles, like a thick, hostile spider's web; there are so many of them that they have become a part of the street, a permanent art installation. It is a miracle that power outages are as rare as they are.

When I visited, the narrow, twisting streets of Qissa Khwani Bazaar, the storytellers' bazaar, were just as chaotic as the rest of the city, a jumble of colours and smells. The selection of goods, however, was very orderly. Each street was dedicated to one thing, so in one, they sold only kitchen utensils, in another only spices, and in a third, women's clothing. All the vendors were men, even in the shops offering lace knickers and sexy bras. As the only Westerner in the bazaar, and the only woman without a face covering, I caused quite a stir. The vendors waved and called to me as I passed. In the kitchen utensils street, a man in his forties came over to us, took Akhtar to one side and talked to him very earnestly for a long time. And from their sideways glances, I guessed that they were talking about me.

"What did he say?" I asked, when the man had gone.

"Nothing," Akhtar said, evasively.

"Come on, what did he say?"

"He was worried about your safety," Akhtar said, with some reluctance. "He didn't think it was safe for you here. He advised us to get out of here as quickly as possible."

Suddenly I saw potential danger everywhere. Men who passed a little too closely, despite there being plenty of space on the pavement. Men staring at me from windows, from street corners. Were they concealing knives in their waistcoats, or guns? Did they have a machine gun hidden under the till? At one of the many checkpoints on the way into town, we had been offered armed guards by the police, free of charge, but I had declined. My reasoning was that guards would make me even more obvious, whereas, in fact, I could hardly be more obvious than I already was. Had I made a mistake when I said no to being escorted?

By the exit from the bazaar, another man came over and started to talk to Akhtar and gesticulate enthusiastically. He had a reddish beard and thick glasses.

"He says he has a Hindu temple in his backyard and wonders if we'd like to go and see it," Akhtar said.

"Do you think it's safe?" I asked.

"Absolutely," Akhtar said with total confidence. "He's from the mountains, like me. From Kashmir."

We followed him into the backyard, and, sure enough, there was an old Shiva temple there. It was shaped like an oval dome, grey, almost black, due to the air pollution, and surrounded by rubbish. There was a small, shining white Sikh temple opposite, which was pristine and beautifully kept. The women in the family greeted Akhtar and me warmly. None of them had their hair covered, and the younger ones were wearing lipstick and nail varnish. On a small platform outside the house, a thin, white-haired man sat supported by cushions. His name was Saeed Muhammad, and he told us that he was seventy, but he must have been older, as he had fled from Kashmir in 1947.

"My father led us here," the old man told us in a high, tremulous voice. "I was very young, so I don't remember that much. I was born in Jammu, in the southern part of Kashmir. The Muslims were slaughtered by the Hindus. I remember the killings, I remember those things. I remember how sad it was to leave our house, our country, everything we owned. We took nothing with us, apart from our animals. We had to hide during the day; we hid by the riverbanks and in the forest. We travelled slowly through the night. The whole family fled together, my three brothers, my four sisters, my uncles and aunts. We walked and walked for more than two weeks."

The old man smiled sadly. One of the young women came out with milky tea and biscuits for us.

"All my brothers and sisters are dead," Saeed Muhammad said, as he sipped at the hot tea. "I am the only one in the family who now remembers where we come from. Kashmir is a paradise. In Kashmir, people don't drink as much tea as they do here, they drink milk. All this tea has made my skin darker. I miss Kashmir every single day, let me tell you. It was cooler there, everything is so different here, and we have had to learn how to live here. When we first arrived, we were given a house and everything we needed by the Pashtuns who lived here. We thought we would soon be able to go home again, but I no longer believe it. *Insh'Allah*, there will be an end to the conflict. If God so wishes."

The partition of India and Pakistan in 1947 led to what is possibly the largest and most dramatic migration of people in the history of humanity. Punjab, one of the most populous regions in India, with a large number of Muslims, Hindus and Sikhs, was divided in two. About fourteen million people ended up on the "wrong" side of the new border and had to leave their houses and homes. Millions of Sikhs and Hindus left Pakistan, while millions of Muslims on the Indian side of the border fled to Pakistan. The refugees used any means of transport available: train, bus, car, bicycle, horse, donkey, camel, their own legs – and many never made it. Estimates of the number of people killed following partition vary from two hundred thousand (the figure the British authorities worked with) to two million. Presumably the real figure is somewhere in between.

Pakistan, which means "Land of the Pure", has been dogged by unrest since its dramatic inception. Clan wars, military coups, widespread corruption and border conflicts with India have made their mark on the young state. The porous border with its war-torn neighbour, Afghanistan, has at times experienced a free flow of refugees, as well as extremists and weapons. Following the Soviet invasion of Afghanistan in 1979, hundreds of thousands of refugees streamed over the Khyber Pass to Peshawar every month. And in this century, after the attack on the Twin Towers in New York and the subsequent invasion of Afghanistan, led this time by the Americans, Pakistan imploded into chaos. This peaked in 2009, when terrorists and rebels carried out more than 2,500 attacks. More than thirty thousand people, most of them civilians, have been killed in terrorist attacks in Pakistan over the past two decades, primarily in the unstable border region to the north-west, but terrorists have been active throughout the country. No-one has been spared. The Qissa Khwani Bazaar in Peshawar has been bombed twice by extremists, once in 2010 and again in 2013.

And every person killed leaves behind a devastated family.

Parents and grandparents, wives, husbands and siblings. Plus all the uncles, aunts, cousins, friends, classmates, neighbours – hundreds of thousands of people have been affected.

One of the bloodiest and most brutal attacks in the history of Pakistan took place in 2014. On the morning of December 16, six armed terrorists or more stormed into a primary school in Peshawar and opened fire, killing 130 schoolchildren.

One was fourteen-year-old Omar.

When I returned to the hotel after visiting the bazaar, I met Omar's father, Fazal Khan, a soft-spoken man with kind eyes and a thick, well-groomed beard. He talked non-stop from the moment he sat down at the table until he stood up again, exactly one hour later.

"I chose to send my son to the Army Public School because I presumed he would be safer there." His English was fluent as he had lived abroad for many years. "Security in Pakistan was appalling at the time, with bombs going off everywhere. The Army Public School was run by the military, and normally security at the school was very good. For example, women in burkas were not allowed in. Every time the children were going to do something special, like get a vaccine, or visit a museum, we parents had to provide signed permission. But on the day of the attack, they were being taught first aid in the auditorium, without it being on the school year plan, or our having been told. And absolutely everything was written down in the year plan, down to the smallest detail. First aid was normally only taught to classes eleven and twelve, but for some reason all the pupils had been called in. The class started at ten o'clock. At a quarter past ten, the terrorists stormed the auditorium. Now tell me something: how did the major, who was in there at the time, escape the attack without so much as a scratch? Not one. If it was the military the terrorists were after, he would have been an obvious target, and easily identifiable in his uniform. But he escaped without a scratch ..."

I ordered tea and water for myself; Fazal did not want anything. We were the only guests in the small hotel restaurant.

"I'm a lawyer, and I now head the parents' group," Fazal said. "All the parents have a right to know what happened to their children. The police had been warned by the security services beforehand that an attack was imminent, that a group of terrorists were planning to attack the Army Public School. There is only one Army Public School in Peshawar. They should have doubled their patrols at the school after the warning, but instead they reduced the police presence from twenty to two. Most of the parents and I are convinced that the government was behind the attack. The whole thing is a sham. We should at least have been allowed a proper investigation. Almost four years have passed now, and we still haven't achieved justice."

I cannot count the number of kitchen tables where I have sat and listened to these same words and accusations, spoken with the same endless grief and pain, only in another language, in another country. On September 1, 2004, a group of terrorists took more than one thousand pupils and teachers hostage at School Number One in Beslan, in North Caucasus. On the third day of the siege, Russian special forces stormed the school and more than three hundred people, most of them children, were killed in the chaos and fighting. I spent many weeks and months in Beslan in the years that followed; I kept returning again and again, and every time I was invited to homes where the dead child's bedroom stood untouched, like museums of a lost childhood, of a wasted life. I met mothers who went to the cemetery every day; their lives had stopped on September 3, 2004 – they were no longer alive, they simply existed. One of the fathers I met had moved into the cemetery to be with his dead daughter every hour of the day.

The Pakistani special forces stormed the Army Public School fifteen minutes after the attack became fact, but did not manage to prevent the terrorist attack turning into a bloodbath. Most of the children were killed in the auditorium, peppered by the terrorists' machine guns.

"Lots of questions remain unanswered," Fazal said. "The authorities can't even tell us how many terrorists were involved in the attack. The official answer is six, but the children who survived say there were more, with numbers varying from eight to twenty-four. I have arranged protests and demonstrations, not just for the victims of the school attack, but of acts of terrorism all over Pakistan. I've given all my time to this, I can't work anymore, I can't concentrate. Fortunately I don't need to worry about money. The authorities don't like me and have levelled various charges against me for anti-government activities, which carry a maximum sentence of ten years. But I'm not afraid. We will continue to fight, even though I am no longer an optimist but more of a realist as a result. I no longer believe we'll achieve justice, but we must try all the same. We have to do everything in our power, absolutely all that we can."

The saying goes that time heals all wounds, but I no longer think that is the case. Every time I have returned to Beslan, things have got worse for many of those left behind. The mothers are ill, depressed and bitter, and the fathers have started to drink. Like Fazal Khan, many of them have dedicated their time to finding answers to their questions. How could this happen? Why were the authorities unable to prevent it? And the most terrible question of all: could I have saved my child if I had done something different?

"I was in court when I heard there had been a terrorist attack," Fazal said, quietly. "My brother rang me to say that the school was under fire. I went straight to the hospital. God forbid that he's among the wounded, I thought. I was at the hospital for more than three hours, but did not find Omar. At four in the afternoon, my brother found Omar in another hospital. It was a black day. A day that changed all our lives. I'm forty-eight and I have four children. The eldest is fourteen now, and goes to the Army Public School, like his elder brother. We could have left Pakistan, we could have changed schools, but that would have been cowardly. Our youngest is only three – he was born twenty days after Omar was killed. We Pakistanis invest our lives in our children, we live out our dreams through them. My wife cries every night. Our life has changed for ever, there is no more normal, any routine has been destroyed. We are stuck at December 16, 2014. Omar was always smiling, no-one can remember having seen him in a bad mood. Everyone who died that day was perfect. Omar would have turned eighteen just over a week ago, on August 19. He was shot five times. I still have the clothes he was wearing that day. I keep them folded in a drawer."

Two years before, Fazal had opened a hospital, named after his son, in a poor district on the outskirts of Peshawar that did not have a hospital. The hospital is open to everyone and is free for those who cannot afford to pay.

"Omar wanted to be an actor, but I didn't think it was a proper profession," Fazal said. "One Sunday he said to me that he wanted to become a doctor, and I promised to open a hospital for him. On the following Wednesday, three days later, he was dead."

Tehrik-e-Taliban claimed responsibility for the terrorist attack on the Public Army School and stated that the attack was revenge for the Pakistani army's military actions in North Waziristan, on the border with Afghanistan. After the attack, military activities in the area intensified. There is no exact figure for how many people have died as a result of these activities, often called clean-up operations. The state of emergency lasted for nine years until autumn 2018 when the Pakistani authorities declared that they had finally destroyed all the Taliban's hiding places in Swat and the surrounding areas, and civil rule was reintroduced. Tehrik-e-Taliban's supporters have now largely been exiled to the Afghan side of the border, but the border is still porous, and explosions are still rife in the Land of the Pure.

Border Crossing

The border crossing at Lahore (217 MSL), about five hundred kilometres south-east of Peshawar, is one of the most famous in the world: every day at sunset the Pakistani and the Indian flags are lowered with great pomp and ceremonial aggression, the gates are closed and locked and the border between the two nuclear powers remains shut until the following morning.

By early afternoon there were long queues on both sides of the border. The Indian stand was far bigger than the Pakistani one, with room for many more spectators. The flags, on the other hand, hung at precisely the same height, each on the relevant side of two securely locked iron gates. Powerful loudspeakers bombarded the public with patriotic pop music. *Pakistaaaan! Pakistaaaan!* was the monotone chorus on our side of the border. On the other side, hundreds of young men and women clustered together happily in front of the gate, in a chaotic dance, as they bellowed *Indiaaa! Indiaaa!*

I was soon to go there too, to the other side, and I looked forward to leaving the seriousness of Pakistan behind, with its severe Islamic rules. The Pakistani audience sat with straight backs, holding green flags in their hands, the women in one stand and the men in another, shouting *Allahu Akbar*, God is most great, and *La ilaha illallah*, there is no God but God. As one of the few foreigners present, I was immediately shown to the front of the VIP section, where, exceptionally, women and men were mixed. The security guard had requested that I keep the seats either side of me empty so that I did not sit too closely to a stranger of the opposite sex.

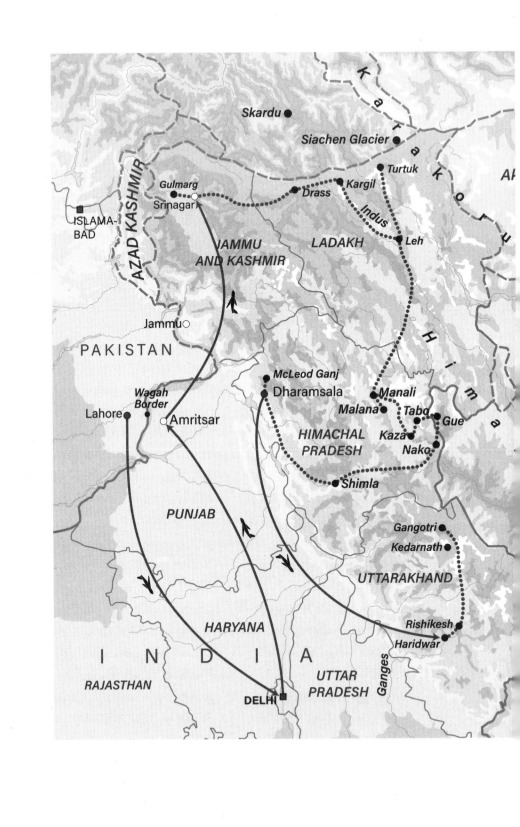

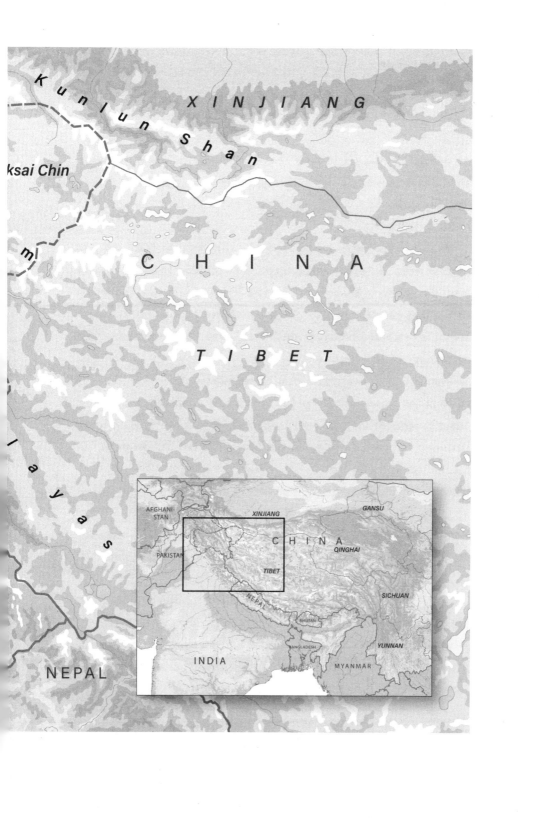

I was positively dripping with sweat by the time things finally got going. Soldiers in black, fitted uniforms and turbans decorated with a kind of tall, stiff fan marched with high kicks towards the border gate, theatrically brandishing their fists at the Indians on the other side. The Indian soldiers, who included two women, returned the gesture. In many ways, this ceremonial taunting was quite sweet, until one remembered that the conflict between India and Pakistan has at regular intervals become only too real, and not simply a military drill.

The ceremony went on and on. The soldiers marched back and forth in front of the gate, accompanied by military roars and cheers from the sweaty audience. The air was humid and heavy and it was so hot that even the insides of my eyelids were sweating, and condensation gathered between my corneas and contact lenses so that everything became blurred.

The first calls for a separate independent state for India's Muslims came in the 1930s from the political party All-India Muslim League. Great swathes of India had been ruled by Muslim Mughals for more than two hundred years when the British started to take power in the Indian subcontinent in the mid-eighteenth century. Bahadur Shah Zafar, the last Mughal emperor, was deposed by the British and sent into exile in Burma in 1858, marking the end of Muslim dominance in India. Under British rule, the Hindus, who were the majority, were given increasing power and influence, and the Muslims felt more and more overlooked.

The All-India Muslim League was founded in 1906 to ensure that Muslim voices were also heard. To begin with, they worked towards peaceful coexistence between Hindus and Muslims in an independent India. However, all their proposals, even the most moderate, were invariably defeated by the Hindu-dominated Congress Party. As the likelihood of independence from Great Britain increased, there was growing concern among the Muslim population: how would they be treated in an independent India, where Hindus were clearly in the majority?

In 1933, a Cambridge student, Chaudhary Rahmat Ali, published the pamphlet *Now or Never. Are we to live or perish forever?* Here he made the suggestion that a separate state should be established for Muslims living in the north-west provinces of British India: Punjab, Afghania (the North-West Frontier Province, which is now known as Khyber Pakhtunkhwa), Kashmir, Sindh and Balochistan. By taking the first letter from the first four provinces and the last three letters from the fifth, he made the acronym PAKSTAN. *Pak* means "pure" or "virtuous" in Urdu, and *stan* is Persian for "land" or "place". The "i" was added later for the sake of pronunciation. The idea of Pakistan was born.

When the Second World War broke out a few years later, the Muslim League, led by the lawyer Muhammad Ali Jinnah, passed a resolution to establish a separate Muslim state. Mahatma Gandhi, the powerful, symbolic figurehead of the Indians' fight for independence, was adamantly opposed to dividing India along religious lines, but the idea of Pakistan resonated with the Muslim population, and in the course of the war years, the two-state solution became an absolute demand. The British yielded and on August 15, 1947, India was divided in three: the Muslim-dominated area in the north-west became West Pakistan, and the densely populated, largely Muslim area on the Bay of Bengal, 1,600 kilometres east, became East Pakistan.

Borders are like sausages – it is sometimes best not to know how they are made. Drawing up the border between India and Pakistan was complicated and done in a rush: it was not until July 1947 that the British appointed two border commissions, one for Punjab in the west and one for Bengal in the east. The commissions were both headed by the lawyer Sir Cyril Radcliffe, and otherwise comprised representatives from the Indian National Congress and the Muslim League. But as the latter two were unable to agree, the border was in effect left to Radcliffe, who until that point had never set foot in South Asia, as is evident in the result.

The other provinces were easier to deal with: Balochistan and Sindh both had a Muslim majority and therefore automatically became part of Pakistan. To the east of the North-West Frontier Province, next to Afghanistan, they held a referendum to decide whether the province should become part of India or Pakistan. Over 99 per cent voted to become a part of Pakistan. In Punjab, however, only 55.7 per cent of the population was Muslim and in Bengal the share was 54.5 per cent. How should one draw a line between these two provinces that covered a total area of 450,000 square kilometres and had 88 million inhabitants so that the territory was fairly divided between the two new states, with as many Muslims as possible ending up on the Pakistani side, and as many Hindus and Sikhs as possible on the Indian side?

It was basically an impossible task, and the tight deadline did not make things any easier. Should Lahore, where Hindus and Sikhs dominated the business sector, but the majority of inhabitants were Muslims, become part of India or Pakistan? And what about the Sikhs' most sacred city of Amritsar, which in terms of administration was part of the Lahore district? The solution was that Lahore, which was also considered a holy city by the Sikhs, was given to Pakistan, so the new nation would have a proper city, and Amritsar remained part of India. It was by no means a perfect solution, but there was nothing better.

As the new border was so controversial, it was not announced until August 17, 1947, three days after the declaration of independence. Months of anguish and bloodshed followed. Gandhi tried as best he could to calm the riots and stop the violence, but with limited success. On January 30, 1948, he himself was shot and killed by a young Hindu extremist in Delhi.

Jinnah, the leader of the Muslim League, became the general

governor of Pakistan. However, the *pater patriae* was in poor health – a heavy smoker, he suffered from both tuberculosis and advanced lung cancer – and died on September 11, 1948, barely a year after taking office.

Radcliffe never returned to India.

The border-closing ceremony between India and Pakistan is not only the best known in the world, but, in all likelihood, also the longest. A good deal of high kicks, fist waving and excessive parading back and forth in front of the gate, and after many shouts of *Allahu Akbar!* and even more of *Pakistaaaan!* the sun finally went down, and the two flags were lowered at exactly the same tempo before being folded with furious speed and marched out without further ado. The remaining soldiers ensured that the gates were locked with due care before they turned on their heels and marched to their own side.

The spectators stood up from their seats and wandered towards the car park, all showing damp patches on their loose-fitting clothes. Only a very few of them would ever have more contact with India than this. For them, the border might as well be closed during the day as well; it was an invisible line they were not allowed to cross, and nor was I. For some reason or other, I had not been granted an ordinary visa to India, though not for want of trying. The Indian Embassy in Islamabad had been even less helpful than the one in Oslo, and, in the end, it was a slow, bureaucratic tug-of-war for me even to get my passport back. As a last resort, I applied for an electronic visa instead, and less than twelve hours after I clicked on "pay", the magic document popped up in my inbox.

The disadvantage of an electronic visa is that you can only arrive in India through an international airport, and so I would have to fly from Lahore to Amritsar. The journey would only have taken around an hour by car, but by plane it would take almost a day, as I would have to fly via **New Dehli**, which was five hundred kilometres away.   216 MSL

I said I was a teacher at passport control.

"So how can you stay here so long?" the officer asked suspiciously. "Don't you need to get back to work?"

"I'm a private tutor," I lied. "I can work whenever I want to."

The officer was clearly sceptical, but eventually gave me a stamp. The few Pakistanis who had been on the flight had all made straight for the duty-free shop, where they filled their baskets with Indian whisky.

234 MSL   In the taxi on the way into **Amritsar** I sat staring out at all the people. Women walked along the side of the road alone, most of them bare-headed, with their long hair hanging loose. Not only were there many women walking alone, a large number of the people on motorbikes and scooters were women. And most of them were dressed in Western clothing – jeans and a T-shirt. I had not seen so much skin for weeks. When I arrived at the hotel, I was greeted by three female receptionists. The culture shock was complete.

I was finally returning to the mountains the next day, after this long detour to get over a border I was not allowed to cross on foot. I looked forward to leaving the suffocating heat of the lowlands behind, and spent the rest of the afternoon in the hotel room, which was blessed with air conditioning. When the sun went down and the air cooled marginally, I took a taxi to the Golden Temple, Amritsar's most famous landmark. As it was not possible to drive right up to the temple, the driver let me off at Jallianwala Bagh, the park where many hundreds of defenceless people were massacred by British soldiers in 1919. Other than the Golden Temple, Amritsar is best known for the massacres that took place here in the twentieth century.

The British blocked the entrances to the walled park before they started to shoot, so it was impossible to escape the bullets. Between fifteen and twenty thousand people, including women and children, had gathered in peaceful protest against the arrest of two Indian leaders, but also to mark the festival of Baisakhi, celebrated by both

Hindus and Sikhs. The British, led by Colonel Reginald Dyer, were determined to crush any nascent opposition, and he ordered the soldiers to shoot into the crowds until they had run out of ammunition. Thanks to the author, Rudyard Kipling, Dyer became known as someone who saved India, whereas in reality the massacre marked the beginning of the end for British rule. The jewel had been loosened from the British crown, and it was only a matter of time before it was lost. After the bloodbath in Amritsar, Gandhi, who had supported the British throughout the First World War in the hope that the Indians would gradually be given more self-determination, was convinced that complete independence was the only solution.

A handful of families were clustered in front of the memorial – a stylised, oval flame in red marble – taking selfies. The lawns were full of young people surfing the internet on their mobile phones or just relaxing in the twilight.

I followed the flow of people down the road to the large, immaculately clean white plaza at the entrance to the Golden Temple. People sat in small groups, chatting and eating; some lay sleeping on blankets they must have brought with them. I handed my sandals in at one of the cloakrooms and covered my head with a thin scarf, then waded through a foot pool and through the white entranceway.

When I came down the steps, I was facing the temple, which lay in the middle of a large pool. The golden building seemed to float on the water, and was lit in such a way that it looked luminescent in the September dark. The building itself was much smaller than I had imagined, but the temple complex was enormous. Pilgrims sat along the walls resting or meditating; some slept. There were men getting changed everywhere, with towels around their waists, having bathed in the holy water of the pool, which they shared with the fat, red carp that swam lazily around.

I walked around the temple before I dared venture into the community kitchen. There was a long queue to get in, but everything was well organised and efficient. While we waited, we were given a spoon, a tea bowl and a metal plate with different compartments for the various dishes. The big door into the canteen opened to allow a couple of dozen people in, then it closed again. The queue was pushing from the back, and we were pressed towards the closed door and up against each other's bodies. A few minutes later, the door opened again, and elbows and legs pressed in from all directions. There was no choice but to go with the flow.

The gigantic canteen was run with military precision. People sat in long straight lines on the floor, squeezed together, eating. A volunteer led us into the room and asked us to make a new line. A tall, thin young woman dressed in a faded sari sat down beside me. She was Christian, she said, but she and her sisters came here regularly. A rotund, middle-aged businessman in a red turban sat beside her. He was from Kolkata and had traversed the country with the sole aim of visiting the temple. Volunteers served us rice, lentils and chapattis from enormous metal buckets. The food was simple but tasty, and the young woman beside me accepted a second portion with a smile. As soon as we got up to leave, a man with a big mop came over and washed the floor where we had been sitting. On the way out, we filed past the washing-up station where volunteers took our dirty plates and bowls and washed them with a clatter and tinkle in the longest sink I have ever seen.

I walked around the temple area again, past thousands of bathing, meditating and sleeping pilgrims. The golden temple still shone like a floating jewel in the water. The atmosphere was friendly; people nodded to me and smiled, but I still felt like an alien. Mentally, I was still in puritanical Pakistan. I had started to get a grip on the different schools of Islam, but what did I know about Sikhism?

I had noticed a sign by the entrance to the temple area that said INFORMATION OFFICE. I made my way there. A friendly man in his twenties welcomed me and offered me a seat.

"How can I help you?" he asked.

"I'd like some information," I said.

"Ah, I'm afraid my superiors are not at work today." He shrugged apologetically. "But we have an excellent multimedia show in the multimedia section. I recommend that you go there. You'll get all the information you need there."

"I'll go there afterwards," I said. "But could you perhaps give me some background information first?"

"I recommend that you come back tomorrow," the young man said. "My bosses will be back at work then. They can give you all the information you need."

"I'm travelling to Kashmir tomorrow," I said.

"Oh." The young man looked at the floor. "Well, then I recommend that you watch our multimedia show, as I said."

"Could you maybe tell me a little about the history of the temple first?"

"Of course," the young man said, "but the complete background is given in the multimedia show."

"I'll go there afterwards," I said, again.

The young man cleared his throat. "Okay, our fifth guru, Guru Arjan, started to build Harmandir Sahib, the Golden Temple, in 1581, and it was completed in 1589. The pool was already here, as it had been made by our fourth guru, Guru Ram Das, in 1577. He is also the founding father of Amritsar."

"Sorry, can you wait a moment?" I said, and got a pen and notepad out of my bag.

"Don't take notes," the young man said.

"But if I don't take notes, how can I remember what you're telling me?" I said.

"That's not a problem," the information officer said. "Just listen for now. You can make notes afterwards."

I obediently put down my pen as the young man rattled off

foreign names and dates that I immediately forgot. Only when he had finished telling me the long and intricate history of the temple was I allowed to take notes again.

"There are four entrances to the temple," the young man informed me. "From the north, south, east and west. That is so that everyone can have access. Everyone is welcome here, we are all children of the same God. When Sikhism was established in the sixteenth century, people of low caste were not allowed into the temples. And for Guru Nanak, the founder of our faith, it was important that everyone should be able to come to the temple, that there should be no differentiation between people. Have you been to the community kitchen?"

I nodded.

"Good," the young man said. "That's the first place you should go when you visit the temple. We are not able to concentrate on spiritual matters unless our bellies are full. We all eat together in the canteen, high and low, there is no difference between us."

Erst kommt das Fressen, dann kommt die Moral, as Brecht so aptly put it.

"How many people normally eat here in a day?" I asked out of curiosity.

"Between fifty and sixty thousand. Sometimes at the weekends it can be as many as two hundred thousand, and on special occasions, such as festivals and the new year, we can serve up to half a million people. We don't actually count, so that's an estimate based on the amount of food we use. We spend more than one and a half million rupees – a little more than twenty thousand US dollars – on food every day. We always serve rice, lentils, vegetables, chapattis and something sweet. We've got our own chapatti machine now. Did you see it?"

I shook my head.

"It's made it all so much easier," the young man said with a smile. "Anyone can stay at the temple for three days, for free. They don't need to be Sikhs, everyone is welcome. By the way, I would recommend that you try to see the sukhasan ceremony before you leave. It's when our holy book, Guru Granth Sahib, is wrapped in a cloth and carried from the Golden Temple to the inner chambers, where it is kept overnight. It's then carried back to the temple at the break of day."

"Thank you for that tip and the information," I said, and started to put away my notebook and pen. "What's your name, by the way?"

"I'm afraid I can't tell you my name," the young man said, with an apologetic shrug. "I'm actually not supposed to give interviews. I hope you enjoy our multimedia show. Like I said, it will give you all the information you need."

I said goodbye to the young, nameless information officer. When I stepped back out into the large stone plaza, I turned right, as recommended, and followed the steps down to the multimedia centre. But I didn't get any further than that. The doors to the multimedia world were locked – I was too late, the screens had been turned off, and there was no information to be had.

There were now even more people than before in the temple area. The place was teeming with colour, bodies and voices. I found a relatively quiet corner and started to read up on the temple's history. The Sikhs had had a strained relationship with the British, and it seemed that their relationship with local rulers had not been much better. In 1737, the then mughal had transformed the temple into a pleasure pavilion with dance and music. Nine years later, another mughal filled the pool with sand. When the Afghan king Ahmad Shah Durrani conquered Amritsar in 1757, he filled the pool with rubbish and the innards of slaughtered animals. The locals cleared the pool and returned it to its former state, but five years later Durrani returned to Amritsar, and this time he blew up the temple. The Sikhs gathered enough money to build a new one, and thanks to these generous donations, they were in time able to cover the entire temple in gold.

But the troubles did not stop with independence in 1947. In the 1980s, the fundamentalist Jarnail Singh Bhindranwale ensconced himself in the temple, and turned it into a headquarters and training camp for a separatist movement. The Khalistan movement, which campaigned for an independent Sikh state in Punjab, was responsible for a number of killings and attacks that had cost hundreds of lives. In the summer of 1984, the prime minister, Indira Gandhi, abandoned any attempt to negotiate with the rebels and ordered that the temple be stormed. The military operation, which involved more than ten thousand soldiers and lasted for a week, was called Blue Star. The temple was at the time full of pilgrims who had come to celebrate the anniversary of the death of Guru Arjan, its founder. According to official records, 493 rebels and civilians and 83 soldiers were killed in the operation, but Sikh sources say the number was closer to five thousand. Bhindranwale was also killed and the separatist movement was driven from the temple for good. A few months later, on October 31, 1984, Indira Gandhi herself was killed by two of her bodyguards, both Sikhs, in revenge for the massacre. At least three thousand Sikhs were killed in the rioting that followed throughout India.

It can often seem that history is nothing more than massacres and destruction. However, any traces of the bloodbath were long gone, and the temple and associated buildings have been restored and returned to their former glory. Such is the unending and exhausting cycle of history: destroy, rebuild, destroy, rebuild.

I was stiff when I got up from sitting on the hard floor, and tottered over to the long queue of pilgrims and spectators who had come to watch the nightly ceremony. There were arms and bags and hips everywhere, men and women all jumbled up. The queue inched forwards in short bursts of sudden movement. And then I felt fingers stroking my behind. I pulled away, but the fingers returned. I turned around and met the intense gaze of a young man.

"Excuse me, could I stand in front of you?" I asked the woman ahead of me in the queue, a voluptuous lady of around fifty. She nodded and let me past, and from then on all I felt against my thighs was her large handbag. By the time I reached the Golden Temple, it was ten o'clock, bedtime for the holy book.

The pilgrims sat like sardines on the temple floor. The inside of the temple was gilded as well – no expense had been spared, that was clear. The high priest, dressed in white with a black turban, waved a large rod with white plumes over the holy book. Musicians played the drums, and priests and pilgrims chanted and sang gentle, repetitive kirtans. I was just in time to see the book being wrapped in white cotton and covered with a colourful, embroidered cloth. A steward tried to move me on, out of the temple, everyone had to keep moving so everyone had a chance to see, but the entrance was blocked by pilgrims who were standing completely still in silent prayer. When the prayer finished, the book was ceremoniously carried out of the temple, followed by the priests, pilgrims and musicians. Meanwhile, the remaining pilgrims thronged to the grey, cloudy holy water that ran down a channel in the paving behind the temple, filled their hands and drank.

I did the same as the others, filled my hands reverently with water, but did not drink.

To cross a border is to throw yourself into another reality. I was only a few kilometres from Lahore and the closed Wagah border, and yet everything was different, from the alphabet to the headwear. The historical scars were largely the same, as the border was still relatively new, but other than that, there was little that was familiar.

I was nineteen the first time I came to India. I had never been so far from home and was utterly overwhelmed. All the people, smells, colours, noise – it was as though my senses were unable to digest it all. I travelled around for two months, from one place to the next, first south, then north again, getting thinner and thinner, my stomach full of amoebas. In the end I tired of it – not my dodgy digestion, but the endless travel without purpose, eating pancakes in backpacker cafés, hanging out with other young Western travellers, haggling as if our lives depended on it; the backpacker existence boils down to logistics, money and a few limited topics of conversation. It was a strangely vacuous existence. I tried to remember who I had been back then, tried to imagine how I had thought and felt at the time, but all I could remember were vague snapshots: a cockroach, a spider, the funeral pyres in Varanasi, a coconut pancake in Kerala, a temple full of rats. These memories might as well have belonged to someone else.

Back then, the first time, I was travelling with my boyfriend, but I have generally travelled alone ever since. When you travel with someone else, even if it is only one other person, you are immediately in a bubble, a private micro-world. When you travel alone, you are at the mercy of what is around you, you are vulnerable, naked.

The question is, why do we travel at all? Why do we subject ourselves to the discomfort, the logistics, the cost that a journey invariably entails? It is a question that can quickly become stiflingly existential, but in my case, the answer is simple: I can't not anymore.

And there I was, back in India, half my life later. I had returned, but it was still unknown territory. I had never been to Punjab before, I had never been to Amritsar, and I had never been to the Indian mountains. India is not simply a country, it is a subcontinent, and it comprises not one reality, but myriad parallel worlds.

There was a Krishna temple next to the hotel where I was staying. Krishna, the god of love and compassion, is recognised as one of the avatars of the almighty god Vishnu, and is himself one of the most popular gods in Hinduism. The temple was not hard to spot, even though it was not particularly big or old. But the entire neighbourhood had gathered outside to celebrate Janmashtami, the birth of Krishna.

There were people everywhere inside the temple too. The rooms were decorated with colourful garlands and balloons, and in the largest room a group of musicians were singing and beating their drums. A powerful loudspeaker system ensured that everyone in the neighbourhood could enjoy the festival. I let myself be pulled along by the crowd, past the priests handing out sweets and past the small cradle that everyone touched fleetingly. It was close to midnight and nearly time for the moment of birth. Girls and boys jostled around me, all wanting a selfie – I smiled to my left and then to my right. Two elderly policemen, both Sikhs with long beards and neat turbans, marched over and positioned themselves a stone's throw from the temple. They kept a keen eye on me. A young, well-dressed couple came over after a brief exchange with the policemen.

"They're concerned for your safety," the man said, nodding towards the two Sikhs. "They think it would be best if you left. But not on foot. This neighbourhood can be dangerous, there are lots of street children and thieves here."

"But it's nearly midnight, there's only ten minutes to go," I said. "I'll leave straight after, my hotel is nearby."

"You can come home with us," the man said. "We live a couple of minutes away and we have a car."

"Yes, come home with us," his wife said. "You take part in our celebration and ritual. We've got our own altar – everyone has. It will be quieter than here."

The police noted down the young man's address, telephone number and registration number, and I got into the back seat. Three minutes later we turned in through a large gate. The young man's mother came out to welcome us. A small dog barked furiously at her feet. The mother did not seem to be in the slightest bit surprised that her son had picked up a foreigner on the way, but the little dog was so agitated by my presence that it had to be left out in the garden. We went up to the first floor, where the mother had spent the whole day decorating the small house altar. The little Krishna in a cradle had been given new clothes and jewellery, and petals of all colours had been laid in an intricate pattern on the altar table. The mother lit an oil lamp and picked up a spoon and a dish of broken nuts and dried fruit. She dipped the spoon in the nuts and held up it up to the colourful statues, which portrayed the various incarnations of Krishna. Then her daughter-in-law did the same, and, finally, I did too. The short ritual would have been peaceful and reverential, had it not been for the small dog that was now going berserk at the front door.

It was only as I walked backwards out of the room with the altar that I realised I had stepped on the elaborate flower decorations the mother had spent all day making. I had not noticed that she had decorated here as well, and now the soles of my feet were covered in petals and coloured powder. I apologised profusely, and they reassured me over and over that it did not matter, but I found that hard to believe.

We went downstairs to the living room, where the mother gave each of us a small dish with the same mixture of nuts and dried fruit that Krishna had just been given. When we had finished these, the couple drove me back to the hotel, and for a moment, intoxicated with impressions and rituals, I was a little sad that I was leaving the next day to head north, to the mountains.

Paradise with a Curfew

"Welcome to **Srinagar**!" A small man with spectacles and a pot belly trotted towards me and grabbed my rucksack. "I will do my *utmost* to ensure that you leave with a positive impression of Kashmir!" he said, and hurried off with what little luggage I had.

I had briefly discussed my travel route in north India with a local travel agent a few weeks before, but had decided to go it alone. I was tired of following itineraries, of having everything planned beforehand and not being able to decide myself where to stay. Javid Iqbal, the head of the travel agent's Kashmir section, had insisted on coming to the airport to pick me up and show me around, all the same.

"I will do all that I can to ensure that you have a successful visit, so you will tell your friends and family that they must come to Kashmir," he said. "That would be reward enough for me! We're very welcoming in Kashmir. I already see you as a friend of the family, a relative!"

Javid was a year younger than me, but the sort of person who will always look middle-aged. His hair was already thinning and he had obvious frown lines and wrinkles around his eyes. His teeth were irregular and crooked. His van was a classic, and it suited him. On the short trip into the city centre, we saw so many soldiers that I lost count, all wearing helmets, knee pads and bulletproof vests.

"I hope, with all my heart, that you will be happy here in Kashmir," Javid said, as we drove past some more heavily armed soldiers. The traffic was chaotic, with cars, pedestrians and scooters all jostling for room in the narrow streets, horns blaring. There was rubbish everywhere, as there is all over India and Pakistan, but the houses were different from the plain, concrete boxes that are otherwise so prevalent in the cities in this part of the world. They were made from bricks, with beautifully carved woodwork; practically all the buildings had decorated windows and verandas.

"My greatest wish is that Kashmir will be independent one day," Javid said, and scowled at a group of Indian soldiers. "Preferably with Sharia law," he added, vehemently.

"Isn't Sharia law rather brutal?" I asked.

"No, that's a myth," Javid said.

"But it often entails physical punishment," I said.

"Yes, that's right, but it's only for the best," Javid almost shouted with enthusiasm. "For example, according to Sharia law, a rapist should be buried in the ground so only his head sticks out, and then stoned. When people know they risk getting such punishments, they won't be tempted to rape someone. And no-one will steal because all thieves get their hand chopped off!"

Javid invited me back to his house for tea. He showed me into the living room, a small room with carpets but no furniture. His mother, a friendly woman with pale skin and big blue eyes, could not do enough for me. She sat beside me, smiling, as I drank my tea, and every time I put down my cup, she gave me more. To her disappointment, I could not stay long, as I had a lunch meeting with Sohail, a young local businessman I had been put in touch with through a mutual friend. Javid insisted on driving me to the restaurant, and then coming along to the meeting.

"I'm worried about you," he said. "I want to see this man you're meeting, to make sure he's a good man. I don't know him, I've never met him before, so it's only natural that I should worry and want to see him."

"You don't actually know me either," I said.

"I have already said that I see you as part of the family," Javid said.

"I'm divorced, by the way. My wife left me when our daughter was only three months old. All she wanted was two hundred thousand rupees, and she got it. She married another man soon after and has a son with him."

"And do you plan to get married again?" I asked.

"My mother nags me about it every day, but I'd rather not have anything to do with women anymore," Javid said. "Being a father is all I need. My daughter is nine now and she's a very good student. She picks things up very quickly, so much brighter than me! My wife was keen to have a son, but personally I think daughters are best."

I immediately warmed to Sohail. He was twenty-seven and dressed in jeans and a T-shirt. His dark wavy hair glistened with styling products. He was sitting with two friends, the jovial Mir Saqib, who was thirty-two and broad-shouldered, and the more taciturn Muzaffar, who was thirty-six. All three were owners of juice and mineral water factories in the south of Kashmir. I had barely sat down before Aijaz Hussain, the vice-president of the youth wing of BJP, the Bharatiya Janata Party – Prime Minister Narendra Modi's party – appeared and sat down at our table as well. Even though everyone had just arrived, I felt that I had landed in the middle of a heated discussion. Javid sat wide-eyed listening to the debate, but fortunately kept his mouth closed.

"India is a secular, democratic country," Aijaz said with passion. "Let me put it another way: a bouquet of flowers is more beautiful than a single flower! We have seventy years of shared history with India, and lots of people from Kashmir have served in the army or studied in India. In my opinion, people should love their country. We, the members of the BJP, want to build a bridge between India and Kashmir."

"What about the millions of people who have been killed by India?" Sohail challenged him. "Can you tell me that?"

"That was before we came to power," Aijaz replied. "I'm not saying that everything is perfect. We have administrative problems. We're struggling with corruption. The public sector is weak."

"What about the relationship with Pakistan?" I asked.

"I often say we can improve our friends but not our neighbours," Aijaz said. "We would like to have a better relationship with Pakistan, but we don't want to be part of Pakistan. Pakistan is a Muslim state. We are a democracy."

"The minorities and Shia Muslims feel they are safer in India than as part of Pakistan," Sohail explained. "Seventy per cent of the population in Kashmir are Sunni Muslims, and the rest are Shia Muslims, Christians, Hindus and other minorities."

"Do you belong to a minority?" I asked Aijaz.

"Yes, I'm Shia," he said. "The freedom fighters always talk about a new dawn, but the new dawn is always tomorrow, and will never come. So it's better to live for today, to look at the situation now."

"The situation now is that people are being killed every day," Sohail said. "Ten days ago, a friend of mine was shot in Pulwama, not far from here. Shabir Bhat was his name, he was also a member of the BJP. I met him three hours before he was killed. He asked me if I had any money to give to the poor, for Eid. He was only twenty-six or twenty-seven. Imagine, he was killed during Eid! We offer goats to Allah during Eid. His mother had to offer her own son."

"Who killed him?" I asked.

"Hizbul Mujahideen," the young men around the table chorused.

"They're supported by Pakistan," Sohail explained. "They have a base in Muzaffarabad, the capital of Azad Kashmir, the Pakistani part of Kashmir. Everything that goes on here has to be approved by the headquarters first."

"Pakistan is the greatest threat to Kashmir," Aijaz said. "They want to destabilise the entire region. An unstable Kashmir is in their interest, not India's. Gilgit-Baltistan in north Pakistan is also a part of Kashmir. And in my opinion, it should be Indian."

"Do many people share your opinion?" I asked.

"Most people think with their heart, not their head," Aijaz said, with a sigh. "They're not rational."

"He has *twelve* bodyguards," Sohail said, and laughed.

"I'm serious, don't laugh," Aijaz chided him. "People in Kashmir are being kept in the dark. They don't understand that there are people earning a fortune from the bloodbath. A gun can't broker peace, it can only kill. Those who believe weapons will bring peace to Kashmir are wrong."

"Have you ever been in danger of your life?" I asked.

"Of course. Why do you think I have so many bodyguards? I've been attacked a few times. And one time, three terrorists were shot and killed outside my house. I've had bodyguards for a year now."

"Isn't it tiring never to be alone?"

"No, I would rather be safe. The truth is, the region is dangerous. I risk being killed tomorrow."

We moved out into the café garden, and having promised not to reveal his identity I was allowed to speak to one of Aijaz's bodyguards. He had a narrow face and full beard, and smiled all the time, but seemed shy. Aijaz sat beside him, flanked by three other bodyguards. Now that we were outdoors, he was an easier target for any would-be assassin.

"I'm thirty-eight, and married with two children," the bodyguard said. "My son is nine and my daughter is three. I've been in the police for twenty years. There weren't any other jobs to be had. I like my job, but it's dangerous. My brother, who was also in the police, was killed earlier this year in a clash with the rebels. And at Shabir Bhat's funeral, we had stones thrown at us and had to run away so the situation didn't escalate."

"Your family must be very worried for you," I said.

"Yes, my wife and my mother phone me at least fifty times a day to check that I'm safe."

"Do you want your son to join the police, like you?"

He thought about this for a long time.

"It would be fine if he was a high-ranking officer," he said, in the end.

"If you could choose any profession in the world, what would you want to be?" I asked.

"A teacher," he said, and smiled bashfully into his beard.

"Has your job put you in situations where you've had to kill?"

"Yes, of course." He looked at me in surprise. "It's seen as collateral damage, but it doesn't feel good."

"What are your views on the Kashmir question? Would you rather Kashmir remained part of India, became part of Pakistan, or became independent?"

"Independent." He looked down at his shoes. "Because people in Kashmir are suffering," he said, quietly. Everyone at the table erupted with laughter at this comment, which was so surprising from someone who was a bodyguard of one of the ruling Indian party's local leaders.

"Do you think you will ever experience a free Kashmir?" I asked.

"No," was the immediate answer. "It's been like this since 1947. I don't believe that it will change."

The history of how Kashmir became part of India is complicated.

When the Muslim warlords from Central Asia conquered northern India step by step in the fourteenth century, the people living in Kashmir were largely Hindus and Buddhists. In the centuries that followed, more or less the entire population converted to Islam. Then, in the eighteenth century, Kashmir fell under the brutal rule of the Afghan Durrani kings, and in 1819 the region was annexed by Ranjit Singh's Sikh army, which had already conquered Lahore and large parts of Punjab.

Thanks to the skilled military leadership of General Gulab Singh, Kashmir expanded considerably under the Sikh empire. Ladakh in the north, on the border with Tibet, became part of Kashmir, as did Baltistan in the north-west, which is now part of Pakistan. Gulab Singh was himself not a Sikh but a Hindu, and came from a Dogri-speaking family from Jammu. As a reward for his efforts, he was appointed raja of Jammu and Kashmir by Ranjit Singh.

When Ranjit Singh died in 1839, his considerable empire immediately started to crumble. Six years after his death, the British East India Company declared war on the Sikhs, and a few months later their empire was history. But the British were not interested in direct rule in the newly conquered territories, and Gulab Singh, the raja of Jammu and Kashmir, had shown restraint in the war and served as a useful middleman between the British and the Sikhs, so the British let him buy back the territories he had ruled. And thus it was that Gulab Singh became the first maharaja – great king – of Jammu and Kashmir, the largest vassal state in British India.

When Gulab Singh died in 1857, his son, Ranbir, took over as maharaja, and during his reign, Gilgit, Hunza and Nagar, in what is now north Pakistan, were also claimed as part of Kashmir. The British did not involve themselves in these local expansions on the peripheries of their empire, as they ruled the whole of India, after all.

The Singh family, otherwise known as the Dogra dynasty, ruled over a complex outpost of India: the Hindus formed the majority in Jammu, in the south, with the Sikhs making up a sizeable proportion of the population, whereas the Sunni Muslims dominated in Kashmir. And in Ladakh, to the north, the sparse population was mostly Buddhist, whereas in Gilgit and Hunza, to the north-east, the Shia Muslims were in the majority.

In 1947, Hari Singh was the fourth Singh maharaja of Jammu and Kashmir. He was primarily known for his high spending and turnover in wives, but that year he had to make a choice that would become his legacy: as the maharaja of an independent princely state, he could unilaterally decide whether Jammu and Kashmir should become part of Pakistan or India. As the majority of the population were Muslims, Pakistan would have been a natural choice. However, Hari Singh's hope was that the principality might retain its independence, and he delayed his decision for as long as possible. The maharaja was already very unpopular due to the high taxes he imposed on his subjects, and a rebellion broke out in western Kashmir. After a number of weeks, the rebels announced that they would no longer be dictated to by Hari Singh, and they established their own government. This part of Kashmir is now incorporated into Pakistan, and is called Azad Kashmir, or Free Kashmir.

The situation then deteriorated from difficult to dangerous when a large group of armed Pashtuns from western Pakistan, supported by the Pakistani authorities, crossed the border to carry out jihad on the infidels and to force the maharaja to let Jammu and Kashmir become part of Pakistan. The invasion provoked the opposite response: a desperate Hari Singh asked India for assistance in quelling the revolt, and on October 26, 1947, he signed the Instrument of Accession, thereby sealing the territory's fate.

Jammu and Kashmir then officially became a part of India.

It was dark when Javid drove me to Nigeen Lake, the most peaceful of the lakes in Srinagar. A shikara was waiting for me by the jetty, to take me over the lake to the houseboat where I was going to stay. Shikaras, a kind of less luxurious Venetian gondola, are the symbol of Srinagar. As in Venice, the boatsman stands in the stern with an oar that he uses both to propel and to steer the boat. Before he left, Javid promised to come back the following morning to show me the most beautiful place in Srinagar. The sound of the van's engine faded into the distance until finally all that could be heard were the cicadas and the splash of the oar. The moon was reflected on the still surface of the lake.

Srinagar is famous for its houseboats, a legacy from the British, who flocked to Kashmir in the summer to hunt, fish and relax in the relatively cool mountain climes. The maharaja would not allow outsiders to buy land or property in Kashmir, so houseboats were an obvious solution. Some of the boats were also used as transport back then, but most are now permanently moored, like floating hotels.

"Why are you so late?" Ajaz, the boat owner's son, asked. He was standing on the deck waiting for me. "The boatman has been waiting for hours. Do you realise how much that costs?"

He showed me to my cabin and said that dinner would soon be ready. I was the only guest and had the whole boat to myself. The cabin was like a time capsule, with red wall-to-wall carpet, flowery curtains, and black-and-white photographs on the walls. Little had changed since the British holidayed here.

Not many people holiday in Kashmir these days. Following the revolt against the Indian administration in 1989, the number of international tourists plummeted. Then in 1995, six Western tourists, who had risked going there all the same, were kidnapped by Islamist terrorists, and the conflict in Kashmir was promptly headline news throughout the world. Hans Christian Ostrø, a Norwegian, was one of those kidnapped. The 27-year-old was executed after being held captive for one and a half months. One of the hostages managed to escape, and it is presumed that the other four were shot. Most Western countries still warn their citizens against travelling to Kashmir.

About an hour and a half later, Ajaz knocked on my door to say that dinner was served. The dining room was small and cosy, with furniture in beautifully carved, light wood. Ajaz sat down on a chair and watched me eat.

"Is it true that the American president, Theodore Roosevelt, stayed here?" I asked. I had read somewhere on the internet that President Roosevelt had stayed on this very boat, which was why I had booked a cabin here. I hoped I might hear the hum of history in the walls.

Ajaz brightened and went to get a framed photograph from the counter.

"This is a copy of the thank-you letter that the president sent to my grandfather," he said. "He stayed on the boat for a whole month in 1925."

As President Theodore Roosevelt died in 1919, it must have been his eldest son, Theodore Roosevelt Jr, who never made it as far as his father. The letter was also signed by his wife, Eleanor Butler Roosevelt, and two other Roosevelts, whose names were hard to decipher.

I thanked Ajaz for showing me the thank-you letter and retired to my cabin, full of basmati rice, curry, British history and Indian politics. Other than the intense sound of cicadas from the shore, all was quiet on the houseboat.

At the crack of dawn the next day, even before it was light, I stepped into the shikara that was waiting. The boatman immediately started to row me across the lake. The first call to prayer could be heard from several mosques, nearby and further away. The boat glided peacefully over the water, under a bridge and through narrow channels lined with lotus flowers and water lilies. Ducks and other small birds tiptoed over the large green leaves looking for food.

"Is it alright if I pray?" the boatman asked. I nodded, of course, and he started to mumble quietly as he knelt down, stood up, knelt down and stood up. The sky changed from black to grey, before slowly turning blue, then golden red and finally milky white. A new day had begun, and when the boatman finished his prayers, we carried on rowing between the flowers and floating gardens. Srinagar's famous floating gardens are made from weeds and roots that are trampled hard until they become a kind of floating mat, about a metre deep, that can be used to cultivate anything from melons to cucumbers. Back in the day, British officers frequently recorded complaints from the locals that they had been robbed of their livelihood, as their gardens had been towed away by thieves.

Just after six o'clock, it was fully light, and we arrived at the floating vegetable market. Gardeners and farmers from near and far had rowed there in the dawn light, their shikaras loaded with onions, cabbages, lettuces, cucumbers and other vegetables harvested from their floating gardens, and were now selling them to the greengrocers who would in turn sell them to housewives and restaurants in the city. Everywhere, people were bargaining and buying, wads of money changed hands, and vegetables were lifted from one wooden boat to another.

A handful of traders had focused their business on the few tourists who sometimes found their way here, and quickly made their way towards me. An elderly, white-haired gentleman was selling *kahwah*, a Kashmiri speciality. It is a drink made from green tea flavoured with saffron and cinnamon, sweetened with honey and garnished with chopped almonds. I bought a cup for myself and the boatman; the sweet, warm drink tasted as golden as the sunrise I had just seen. A serious young man with a narrow, angular face tried to sell me papier mâché figures. And his friend, who seemed a little more light-hearted, tried to tempt me with small boxes of saffron.

"Papier mâché is light, it weighs nothing, the perfect souvenir to take in your luggage!" coaxed the young trader, who I soon found out was called Amir.

"Kashmiri saffron takes no room whatsoever and is famous throughout the world," his friend argued. I never discovered his name.

We discussed papier mâché and saffron for some time. The two friends outdid each other in extolling the merits of their wares, claiming the quality was unsurpassed.

"Would you prefer independence, or to be a part of India or

Pakistan?" I asked, when I finally managed to turn the conversation.

"Independence, obviously." Amir did not even need to consider his answer. "I want Kashmir to be free, as it was before. The Indians keep killing us. They've killed millions of Kashmiris since 1947! And India is also full of rapists – they gang-rape women there. Pakistanis aren't much better. They're just interested in our land, like the Indians. And Pakistan is backward. They haven't realised that we're living in the twenty-first century and that women have been liberated as well."

"Speaking of women, what kind of marriage is most usual in Kashmir? Arranged marriages or love marriages?" I asked.

"Arranged love marriages," the saffron seller chortled.

"I don't believe in love," Amir said, and a shadow passed over his face. "I had a bad experience, once, with a girl. Really bad. I just cried and cried when it was over. No more love. Never again! Love is not for me."

Someone who must have believed in love, however, is the Mughal emperor Jahangir, who reigned at the beginning of the seventeenth century. He gave his queen, Nur Jahan, Light of the World, a garden of love. Srinagar is known for its extravagant Persian gardens, and Shalimar Bagh, the one made by Jahangir, is perhaps the most beautiful of all. *Shalimar* means "abode of love", and *bagh* is Persian for "garden".

Jahangir was the son of the Mughal emperor Akbar, who annexed Kashmir in 1586. Jahangir was so captivated by Kashmir that he made Srinagar his summer capital. Every year, he and his entire court and government crossed the mountains on elephants to spend a few summer months in Shalimar Bagh, surrounded by trees, flowers and fountains, with the Himalayas as a backdrop. He had a quotation carved into the uppermost pavilion, lines that are generally ascribed to the poet Hazrat Amir Khusrau: "If there is a paradise on earth, it is this, it is this, it is this." It is said that when he was on his death-bed, Jahangir was asked what he desired most in the world. "Kashmir, the rest is worthless," was his reply.

The garden was an entire small world of fountains, canals and the slender, elegant trees that are typical of Kashmir, unlike any others I have seen, and well-tended beds of roses and other colourful flowers. Some small boys and girls were splashing happily around in a pool that was surrounded by NO SWIMMING signs. Families and friends sat on the lawns drinking tea and chatting. Behind a tree with magnifi-cent pink flowers, four men were shaking their fists at each other, tense and red in the face.

"What are they fighting about?" I asked Javid, who had kept his promise from the evening before and taken me to the most beautiful place in Srinagar.

"I don't know," he said, with a shrug. "Maybe about tea." He squinted at me. "What do you want to see now?"

"The grave of Jesus," I said.

Javid sighed.

"Everyone wants to see that," he said.

The theory that Jesus did not die on the cross, but is in fact buried in Srinagar, was launched by the self-declared prophet Mirza Ghulam Ahmad in 1899. Ahmad claimed that he was the Messiah and Mahdi, a messianic figure who Muslims believe will appear to rid the world of evil and tyranny. Ahmad founded the controversial Ahmadiyya movement, which currently has several million followers but is not recognised by other Muslim schools. Ahmad travelled extensively through Punjab to gather disciples. He also wrote more than ninety books, including *Jesus in India*, in which he argues that Jesus survived the crucifixion and fled to Kashmir, where he died a natural death at the age of one hundred and twenty. According to Ahmad, Jesus is buried at Roza Bal, the Tomb, in the centre of Srinagar.

The disputed tomb was in a dilapidated, whitewashed building.

As the gates were closed, I had to be satisfied with a glimpse of the sarcophagus, which was covered in green cloth, through meshwork on a window. There was a sign at the gate, with verses 4:157 and 4:158 from the Koran, on it, in both English and Arabic: *And they [Jews] said in boast we killed Christ Jesus, the son of Mary, the apostle of Allah. But they killed him not nor crucified him; but so it was made to appear to them and those who differ therein are full of doubts with no (certain) knowledge, but only conjecture to follow, for of a surety they killed him not. Nay, Allah raised him up unto Himself. And Allah is exalted in power, wise.*

Officially, it is Yuz Asaf, a Sufi Muslim sage from the Middle Ages, who lies buried in Roza Bal, but millions of people, and by no means only Ahmadiyya followers, believe that Yuz Asaf, or Youza Asaph, is another name for Jesus of Nazareth. Since *Lonely Planet* wrote about this theory in 2010, Roza Bal has become a popular attraction for any foreign tourists who dare to visit Kashmir, much to the delight of the local shop owners, who no doubt are behind the Koran quotations.

Javid looked at his watch.

"It's still early," he said. "We have time to visit the floating market, if you're interested."

We went down to the harbour and Javid negotiated for a long time with one of the boatman about the price of the trip. When they finally agreed, we settled down on the soft cushions in the narrow wooden boat. Once again, I slid through a network of floating streets, this time more like a town on water: small kiosks, hardware stores, grocery stores, cafés and souvenir shops built on timber rafts that shaped the waterways, only accessible by boat. Javid asked the boatman to stop outside a papier mâché shop, so I went in and looked politely at the carefully made objects for a couple of minutes before heading back out.

"Is there really nothing you want here?" Javid asked.

"I can't carry big papier mâché figures in my rucksack," I said. "It's full enough as it is."

"We send our goods all over the world," the trader said, obviously having listened to our conversation.

"What about this, for example?" Javid pointed at a garish vase.

I shook my head firmly and settled back down into the cushions. A few minutes later, Javid asked the boatman to stop again, this time outside a shop that specialised in shawls.

"Our pashmina shawls are the best in the world," Javid said, and smiled. "And they won't take up much room in your rucksack. Lots of tourists buy shawls here, they are very popular."

I obediently followed him in and was warmly welcomed by the two sellers, one young and one old. The young one immediately started to unfold shawl after shawl. They were made in every conceivable colour and pattern, and some of them were so soft that they moulded round your shoulders like an extra layer of skin.

"You're lucky," the young salesman said. "The gentleman who is with you today says that he won't take a cut. He wants you to get the best price, he says, so I am willing to give you a very good discount. We normally pay a twenty per cent commission to all the guides and boatmen, because we're completely dependent on them to bring people here, but as this man doesn't want anything, we can cut out the middleman."

Kashmiri shawls are indeed famous throughout the world, and in a flash of inspiration I decided to do my Christmas shopping. The young man lit up and helped me find shawls for the whole family. With great enthusiasm, Javid haggled the price down on my behalf – in English, so that I could follow the negotiations. The figures flew like missiles between him and the seller: *9,700, 9,500, 9,450, 9,300, 9,150, 9,000 . . . final offer, come on now, no, give her a good price, forget it, she's the first customer of the day, but I have to make a living as well, so I can't be left with nothing, oh, come on, she doesn't have much money, 8,800, 8,750, 8,700 . . .* In the end, they reached agreement and looked at me expectantly. I thought the price was fine and paid the amount they had agreed on. The salesman folded the shawls with great solemnity and handed them to me, then he and Javid disappeared behind a curtain into a side room. I stood up and followed them.

"You stay where you are, he's just showing him to the toilet," shouted the old man, who thus far had said nothing. I ignored him and pulled the curtain to one side, just in time to see Javid accept a banknote from the trader.

"We're just swapping business cards!" Javid said, with a wide smile.

"Yes, I wanted to give this honest man my card, so he can bring other tourists here," the young man said, with an equally broad smile. He followed us out onto the jetty where he shook my hand one last time.

"You are so fortunate to have this honest man with you, who doesn't ask for a commission," he said again as I stepped into the shikara. "I don't know why he does it, but you are truly blessed."

*

A security guard opened the gate, and a servant opened the front door and showed me into a reception room, where the walls were lined with diplomas and awards. Not long after, Nayeema Mahjoor came down the stairs. Until the regional government had been disbanded a few months before, she had been chair of the State Commission for Women on behalf of the PDP, the People's Democratic Party. She spoke slowly and articulately, without ever losing track – it was easy to see that she had twenty years' experience as a radio journalist. And like most good journalists, she preferred to talk about others and the general situation, rather than herself.

"We're still stuck in 1947," she said. "The conflict is still not resolved. India was not honest with us. Paragraph 370 was supposed to give Jammu and Kashmir a degree of self-rule and its own constitution, but the paragraph has been systematically diluted over the years, and the regional governments have been puppet governments, put there by India."

The servant came in with tea and biscuits.

"Have you seen Fox News?" Nayeema asked. "We only have Fox channels here in India. The only thing the Indian authorities have done is to create chaos and distrust. In the past few years, the Modi government have held a very confrontational position: Modi or nothing. There has been a series of raids and mass arrests, just like those in the 1990s. Many thousands of people have lost their sight, thanks to Modi's rubber bullets, and the so-called non-lethal weapons that the soldiers use at demonstrations. We have an Armed Forces Special Powers Act, which means the military here can do what they want, they are never held responsible for anything. They can rape and kill without having to face the consequences. You have no idea how many rapes there are. In the 1970s, none of the women here wore veils, but now nearly all of them do. I don't think it's due to radicalisation, they're just trying to hide themselves from the soldiers."

Nayeema sighed.

"The women of Kashmir lose their sons, their husbands, their fathers. Whether he works for the security forces or is a rebel, she is constantly worried about what might happen to him. According to a survey, sixty-five per cent of women have psychological problems. When the violence was at its peak, a lot of young girls had to stop their education. Reproductive health is a huge issue. Many women have had to have hysterectomies, often as a result of rape. Domestic violence is another problem. Men take out their frustration with the situation on their wives within the four walls of home."

"Has being a high-profile woman in a male-dominated society created problems for you?"

"Oh, good God, yes! I have lots of sisters and my father was a well-educated man. He always supported us. He was liberal, but sadly our relatives were not as liberal. When I was seven years old, I played a little girl in a family play on the radio. This was like an earthquake in the family. I was told I had to say goodbye either to the family or to the radio. I was only a child, and asked my father: "What do you want me to do?" His reply was: "Let's say goodbye to the family, because what will be next? That none of you are allowed to go to college?" He added that I had to promise him that I would do my best in life, not waste any opportunity. My sisters and I have all done as he asked. My sisters are doctors, theatre directors. I worked for the BBC World Service for twenty-two years, so you could say I stayed in radio."

"Are you in contact with the rest of the family now?"

"No. Some of my sisters are reconciled with them, but not me. I have a new family, my own friends. I work for the people of Kashmir, for everyone here who needs me. They are my family. I moved back here from London three years ago, and in the course of those three years the situation has gone from bad to worse. Now everyone is waiting for 2019 and the election. God forbid that Modi is re-elected, but we have to be prepared for the worst. I published a book called *Lost in Terror* three years ago, and I'm working on a new one now. It's going to be called *Lost in Peace*."

"Why do you have security guards?" I asked when my allotted time was up.

"It's been necessary since I started working for the government," Nayeema said. "I don't normally take them with me when I go out. When I'm alone, I'm safe. If they're with me, I'm a target."

She stood up and followed me to the door.

"Getting involved with politics is the biggest mistake I've made," she said, as we said our goodbyes. "I don't believe there's a political solution for Kashmir anymore."

Sohail and Muzaffar, the two mineral water factory owners I had met the day before, had taken it upon themselves to be my personal guides in Srinagar, just as Javid had done. While Javid took me to the tourist attractions and shops, Sohail and Muzaffar introduced me to politicians and activists. After my visit to Nayeema, they drove me to the office of Kashmir's best-known human rights activist, Khurram Parvez.

"I've just had a death threat," Sohail said from the front seat. He let out a nervous laugh; the words came fast and frantic. "Some extremists have posted a sound file on YouTube threatening all factory owners who employ women. They've given us three days to get rid them. And *all* my employees are women, with the exception of the drivers. So that's ten in all! It's a hopeless situation."

Sohail shook his head in despair.

"My sister is married to a man who refuses to divorce her, even though he's married three other women! I've tried talking to muftis and imams, but no-one wants to help me, they all say that Islam allows a man to have four wives, so my sister's husband is living in accordance with Islam. In my opinion, Islam is full of intellectual nonsense! I'm probably one of those who is hardest hit by the conflict," he said, gloomily. "I can't criticise Islam, because then the mullahs will threaten to kill me. I can't do anything that's fun. I can't have female employees. Everything is forbidden here! If Kashmir had been part of Pakistan, I would have been dead long ago, but because we're part of India there's at least a modicum of democracy and freedom of speech. I can say what I like – even if I risk being killed . . ."

"Why don't you just leave Kashmir?" I asked. "Wouldn't that make everything simpler?"

"No, no, I can't do that," Sohail said with a sigh. "My family lives here. My factory is here. I can't just leave. But if Kashmir ever becomes independent and is left to its own devices, I'll be the first one to leave, believe me!"

*

Khurram Parvez welcomed us into his tiny office in an ordinary, low-rise block of flats. I held out my hand, but instead of his hand, he gave me a telling-off.

"You have to be careful in Kashmir! Journalists without their papers in order can be deported – a French journalist who was here on a tourist visa was arrested just recently. And you called me from your own mobile phone! You didn't even use the encrypted service!"

"The SIM card isn't registered in my name," I said, sheepishly.

"Makes no difference. You said your name and my phone is tapped. When I have meetings, like now, I often put it under my thigh, so they can't hear what I'm saying." He made a point of putting his phone under his right thigh.

Following this initial reprimand, Khurram started to tell me about all the human rights issues in Kashmir. Like so many other human rights activists that I have met, he was unstoppable once he got going.

"The conflict here has cost more than seventy thousand lives since 1989, and more than eight thousand people have disappeared. The police are highly militarised. According to the authorities, there are only around three hundred insurgents left. More than six hundred and fifty thousand soldiers have been deployed to fight them! That is the biggest armed force in any region in the world – that many soldiers were not even deployed during the wars in Iraq or Afghanistan. Torture is one of the biggest problems here – we know about at least a hundred thousand cases of torture. The torture in Guantánamo was discovered through the drawings, but we have no whistleblowers here in Kashmir; if we did, you would have heard far worse stories. One man had his tongue split because he'd warned people in his village that the army was on its way. Another man had both his legs chopped off, and before that they barely gave him food for a month. Then they cut pieces out of his buttocks and belly and forced him to eat them. That's the worst case we've come across."

Khurram started to work in human rights in his early twenties, but his passion was born even earlier than that, in the 1990s, when he was thirteen.

"There was a demonstration that year against the soldiers' abuse of women. My grandfather took part in the demonstration and was killed. The officer who ordered the soldiers to shoot was our neighbour. Every day I had to see the face of my grandfather's killer. I was an angry young man. At first I wanted to join the insurgency, become a militant, and I read the Koran and other religious writings. Gradually, I realised that anger was not the answer. Angry people make bad decisions. I learned to manage my anger and got in touch with human rights activists."

Khurram took a sip of coffee and continued his monologue. I realised that there was no need for the questions I had prepared.

"Six thousand families in Kashmir are blacklisted and can't get a passport. The head of our organisation was refused a passport for eleven years, as was his deputy. We all have major issues because of our work. I lost a leg in 2004. I was with six others on our way to Lolab Valley to be election observers when a roadside bomb exploded. My best friend and the driver were killed. Everything points to the authorities, that they were behind it, but we don't have conclusive evidence, so can't prove it. I had to have my leg amputated, just below the knee, and spent three and a half months in hospital. If I dwelled on it, I would be a psychological wreck, but I've just continued as before. I can't run or play football anymore, and I loved playing football, but I can still be an activist."

A young woman came in with a pile of documents, then quickly disappeared .

"There have been other things too," Khurram said. "On September 16, 2016, I was arrested and imprisoned for seventy-six days, charged with inciting protests and the like. It was an opportunity to meet other prisoners and see what conditions were like on the inside. The prisons here are awful. The food was bad and it was unbearably hot. In my section, twenty-five people shared one toilet."

Khurram drank some water and I took the chance to squeeze in a question. "It's not easy to be optimistic about the situation in Kashmir," I said. "How do you see the future?"

"If Europe could become a peaceful place after a hundred years of war, and if Germany could rid itself of the Nazis, then there's hope for Kashmir as well," he said. "I believe Kashmir will be free, sooner or later. I sincerely hope and wish that for my children. To lose hope is a crime. It's not all bleak, not at all. Two hundred million Indians are malnourished, but here in Kashmir no-one is starving, despite all the other problems."

"And is it a good thing that I could meet you here, in your office, and speak to you?"

Khurram shook his head.

"India wants to be seen as a democracy, but the authorities have done everything they can to destroy us. We can't register our organisation, which means we can't receive financial support from abroad, and have to keep our costs to a minimum. This office, for example, is the boss's personal property. I don't earn any money from my work with human rights; it's my wife and mother who pay for the family. But as I love my children, I have to carry on with my work. I work so that my children may one day live in a free and peaceful Kashmir."

Javid was not convinced that I had fully understood how beautiful Kashmir was. Later that afternoon, my last in Kashmir, he took me 2650 MSL to **Gulmarg**, one of India's best ski resorts. It took two hours to drive there, through green, rolling hills, past orchards and apricot plantations. We stopped at a prolific orchard and the farmer let us pick as many apples as we wanted from trees that were laden with fruit. Kashmiri apples are juicy and red, and the most popular variety in India, accounting for more than two-thirds of total consumption.

As much as half the population of Kashmir depends on apples to make the wheels go round.

Even though the skiing season was a long way off, the ski lifts clanked and whirred all day long. Javid and I swayed over small settlements of nomads, grazing sheep and lethargic horses. The sky above us was deep blue.

Javid was beaming.

"Isn't it beautiful here? Isn't Kashmir the most beautiful place in all the world?"

Even at the top, four thousand metres above sea level, the landscape was lush and the green-clad mountains stretched out in all directions, as far as the eye could see, with no regard to troubled borders, military road checks or control lines.

I still regret that I did not stay longer in Kashmir, and at several points on my onward journey, I was tempted to order a flight back to Srinagar, if nothing else to experience one more day on a houseboat on Nigeen Lake.

*

Pessimistic postscript

Since I left India, the situation in Kashmir has deteriorated even more. In spring 2019, the BJP won more than thirty-seven per cent of the votes, almost twice as many as the Congress Party, and Modi remained in office as prime minister. On August 5 that year, the government revoked Article 370, thus stripping Jammu and Kashmir of the special status it has held since 1947, including the right to pass its own laws. Outsiders can now buy land and property in Kashmir, which, in the long run, could change the population composition dramatically. In addition, the region of Ladakh, to the north, which is largely populated by Buddhists, was separated from Jammu and Kashmir and designated "union territory". Constitutional amendments were passed and tens of thousands of soldiers were sent to the already highly militarised region, several thousand civilians were jailed, foreigners and tourists were ordered to leave Kashmir, a long-term curfew was introduced, and all telephone lines and the internet were shut down. Tons of overripe apples were left to rot on the ground as seasonal workers from other parts of India could no longer get there to pick them.

Before the coronavirus crisis peaked and the whole of India was locked down, some communication lines were reopened, but large parts of Kashmir, a paradise on earth, are still cut off from the rest of the world. Many of the apple farmers were able to save some of the 2019 harvest and put the apples into cold stores in the hope of better times.

They may have to wait a long time.

The Highest Battlefield in the World

Who knows how many military bases we passed on the way from Srinagar to Kargil; one military camp after another, walled in, sealed up, like camouflage-coloured monasteries in the mountains. Soon the green mountains of Kashmir were behind us, replaced by inhospitable, barren peaks. The young driver was silent he spoke very little English – and the car was small and rickety. With sheer determination, he forced it up the narrow, twisting roads. It was raining heavily and the ground was slick and muddy, the wheels spun, the car skidded, but the driver kept his eyes on the road and his foot on the accelerator. If we stopped here, we would never get over the pass. If we skidded off the road, we would get no further, meeting our end with the other rusty wreckages that lay on the mountainside far below. A minibus had broken down in the middle of a sharp bend; the passengers sat resting their stony faces against the windows, as though they reckoned they too might have to stay here for ever. Somehow, miraculously, the driver managed to squeeze the car past the stranded minibus, on the outside of the bend where the mountainside was so steep that I could not see the bottom. I closed my eyes and did not want to open them again.

J&K TOURISM WELCOMES YOU TO **DRASS**, THE SECOND 3300 MSL COLDEST INHABITED PLACE IN THE WORLD, said a battered, blue sign. Drass appeared to be one long street with some small shops and cafés, and the odd guest house.

"How cold does it get here?" I asked the driver.

"Minus six," he said, proudly. He was clearly not pleased with my reaction, as he immediately dropped the temperature. "Perhaps minus seven or minus eight."

The driver was in fact out by a long shot. On January 9, 1995, the recorded temperature in Drass dropped to minus sixty degrees.

The war monument outside Drass is dedicated to the first war in history between two nuclear powers. The weapons that were used to force Pakistan into retreat were displayed on signs with lengthy information panels about the Indians' greatest feats. Indian flags formed an avenue between the headstones for all the soldiers who lost their lives fighting for the fatherland high up here in the Himalayas – thousands of them. And even though the memorial was dedicated to the Kargil War in 1999, there were dates from every year since 1947, right up to 2018. Even in times of peace, bullets and grenades crossed the line of control; in the past two years alone, more than two hundred soldiers had died in border skirmishes.

The borders in the Himalayas are not only still dotted lines and debated, they are also soaked in blood.

India and Pakistan have engaged in four wars since the two countries separated. The first was already under way when the desperate Maharaja Hari Singh signed the agreement that made Kashmir part of India, in 1947. The fighting lasted for over a year, until the UN successfully negotiated a fragile ceasefire on New Year's Eve 1948. Technically, India was the winner: two-thirds of the territory that made up the state of Jammu and Kashmir remained in Indian hands. Azad Kashmir, which is comparable in size with Montenegro, and Gilgit-Baltistan to the north went to Pakistan.

Peace prevailed in the mountains until 1962, and this time it was China that tried to resolve border disputes with violence. The cause of the conflict was Aksai Chin, an area about the size of Switzerland, between Xinjiang and Tibet. The relationship between India and China was already tense, as India had granted asylum to the Dalai Lama three years earlier. However, the roots of the war between the two giants went back to the nineteenth century and the border demarcation by the British.

When the first border between China and Kashmir was drawn in 1865, the Chinese were not even informed. Known as the Johnson Line after the British man who mapped the area, this border showed Aksai Chin to be part of Kashmir. But in the 1890s, China started to show an interest in Aksai Chin, and as the British had no representation in the sparsely populated, inaccessible mountain region, it was felt in Calcutta that allowing the Chinese to take control might in fact not be such a bad thing. The fear of Russian expansion was a decisive factor – the Russians had at the time taken control of the greater part of Central Asia and were prowling around the Pamir Plateau, dangerously close to the border with British India. In 1899, the British therefore proposed a new border that would make Aksai Chin a part of China: the Macartney–MacDonald Line was named after the British consul in Kashgar and the diplomat who was given the task of presenting it to the Chinese. Beijing never gave an answer, and during the First World War, the British reverted to the Johnson Line. They maintained this border until they withdrew from India in 1947, so Aksai Chin was again part of Jammu and Kashmir, which in turn became part of India.

In 1962, the Pakistani authorities agreed to yield territories to China in accordance with the Macartney–MacDonald Line, but the Indian authorities were insistent that Aksai Chin had always been a part of India and would remain so for evermore, even though hardly any Indians had ever set foot there. The Chinese were not happy with the McMahon Line either, the 890-kilometre border that the British had drawn in the eastern Himalayas, in the remote area between Bhutan and Burma. They were particularly upset that the demarcation had been agreed directly with the Tibetans, without the Chinese even being asked. But the Indians were unwavering.

Mao's China in 1962 was a far more powerful and assertive state than the China under the floundering Qing dynasty that the British officers had known at the end of the nineteenth century. In 1950, Chinese soldiers had marched into Tibet, and a few years later work had started on the construction of a road that would link Tibet with Xinjiang. Parts of the road passed through Aksai Chin, just south of the Johnson Line. And it was this road that was the direct cause of the war in 1962: the Indians did not know it existed until it appeared on Chinese maps.

On October 20, in the middle of the Cuban Missile Crisis, China attacked the border with India in both the east and west. The Indians were totally unprepared for the attack, and as the Soviet Union had more than enough on its hands with the crisis in the Caribbean, India had to manage alone, without any help from its allies. Most of the fighting took place at four or five thousand metres above sea level, in extremely demanding conditions. More than three thousand Indian soldiers were killed in the war, which lasted no more than a month. Many of them died from frostbite, rather than in combat.

On November 21, the Chinese unilaterally declared a ceasefire. They announced that they would allow the "unlawful" McMahon Line in the east to remain unchanged so long as Aksai Chin was ceded to China, behind the line that was called the Line of Actual Control, which is now the de facto border. Neither border, to the north-east or the north-west, has been ratified by any party, but nor have they been changed since 1962. And there have been no more wars between China and India.*

There have, however, been wars between India and Pakistan.

---

* In summer 2020 there was, however, a close call. On June 15, hundreds of Chinese and Indian soldiers clashed in the dark on the steep mountainsides of Galwan Valley, along the disputed border with Chinese-controlled Aksai Chin. The soldiers fought man-to-man for several hours, as soldiers in the area do not carry firearms, owing to the volatile situation. Twenty Indian soldiers died as a result of the melee and there were fifty-three Chinese casualties. It was the first confrontation with fatalities along the India–China border since 1975.

In 1965, three years after India had lost Aksai Chin to China, Pakistan sent more than twenty thousand troops over the border into Jammu and Kashmir. The soldiers were disguised as Kashmiri rebels; the plan was that they would foment a rebellion against India, but this was soon discovered. India responded with a large-scale military attack on West Pakistan. Following intense negotiations led by the USA and Soviet Union, the parties agreed to a ceasefire. The war only lasted for seventeen days, but cost more than six thousand lives. A few hundred square kilometres changed hands, but, by and large, the line of control stayed the same.

The war between India and Pakistan in 1971 is the only one that was not about Kashmir. There had long been feelings of discontent in East Pakistan and a secular independence movement had recently emerged. The Pakistani authorities did what they could to crush the independence movement, by any means possible. In the months that followed, hundreds of thousands of people were killed and several million Hindus fled over the border to India. Towards the end of the year, India got involved in the conflict, and on December 16, the Pakistani army in East Pakistan surrendered. With the stroke of a pen, Pakistan lost over half its population, and the state of Bangladesh was born.

During the short, intense war, there had also been fighting in Kashmir, and India had occupied some territories on the Pakistani side. When the war was over, most of those reverted to Pakistan, but India retained a couple of strategic areas by the north-west border.

In the ensuing peace treaty, India and Pakistan promised that they would henceforth respect the line of control and not attempt to change it. The Pakistani authorities managed to keep this promise for thirty years. Then, on May 3, 1999, Pakistani soldiers crossed the border by the small town of Kargil, just north of Kashmir. They tried the same old trick, using soldiers disguised as Kashmiri rebels, but once again it failed. The short war that ensued was an even greater humiliation for Pakistan. Young men had put their lives on the line in an attempt to control the border, but achieved nothing other than an early grave.

2676 MSL In **Kargil**, traffic jams are a permanent feature. No amount of frenzied tooting helps. The small, drab town is surrounded by the Himalayas, hemmed in by steep brown mountains. Some of the buildings are concrete and characterless, but most are constructed with a mixture of brick, clay and wood and look as though they might collapse at any moment. The women wear hijabs and long clothes, but almost none of them cover their faces, as I had seen daily in Srinagar and Pakistan. I checked into the hotel, then went to the Roots café, which not only is the only café in the town, it also doubles as the only travel agency. A chubby man in his twenties was sitting in front of a computer in the small office below the café. I soon realised he was responsible for both the café and the travel agency, and I asked if it would be possible to book one of the guided tours that were advertised on their homepage.

He was slow to answer. "The truth is, we stopped doing guided tours last year," he said, eventually. "There's nothing to see here. All the old stuff has been destroyed."

"What about the caravanserai?" I asked. It was listed as one of the highlights of the tour.

"The caravanserai is sadly in such a state that I would not recommend going in," he said. "But try the Central Asian Museum," he added helpfully. "It's run by the family that owns the caravanserai."

The museum lay beyond the traffic chaos, in a residential area. The door was open, but there was no-one there, not even a ticket seller. The rooms were full of colourful objects: saddles from Kyrgyzstan, pointed hats and detailed Buddhist paintings from Tibet, jewellery and silk fabric from Xinjiang and hand-knotted carpets from Bukhara, each object a reminder that, until relatively recently, Kargil had been a Himalayan hub on the trade route between Tibet, Kashgar and Central Asia. The collection also included European soaps, American medicine in brown bottles, oil lamps and toothbrushes, all Western luxury items that had been transported along the traditional caravan routes from the port in Bombay.

"Everything you see here belonged to my grandfather," said a man's voice behind me. I jumped, turned around and saw a middle-aged man with narrow eyes and a trimmed, short moustache. He introduced himself as Gulzar Hussain Munshi.

"My grandfather, Munshi Aziz Bhat, started the caravanserai in 1920," he said. "My grandfather was born in 1866 in Leh, the capital of Ladakh. His job was to help merchants on the caravan routes organise their journey. As he was one of the few who could speak English at the time, he became an important person in Ladakh and socialised with princes, officers and even the maharaja himself. In fact, he became the maharaja's official clerk up here. Anyone who wanted to raise an issue with the maharaja had to visit my grand-father, who then wrote an official letter on his or her behalf. My grandfather died in 1948, just after partition. It was a difficult time for our family. There was an abrupt end to trading and the family was without work for several years."

The partition of India and Pakistan saw the demise of the trade route that had been used for centuries. It is a little more than a hundred kilometres from Kargil to Skardu, which now lies on the Pakistani side of the border. From Skardu, the caravan routes went up over the mountains to Kashgar and Central Asia, but suddenly it was no longer possible to get from Kargil to the neighbouring town. When the Chinese occupied Tibet in 1950, that trade route was also cut off.

"In winter, the roads to Srinagar and Leh are closed," Gulzar said. "The only way to get in and out of Kargil then is to fly. Other than that, we are completely isolated."

"Were you here during the war?" I asked.

"I experienced the bombardment. It started at two o'clock in the afternoon and went on until five. The Pakistanis weren't actually targeting Kargil as such, the real target was the weapons depot and military camp outside the town. But many of the projectiles and splinters hit here too. About fifty people were killed that afternoon. The hospital and the school were both hit, and there were bodies in the street. Everyone who could flee did so that very evening, and Kargil became a ghost town. My family and I stayed away for six months, until the war was over."

"Lots of people I've spoken to would like independence for Kashmir," I said. "What about you? Would you prefer independence, Pakistan or India?"

"India," he said, without hesitation. "Most of us here in Kargil are Shia Muslims. And we're safer in India."

An acquaintance of Mir Saqib and Sohail, the mineral water producers in Srinagar, had given me the telephone number of Anayat Aali Shotopa, a local journalist who worked for the radio station Air Kargil. When I called Anayat and introduced myself, he dropped everything he was doing and ran to the hotel to meet me.

"We had guests for lunch, but I told them that this was more important," he said, out of breath. "So little is written about Kargil, it's like an empty chapter."

Anayat talked non-stop and was as helpful as could be. He was thirty-four years old and already had a little pot belly, which he planned to lose.

"I never get to move in this blasted job," he said. "Everything is always urgent, so I just have to jump into a car."

We too jumped into a car and headed for the old Pakistani border. As we sat, locked in Kargil's eternal traffic jam, Anayat told me about the war in 1999.

"I was fourteen years old and on my way home from school when the bombardment started. There was a sudden explosion right beside me. I threw myself down flat on the ground, as we had been taught at school. It was all quite exciting and interesting to begin with, a completely new experience, but then a woman came towards me, crying. I comforted her. Another projectile hit, another explosion. I lay down again, then spotted a man in his thirties crying, with a bleeding nose. I remember it was a real shock, because I had never seen a man cry before, I didn't even know it was possible! Not long after that, I met an old man I knew, who followed me home. When I got there, my mother was crying and she hugged me and hugged me and wouldn't let go."

The traffic slowly eased and we eventually got out of the centre of town. The driver turned onto a narrow road that climbed up a steep mountainside.

Anayat proposed a stop by a very basic tea shack that boasted binoculars for hire, and leaped out of the car.

"Can you see that white house over there?" He pointed to a small, white building a few hundred metres away as the crow flies.

I nodded.

"It's a holy shrine for Muslims. But we can't go there, because it's in Pakistan."

We could see small clusters of run-down houses beyond the shrine. The brownish-red, rugged mountains stretched seamlessly down the valley, without any indication of where they changed nationality. There was a gravel track beside the river, the old road to Skardu.

"The road doesn't go over any high passes, so it could stay open all year round, but instead it's been closed for almost seventy years now," Anayat said. "We're actually standing on what used to be Pakistani ground. The border passed just below where we are standing now, prior to the war in 1971."

I looked down to where he was pointing, and saw some low stone walls on the mountainside. The foundations were all that remained of the Pakistani border checkpoint. Small signs warned that there were still landmines in the area.

"Every so often animals get blown up," Anayat said.

We got back into the car and a few minutes later came to an abandoned village. Low, square wattle-and-daub houses climbed the mountainside like steps; many of them had partially collapsed.

"The village was abandoned in 1971," Anayat said, as we scrambled down the slope, crossed the narrow river and walked over to one of the houses furthest down. He showed me where the key was and opened the door.

"This has been made into a kind of museum," he said, as we entered.

Inside, it was low under the ceiling. A small opening let in strips of light, and there was a hole in the roof to let out the smoke from the fireplace. Colourful jewellery and earrings were displayed in a glass case; the family who had lived here must have been wealthy. Why had they not taken their jewellery with them? The domestic artefacts were timeless: an iron pot, two clay jars, a scythe, a carding comb. The village could equally have been abandoned a hundred years ago.

There was a copy of a letter hanging on one of the walls. "How are things over there? Tell me about the family and your children. I have lots of letters for everyone here. But I haven't had any replies. If I have done something wrong, I beg, from the bottom of my heart, for forgiveness. [. . .] Please write to me soon. I am waiting for your reply. [. . .]"

Following the Indian–Pakistani war in 1971, India, as mentioned, retained a couple of strategic areas on the Pakistani side of the line of control. The village of Hundarman was one such place. Some of the inhabitants ended up on the Pakistani side, and the others moved over time to the settlement in Upper Hundarman and left Lower Hundarman as a time capsule.

We drove on to Upper Hundarman, which was only about a kilo-metre higher up. The village was again made up of simple, low mud houses, like Lower Hundarman, but there was colourful washing hanging out to dry, goats and hens wandered between the houses, and women peeped shyly out of doorways and windows as we passed. A tiny man with a long white beard was sitting on a mat outside a very modest house, watching village life. He had lost most of his teeth, and his face was furrowed and lined, but his body was lithe and supple. His name was Haji Hassan, and while he said he was eighty-one, Anayat, who was translating, said he must be older.

"I have lived through four wars!" Hassan shouted, waving his arms around. "In 1947, 1965, 1971 and 1999. I saw all those wars! I also experienced the delegations from the East India Company, the Dogra dynasty, partition, then Pakistan and now India!"

He looked at me with small, bright eyes.

"Are you British?" he asked.

I shook my head.

"You look British, but then I haven't met any white people who were not British!" Haji Hassan's tiny frame shook when he laughed. "I was born in this village! There was no Pakistan then, and nor was there an India! The Dogras ruled! They didn't have policemen or soldiers, but it was still an authoritarian regime! The maharaja liked to collect taxes from people. A lot of taxes! In 1947, there was fighting just by the village. The border was just down there! Our village was left untouched, as the army used roads and we didn't have a road back then. No road, no school, we had nothing. Then there was another war in 1965! The soldiers stood up on that outcrop over there. Up there, and down there!" He leaned forwards and pointed first up the valley, and then down.

"What was life like when you were part of Pakistan?" I asked.

"We lived just as we do now, only we were in Pakistan!" He laughed again with a twinkle in his eye. "It wasn't a problem. The closest town then was Skardu, and we went there often! Then, in 1971, there was a new war!" Hassan waved his arms around as he spoke. "We stayed in our homes throughout the war, because the fighting wasn't actually here. But five hundred Indian soldiers came. They were nice, the Indian soldiers. Their leader was even a Muslim! We discovered later that we'd become a part of India. When there was a drought here, we got food from the Indian army. Modi has cut the food subsidies now, but we have a good relationship with India and the army. There's been development under India, which we didn't have under Pakistan. But otherwise, there's not much difference!"

"Were lots of families separated in 1971?" I asked.

"Yes, lots of families were split up. Some people died of heartbreak because they were separated from their family, but there wasn't much we could do. We had to accept the situation as it was! My wife's brother lives in Pakistan! And my wife and children have cried so much because of that . . ."

"An uncle on the mother's side is very special," Anayat explained. "Maternal uncles are extremely important in our culture."

"Do you have any more children?" I asked Haji Hassan. When he introduced himself, he had said that he had one son and four grandchildren.

"Yes, I have six in all," he said. "Four boys and two girls! Five of them are dead! One boy died when he was in tenth grade, in India. One was twelve. One was very young. One girl died when she was eight, the other straight after she was born! We don't have a doctor here, we're so isolated! My wife is also dead! She died a long time ago! Ten years ago, at least! I'm the only one left, I'm the only one who can tell these stories! Ten years ago, I went on Hajj, and I've also been to Syria, Iraq, Iran and Delhi! I've worked all my life. I've worked as a weaver, a bricklayer and a porter for the army. In 1999 there was another war!" he shouted. "Everyone else fled, but those of us here in Hundarman stayed. We all supported the Indian army. The sky went dark, there were so many grenades and bombs! When they started bombing, we all sheltered in a cave below the old village. We didn't know if we'd find our houses standing when we came back!"

"Just take a look at his house," Anayat said and pointed at all the bullet holes in the walls. They were tightly packed, almost like a designed pattern. Haji Hassan had lived in the house all his life while rulers and borders came and went, and one war took over from another. From here, on the flat ground in front of his house, he had watched the geopolitical drama unfold from the best seat in the house.

"Are you worried that there might be another war?" I asked, before leaving.

"Yes," Haji Hassan said. "I'm worried for my grandchildren. Because there will be another war, you can be certain of that!"

Some distance north-east of Kargil, there are four small villages that were also a part of Pakistan until the 1971 war. To get there from the Indian side, which is the only way now, proved to be a protracted affair. From Kargil, we first had to drive five hours south-east, to the tourist hub of Leh, and then we had to cross the Khardung-La Pass, at 5359 MSL, and then head north-west, past enormous Buddha statues and small, modest monasteries, until we were almost at the border with Pakistan. The road was in excellent condition, and open all year round, as it led to the seventy-kilometre-long Siachen Glacier, the second longest glacier in the word, excluding the polar regions. But the glacier is even better known for being the world's highest and most expensive battleground. The peace treaty that was signed following the 1971 war stated that the border should continue to the Siachen Glacier, but did not specify how the glacier would be divided. The UN envoys clearly assumed that there was little potential for armed conflict on the glacier. They were wrong. In 1984, the Indian military invaded and occupied the entire glacier, pipping Pakistan to the post, as they also had ambitions to occupy the ice mass. The Pakistani military, however, had arrived a week too late and were forced back down the mountainside. And since then, for more than thirty years, Indian and Pakistani soldiers have remained in more or less the same positions, fiercely guarding the ice at 6000 MSL. And over the years, more than two thousand soldiers have lost their lives on Siachen Glacier, some in the intermittent fighting, but most as victims of nature rather than each other.

3001 MSL Late in the afternoon, we got to **Turtuk**, a village with about three thousand inhabitants that creeps up the slopes on either side of the Shyok River. The village was almost invisible, the flat stone and mud houses hidden behind leafy, green trees. It was only a matter of years since Turtuk had opened up to tourists, as the village lies so close to the line of control that the authorities preferred to keep a check on who was going there. But cafés, restaurants and a number of small guest houses had already popped up. I checked in to a guest house that had been recommended to me, and asked the young host, Salim, if he knew anyone in the village who had family in Pakistan.

"Everyone here has family in Pakistan. I do too," he said. "But you should talk to Muhammed Ali, whose father has just recently visited from Pakistan."

"Is there anyone here who speaks English and could interpret for me?" I asked.

"I'm afraid there's only me," Salim replied. So he accompanied me to the other side of the river, where Muhammed Ali lived in a low-ceilinged house on a narrow backstreet. Muhammed appeared in the doorway almost as soon as Salim knocked on the door. He was wearing a down jacket and a large brown suit jacket on top of his dirty tunic. His hair was grey, his long, narrow face deeply furrowed, and his lips were dry and split. He did not invite us in, but rather indicated that we could sit on the stone slabs just outside.

"It's full of children in there," he said. "It's impossible to speak in peace."

He told us he had five sons and two daughters. Salim then explained why I was there.

"I was four in 1971, or maybe five, possibly even six, I have no idea, but I was young, so I don't remember much from that time," Muhammed said.

A donkey and a cow wandered towards us. The cow stopped and looked at us uncertainly, but was soon chased into the byre by one of Muhammed's sons.

"Three days before the war broke out, my parents went to Khaplu, which is about seventy kilometres from here," Muhammed said. "Mother often had aching joints, and there was a hot spring in Khaplu that was good for her. The war broke out when they were there, and when the war was over, Turtuk was part of India. My parents were on the Pakistan side of the border and didn't manage to get back. I only remember them from photographs. My uncle and his wife looked after me and my two brothers."

Muhammed cleared his throat and stared straight ahead with a dejected look on his face. He spoke slowly, as though he had to pull the words up from a deep place.

"Some years later we were told that Mother had died. I was nine. We found out from a letter that was sent to someone else in the village. My father remarried in Pakistan, and had three more children – two sons and a daughter. I have never met them. In 2014, I met my father again for the first time. One of my sons went to the border to welcome his grandfather. I met him in Leh."

He gave me a gentle smile, but was quickly serious again.

"I was so happy to meet my father, but also saddened to see how old he was. When I was finally reunited with him, he was an 86-year-old man with a white beard and a stick. I knew that he would not be able to stay here more than three months, then he would have to go back to Pakistan. So I had very mixed feelings when I met him."

"It must have been strange to see your father again after such a long time, perhaps having only spoken to him on the phone," I said.

"I had never spoken to him until then," Muhammed said. "We didn't get a telephone line here until 2006, but that didn't make much difference anyway, as it wasn't possible to call Pakistan from here."

He looked down.

"I am angry with the border authorities," he said in a quiet voice. "Because of a couple of lines in the map, I couldn't meet my father. It's only forty-five kilometres from here to Skardu – that's half an hour in a car – but it's not possible to cross the border. My whole life has been marred by this dividing line they put in place in 1971. If Father had been here, he would have been able to give me advice as I grew up and became an adult myself. But there was no-one who could give me advice. My life has been difficult."

"What is your greatest wish?" I asked.

"I wish there was a place at the border where we could meet our relatives, so that they didn't need to come here, and we didn't need to go to Pakistan. A place where we could meet. That's my only dream."

"I hope that it comes true," I said, and immediately heard how hollow my words were. Not because I didn't mean it, but because I could not believe that it would ever happen, no matter how simple his dream was.

"After my father left, I didn't touch the bed where he had slept for three months," Muhammed said. "I left it just as he had. He gave me this jacket before he went."

He pointed to the brown suit jacket that he had on under his down jacket.

"I wear it every day, and only take it off when I go to bed. I've never washed it. I don't want to lose the smell of my father."

Of Gods and Men

Leh was like a Himalayan Disneyland. The souvenir shops and travel agencies jostled for room, and it seemed the latter were trying to outdo each other when it came to clichés: *Mystic Ladakh Tour, Ladakh Exotic Tour, Authentic Ladakh Tour, Marvels of Ladakh, Ladakh – the last Shangri-La, Discover the Secrets of Ladakh* . . . Less spiritual tourists might be tempted by offers of paragliding and offroad motorbike tours with a "guaranteed adrenaline kick". The outdoor shops, of which there were many, all advertised dirt-cheap copies of the most expensive brands, and the cafés lured customers in with the promise of banana pancakes, milkshakes, pizza, spaghetti and "real coffee". There was a German Bakery on every corner – a sure sign that you had arrived in a tourist Mecca. Foreigners crowded the streets, most of them clearly outward-bound types in hiking books and the most advanced hiking clothes on the market. But there were also droves of their anti-materialist counterparts, who wandered around in baggy, colourful clothes with blissed-out smiles on their Western lips. Their dreadlocks had probably not been washed since they were stamped into India.

Until relatively recently, Leh was a destination for only the hardiest of adventurers. The Ladakh capital lies in between the Karakoram and Himalaya mountains, just south of the disputed Aksai Chin region and equally controversial Chinese border. In cultural terms, Ladakh has close links to Tibet, but it is now ruled from Delhi. The region, which is often called Little Tibet, has been a part of India since the 1800s, when the people who lived in this corner of the Himalayas generally had more contact with their neighbours than with the ruling powers in India. Because of its strategic position, nestled between Tibet and Xinjiang to the north, Baltistan in north Pakistan to the west and Kashmir to the south, Leh was an important stopping place for the Himalayan caravans. Local products such as wool, salt and dried apricots were exported from Leh, as well as Indian goods such as cotton fabric, beads, spices, rice, sugar and tobacco. Money was a rarity in these parts, and goods were generally bartered for other produce.

Following partition in 1947, and China's occupation of Tibet in 1950, Ladakh became culturally and geographically isolated. For people like me and the other foreigners who enjoyed a beer or a cappuccino at one of the panoramic cafés in Leh, the world has become more accessible than ever in the past decades, thanks to cheap plane tickets and passports that are welcomed everywhere. However, for the local people, who have been crossing mountains and valleys for centuries in order to exchange goods, the world has become smaller and full of restrictions, despite the fact that the roads and means of transport themselves have never been better.

These days, it is almost *too* easy to get to Leh. Before the road was completed in about 1950, the journey from Srinagar to Leh took more than two weeks, whereas it now takes a day in a car, or a couple of hours by air. Altitude sickness is a common side effect of these modern means of transport, as Leh lies at 3,500 MSL, which is almost as high as Lhasa, the capital of Tibet. Even though I had travelled more slowly than most, I could feel the altitude. There was a constant gentle thrumming in my head, and I was left breathless by the slightest exertion. Having trundled around the busy shopping streets for an hour or so, I turned back – my hotel bed was calling.

A small French girl was sitting with an enormous oxygen mask over her face in reception. There were traces of tears on her cheeks, and her mother was holding her close, telling her to breathe deeply and slowly. I bumped into a tall, sinewy Swedish man in the hotel garden. He had shoulder-length white hair and a trim beard, and was wearing a T-shirt with his participant number for the Ladakh Marathon. He moved stiffly towards one of the tables in the sun and moaned as he sank down on a chair.

"Oh my God, that is the hardest marathon I've ever run!" he exclaimed. 'Even tougher than the one in Antarctica."

"Because of the altitude?" I said.

"No, no, I've acclimatised. It was just so damn hilly! The last five kilometres were uphill all the way. No-one ran the final stretch, everyone walked. Some crawled."

The tall Swede was called Håkan Jonsson; he was sixty-eight and was a radiologist, but spent most of his time running marathons in strange places in order to raise funds to fight child mortality in South Africa.

"Do you know of any other places I could run a marathon?" he asked, and took a swig of beer. "I've already run on all the continents. There's a challenge where you can run a marathon on every continent in seven days, but I think that might be pushing it."

He invited me to sit down, and we chatted about this and that. I told him about my most recent travels, and he lit up when I mentioned Mongolia.

"I've always wanted to go to Mongolia," he said.

"Maybe there's a marathon there," I said.

Håkan was already busy searching on Google.

"There is, but it's in winter," he said with audible disappointment. "Having run a marathon at the South Pole and the North Pole, I don't think I can face going to Mongolia to run in the ice and snow. It's so damn difficult to run in snow."

I saw no reason to argue with that.

The palace in Leh perches on a rocky outcrop above the centre. The impressive building is nine storeys high and made from wood, stone and clay. It is remarkably like the Potala Palace in Lhasa, which is from about the same period. The palace was built in the seventeenth century, during the reign of Sengge Namgyal, who was known as the Lion King. He was the son of a Muslim princess from Baltistan, the neighbouring region to the west, but was himself a devout Buddhist. In the course of his life, he built and restored monasteries throughout his kingdom. The Lion King's descendants lived in the palace for more than two hundred years, until Ladakh was annexed by the Sikhs in 1834 and the local royal family was evicted, never to return.

From the roof, there was a panoramic view of the town and the blue mountains that surround it. The bustling streets looked curiously small from up there.

The Hemis Monastery lies forty kilometres from Leh, and is one of the monasteries that was restored to its former glory by the Lion King. Today, it is one of the largest and wealthiest in the region. Like so many before me, I went there in search of Jesus's secret testament, albeit without much hope of finding it.

In 1894, five years before the self-declared prophet Mirza Ghulam Ahmad launched his theory that Jesus did not die on the cross but is buried in Srinagar, the book *La vie inconnue de Jésus-Christ en Inde et au Tibet* was published. The author, a Russian adventurer called Nicolas Notovitch, wrote that a few years earlier, when travelling in Ladakh, he had come across an old, secret book in the Hemis Monastery about the travels of Jesus, or Issa, as the Buddhist monks called him, when he came to India to study Buddhism and Hinduism as a young man. Notovitch said the abbot had at first been reluctant to show him the book, as only venerable lamas had access to it. However, on his way back to Leh, Notovitch broke his foot in a riding accident, and had to stay at the monastery for three days until he had recovered sufficiently to travel on. To entertain him as he convalesced, the abbot read to him from Issa's biography. In the short time that he was there, Notovitch managed miraculously to complete a translation, which was then published in the book, and largely focuses on Issa's years in India. In the fourth chapter, the fourteen-year-old Jesus sets out on his journey east: "Then Issa secretly absented himself from his father's house; left Jerusalem, and in a train of merchants, journeyed towards the Sindh, with the object of perfecting himself in the knowledge of the word of God and the study of the laws of the great Buddhas."[5]

According to Notovitch, Jesus travelled around India for the next fifteen years; he learned the languages and customs, and tried to convince the Buddhists and Brahmins that he met that there was only one eternal, indivisible God. Then he went home to Palestine and was crucified.

In the long foreword, Notovitch claims that he took a number of photographs, but when he returned to the lowlands he discovered to his horror that the negatives were ruined. But this did not stop the book from becoming a sensation. In its first year, the French edition was reprinted eleven times and the astonishing story featured extensively in the *New York Times*. However, people soon started to voice their doubts about the veracity of Notovitch's incredible story. The kindest critics believed that the lamas in Ladakh had been having fun at expense of the naive Westerner, telling him wild tales, but a couple of scholars made the effort to contact the abbot of the Hemis Monastery, who said that they had received no European visitors for fifteen years, and dismissed Notovitch's book as pure lies. However, the theory that Jesus spent much of his adult life in India persists, and every now and then books are published that still argue that Jesus was in India in those mysterious years that are not described in the Bible. The idea that he may just have been at home with his mother and father, working as a carpenter's apprentice is, undeniably, more mundane.

The monastery buildings were big and well maintained. They were painted red and white and arranged in a rectangle around an open square, which was teeming with young monks. A group of women dressed in black woollen dresses stood talking in one corner. I headed towards the monastery's well-stocked bookshop, but the Notovitch book was nowhere to be seen among all the Dalai Lama's publications and books on Buddhist philosophy.

"Do you have the book by Notovitch anywhere?" I asked the monk behind the counter. He shook his head. He had never heard of Notovitch. I went back out into the square and asked one of the monks who were sitting chatting in the shade if he had heard of Notovitch. He had not. I had more or less given up hope of finding someone who could help me when I asked a third monk, a tall, slim man in his thirties.

"Yes, of course I've heard of Notovitch," he said. "What is more, I've got his book."

"Is what he writes about in the book true?" I asked.

"Of course it is all true," the monk said. "You are not the first to ask. Over the years, many Russians have come here and asked about Notovitch and Jesus, so one day I asked my teacher, the head lama, if it was really true that Jesus had lived here. He said of course it was true. Jesus meditated in the same cave as Padmasambhava, on the mountainside behind the monastery. It was a holy place already then, but, obviously, the monastery wasn't here. You can go up to the cave yourself, if you like."

"So the manuscript about Jesus's life is here in the monastery?" I asked, enthusiastically.

"Yes, in the library."

"Have you seen it yourself?"

"No, only the head lama is allowed to see it."

"Would it be possible to meet him?"

"He's in Tibet, so it would be difficult."

"I'm going to Tibet soon," I said. "Perhaps I could meet him there."

"You could try, but it would be difficult," the monk said again. "The Chinese authorities keep a strict eye on tourists."

"Have you read Notovitch's book?" I asked.

"No, unfortunately not," the monk said. "I've got the book, but it's in Russian."

"Many people in the church disagree with what it says in the book, and there's nothing in the Bible about Jesus coming to India," I said.

"We also have the Bible in our library," the monk said. "We have all kinds of religious books there. But there are lots of people who believe that Jesus was in India. Have you googled it? If you search on Google, you'll get lots of hits. But for me, the most important thing is that my teacher has confirmed it. If he hadn't said it was true, I would never tell you that Jesus was here, but as my teacher has said that it's true, I can now stand here and tell you that it's true. Jesus was here."

I was flabbergasted. I had not expected to have Notovitch's theory confirmed. Though perhaps confirmed is not the right word. Other than possibly the head lama, who I did not meet, no-one had actually seen the mysterious manuscript with their own eyes. And the only one that existed was a dubious super-fast translation by a discredited Russian explorer. But the myth lives on, as does the myth that Jesus is buried in Srinagar. The Himalayas are teeming with stories like these, not just about a Christian saviour, but also about levitating lamas, abominable snowmen and hidden valley paradises where people live happily in harmony and are not plagued by worldly sufferings like ageing and illness.

The Western notion that these misty, ice-covered, inaccessible mountains of Asia hold deep secrets, magic and sages goes back a long way, and was perhaps reinforced by the fact that the Himalayan kingdoms were so closed: until the middle of the last century, Nepal, Bhutan and Tibet, in particular, were as good as hermetically sealed to foreigners. This of course just galvanised intrepid travellers all the more: Lhasa became the ultimate destination. Tibet was a blank spot on the map, a fairy tale land east of the sun and west of the moon, a mirage. For a good part of the twentieth century, explorers continued to risk their lives in their attempts to get into Lhasa, dressed as monks or merchants, crossing the plateau by foot, exposed to the elements. Almost none of them succeeded, but the few that did were guaranteed an income for the rest of their lives from book sales and lecture tours.

One did not necessarily need to contract hypothermia at six thousand metres or have infected blisters or live on dried yak meat to ride the Tibet wave. Western audiences were so insatiable that they would swallow anything hook, line and sinker.

In 1956, a book called *The Third Eye* was published in England, in which the author, a lama by the name of Lobsang Rampa, tells about his childhood in Tibet. He was born into a rich family, he writes, and was sent to a monastery when he was seven. Life in the monastery was hard, but it was discovered early on that he had exceptional abilities. He describes in detail an operation that the older lamas performed on him one day, where they drilled a small hole between his eyes in order to open the third eye. The book was an instant bestseller.

An Austrian mountaineer, Heinrich Harrer, who was one of the few who had actually been in Tibet at the time, found Lobsang Rampa's story hard to believe. He himself had spent seven years in Tibet, having fled over the mountains in 1955 to avoid becoming a prisoner of war of the British Indian authorities, and he had become one of the Dalai Lama's closest companions. Harrer hired a private detective to investigate, and the detective concluded that Rampa was in reality called Cyril Henry Hoskin, and came from the south coast of England, where he had previously worked as a plumber. Hoskin had never been in Tibet – he did not even have a passport – and could not speak a word of Tibetan. In his third book, *The Rampa Story*, the lama plumber explained what had happened: one day he had climbed up a tree in the garden to take a photograph of an owl. He fell and knocked himself out and when he came to he saw a Buddhist monk coming towards him. The monk was Tuesday Lobsang Rampa, whose body was worn out after a lifetime of many inhuman trials. Rampa therefore wanted to take over Hoskin's body, and Hoskin, who had not achieved much in life, generously allowed Rampa's soul to move in.

Rampa wrote a further seventeen books in his plumber's body, and they were all bestsellers. More copies of *The Third Eye* have been sold than of any other book about Tibet ever published in the UK.

*

I travelled south to the holiday town of Manali in the state of Himachal Pradesh in a packed minibus. The sun was setting as we left the bus station in Leh, and soon the dark enveloped us. Evening turned to night and I shivered in my seat. We had to cross two mountain passes; the minibus clattered and bounced along the narrow, muddy, twisting road – apparently one of the most dramatic in India, amid a spectacular landscape. But all I could see was the sides of the road whenever they were illuminated by an oncoming vehicle. The driver played loud music all night, an eclectic mix of Indian pop music and Buddhist meditation music. I put in my earplugs, buttoned up my jacket and pulled the hood over my head. I slept intermittently, but whenever I dropped off, we stopped at yet another checkpoint, and the driver turned on the lights and asked for yet another photocopy of my passport. Before I fell asleep again, I thought of all the Westerners who are still drawn to the East, to the Himalayas, in search of inner peace, harmony and spiritual insights that they are unable to find at home. Literature about the Himalayas can be roughly divided in two: books about daring attempts to climb one of the mountains, or books about the search to understand the peaks and troughs of the soul, often the author's own.

Then sleep took over; floating lamas, abominable snowmen and surly passport officers all blended into one.

I woke up as the day was dawning and discovered that I was in

Switzerland. The steep mountains that ran down into the valleys were no longer brown and bare, but green and lush and covered in trees. The Kullu district, which for centuries was its own kingdom, was only connected by road to the rest of India after 1947. The women here wore colourful headscarves and many of the men still wore round, embroidered felt hats. In the course of my travels through the Himalayas, I visited five countries, according to the atlas, though in reality I went to many more. I could hardly move from one valley to the next without coming across different traditional clothing and building styles, different gods and completely different languages.

2050 MSL   In **Manali** there were even more hotels than in Leh. Most of them were targeted at the Indian tourist market, those who come to enjoy the mountains and the fresh, clean air.

And to smoke hash.

It is said that the world's best cannabis is grown in the mountain 2652 MSL village of **Malana**, which lies about eighty kilometres from Manali. The driver had not been there before, or he would never have said yes. The last hour of the journey was on a narrow, stony road up a steepening valley; the stones knocked and scraped against the undercarriage of the car. There had been rockfalls in several places and the driver had to inch past the boulders along the very edge of the road, with a clear sightline down to the tumultuous river far below.

"Very dangerous road," he said, with feeling. It was the first time I had heard an Indian complain about the state of a road.

The start of the path that led up to the village was marked by an archway. In the past, one had to walk for days to get to Malana, but now, thanks to the new dam and accompanying hazardous road, it took no more than an hour. The path and steps had been laid with concrete. On the way up, I passed three Indian tourists who were resting, out of breath, on a bend. At the entrance to the village there was a small kiosk. The smoke hung heavy around the shack and the young man who worked there.

"Would you like Malana Cream?" he asked, with a smile, and held out a substantial lump of hash.

"No, thank you," I said, politely.

"How about a meal? Some soda water? Chocolate? Are you planning to stay here overnight? If so, I can recommend a small guest house at the other end of the village." He looked at me with bloodshot eyes.

"I'm not staying the night," I said. "Is it true that the people here are descendants of Alexander the Great's army?" I had read everything I could about Malana on the internet, and it said in all the articles and blogs that the people here believed this to be the case, and that that was why they had so many peculiar rules.

"Alexander the who?" the kiosk man said in a bewildered voice.

"The Great."

"No, no, we're not descendants of the Great, we're descendants of our god, Jamdagni Rishi."

I thanked him for the information and continued into the village.

I was careful to stick to the path that led through the village. On the surface, Malana was like any other Indian village, with houses that were two to three metres high, built in stone and timber, with corrugated metal roofs in vibrant colours. There were lots of people about, and at regular intervals I passed groups of men and women standing around talking, but no-one returned my smile. Indian pop music was blasting out full volume by a wooden platform that presumably was the village dance floor. A large yellow sign warned in both Hindi and English that there was a 3,500-rupee fine for touching the temple.

No-one took any notice of me. I was invisible. It was a rather odd feeling, as I had been noticed constantly for the past two months. Women and even children stepped to one side in irritation when I approached them and ignored me completely. As I had read everything I could before coming there, I knew that it would be like this, but still it upset me. I pulled myself together and went over to a group of men and asked if any of them could speak English. They did not even bother to answer.

I was almost in tears when I bumped into the three Indians I had passed on the way up to the village. They were about to buy three small Malana Cream cakes from a middle-aged man. The Indians greeted me cheerfully, and I asked if they could help me with some translation. They were more than happy to do this, so I asked if they could get the seller to tell us a little about Malana culture.

"I can't say much about the place, as we are reserved and private people," the seller said. He did, however, tell us a bit about himself. His name was Moti Ram, he was forty-one, and was the first person in the village to complete twelve years of education, so he was held in great respect.

"We have our own king," he said. "We're not part of the Indian democracy. I'm sure you've noticed all the signs that say you'll be fined if you touch our temple? We're not allowed to touch it either. Only ten men, who are selected every second year, are allowed to go into the temple. And only these ten men can make hash from our cannabis plants. Our religion tells that the mughal king Akbar came here. He made off with our treasures, but then fell ill and had to come back. And so he became our king. We have a special day when we fast in honour of him. For one day of the year, we worship Akbar like a god. And on all the other days, he's our king. We also have our own language, Kanashi, but everyone can speak Hindi as well."

"Why are you not allowed to touch foreigners?" I asked.

"The problem with foreigners is that we don't know which caste they are from," Moti said. "They don't even know themselves. We belong to the Thakur caste, just below the Brahmins. Indians, on the other hand, are like us, so we can touch them. I can shake your hand, but then I have to cleanse myself before I can go into my house. Our houses are sacred."

"Is it true that you are all descendants of Alexander the Great's army?" I asked again.

"That's a myth that was created elsewhere," Moti said. "People like good stories, but we don't have any Greek blood in us. We're Indian."

"That's not what it says on the internet!" said the young Indian who was interpreting for me.

"Everything that's said about us on the internet is wrong," Moti said calmly. "The main source of income here is hash," he carried on. "We also have cattle. And honey. Personally, I would rather sell honey. We get 50 euros for 11.6 grams of hash. And in Amsterdam, it's sold for 250 euros a gram. Cannabis is illegal in India, but for us it's sacred."

Not all myths would survive a meeting with the main characters. But the myth that the deeply religious inhabitants of Malana are the descendants of Alexander the Great has, like all good and exciting stories, a life of its own. If one were to believe all the stories, Alexander the Great's virile soldiers left behind them blue-eyed descendants in the greater part of Eurasia: the legion of Greek genes apparently stretches like a great blond swathe from the Black Sea to the mountain valleys of the Himalayas.

I stopped by the small kiosk to buy a packet of crisps as I left the village. I took out the money to give to the man, but he refused to take it.

"You have to put it on the ground," he said.

I did as he asked, and he bent down to pick up the notes, then indicated that I could take a bag of crisps. He put the change down on the ground in front of me. There were crisp packets and soda bottles everywhere around the kiosk and entrance to the village.

"I studied English, history and lots of other subjects in Manali," the kiosk seller told me. "You can call me Jack."

"What's your Malana name?" I asked.

"Akshe," he said. "Did you like Malana?"

"No," I said, as it was the truth.

"I don't like Malana either," Jack said. "But I like the hash." He tittered. "My father smokes as well. And my brother."

"What about your mother, does she smoke?" I asked.

"No, women never smoke."

"Why did I have to put my money on the ground?"

"Because that's how we do it here," Jack said. "The village is a holy place." And then added, out of context: "I've got a friend in Australia. I've also got a girlfriend there."

"I thought you weren't allowed to touch foreigners," I said.

"Oh yeah," he said. "I can. I'm not like the others."

Another young man came over. He was darker than any of the other villagers I had seen, and his brown eyes were swimming.

"I'm originally from Kolkata," he said and giggled. "I was adopted by the village four or five years ago. I'm forty-one, but I'm actually only forty because the climate's so good here. It snows in winter," he said, and this was followed by a deep, contemplative silence.

On my way back to the car, I passed five Western tourists with dirty dreadlocks and eager eyes, dressed in colourful, loose clothes.

"Is it much further to go?" one of them asked me, out of breath.

"You'll be there soon," I said, and they carried on with grateful smiles.

A couple of local women were walking behind them. They groaned when they saw me and made a show of stepping out of my way. I found myself longing for the bustle of ordinary Indian streets.

On the way back to Manali, we drove past a small procession. The men at the front were playing drums and pipes, and the ones at the back were carrying incense holders. Four men in the middle were holding a litter with a silver statue on it. The statue was decorated with flowers and pieces of cloth in every colour.

"What are they doing?" I asked the driver.

"They're celebrating their god," he said.

"Which god is that?"

He shrugged. "Oh, some god or other. A local god."

Little Tibet

The Spiti Valley is one of the most remote and sparsely populated valleys in India, and the road there was in a shocking state. The Land Rover bounced down the narrow tracks, over stones and through deep puddles. Rakesh, the good-natured driver, kept an average speed of fifteen kilometres per hour as he hummed happily along to Indian pop songs without ever getting the tune right.

The green forests of Kullu were behind us, and once again the landscape was brown and bare. There were no villages along the road, only a couple of café tents and resting places. We arrived just after sunset at the small, modest convent where we were going to stay the night.

A young monk welcomed me in broken English, and introduced himself as Tenzin, my local guide. He was twenty-eight and a lama at one of the monasteries in Kaza, the biggest village in the valley.

"I hope you can teach me a bit more about Tibetan Buddhism," I said, and smiled. "All the different schools and movements are rather confusing."

We were going to spend a whole week together, but Tenzin wasted no time and immediately started to tell me about the various Buddhist schools and differences between them. He listed the long, complicated names of the main schools, middle schools and sub-groups, the name of the head priest here, and the head priest there, yellow hats, red hats, black hats. I lost track almost straight away. Just as he started to elaborate on the subtle differences between the Nyingma, Kagyu and Gelug schools, I was saved by a young nun who invited us for tea.

The mountain air was cool and clear, but it was as warm as a summer's day in the small kitchen. It smelled of gas and fresh chapattis. Tenzin and I sat down on the big cushions along the wall, while four young nuns poured us tea with warm, sweet milk. They were dressed in T-shirts and long purple skirts, with shaved heads just like the monks. I asked them a few questions – how long they had been nuns, how old they were, what they were called – but they just giggled and looked away.

Tenzin was curious about Christianity and wanted to learn more himself. I told him, as simply and clearly as I could, about the Garden of Eden and Jesus, the son of God, who was born to a virgin, and performed a number of miracles and was then nailed to the cross for our sins, but rose from the dead on the third day, and about the Holy Trinity, which is not actually three, but one. When I was finished he looked just as confused as I had been following his crash course in Tibetan Buddhism.

At some point, Tenzin disappeared on a necessary errand. The nuns moved closer. As it turned out, all four of them spoke good English, and they were dying to ask me a whole host of questions. They wanted to know how old I was, if I had siblings, a husband, children, where I lived, what I did, if I was a Buddhist, if I liked their convent. They were all from the Spiti Valley, which, like Ladakh, is known as Little Tibet. Tibet is within walking distance, on the other side of the mountains, and until China occupied the country, there was close contact between the neighbours, who shared a language, culture and religion. Tibetan culture is probably better preserved in the Spiti Valley than it is in Tibet, where a great part of the cultural heritage was lost during the Cultural Revolution, and the Tibetans are still subjected to strict regulations and extensive surveillance.

When Tenzin came back a few minutes later, the nuns were once again reserved and silent, other than a few giggles.

*

First thing the next morning, two of the nuns were already busy preparing breakfast. They sat on the floor and rolled bread dough into long sausages which they then made into small portions and lowered into a huge pot of boiling water. The oldest girl was nineteen and called Sherab; the youngest was only thirteen, and called Tenzin – in Tibetan, boys' and girls' names are often the same.

"My parents didn't want me to become a nun," Tenzin said, with a shy smile, "but my friend and I decided to become nuns all the same. We left our village three years ago to come here. Life in the convent is simple, and I like it that way."

"So you don't want to get married and have children?" I asked.

"NO!" They both covered their faces in horror, then burst out laughing.

"To be married and have children sounds like too much work," Sherab said.

The nuns up on the first floor were well into morning prayers. A dozen or so young girls sat along the walls of the simple but richly decorated temple room, chanting along with the recording of a lama that was being played on an old-fashioned tape deck. When the recording stopped, the nuns continued to recite their mantras for a while longer – in quiet, insistent, hypnotic voices. One of the older nuns then handed out to each of them a long printed page from the *pecha*, Tibetan religious books, and they started to rock gently as they read out loud. The older nuns rattled their way through the pages with great efficiency, whereas the younger ones, some of whom could not have been much more than seven or eight, sounded their way painstakingly through the difficult words. Half an hour later, the pages were gathered in again and carefully wrapped in an orange cloth. The nuns recited some more mantras, their voices rising and falling, and a couple of the little ones could not suppress their yawns. When they were finished, the sleepy girls got up from their cushions and went for breakfast.

While we ate, I spoke to Dolma, one of the oldest nuns in the convent. She was forty-five and had been there since the convent was established, when there were only a handful of nuns and they lived in small caves up in the mountains.

"There wasn't much room there and it was extremely cold in winter," she said. "We had nothing, not even proper tea cups. The only one we had had a hole in it, hahaha!"

There are now about forty nuns living in two buildings, which are simple, but warm and comfortable. The entire village helped to build them.

"Is there anything you miss from your previous life?" I asked Dolma.

"I was so young when I became a nun that I can't remember anything I might miss," she said with a laugh. "I only remember that I used to walk to school with a small bag over my shoulder."

"Why did you choose to become a nun?"

Dolma burst out laughing.

"I didn't really think about it," she said, and laughed even more.

"She was probably pressured by her parents," Rakesh, the driver, said. "Sending your children to a monastery is part of our culture. The village is very small, and life is hard, especially in winter."

"How many brothers and sisters do you have?" I asked Dolma.

"Two brothers and five sisters," she said. "One of my little sisters is also a nun. I'm one of the oldest here, and do my best to make sure that the young nuns will have an easier life than I've had. I feel like a mother to them all and want them to get a good education."

Friday was a day of rest in the convent, and the nuns did not need to study. They used the time to wash and play. A couple of girls had started to scrub the floor of their cell. Two very young nuns, who were no more than five or six, had let a newborn calf out of the barn and were playing with it in delight. A couple of lads from the village cycled back and forth across the hay that the nuns had laid out to dry, to break it up into smaller pieces.

When Tenzin, Rakesh and I set off for Kaza later in the afternoon, the car was full of giggling teenage nuns who had to go to the village on "urgent business", as they put it. They sat squashed in the back seat, laughing and chatting, with their mobile phones and handbags to accessorise their plain nuns' habits.

The muddy streets wound between the low houses in **Kaza**, which   3650 MSL
is the only place in the Spiti Valley with any kind of decent mobile phone coverage. People in other villages simply had to manage without any satellite connection to the rest of the world. The sky was intensely blue and there was not a cloud; the air was thin and pure. The Spiti River, which divides the village in two, sparkled in the sunlight, and the reddish-brown mountains that flanked it were exquisitely topped with snow.

Over lunch, I got talking to an *amchi*, a practitioner of traditional Tibetan medicine. His name was Norbu; he was in his fifties and radiated the calm authority that is so typical of doctors the world over. He had perfect white teeth – a rarity in these parts – and spoke excellent English. He introduced me to the workings of an *amchi*, while I enjoyed my steaming momos, big, fat dumplings filled with potato and cheese.

"Traditionally, the *amchi* gathers the herbs from which he makes his medicine," he said. "An *amchi* is a one-man operation, he does everything himself. It's a long training. I studied Tibetan medicine at the Men-Tsee-Khang Institute in Dharamsala for five years and then did a two-year apprenticeship. My mother forced me to study medicine. I was only seventeen or so and didn't really have any idea what I wanted to do in life. At the institute, we learned about illnesses and symptoms, diagnosis and what kind of medicine to use. When we make a diagnosis, we measure the pulse rate, look at the colour of the urine, tongue and eyes. An *amchi* can normally cure chronic afflictions like rheumatism, but sometimes he has to send the patient to hospital."

"Tibetan medicine is closely linked to Buddhism," Tenzin added.

"Yes, we often advise the patient to recite special medicinal mantras," Norbu said. "We believe it helps. We also treat psychological illnesses. We call it *lungat*, which is often translated in the West as depression, but it's not quite the same, as *lungat* doesn't necessarily have an external cause. Not long ago, a woman in Kaza committed suicide, even though there was no reason. She had a good family, fine sons, a good life. But she suffered from *lungat*."

"What illnesses are most common here?" I asked.

"Mostly digestive problems. And joint pain. People wear different clothes now, synthetic, and they wash themselves and their clothes too often. Diabetes has become more widespread in the cities. We believe that illness is linked to lifestyle, environment and food. It's cold and dry here, and that affects the body. We also believe that feelings can affect your health. Desire leads to lung problems, whereas hate can give you gut problems. We believe that everything, including your emotions, needs to be in balance."

Norbu had been an *amchi* for twenty-five years and had worked in Shimla, Delhi and Kolkata as well as here at home in Kaza, but had recently given up his practice.

"Tibetan medicine is widely used in the rest of India, but here people prefer to go to an ordinary doctor," he said sadly. "According to tradition here in Spiti, the eldest son inherits everything: the house, the land, everything. I'm the youngest of four brothers and have to make my own living. To begin with, I sold clothes, but now I've started to sell souvenirs to the tourists who come here. And the sad thing is that I earn more from selling Buddha statues and T-shirts than I would from being an *amchi*."

Tsechen Chöling, a brand-new convent that housed fifteen young nuns, lay on the other side of the river. I was given a twenty-minute private audience with Lama Tsewang, who was responsible for study.

The 37-year-old lama welcomed me from a wicker chair at the end of a corridor, where there was a fantastic, panoramic view of the mountains and valley.

"There are several traditions within Tibetan Buddhism, but the exact number depends on how you count," he said, and rattled off the names of the different traditions, which then can be split into further subdivisions. "I am not able to tell you in detail about one of the main traditions, Vajrayana, the Diamond Vehicle, or Tantrayana, as it's sometimes called, as I would need permission from one of the teachers. I would also need permission to read a tantric text. It's very secret. But, in short, tantric Buddhism uses esoteric, spiritual techniques that act as a shortcut to enlightenment and can only be taught by initiated teachers. The Dalai Lama is the head teacher. There are many misunderstandings about Buddhism, because the dharma, or the Buddha's teaching, is often mixed with cultural practices. Buddhism is not a religion; it is a discipline. Buddhism is about your life, the truth of your life, it's about the essential nature of existence and the universe. We have to know how the world works in order to live. The Buddha's teaching is integral to liberation."

Tsewang glanced at his watch.

"On a general level, Buddhism teaches emptiness," he said.

"To me, all the temples, gold statues, rituals and offerings make Buddhism very much a religion," I said.

"Yes, yes, I can understand why you think that!" Tsewang said with sincerity. "Buddhism is supposed to have no caste system, no hierarchy, but our monasteries are full of gold statues of the Buddha! The Dalai Lama has said that Buddhism incorporates three elements: the religious, the philosophical and the scientific. The long texts that we study are part of the philosophy. The pursuit of the true nature of all things is scientific. And when we offer butter lamps, money and water to the Buddha, that is a religious practice. Are you with me?"

I nodded.

"The essential thing is not the action itself, but the inner motivation that drives you to take that action," Tsewang continued, with another glance at his watch. "As I said, Buddhism is not a religion, we Buddhists don't believe in a creator of the world and the soul. Our rituals, statues and offerings are expedient means to perceive the ultimate truth. They are merely symbols, you see? So far, so good?"

He did not wait for an answer, or even a nod, but carried on with great enthusiasm.

"The recitation of mantras and prayers, and the fact that we prostrate ourselves for the Buddha – they're all just methods, practices, you see. *Thousands* of things, *incalculable* ions distract us from our true nature, and at the end of the day, there are only two ways: the accumulation of good deeds and wisdom, and the purification of *kleshas*, which are the life states that prevent us from seeing clearly. You follow? The ceremonies, stupas, offerings are all good deeds. But sadly, many get so caught up in accumulating good deeds that they lose sight of the goal. We *love* symbols here in the Himalayas! People will proudly tell you that they've recited hundreds of thousands of mantras, because they like to have concrete targets, but the ultimate goal is, and always will be, enlightenment."

My allotted time was over, by some margin, and Tsewang had things to do; the duties of monastery life called. I thanked him and stood up to leave, but he indicated that I should stay where I was, and called out various names until he got hold of a nun, who went to get the nun he was looking for. She was called Tashi, and was twenty-four years old.

"She speaks very good English and can explain more," Tsewang said, then hurried off down the corridors with his robes fluttering behind him.

Tashi invited me into a small room that she shared with two other nuns. There were three mattresses on the floor, and a few photographs of parents and siblings on the wall. We sat cross-legged on two thin cushions. Tashi was originally from Kaza and had been a nun for seven years. She had a narrow, oval face and wore thick glasses. And was keen to talk.

"To be honest, it was my mother who thought I should become a nun, not me. My mother has had a difficult life. My father died when I was twelve, and she had to look after me and my brothers and sisters alone. She thought life as a nun would be simpler and better for me than an ordinary life. If I wasn't a nun, I would be consumed by family life, and problems with my husband and children and the like. As a nun, I am free and don't need to concern myself with such worries. Instead I can do something good for all living beings in the world. Before I came to the convent, I didn't know much about Buddhism and what it meant to be a nun. The only thing I knew was that nuns recited mantras, prayed, cropped their hair and wore red robes. But then when I became a nun myself, I realised how much nuns study, how much they learn. And I am eternally grateful to my mother!"

"Could you not have done good for humanity by being a doctor or a teacher, for example?" I asked.

"The ambition to be a doctor or teacher is a very *small* ambition," Tashi said, with a smile. "Being a doctor or teacher means you're only concerned with this one life."

I asked her to describe the daily routine at the convent, and she gave me an extensive answer. The days there were highly regulated, down to the smallest detail.

"We wake up at five, and study Buddhist texts until six. Then there's a thirty-minute *puja*, or prayer, for everyone. After that, there's time for personal meditation, work, gymnastics or more reading until breakfast at eight o'clock. From eight-thirty to ten-thirty there's a Buddhist philosophy class, then a tea break for half an hour. After that we have an hour-long discussion with the teacher, and then an hour of self-study before lunch at one. After lunch, we rest for an hour. There is time for self-study again from half past two to half past three, followed by another tea break. And from four to half past five, we have a religion class where we go through what we learned in the morning, but without the teacher, so only the nuns. Then we have discussion from half past five until half past seven, followed by a short rest and dinner at eight. After dinner there is self-study again until ten o'clock, and then the day is over, and we are free. We wash our faces and brush our teeth and things like that, and are in bed by half past ten."

"There's a lot of philosophy and discussion," I said. "I thought meditation was the primary activity of monks and nuns."

"So did I! But we actually don't meditate for more than thirty minutes a day. The Buddha said that there are three stages to understanding: listening, contemplation and meditation. I'm still at the first stage. Buddhist philosophy is an enormous field. There's so much to discuss! The Buddha said that we should not accept his teachings and writings just because it was he who said it. When we buy gold, we check the purity before we pay, don't we? And we have to do the same with the Buddha's teachings. I've only studied Buddhist philosophy for two to three years. And that's a very short time in Buddhist terms. I've probably only learned a tiny fraction of all there is to learn."

"What's it like living at such close quarters with all the other nuns? Do you ever get sick of each other?"

"No, we never get sick of each other!" Tashi assured me. "We have new things to discuss every day. We argue every now and then, of course, because we're all caught in *samsara*, the eternal cycle of birth, death and rebirth, but we're friends again after a few minutes."

"Is there anything you *don't* like about life in the convent?" I asked.

For the first time, Tashi was still. She thought about it for a minute or two.

"I don't think so, no," she said, eventually. "I like everything here. Before I became a nun, I used to love to sleep. I slept until half past eight every morning. So to start with it wasn't easy getting up so early, but now I'm used to it. I'm happy here."

"You live in a kind of bubble here," I said. "Do you ever get depressed when you see the news? There are so many terrible things happening in the world, it's full of suffering. Global warming, war, terrorism . . ."

"I have to confess that we don't watch much news," Tashi said, and smiled apologetically. "Our teacher says that we should watch the news, that the whole world is available to us on television. He watches the BBC and tells us about the most important events. We prefer to watch films rather than the news. We're only allowed to watch TV on Sunday and Monday evenings and we generally watch Bollywood films. Not the romantic ones, though." She laughed. "Sometimes we even watch action films! But we like reality shows best, especially the singing ones, those are our favourite."

It was getting late and the nuns would soon start to get ready for bed. It was some time since dark had fallen. As I got up to leave, Tashi let out a sad sigh.

"I regret wasting so much time! For the first five years, when I was at the other convent in Dehradun, we didn't study philosophy, we only learned the practical things, like how we should pray, give offerings and recite the mantras. We had a lot of free time there, but wasted it gossiping with friends and surfing on the internet . . . I didn't know then how little time there was. How much there was to learn."

When I woke up the next morning, the mountains had disappeared. A thick mist hung over the valley, hiding the village, the mountainsides, the river, everything. It was raining heavily and it felt cold and raw, both inside and outside. We shivered as we said goodbye to the nuns and drove on down the valley to **Dhankar**, a small   3894 MSL village that had once been the seat of the kings of Spiti, in the short periods that the valley was independent.

The old monastery in Dhankar was built on the edge of a cliff over eight hundred years ago, but looked more as though it had grown out of the rock. A goat carcass stuffed with straw dangled over the steps at the entrance to the complex. Tenzin took me to the room where the monks stored the terrifying masks that they used for their tantric dance rituals: red demons with gaping mouths and sharp fangs, skulls and sneering deer faces. I could not go into the monks' prayer room, as women were not allowed. Down in the cellar, the ceiling was so low that we could not stand upright. Ancient, faded religious paintings, *thangkas*, hung side by side along the wall, framed with colourful silks.

One of the monks noticed us looking round, and invited us for tea. The floor and walls of the cave-like common room were covered with simple rugs. A handful of monks were sitting around the wood stove in the middle of the room, each with a cup of tea in their hands. As the stove did not have a pipe, the air was thick with smoke. I could feel the warmth slowly returning to my toes and fingertips, and soon my skin started to prickle.

"We sit like this all winter," Tenzin said.

We spent the night in the monastery guest house, which was next to the new buildings. For the third day running, there was no power and the rain continued to pour. None of the monks had time to talk to me, as they were all preoccupied with trying to keep the warmth in and stop the roofs and walls of their small, basic houses from leaking.

The following morning was greyer and colder than the day before. I could barely see the outline of the white and red main building on the other side of the square. Morning prayers had been cancelled as the monks were still busy trying to keep the rain out. Despite the grim weather, a group of young monks were splashing in the puddles playing football. The tiny monks dashed after the ball, engrossed in the game, concentration etched on their faces.

Tenzin and I hurried to the car and drove on through the rain

China

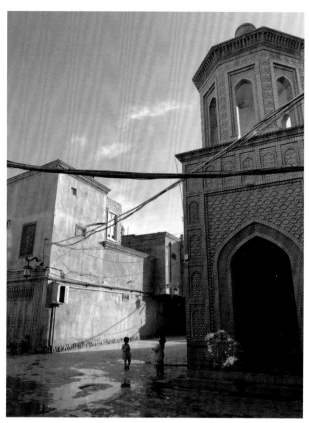

Right: Brand new past: Kashgar's famous Old Town is in fact a recently constructed set.

Below: Smooth as silk to Pakistan: the Karakoram Highway is part of the New Silk Road – the future lifeline for China's trade with the rest of the world.

Pakistan

Left and above: North Pakistan: author as novelty.

Colourful freight transport: decorative Pakistani trucks waiting for freight from China.

One of the countless landslides on my travels: stop, get out of the vehicle and watch the clear-up operation with crossed arms.

Viewpoint in Karimabad: some viewpoints have better views than others.

The Fairy Meadows: wild polo match at dusk. The British colonial rulers liked the sport so much that they took it home with them.

Juglot: two important rivers and the world's three largest mountain ranges meet here. The Karakoram Mountains can be seen on the left side of the Gilgit River, and the Himalayas are on the right side of the Indus River. The Hindu Kush can be seen to the far left.

The Kalash women are not required to cover up. I got a warm welcome from Zaina.

Above: The two local pop stars, Amrina and Ariana (centre), surrounded by loyal fans and friends.

Left: New outfit for the harvest festival.

Above: Recently restored calm: thanks to the work of Italian archaeologists, the Buddha of Swat is once again whole and well after it was blown up by the Taliban in 2007.

Right: Peshawar: this old man still missed his real home in Kashmir, which he had not seen since the border was drawn in 1947.

India

Kashmir: the floating vegetable market in Srinagar

Kashmir: "If there is a paradise on earth, it is this, it is this, it is this."

The Golden Temple in Amritsar floats in the dark.

Haji Hassan has stayed in the same place, despite the wars that have come and gone and the borders that have moved back and forth.

Regimented in death: the Indian military cemetery in Drass, a memorial to the first war between two nuclear powers in the history of the world.

The Spiti Valley in India, "Little Tibet": the road into the valley is, if possible, even more dramatic than the scenery.

Altitude with attitude: all the roads were closed and the valley was cut off by unexpected extreme weather.

Above: A young boy on the threshold of monastery life.

Opposite: The author chose not to share this photograph with her family until she had returned from the Spiti Valley.

Above: Mini nuns reading diligently during morning prayers.

Above: The Fab Four: spiritual tourism in Rishikesh.

Below: The young Ganges flows down to the lowlands: sunset ceremony in Haridwar.

A pilgrim washes himself in the clean, ice-cold water.

Royal hospitality: Semla, the former princess of Sikkim.

and mist. Rakesh, our driver, hung over the steering wheel and said nothing for once. The valley, which had been bathed in sunlight when we arrived, had been erased and we could only see a few metres ahead. The narrow road was full of stones that had fallen from the mountainside during the night, and continued to do so as we drove along. Rakesh had to dodge the stones, and he kept a keen eye on the misty mountainside, ready to slam on the brakes or accelerate at any moment.

Around mid-morning, we reached the tiny village of **Tabo**. Several 3280 MSL of the temples in the monastery there were more than a thousand years old, built of dried grey mud and decorated by some of the best painters and sculptors to be found at the time, in a mixture of Tibetan, Indian and Kashmiri traditions. The temples in Tabo alone made the difficult journey to the Spiti Valley worth it. The walls were covered in ancient paintings in gold, red and blue. The colours had withstood time remarkably well in the dimly lit temple rooms. The painted clay Buddha statues were both timeless and crumbling. The dark rooms with deep shadows were lit only by candles, so the past came alive in flickering flashes.

There were shoes everywhere outside the main temple: boots, sandals, trainers, fur-lined boots. And inside the temple, the old men and women from the village sat in long rows, laughing and chatting with the head lama, who was giving a lecture on Buddhism. The steep, barren mountain above the monastery, barely visible though the milky white mist, was full of small caves where, through the centuries, monks had sat and meditated alone on the inherent emptiness of the world.

It is perhaps not so strange that Buddhism became so deeply rooted, and still has such a strong hold, in these remote mountain valleys where practically nothing grows. Life here has always been hard, in winter in particular, when the snow renders the isolated villages even more isolated. In surroundings like this it is surely easier to think about emptiness and the insignificance of human life. And the land itself has contributed to Buddhism's popularity here: people are poor and arable ground for the eldest son to inherit is a scarcity. The monasteries are part of the social fabric of these small, impoverished communities, and have doubled up as children's homes and schools, relieving parents who are struggling to feed all their children, and offering a means of survival for children who have no other way to make a living.

3200 MSL **Gue** lies only nine kilometres from the Tibetan border. It is a sleepy little village with only one attraction: a 500-year-old monk, by the name of Sangha Tenzin. The monk was found after an earthquake in 1975, and now sits in a glass box in a small white house at the end of Mummy Road. The tiny, emaciated monk is seated, curled like a foetus, on a bed of banknotes, his dark-brown, parchment-like skin wrapped in white silk. The monk has his chin resting on his left knee, and his arms clasped around his legs. A row of white teeth is visible behind his open lips. One eye is open, and the eyeball is still intact, as are the eyebrows. And the mummified remains of hair are still visible on the monk's head.

"He mummified himself," Tenzin said, with great reverence, and bowed in front of the case.

The legend is that Sangha Tenzin mummified himself in order to free the village of a plague of scorpions. It is said that when he died a rainbow appeared and the scorpions all disappeared. The monk in Gue is the only mummified lama that has been discovered in the Himalayas, but in Japan the remains of sixteen self-mummified monks have been found. First they starved themselves over a thousand days to get rid of all the fat in the body, then they drank a poison that would eventually kill them but which helped the internal organs not to rot after death. As they approached the moment of death, they were buried in underground tombs where they continued to recite the mantras and ring a bell. When the other monks no longer heard the bell, they knew that the monks were dead.

Until quite recently, traders and travellers regularly crossed the pass, and Tibetans came over to Gue and the other villages in Spiti to sell rugs and other locally produced goods. But about a decade ago, the Indian authorities set up a military checkpoint just outside the village, and thus put an end to the illegal border trade. The story is the same throughout the Himalayas: the borders are closing as nation states pull back to protect themselves and plug any holes with military posts.

The small village felt desolate and abandoned. Only a few hundred people were left. A woman in her fifties with a wrinkled face spotted us and asked us into her tiny kitchen. Her daughter-in-law served us boiled, sweet milk. There was a poster illustrating the Indian Devanagari alphabet – a reminder of which country we were in.

"What is it like here in winter?" I asked. Even though it was still only early autumn, the snow had made its first appearance the night before and covered the ground in a thin, white blanket.

"We certainly don't need freezer boxes here in Spiti," the woman said, with a rattling laugh.

The weather was so bad that we decided to leave Spiti Valley while the roads were still open. We drove on to **Nako**, a little village   3625 MSL with traditional dried clay houses, and wood and hay on the flat roofs. The small pathways between the houses were muddy and slippery after all the rain, and also full of cowpats. Tenzin wanted me to see the monastery in Nako, which was also from the eleventh century, but the doors were closed and secured with a heavy pad-lock. The monk who had the key had vanished.

The following day it was raining even harder. It felt as though the entire area was drowning. We had to dodge between large stones and deep puddles on the road. A bus had been abandoned on a bend, the road ahead divided by a river of water. How had the passengers carried on their journey? Were they forced to walk? A sign informed us, rather unnecessarily, that this was THE WORLD'S MOST TREACHEROUS ROAD.

It continued to pour with rain and there was remarkably little traffic on the road. After zigzagging along the valley for several hours, we discovered why: a huge piece of rock had fallen onto the road and there were enormous queues on either side of it.

"What do we do now?" I asked. Turning round was not an alternative as the road back to Kaza was closed.

"Wait for the dynamite," was Rakesh's level-headed answer.

And it arrived with astonishing speed. The boom from the explosion caused even more rocks to fall onto the road and people ran back to their cars in panic. Rakesh watched it all with stoic calm.

"Have you experienced things like this before?" I asked.

"That they have to use explosives, you mean?" He let out a hearty laugh. "Many times. Far too many times!"

Two hours later the road had been cleared and we could drive on. Dark was falling, and it was still raining heavily. When we eventually got mobile coverage again, I received worried messages from my new friends in Kashmir. There was bad water throughout Himachal Pradesh, and hundreds of roads had been closed, people were drowning like cats, and towns and villages had been cut off. Foreign tourists had even been evacuated from the Spiti Valley by helicopter.

2206 MSL   I have seldom been more pleased to see a glimmer of urban light pollution in the distance. I stayed in **Shimla**, the summer capital of the British Raj, for five days, enveloped in imperial nostalgia and the scent of freshly made tea.

When we woke the next morning, the sun was beaming down from a blue sky and the mountains were visible once again, lush, green and gentle.

Emptiness and the Pursuit of Radio Waves

The queue outside the Dalai Lama's security office in **McLeod**
Ganj ran down the street, round the corner, then continued down
some steps. It moved at a snail's pace. Hundreds of brightly clad
visitors were there to get their tickets for the Dalai Lama's lecture
series later in the week. I was still exhausted from my journey the
day before: nine and a half hours in a packed, rickety bus had taken
their toll. The bus stopped at every tiny shelter on its way from the
British summer capital to the Tibetan exiles' capital, and I didn't
have the energy to engage in all the socialising around me. The other
people in the queue appeared to have embraced the new day with
fully charged batteries and the atmosphere was buoyant; complete
strangers chatted away, united by a shared spiritual yearning. The
German woman in front of me described her eating habits in great
detail to her queue mate, a Thai woman who was studying Tibetan
medicine.

"I only eat between eleven in the morning and four in the afternoon, never later, and generally only boiled rice and curry, mostly
vegetarian." She had a loud, grating voice, and every sentence was
followed by a nervous laugh. She was tall and thin, and had grey,
shoulder-length hair. Her nose and mouth were covered by a cotton
mask. When she had given enough information about her diet, she
segued seamlessly to her mother, who was dead, and talked about
the post office in Germany where she had worked before she retired,
her pilgrimage to Bodh Gaya, where the Buddha attained enlightenment, her asthma, which had bothered her for years, and the German

doctors and Western medicine that couldn't help her when she was bloated and full of water.

"What are your toilet routines like?" the Thai woman asked with interest.

"My toilet routines?" the German woman shrieked. "*Ach!* Let me tell you."

She had relatively normal toilet routines, defecating in the morning, good consistency. Before she got started on her urine, I mercifully spotted another, much shorter queue ahead: the queue for those who had already registered online. I slipped over to that queue and was the last person to be served before lunch.

McLeod Ganj is home to the exiled Dalai Lama and the seat of the Tibetan government in exile. The small town has an idyllic location, lying as it does on a forested hill just south of the Himalayas. It also functions as a suburb of a much larger town, Dharamsala, which lies a few kilometres lower down on the plain.

The centre of McLeod Ganj was not big, but it was impressively noisy. With a little goodwill, the narrow streets were wide enough for one car, but that did not prevent drivers from making bold attempts to pass, honking aggressively as they did so. The losers were, as usual, the pedestrians who were constantly forced to the side of the road while two or more drivers argued about who should let who pass.

The shops sold pashmina shawls, Indian gods and Tibetan jewellery. Japanese and Italian restaurants stood side by side. Outside the cafés, white-haired monks with red robes sat next to American ladies in loose-fitting tunics, and young French couples in their twenties wearing turbans and harem trousers in clashing colours. In stark contrast to the Western tourists' lack of elegance, the Tibetan women walked by with straight backs, dressed in traditional long dresses, with woven aprons and silk shirts in soft, dark colours.

Tsuglagkhang Temple lies close to the Dalai Lama's residence, and looks rather like a Spanish municipal building from the Franco era. But it was actually a very pleasant place to be and delightfully calm after the traffic chaos outside. I sat down in the shadow of a tree and watched the tourists lining up to be photographed in front of the steel and concrete building.

The government in exile's main offices lay a little further down the hill, in another building that met the aesthetic requirements of sixties brutalism. Even though I did not have an appointment, I was able to have a long conversation with Sonam Dagbo, Secretary of the Department of Information and International Relations. He started by giving me a quick introduction to the history of the Tibetan diaspora and the work of the government in exile.

"On March 10, 1959, there was an uprising in Lhasa, and His Holiness the 14th Dalai Lama left the Tibetan capital on March 17. In 1960, the Indian government gave His Holiness permission to settle here in Dharamsala. Back then, Dharamsala was a very small town that had been established as a holiday destination for the British, but then it became the main seat for Tibet's central administration in the 1960s. His Holiness the 14th Dalai Lama has reformed this institution and introduced democracy with elections every five years, when all Tibetans living in exile can vote. The diaspora is spread over more than forty countries, but the vast majority live in India, with around twenty thousand here in Dharamsala. When we came here, priority was given to the refugees, especially children, and we had to make sure that everyone was given healthcare and an education. Our original goal was the liberation of Tibet, but since 1974 we have worked for self-rule within the Chinese state. Tibet is today divided into several regions and some two to three million Tibetans live in the autonomous region of Tibet. The majority live in the neighbouring regions. We want these regions to be united as one region with self-rule, where we have religious, cultural and political freedom. We call it "The Middle Way". The Chinese claim that we already have self-rule, but that's only on paper. The situation is, as I'm sure you understand, complex."

"Do you see any parallels between what is happening to the Uighurs in Xinjiang and what has been going on in Tibet for a long time now?" I asked.

"Chen Quanguo, the secretary of the Communist Party in Xinjiang, was the secretary of the Communist Party in the Tibet Autonomous Region before he was given the post in Xinjiang," Sonam Dagbo said. "The Tibetans have suffered the same traumas that the Uighurs are suffering today. The re-education camps, surveillance, forced sterilisation, the systematic destruction of culture and religion, and so on, it's all happened already in Tibet. Same system, same man. He got plenty of practice in Tibet, so now he's an expert."

Sonam Dagbo had spent his earliest years in Tibet. His family fled to India in 1962, when he was six years old.

"My father was arrested and sent to prison for one year. When he was released, we escaped over the border to India. We didn't live far from the border, and the Chinese were not in such good control of the border back then, so our escape route was not that complicated. It is much harder to escape Tibet today, well, more or less impossible since 2008."

"Have you been back to Tibet?" I asked.

"I was there with a delegation that went to negotiate with the Chinese, so yes, I have been back, but I couldn't visit the place in the south where I was born," Sonam Dagbo said. "I still hope that I will be able to see my birthplace again, one day. We have held on to our hopes for more than sixty years and continue to hope. Tibetans have lived in Tibet for more than two thousand years, we have our own alphabet, and a deeply rooted culture. The Chinese can repress us physically, but they can't break the Tibetan spirit. And what's more, we Buddhists believe in transience, that nothing lasts for ever. In Europe, you have had the Roman empire, the Austrian empire, the Russian empire, the British empire, and so on. They no longer exist. The China we know today will not be like this for ever."

*

Gu Chu Sum is an organisation that works to raise awareness of political prisoners in Tibet. The staff have all been political prisoners themselves. The offices are in one of the backstreets of McLeod Ganj. I received a warm welcome, even though I turned up without an appointment here as well. The English-speaking international secretary was, however, out of the office, and no-one knew where he was or when he would be back.

"Perhaps you could come again tomorrow?" said the bookkeeper, a rather severe-looking woman in her thirties, who spoke a little English. "Everyone here has a story to tell, but no-one apart from the international secretary speaks good English."

"I can't tomorrow, as I'm going to the Dalai Lama's talk," I said. "Could you perhaps translate for me? It won't take long."

She was happy to do it, and so I was able to talk briefly to Gyalthang Tulku Kunkhen Jamchen Choeje, the 48-year-old general secretary. He wore a white shirt and tie, and spoke in a slow and dignified manner. The bookkeeper translated as best she could.

"He says that there are currently about two thousand political prisoners in Tibet, and the number is growing. The economic situation in Tibet has improved, he says, but the human rights situation has got worse. We have no freedom of speech and are not allowed to say the Dalai Lama's name. He says that Tibet has historically never been a part of China."

"Whereabouts in Tibet is he from?" I asked.

"Eastern Tibet."

"When did he come to India?"

"In 2010."

"Can you ask him to tell me a bit about his childhood in Tibet?"

The bookkeeper translated and was given a long answer that she summarised in three sentences: "His father has two wives, and twelve children. The family had a lot of financial problems. They didn't have enough money for school, clothes or food, but out of all the children, he's had the most problems."

"Could you ask him to say a little more about his childhood?" I asked. "I want to understand how and why he became a political activist."

This time the bookkeeper condensed the answer into two sentences. "He started to put up banners saying that all Tibetans should support the Dalai Lama and pray for a free Tibet. He was arrested on October 12, 2007."

"Can we rewind a moment?" I said. "When did he become politically aware? Were his family interested in politics?"

"No, he is the reincarnation of Gyalthang Tulku. Both the Dalai Lama and the Chinese authorities have recognised him as the reincarnation of Gyalthang Tulku." The bookkeeper stopped translating my questions and simply answered herself.

"Okay," I said, without feeling any the wiser. "Did he go to school in his hometown? What is his education?"

"To ninth grade. And four years at high school."

"And did he get a job after that?"

"No, he became a political activist," the bookkeeper said, with obvious impatience. "He spent a long time planning his campaign, more than two years."

"And where did the need to be a political activist come from?" I asked again. "He must have known that it was dangerous and would have consequences."

The bookkeeper sighed.

"I've already told you. He is the reincarnation of Gyalthang Tulku."

"Right." I decided to drop the subject. "What did his family think about his activism?"

"That's been the hardest thing," the bookkeeper translated. "There have been many problems with his family. His father did not support his activism, he said that what he was doing was too dangerous.

The family got into trouble as well. When he was in prison, his family and friends started to look on him as a bad person. That's been the worst thing for him, so far. That his family, his father and friends no longer supported him."

She looked sharply at the clock. It was almost five.

"Are we running out of time?" I asked.

"Well, we've got five more minutes."

"I'll be quick," I promised. "How was he arrested?"

"They couldn't arrest him on the street, so he was arrested during a meeting, in an office. When he went back out onto the street with them, there were more than a hundred Chinese soldiers there waiting for him."

"What was he officially charged with and sentenced for?"

The bookkeeper gave me an exasperated look. We had two minutes left.

"Illegal political activity, perhaps," I said.

"Yes, obviously," the bookkeeper sighed.

"How was he treated in prison?"

"Not too badly, as the Chinese knew he was the reincarnation of Gyalthang Tulku."

"How did he manage to get out of Tibet in 2010?" I asked.

"He tried many different ways. Eventually he found a travelling salesman close to the border with Nepal who could help him. He hid in his truck, in among all the goods."

"What kind of goods were in the truck?"

The bookkeeper looked at me in desperation. It was three minutes past five.

"All kinds of things! It was a big truck! And there were lots of goods in the truck."

I realised that my time was up, and some, and thanked them for their help. The bookkeeper and general secretary were both visibly relieved.

*

The Tibetan community has done its utmost to maintain Tibetan traditions and institutions in Dharamsala. The Men-Tsee-Khang Institute, which was established in Lhasa in 1916, was resurrected in its new concrete home in Dharamsala in 1961. The institute offers five-year courses in both Tibetan medicine and astrology.

"We call it astro-science," said 53-year-old Tsering Chözom, the head astrologer at the institute. Like all the other women who worked at the institute, she was dressed in traditional Tibetan clothes. Tsering was the first woman to have a formal education in Tibetan astro-science, and she gave me an instructive introduction to the field, with the natural authority and patience of a pioneer.

"We practise a mixture of astronomy and astrology based on ancient traditions passed down by our ancestors," she said. "Even though we have learned astrology from the Indians and the Chinese, we have our own unique Tibetan system. Our system is more about climatic conditions and the Tibetan way of life and is closely linked to nature. We can predict changes in nature, but our predictions are more about what *ideally* should happen. Nature confuses us these days because of man-made changes, and our predictions don't come true . . ."

Her spacious office was decorated with beautiful paintings of the Buddha and Tibetan protective deities.

"As Buddhists, we believe in karma," she said. "We believe that an individual has to go through certain difficulties because the causes already exist, but we don't believe in fate. We believe that everything can be changed by our own actions. If we do good things, our lives will improve. One can be born into excellent circumstances and with good health, but then destroy everything with bad conduct. One should generally do good deeds and not harm others. Those who behave badly may not experience the effect in this life, but sooner or later their actions will have consequences."

"What is the difference between Western and Tibetan astrology?" I asked.

"Western astrologers focus more on the solar system, whereas we look at the moon," Tsering said. "A Tibetan and a Western horoscope should contain the same information and give the same result, but our astrology is closely linked to Buddhism. We believe in karma and treatment in the form of prayer. Astrology is highly important in Tibetan culture. Based on the month, day and place that you were born, we can tell you something about your whole life. Tibetan parents usually order a horoscope for their children as soon as they're born, because they want to know if their baby will be healthy, intelligent and live a long life. They often come back for more detailed information later, when they're starting to think about marriage, for example. Before a couple gets married, they usually visit an astrologer. The couple may not always be a good match – for instance, they may have different views on things, or temperaments that are not suited. When people who are already married come to us for advice, we can't tell them to get divorced, but we could for example advise them to be careful with their money or take better care of their health."

She rested her chin on folded hands and smiled.

"We're all sorts, you see. Marriage counsellors, psychologists, doctors. But the training is not as long as for a doctor: five years plus one year's practice. If people have already been to the doctor and the medicine is not working, they come to us."

"What personal qualities should a good astrologer have?" I asked in closing.

"A good astrologer should first and foremost be loving and compassionate," Tsering said. "He or she should care about other people. We often have to tell them things that are not particularly pleasant, as people come to us when they are uncertain or in doubt, and some come to us with very difficult issues. Our job is to find the antidote. There's always a cure."

*

I did not feel that the astrologer who drew up my horoscope was especially loving and compassionate. Her name was Sonam, and she rattled off one bad thing after another.

"You are a devoted and loyal person," she started. "Cheerful and easy going. If you have a plan, you follow it through and don't give up. But you have a lot of health issues. Problems with your spine, headaches, muscular pain. And you're prone to accidents. You fall."

"I don't actually have many health issues," I said.

Sonam frowned and looked quickly through her notes.

"I have gone over the calculations a couple of times. There are no mistakes here." She carried on. "There's not much good to say about your finances. They fluctuate. And with regard to relationships, you have love. Things are a bit up and down with friends though. I see arguments, later on in your marriage, in particular. You don't share fundamental values. That's not good."

"No, that doesn't sound good," I conceded.

"And I see problems when it comes to children," she said. "This may be in relation to their health or upbringing. So you should be very careful. And in general, you should be careful in dangerous places. If you take part in high-risk activities or find yourself in dangerous places, there's a greater chance that an accident will befall you."

"That sounds pretty obvious," I muttered.

Sonam looked up from her papers.

"Sorry, did you say something?"

"No, no, carry on!"

"Professionally, there will be positive changes, but it may lead to conflicts with your colleagues or superiors," she said.

"There's a lot of negative things here," I said.

"Yes, but there's some positive things as well," Sonam said. "You are under a favourable influence from now until you reach thirty-eight. Your love life is good. Your finances are stable. You need to be careful next year. Then you will be influenced by what we call the winds of transition. Your thirty-seventh year is a year of obstacles. There will be another year of obstacles between the ages of forty-eight and forty-nine, when changes will occur. Have you managed to write all this down?"

"Yes, I'm writing it all down," I assured her.

"Good things will happen," Sonam promised. "Between thirty-eight and forty-two, both good and bad things will happen. You will experience problems with your health. You will lose what you had. Whether that's money or a man is not easy to say. I can see an argument with a person in authority, maybe your boss."

"That really doesn't sound good," I said.

"But between forty-two and forty-eight, things will go well," Sonam said quickly. "Your finances will be stable. If you want to get pregnant in this period, you will. But you need to be wary of a woman. You can come into conflict with a woman. Be careful."

She carried on. "Between forty-eight and fifty-three is not so good. You will have both health and relationship problems. Arguments for no reason. People you are close to will disappear. You won't achieve what you want to in your professional life. I see a lawsuit as well. You will, however, have a good period between fifty-three and sixty-four, certainly compared with what's gone before. You will do well in your career, though I do see some disharmony. Problems with someone close to you. Financial ups and downs. Someone talking about you behind your back. You must be on your guard."

Fortunately, she had now reached the last page.

"Between sixty-four and seventy-nine, you will become a grandmother. Your children will give you love, but you are not satisfied. A new person will come into your life. You have someone who will look after you when you are sick." She folded the pages and looked straight at me. "And when it comes to the immediate future, 2019 will not be good."

"None of it sounds particularly good," I mumbled.

"You must be careful, with regard to both money and relation-ships," Sonam said. "In 2020, things will get better, but you may experience health problems. I would advise you to buy an amulet against bad years: a health amulet or a life-force amulet. But, of course, it's up to you whether you do or not."

I thanked her for the consultation and wandered, amulet-less, out into the traffic chaos of McLeod Ganj. Even though I did not believe in horoscopes, I decided to get another one from another astrologer, somewhere else in the Himalayas. No harm in getting a second opinion.

Early the next morning, the queue outside the Tsuglagkhang Temple stretched far up the one-way street. Thousands of Tibetan exiles, monks, nuns and tourists from all over the world were there to hear the Dalai Lama's lectures. There were people everywhere; every tiny piece of the concrete floor inside the temple was covered in cushions and pilgrims. I had to search for a while to find a tiny, vacant space on the square outside the temple where I could sit down. When everyone had found somewhere, the crowd started to chant *Om mani padme hum, om mani padme hum* . . . The temple resounded with a peaceful hum.

A sigh rippled through the masses when His Holiness the 14th Dalai Lama came out of his residence and was escorted across the square. Everyone craned their necks to catch a glimpse of the living god of mercy in his plum robes. The energetic 83-year-old took time to greet the pilgrims sitting in the front row, who reached out their hands to touch him. The Dalai Lama appeared to be bubbling with good humour, as usual, and had a presence that radiated gentleness and calm. He smiled and chatted with several of the pilgrims, and paid no attention to his companions' discreet impatience.

Like most of the others in the audience, I had to follow the lecture on one of the big screens. Only Buddhists who had travelled from Taiwan, for whom the lecture series had been organised, had places reserved inside the temple itself. The old man settled down on the golden throne with soft movements and a smile on his lips.

Silence fell over the huge temple complex as soon as the Dalai Lama started to speak. He was alive and engaging, and fully present in the moment. Now and then he chuckled at something he had said. The many thousands of Tibetan exiles who were there were enraptured. An interpreter translated from Tibetan to Chinese for the Taiwanese guests, and, in addition, there was simultaneous interpretation available in English, Spanish, French, Hindi and a number of other languages via radios. We had all been instructed to take a transistor radio with us, so we could listen to the translation, but I struggled to get my cheap, newly bought radio to work and only managed to catch fragments: *Emptiness . . . Cosmic beings . . . The Buddha . . . The nature of self.* There was an infernal crackling in my headphones and the sound vanished every few seconds. I was not the only one. Everywhere people were frantically twiddling the knobs on their radios. They may have travelled a long way to hear the lecture, and the only thing they heard was the odd word, and occasional sentence: *Emptiness . . . The Middle Way . . . true compassion . . . emptiness . . . the Truth is that there is no Self . . . the Path to True and Enduring Happiness . . . emptiness . . .* Every now and then the Taiwanese interpreter burst out laughing, and I had no idea why, and the Tibetans laughed heartily and loudly. In the end I gave up trying to get the radio to work, and sat there listening to the unfamiliar Tibetan words as I sipped the sweet, milky tea that the temple monks were handing out.

Enduring happiness. True compassion. Emptiness. Tea.

The Source

While Dharamsala is the capital for Tibetan Buddhism, **Rishikesh** on the banks of the Ganges is the capital of yoga. The busy streets in the centre were cluttered with tightly written signs advertising all manner of variations, from laughing yoga to anapana sati yoga, vipassana yoga, iyngar yoga, jivamukti yoga, bikram yoga, power yoga, yin yoga, et cetera, et cetera. And the offers did not stop at yoga, but included all kinds of spirituality and self-development, such as reiki, chakra healing, tarot card readings, sound therapy, kundalini awakening, ayurveda therapy, palm readings, past life regression therapy, mantrology, rudraksha, crystal healing, hypnosis, distance healing. A handful of travel agencies had specialised in tourists who preferred an adrenaline rush, and offered paragliding, rafting and bungee jumping instead of spiritual insight. The cafés advertised detox juice and American pancakes, and the hotels could provide a peaceful view detox and cosmic energy. The streets were buzzing with backpackers and yoga fans, all dressed in loose, colourful and, by Indian standards, revealing cotton clothes.

The small city at the foot of the Himalayas made its mark on the world in winter 1968, when George Harrison, John Lennon, Paul McCartney and Ringo Starr came here to meditate at the luxury ashram of Guru Maharishi Mahesh Yogi. The Beatles had been introduced to the maharishi the year before when he visited the UK on one of his many world tours. They felt an immediate affinity and accepted his invitation to spend three months at his ashram in Rishikesh.

Little is known about Mahesh before he was given the honorary title of maharishi, which means "great visionary" or "great sage". It is thought he was born in 1917 or 1918, or perhaps even as early as 1911, and studied physics at the University of Allahabad in north India. As a graduate, he became a disciple of Swami Brahmananda Saraswati, also known as Guru Dev, "divine teacher". When Saraswati died in 1953, Mahesh retired to meditate in the mountains. After two years as a recluse, he returned to civilisation to teach the masses a form of meditation he had developed himself and called transcendental meditation, which was shortened to TM. By meditating for twenty minutes twice a day, and reciting a secret mantra, practitioners would, according to Mahesh, or the maharishi as he now called himself, lock into the universe's "Creative Intelligence" and experience "The Inner Self" and absolute peace. The maharishi soon expanded his arena from India to the world, and undertook extensive tours where he guided a spiritually thirsty Western audience in a meditation technique that "everyone could master".

The stay in Rishikesh proved to be a mixed experience for the four musicians and their wives. Ringo Starr and his wife, Maureen, left after only ten days. Starr could not stomach the spicy Indian food and his wife suffered from entomophobia. George Harrison had long been fascinated by Indian culture and gladly embraced the meditation, but none was keener than John Lennon, who meditated for hours every day. After a month and a half, Paul McCartney had also had enough of life in the ashram, and flew home. But Harrison and Lennon stayed on in India, and fans were worried that they might stay there for good.

On April 12, after two months at the ashram, Harrison and Lennon made a hasty exit from India, accompanied by their wives and Alexis Mardas, better known as Magic Alex, a Greek electronics engineer, who was closely associated with the Beatles during this period. The Fab Four obviously had a penchant for self-declared sages at the time, wise men who swathed themselves and others in promises. Mardas had promised them incredible inventions, the one better than the other, from sonic walls to invisible paint and flying saucers. The Greek engineer had come to the ashram after McCartney had left, and started to spread compromising rumours about the maharishi. He eventually managed to convince a sceptical Lennon and even more sceptical Harrison that the maharishi hit on his female disciples, and that he had had sex with one of them, a young American nurse. Deeply disappointed that the ascetic had the same earthly desires as any old rock musician, the two remaining members of the band decided to leave India. In the car on the way to the airport, Lennon wrote a song that he first called "Maharishi", but which Harrison then suggested should be called "Sexy Sadie" instead, to protect the guru: *Sexy Sadie, what have you done? You've made a fool of everyone.*

Harrison and McCartney both continued to practise transcendental meditation and many years later reconnected with the maharishi. The guru died in 2008, and the following year McCartney and Starr played together as part of a charity concert, where the takings were to be used to teach poor children the world over how to meditate. The ashram in Rishikesh stood empty for more than a decade, abandoned to nature. Then, a few years ago, it changed its name to the Beatles' Ashram and reopened its doors. For six hundred rupees (about eight dollars), you can now wander around the large, deserted and overgrown complex.

Most of the buildings were built in traditional Indian style, with decorated, arched window frames. Now that they were about to be engulfed by nature, they reminded me of the Mayan ruins in the Guatemalan jungle. Ruins are timeless; not only has time stopped, it seems to have turned back, so the past is now more than the past, the abandoned buildings are more than themselves, they are now History. Some of the buildings, such as the cafeteria where Ringo Starr had been served spicy food, were built in a more futuristic, sixties style. Surrounded by trees and monkeys as it was, it felt like a miniature Chernobyl in the jungle. The beehive-shaped meditation cells below the cafeteria were covered in a thick layer of moss, hemmed in by the jungle – everything grows fast in the tropics. Once upon a time there had also been a swimming pool and a helipad on the property, but it was no longer possible to find them among all the trees.

I had the ruins to myself, in contrast to those in the Guatemalan jungle. I wandered around with only the monkeys and colourful birds for company. Half a century ago, four lads from Liverpool had walked the same paths. When they were not meditating, they played on their guitars and sitars and scribbled down lyrics. Many of the thirty or so songs that they wrote here, such as "Dear Prudence", "Back in the USSR" and "Blackbird" have achieved immortality, to the extent that pop songs can. The material luxury that the musicians surrounded themselves with is already a thing of the timeless past, a fate shared with all the world's ruins.

I walked on through the jungle, past the posters advertising the scientific effect of transcendental meditation, and into a hall that resembled a derelict garage, with broken windows and a corrugated-iron roof. And there on the walls were John, Paul, Ringo and George, immortalised in black graffiti, with the bearded maharishi between them. Ten or twelve Western women were sitting on the floor in the lotus position. A short Indian man dressed in white clothes, with a long, grey beard, was guiding them through a session without a word.

After a few minutes of sublime silence, I left the meditating women and headed back to the city centre. The path was deserted, other than the odd emaciated cow standing in the ditch eating rubbish. The temples along the riverbank were, however, full of people. Musicians played on drums and other percussion instruments, young boys dressed in orange tunics held out burning oil lamps and dishes as they mumbled their way through the mantras. The oil lamps were circulated to the pilgrims, who passed their hands over the flame to receive blessings. Many of them had taken with them small banana-leaf boats filled with flowers, incense and tea lights that they then sent off down the Ganges – an offering to the gods and to the river itself, which up here in the mountains was relatively clean and unpolluted. A woman in her sixties, with long, grey hair, dressed in white cotton clothes, strode down the steps and chanted and spoke about harmony, peace and holy rituals in a nasal American English. She spoke for a long time, but repeated the same words and points again and again. Holy rituals, harmony, peace. Peace, holy rituals, harmony. Another elderly Western woman, also draped in white cotton, was so caught up in the ritual that the people around her had to move to make room for her wild, ecstatic arm movements.

1968 was only yesterday.

The second horoscope came of its own accord. I was sitting devouring a pancake in a restaurant with the rather dubious name of Holy Crêpe, when a young man with a beard and narrow eyes came over and asked if he could have a photograph taken with me. He waved to his friend, who hurried over to us, and took a picture.

"Is it okay if I sit down for a chat?" he asked. I nodded; I had no other plans. He sat down and introduced himself as Samarth.

"I'm twenty-eight and a maths teacher and writer," Samarth said. "My first book is being published soon. It's about history, economics and Europe."

He smelled of stale sweat, but looked more kempt than many of the backpackers in the restaurant.

"I'm an astrologer as well as a maths teacher, historian and writer," he added.

"Interesting," I said. "I've just had my horoscope done in Dharamsala, and it was nothing but misery."

"I don't see any problems," Samarth said, "but that's what they do. They tell you all the negative things to make you worried."

"Are you a qualified astrologer?"

"I don't have any formal training as such, but if you give me your date of birth, I'll tell you everything."

So I did, and he used a pad to draw up the numbers in complex diagrams, adding and subtracting and moving them around.

"You're very emotional," he said, eventually. "You travel a lot."

"Yes, I mean, I'm here, after all."

"But you've travelled a lot in the last few years, in particular," Samarth said. "It's been extreme. You're restless, full of feeling. You often can't sleep because you're so full of emotions. Do you drink or smoke? If you do, it's to take the edge off these feelings. You fell in love in 2007, is that right?"

I shook my head.

"In two years' time you will have a great breakthrough," Samarth said, unperturbed. "You will have great success and earn lots of money."

"According to the Tibetan astrologer, I can expect misfortune in two years," I said.

"No, no, there will be a change, but it will be a very positive change," Samarth said. "You will earn lots of money. You should invest the money in property – that would be very wise."

He stared at me so intensely that I suddenly felt the need to get up and leave. But before I left, he gave me his telephone number and email address, in case I should need more guidance.

The neighbouring city, **Haridwar**, is even bigger, uglier and holier 314 MSL than Rishikesh. It is where the Ganges meets the Indian lowlands, and, according to Hinduism, where the goddess Ganga first set foot on earth after Shiva had released the mighty river from his hair. Even though Haridwar is only about twenty kilometres from

Rishikesh, the journey took two hours. The traffic ground to a halt for long periods, despite all the drivers constantly sounding their horns with great force.

The car park was some distance from the main temple, but all we had to do was follow the crowds. Tens of thousands of people had gathered on the riverbank to experience the sunset ceremony. I could forget trying to find a space on the temple side of the river, but managed to nudge my way to a space on the viewing platform opposite the temple. I saw no other foreigners in the sea of people and was pushed further and further forward by eager pilgrims. "Move forward so you can see!" they said. "Go, go, don't be shy!"

On the other side of the river, Hindu priests swung fire bowls back and forth in the fresh dark of the evening. Everyone raised their arms in pure ecstasy and tens of thousands of voices rose and fell in song. A fire bowl was passed to me and the young man at my side, a PhD student from the desert state of Rajasthan, insisted that I should do the same as everyone else and hold my hands over the flames. It would bring me good fortune, he promised.

"Now we have to go to the river," he said afterwards, holding up the small banana-leaf boat in his hands. Without any effort, he manoeuvred his way through the crowd, and I followed behind. Down by the water, he got hold of a priest in orange robes and in the course of their negotiations made it clear that the priest should pray for both of us, that I was to be included. The PhD student squatted down and lit the candle that stood up from the tiny boat like a mast without a sail.

"Let's put it on the water together!" He smiled at me, and together we sent the little boat with its cargo of incense and flowers off on its voyage down the Ganges. The fragile vessel bobbed and spun perilously on the fast-running river, but did not capsize. The candle flickered as it was pulled away from us by the current, eager to start its long journey with the mother to the Bay of Bengal.

"Now you have to pour milk into the river," the PhD student told me. A young boy was already there beside us with metal cups and milk. I gave him ten rupees – after strict instructions not to give him any more – and got two cups of milk in return.

"Pour the milk slowly into the river," the PhD student said, as he did so himself. The white liquid was swallowed by the greenish, foaming water. My helper beamed at me. "Excellent," he said. "And now we must bathe!"

The guidebook was full of warnings about people who offer assistance to tourists during the Ganga Aarti and then demand payment. Fortunately, people are often far kinder than guidebook writers make out. The PhD student kicked off his sandals and stood joyfully with both his feet in the water. I did the same. Then he filled his hands with water and splashed it over his head. I did the same and he beamed at me.

"The water here is fresh and cold," he said. "The Ganges was born here, right here, in this very spot. Where are you from, by the way?"

"Norway."

He thought for a moment.

"The Ganges is to us what the Thames is to Europeans," he said. "A holy river. Do you feel happy now?"

"Yes," I said, and I really did. Perhaps my feeling that I had been embraced by all this – the flames, the prayers and the water – was thanks to the crowd and a general euphoria and joy. Who knows? Mother Ganges flowed past us, wide, strong and pure, the noise from the river almost drowning out the pilgrims' happy voices.

"And are you happy?" I asked.

He smiled from ear to ear.

"Yes, it's the first time I'm here."

Even though it was now completely dark, there was still a lot of activity in the water, with many pilgrims bathing. Some were not satisfied with only dipping their toes, and submerged their whole body. There were chains for them to hold onto as the water blessed their body. The young Ganges was tumultuous up here in the mountains, cheered on, as it were, by gravity. A long row of beggars sat against the railings of the bridge with outstretched hands, pleading eyes and all their deformities, their only capital, on display: false limbs, stumps, club feet covered in folds of loose skin.

We drove back at what would have been a comfortable jogging speed. When we got to the large sign that welcomed us to Rishikesh, the driver suddenly stopped and jumped out of the car, with no explanation. Rickshaws, cars and motorbikes stood abandoned by the roadside and across the carriageway. I spotted some long queues in front of two brightly lit stalls. A short while later, the driver came back with a happy expression on his face and two brown glass bottles. As Rishikesh and Haridwar are both designated holy cities in Hinduism, the sale of alcohol is forbidden within the city limits. Just outside the city gates, however, anything is allowed.

The car would not start; the engine spluttered and coughed, then died. This happened a couple more times, and in the end we had to push the car to get the engine turning.

"Instant karma," I quipped.

The driver grunted something in reply, his face no longer radiating satisfaction. The brown bottles clinked as we drove through the gates of the holy city.

Where does a river start and end?

It is perhaps easier to say where the Ganges ends than where it starts. Having run over two and a half thousand kilometres from the Himalayas, across the northern plains, fed by more and more tributaries along the way, the Ganges meets the Brahmaputra River, which has travelled even further, all the way from Tibet. Once combined, they create an intricate network of major and minor rivers which together constitute the world's greatest delta, and are a lifeline for more than one hundred and sixty million people in Bangladesh. Having passed through five holy cities, the Ganges finally empties out into the Bay of Bengal roughly where the enormous Eurasian continental plate meets the Indian and Burmese tectonic plates.

But does a river ever really end? All the world's rivers, including the holy Ganges, are part of the eternal cycle of water. The surface of the ocean evaporates and forms clouds that become rain, snow and glaciers, which in turn become rivers, which then after a longer or shorter journey empty out into the ocean and lakes, and so the cycle begins again.

If we are to believe Hindu sources, the holy river's life began long before it reached earth. According to one legend, Ganga, the river goddess, is the daughter of Himavat, king of the snow and mountains, king of the Himalayas. In Sanskrit, the name Himavat, which means "snow" or "frozen", is also used of the Himalayas, thus the god and the mountains become one. According to another legend, the Ganges was born when Vishnu measured the length of the universe. When he stretched out his left foot, the nail on his big toe reached the end of the universe and made a hole. The ocean that surrounds creation thus flowed into the universe through the hole in the form of the Ganges, which washed the god's saffron-covered feet.

The Ganges did not descend to earth immediately. The legend tells that King Sagara sends his horse to circumnavigate the earth, a ritual he has carried out many times before, but this time it does not return. The king then sends out his sixty thousand sons to search for the horse. They eventually find it tied up outside the cave of Kapil Muni, a hermit. Naturally, the sons suspect that he has stolen the horse and storm into the cave, then start to hurl abuse at him. Kapil Muni, who has been sitting deep in meditation, opens his eyes for the first time in many years, and is so angry that his gaze turns all sixty thousand sons to ash. When King Sagara hears what has happened, he sends one of his grandchildren to Kapil

Muni to find out what can be done to save his sons. He is told that the princes will return to life if they are cleansed by the waters of the Ganges. Another grandchild, Bhagirath, then lives as a hermit in the Himalayas for a thousand years in order to persuade Brahma, the creator, to let the Ganges flow down to earth. Brahma eventually agrees to do this, but first Shiva must be asked to soften the river's descent, or the weight of the water will destroy the earth. Bhagirath has to stand on one toe for an entire year before Shiva agrees to catch the raging Ganges in his hair. Shiva uses his locks to divide the river in three – Bhagirathi, Alaknanda and Mandakini – which he then allows to stream down to earth. These three rivers, or locks of hair, which are all holy to the Hindus, all spring from glaciers in the Indian part of the Himalayas. Alaknanda and Mandakini merge after some seventy kilometres, and further down the Alaknanda and Bhagirathi meet to become the Ganges.

Since time immemorial, the Ganges has been the holiest of rivers for the Hindus, personified as the goddess Ganga, often called Ma Ganga, or Mother Ganges. The Hindus believe that bathing in the Ganges will cleanse them of all sins and thus give them an even greater chance of achieving *moksha*, release from the cycle of death and reincarnation. Thousands upon thousands of pitiful pilgrims make their way to the towns and cities on the riverbanks to die and be cremated next to the holy river, and millions of Hindus have died with water from the Ganges on their lips.

At two and a half thousand kilometres, the Ganges is some way down the list of the world's longest rivers. But if one were to measure the importance of the world's major rivers by how many people depend on them, rather than by their length, the Ganges would top the list. More than a third of the Indian population, and as good as everyone in Bangladesh – which adds up to more than half a billion people – is dependent on water from the Ganges. They drink water from the holy river, they wash in it, and the river is essential for all the agriculture and industry along its banks. Unfortunately, this also means that the Ganges is top of the list when it comes to pollution. The towns and cities on the riverbanks produce close to three billion litres of sewage every day, most of which ends up untreated in the river, and as a result, multi-resistant bacteria flourish in the holy water. Chemical factories, hospitals, slaughterhouses, distilleries and so on, also discharge huge volumes of poisonous waste into the river, including chrome and mercury. All this spews out into the Bay of Bengal at the end of its roughly 2,500-kilometre journey.

But to return to the beginning: where does the Ganges start? Cartographers and etymologists would probably say that the mighty Ganges starts in the small town of Devprayag, about two hours' drive north-west from Rishikesh, where the Bhagirathi and Alaknanda rivers meet and change their names to the Ganges. Hydrologists and geographers might argue that the Ganges starts at the Satopanth Glacier, where the Alaknanda has its source. It would be logical to say that this source is also the source of the Ganges, due to the length of the Alaknanda, and the volume of water.

But most Hindus believe that the Ganges starts at the source of the Bhagirathi River, at the foot of the Gangotri Glacier.

The journey by car from Rishikesh to **Gangotri** took more than   3415 MSL
nine hours. The road was in a shocking condition, but minibuses bursting with pilgrims, decorated with local flags and with statues of local gods on the roof, struggled valiantly up and up towards the sacred destination.

The temperature in Gangotri was around freezing, both inside and out. A narrow street full of shops and stalls that sold incense, flowers and other offerings led up to a small temple. It was already late in the afternoon, and the temple, which dated from the nineteenth century, was closed. The majority of pilgrims had long since hurried on to the next shrine. The temple in Gangotri is one of four pilgrim destinations on the Chota Char Dham circuit, which translates as "the small four abodes", a pilgrim route in the Himalayas that every devoted Hindu dreams of taking one day. Again, those who manage to visit all four of the abodes will have their sins erased and increase their chances of achieving *moksha*. The journey normally takes ten to twelve days by car, but wealthy, busy pilgrims can visit all four temples in two days, with the help of a helicopter.

As the sky over the mountains turned pink, a handful of shivering priests went down to the river, dressed in woolly hats, thick down jackets and white cotton tunics. They dutifully lit the fire bowls, which were then passed round, accompanied by light rhythms on the drums and chanted prayers. Three or four pilgrims were blessed by the flames and then made their way down to the water to launch their little banana-leaf boats. The Bhagirathi, or Ganges, was clean and unpolluted up here and flowed rapidly past the temple. As soon as the sun had set, the priests and pilgrims hurried back indoors to the warmth.

It is possible to get to the actual source on foot. All pilgrims and tourists have to register before they are allowed to set off. In theory, the registration office opened at eight in the morning, but in practice, it only opened when the soldiers who manned it decided to make an appearance. A tired, grumpy, middle-aged officer sat down behind the desk at about half past eight, ready to start the day's business. It was forbidden to go to the source alone, so I was given a porter – a shy, young man who knew about as many words in English as I did in Hindi. I had tried to teach myself Hindi before I came, and struggled valiantly with the consonant-rich Devanagari alphabet and the unfamiliar verb forms. Despite getting good grades in the exams, I could only remember one phrase from all those hours of study and revision: *Ajka mausam ajha hai.* The weather today is good. I could also say the opposite: *Ajka mausam ajha nahi hai.* The weather today is not good. And that was it.

A wide stone and concrete path rose gently up the side of the valley, which was bathed in sunshine, and flanked by high, tree-clad slopes. We walked through forests of evergreen rhododendron, silver fir, autumn-coloured pine and Himalayan cedar, an evergreen conifer that thrives at high altitudes. The plan was to take my time and to chat to the pilgrims I met along the way, but instead I became fixated on passing as many people as possible and getting there as fast as possible – all those childhood Sunday walks in Vestlandet must have left their mark. Not that there were many people I could have spoken to. Most of those I met – and rushed past – were Westerners. The few Indians that I saw were being taken up on horseback. At some point in the afternoon, I saw something I will never forget: a sinewy, hunched man trudging down with a very ample Indian woman in a basket on his back. I assumed that the woman was disabled and felt sorry for her, but then a few kilometres later I spotted another one, only this time the woman in the basket was young and vivacious, dressed in expensive hiking gear. She sat in the basket, dangling her feet, which were equipped with brand-new hiking boots, while the poor porter carried her to the source, step by step, hunched over and bent double.

Dark had started to fall by the time I reached the small camp where I was going to stay the night. I got myself a bed in an eight-man tent, which I shared with backpackers from Canada, France and Israel. It was so cold in the simple café tent that we all crept into our sleeping bags before it was even seven. I woke up during the night with a pounding headache – we were four thousand metres above sea level. The generator was no longer humming and it was pitch black both inside and outside the tent. I crawled out of my sleeping bag and went out to look at the stars. Over my aching head, the Milky Way crossed the sky like a white path. The Indians call the Milky Way Aksaganga: Heavenly Ganges.

The path disintegrated for the final kilometres up to the source.

Horses and baskets would not work here; pilgrims had to use their own two feet. Old, weather-beaten people with sticks and cheap sandals defiantly made their way along the rudimentary path. Eventually we had to climb over and around boulders and navigate slopes of scree where small stones were constantly rolling down.

The old path to Gangotri Glacier was totally destroyed by the great flood of 2013. Unusually heavy rain for several days on end had left many of the rivers blocked by trees and sediment from the mountainsides. When these natural dams broke up, an enormous amount of water raced uncontrollably down the valley, taking with it villages and people. More than five thousand people lost their lives, and Kedarnath, one of the four pilgrim destinations on the Chota Char Dham circuit, was hit hardest. The temple itself survived, miraculously, but pilgrims, porters, horses, hotels, shops and cafés were swept away by the raging water. Rainfall like this is not usual in the mountains, but is likely to become more normal in the future, in line with other types of extreme weather.

I almost missed Gangotri Glacier, as I saw nothing but dirt and gravel. The glacier was covered in black sand and small stones that hid the ice. Cold, fresh water poured out of an oval opening. I had expected a small, trickling stream, but the Ganges was surprisingly rapid even at its source. The Hindus call the head of the glacier 4023 MSL **Gaumukh**, which means cow's mouth, and it does indeed resemble a mouth. Half a billion people are dependent on the meltwater that pours out of this cow's mouth from an apparently eternal source.

But the eternal source is melting. Like nearly all the other glaciers in the Himalayas, Gangotri is shrinking. Two hundred years ago, it stretched three kilometres further down the valley, and with every year that passes, the speed at which it melts is accelerating. The most worrying thing, however, is not that the glacier is retreating, but that it is getting thinner and therefore contains less ice, like all the other glaciers around the world, which in turn makes them more vulnerable. Meltwater from the Himalayas accounts for about seventy per cent of the water in the Ganges, and these glaciers are now melting at an alarming rate. Even if the total amount of precipitation remains the same in the future, the water will not flow as steadily. Floods will be followed by droughts, which in turn will be followed by floods, in a nightmarish cycle.

For the time being, it is easy to say where the Ganges ends, but in the near future, it is not unfeasible that Ma Ganges will no longer reach the ocean for parts of the year.

A thin, young man had squatted down by the water's edge and was washing himself. He had taken off everything except his underwear, but did not appear to be cold. He looked up at me and smiled happily. I smiled back. The sun shone down from a steel-blue sky and the incredibly clean glacial water, still opaque and greenish in hue, cascaded down the valley, heading for the overpopulated plains of north India.

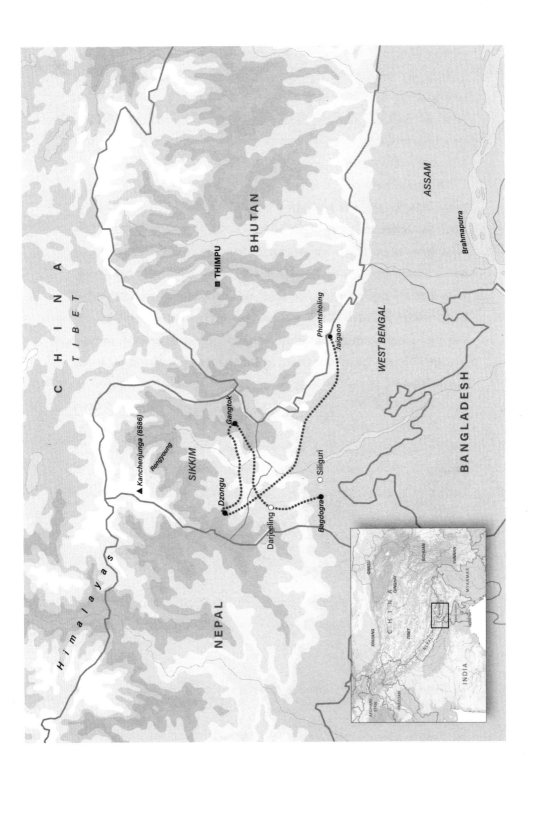

Champagne of the Mountains

The narrow road up to Darjeeling was full of hairpin bends. The nearest airport, **Bagdogra**, was down in the lowlands, about a hun- 136 MSL dred kilometres from the Mecca of tea. Slowly we climbed again, through a hazy, iridescent green landscape. Without warning, the driver pulled in to the side and slammed on the brakes by a dilapidated stall. He slipped out of the car, handed the stallholder a creased banknote and stood there enjoying a sweet, spiced chai.

Indians are, not surprisingly, big tea drinkers. However, if one looks at the population as a whole, annual consumption is not so great, at around three-quarters of a kilo per person. The British drink twice as much, and the Irish almost three times as much. But no-one beats the Turks, who hold the record with more than three kilos, equivalent to thirteen hundred cups of tea per person per year. Many Indians are so poor that they cannot afford tea, but those who can drink a lot.

It was in fact the British who brought tea to India. Tea bushes only grow wild in the Brahmaputra Valley in Assam, and only the small Singpho tribe, who have roots in Myanmar, knew about the drink before the arrival of the British. They had been introduced to tea in the mid-1700s and had been major consumers ever since. At the beginning of the nineteenth century, enterprising British merchants managed to smuggle some tea plants across the border from China to India, and then persuaded experienced Chinese tea growers to come and work for them. The plan was to establish large tea plantations in the lowlands of Assam, to keep import costs down, but they soon discovered that the Chinese tea plant did not thrive on the Indian plains, and tended to die after a short time. Their solution was to cross the Chinese tea plant with the more robust tea bush that was native to the Brahmaputra Valley, which gave a darker, stronger and less refined tea. The result was a huge success: India is today the second largest tea producer in the world.

It took time for the Indians to embrace the new plants. In his book *Key to Health*, Gandhi warns against the drink, which he believed was harmful as it contained tannins, which were used in tanneries to harden leather. Gandhi thought that tea would have a similar effect on the stomach, and recommended that people instead drink boiled water with a little milk and sugar. The Indians only became addicted to tea years after Gandhi's death, during the 1960s. The green revolution involved the introduction of machinery, artificial fertilisers and pesticides in a large-scale drive to make agriculture more efficient, and was not, in reality, very green at all – pollution in the Ganges and other rivers rocketed as a result. A tea-making method using machines also started to gain traction around this time. The tea leaves were placed in machines that either cut or crushed, tearing them into small pieces that were then rolled into small knots. The method is called CTC (crush, tear, curl) and it made it possible to produce tea that could be boiled, which suited the Indian palate, in a far more cost-effective way than the usual time-consuming rolling method. The Indians generally drink masala chai, which is boiled black tea spiced with cardamom, ginger and cinnamon, with added milk or milk powder and large amounts of sugar. These days, tea production is largely mechanical, and the Indians keep more than seventy per cent of all tea that is produced, forcing the British to buy from other markets as well.

In Darjeeling, however, CTC is a profanity, and more or less all the tea that is produced is sold to foreigners at a premium.

No matter where I looked, the view from the car window was

of tea bushes. The undulating hillsides were covered in the low green bushes. When we reached **Darjeeling**, the traffic ground to a halt, 2042 MSL with the cars standing in long, disorganised queues, caught in an eternal chaotic cacophony. The sides of the road were awash with rubbish and a thick mist had fallen over the city, erasing the silhouette of the mountains.

The smell of newly fermented tea hung heavy over the small Happy Valley tea factory.

"Because of its altitude, humidity and fertile soil, Darjeeling is particularly well suited to growing tea," said Sitam, the young production assistant who showed me around.

Sitam made it sound obvious that Darjeeling was the perfect place for tea, but the truth is that nobody, not even the most experienced botanists, believed that tea would thrive at such high altitudes, in an area with so much rain and so little sun. Darjeeling lies just over two thousand metres above sea level, in the dampest and most fertile corner of the Himalayas, nestled between Nepal to the west, Tibet and Sikkim to the north and Bhutan to the east.

Darjeeling was originally part of the small kingdom of Sikkim. At the end of the eighteenth century, Sikkim had great difficulties with its neighbour to the west, the Gorkha kingdom, which encompassed large parts of what is now Nepal. In the space of a few years, the Gorkhas had conquered large tracts of land, but when in 1814 they wanted to subjugate the rest of Sikkim, they were stopped by the British East India Company. The British later gave the liberated areas back to Sikkim, but not without a price. They had a predilection for the so-called hill stations, up in the mountains. The air there was fresher and cooler than down on the plains, where it could get unbearably hot in summer. The lush hills of Darjeeling were the perfect place for sanatoriums, and the position was also strategic, lying as it did on the border with Nepal and the closed, mysterious

Tibet. It was originally called Dorje Ling, the Land of Thunder, after a Buddhist monastery that was there. With the exception of a few small villages, the area was uninhabited. The chogyal, or king of Sikkim, was at first not willing to lease the territory to the British, but when the British once again stopped the Gorkhas from taking over Sikkim in the 1830s, an agreement was soon drawn up.

A few years later, in autumn 1849, Dr Archibald Campbell, the enterprising Scottish superintendent of Darjeeling, set off on an expedition to Tibet. He travelled with the legendary botanist, Joseph Dalton Hooker, who was also a Scot. Despite warnings from the king's guard in Sikkim, the two adventurers managed to cross the border into the promised land. When they re-entered Sikkim, they were arrested for illegally crossing the border, and it is said that Campbell was tortured in prison. The two Scots were held for one and a half months and it was Christmas Eve by the time they returned to Darjeeling. In retaliation, the British annexed the fertile lowlands south of Darjeeling, and stopped paying the rent. Sikkim was thus reduced to an isolated mountain kingdom, caught between Tibet and British India. Darjeeling, on the other hand, was no longer an enclave, but was linked to the rest of India, and in due course connected by train. In 1881, the Darjeeling Himalayan Railway opened; it is a major engineering feat and is now listed as a UNESCO World Heritage Site. The narrow-gauge railway crosses 554 bridges and has 873 curves and three loops to allow the train to pick up enough speed. The track follows and criss-crosses the road in order to manage the tight bends, and sometime passes so close to shops that, if one dared, one could simply stretch one's hand out through the window and help oneself to whatever one liked.

It is thanks to Dr Archibald Campbell that tea is now cultivated in Darjeeling. Shortly after arriving in the sanatorium town, he planted some Chinese tea bushes in his garden to see what would happen. To everyone's surprise, the bushes thrived. In the years that followed, forests were cleared to make way for tea plantations, and the first tea factory in Darjeeling was opened in 1859. The rest is history.

"Making Darjeeling tea is an art," Sitam said, as we stepped into the tasting room. "Each producer makes their own unique tea, there are no rules. Around ninety per cent of the tea we produce is black tea, but green tea, white tea and oolong tea can also be made from the same plant. The Darjeeling season is short, because of the cold climate, and only lasts from mid-March to mid-November. As our plantation is the highest in Darjeeling, our season starts in mid-April, so it's even shorter."

He held out a cup of steaming golden tea. I took a sip, and my mouth was filled with a gentle taste of spring.

"The first harvest is called the first flush, and is light and aromatic," Sitam explained. "White tea is made from the finest leaves. Some people call it expensive boiled water, as it has no colour and very little taste, but it's rich in antioxidants."

I was given a new cup, filled with something that really did look like boiled water, which had a very delicate flavour of light blue, like a Nordic summer night.

"In summer we pick the second flush, my favourite. It's our strongest and most aromatic tea."

Sitam handed me a cup of deep-orange, strong brew. The tannins made my mouth pucker.

"The tea has less taste during the monsoon, so we mix the tea from the monsoon harvest with tea from the other seasons," Sitam said. "And then, finally, we have the fourth flush, which is picked in autumn. We don't make Indian masala chai here, as it's made from another plant. In fact, the way Indians make tea, they ruin it completely," he said, derisively. "The tea drowns in the milk and sugar. And by the way, Darjeeling tea should be drunk without either, perhaps a drop of lemon, that's all."

We wandered through the empty factory.

"The picking is all done manually," Sitam said. "We have one hundred and ninety-two pickers, only women. They are very experienced and only pick the leaves needed for the particular type of tea that we're going to make. When the women come here with the freshly picked leaves, we spread them out on a long drying mesh and they lie there to dry for anything between twelve to eighteen hours. For the first nine hours, there is a fan under the rack that blows out first cold then warm air. We manage to lose around sixty to seventy per cent of the moisture in the leaves in this way, which makes them lighter and much easier to work with. It's crucial that the leaves are not so brittle that they break. The next stage is rolling."

We carried on to three machines that looked like something from the 1950s. Large, shiny metal drums that went round and round, with a heavy stamper mounted on each drum.

"The stampers press the leaves and break down the cells and start the oxidation process," Sitam said. "The leaves are rolled for twenty to forty minutes, never longer. Afterwards, we spread the leaves out on a long table, where they lie oxidising for anything between half an hour and an hour and a half. White tea and green tea are not oxidised, so we're talking black tea here."

In the next room, there was a solid iron drum with a mesh in front of the opening.

"When the leaves have been oxidised, we move them into this machine, which has a steady temperature of one hundred and twenty degrees centigrade. The leaves are dried here for ten to fifteen minutes, in order to stop the oxidation process. When they are ready, there should only be about two to three per cent moisture left in the leaves. The whole process takes between two and two and a half days. The fresh tea will keep in an airtight bag for up to two years."

We carried on to the next room, where there were four oblong sorting trays.

"The largest leaves stay on top. The powder that gathers at the bottom is used for teabags."

A handful of women in white coats were sitting bent over baskets of tea in the last room. With deft hands they picked out all the tea leaves that were not of a high enough quality.

"The quality assurance system for tea is very complex," Sitam told me. "The best quality is complete leaves, SFTGFOP: Super Fine Tippy Gold Flower Orange Pekoe – or, as I call it, Far Too Good for Ordinary People." He chuckled quietly at his own joke, which he no doubt told many times a day.

The estate manager at Happy Valley Tea Estate, Narendra Singh, was only a couple of years older than me, but in these parts, people, especially bosses, assume a kind of permanent middle-aged manner. We sat at a small table in the shade of a tree outside his bungalow, which undoubtedly dated from the British colonial era. A servant came out with a pot and filled our cups with steaming golden tea.

"I have been the estate manager here for eighteen months, but have experience of other estates in Mozambique and Ethiopia as well," Narendra said. "I originally come from Varanasi, but as my father was in the military, I have lived all over India. It was my father who said that I should get into tea, and as I've always been interested in agriculture, I followed his advice."

"When you live in a country that produces the best tea in the world, how is it that people here ruin the tea with milk and sugar?" I asked.

"Easily answered!" Narendra smiled. "Milk is a part of Indian culture. We start the day with a glass of milk and our diet is based on cheese, butter and milk. The British wanted the Indians to start drinking tea, so they introduced us to tea with milk. That's how they like to drink it themselves. Sugar beet also features in traditional Indian food. Indians have a real sweet tooth."

He patted his pot belly to prove his point.

"So what is it that's so special about Darjeeling tea?"

"Taste and see for yourself!" Narendra poured more tea into my cup. "The first flush from Darjeeling is simply the world's best tea. Darjeeling tea is a concept, it has its own culture, and is part of life here. It's also a protected name; only eighty-seven estates can call the tea they produce Darjeeling tea. Our bushes can live to be close to two hundred years old, and in my opinion, the older the plant, the better the tea. All tea production here is manual, because the hillsides are too steep for machinery, and several of the estates have opted to become organic. There are four key factors to making good tea: good soil, the right climatic conditions, rain and labour. The soil here is rich and fertile, the climate is perfect. We have between two and four hundred millimetres of rain a year, but most of it runs off, rather than penetrating the ground. And the plants grow more slowly in the cold climate."

Narendra ignored my protests and poured me yet more tea.

"Please bring a new pot!" he called to the servant, who was standing by the door. "Everyone talks about climate change these days, and we've noticed it too," he turned and said to me. "We used to have snow here in winter. But that no longer happens, which is good for the tea plants as they don't like snow."

He drank some more tea and looked disapprovingly at my untouched cup.

"Please drink! That cup is worth between eight hundred and a thousand rupees."

"But I've already drink four cups," I protested.

"That doesn't matter, you can drink as much tea as you like, it's a healthy drink! I often say it's like drinking oxygen." Narendra laughed, finished his cup and poured another. "As our plants grow at such a high altitude, they are packed with oxygen and antioxidants. And what are antioxidants good for? Well, they're good for your skin, they keep you beautiful. And by the way, I must say, you obviously look after yourself better than my wife, even though she's a nutritionist. But you wouldn't believe it if you saw her, hahaha!"

Another servant came in with a pot of fresh tea.

"How many servants do you have?" I asked.

"Five women and four or five boys." Narendra poured even more tea for himself and filled my cup to the brim. "It's one of the privileges of working here. I'm responsible for several hundred employees, so nine or ten servants isn't that many. Come, let me show you the estate!"

I followed him out to the jeep, where a servant was already waiting behind the wheel. However, Narendra insisted on driving himself, and manoeuvred the jeep down a narrow, winding track, past a small blue stand where a group of women stood nattering. He carried on down the steep track, undeterred, until we were entirely surrounded by low, dark-green tea bushes.

"This is my favourite place!" he said and jumped out of the jeep. The bushes followed the undulations of the hillside until they disappeared into the greenish-white Darjeeling mist in the far distance. High up above us, the colourful houses of Darjeeling were only just visible.

"There's no picking going on today. Everyone has the day off as it's the harvest festival," Narendra said. "Last year, it was almost as quiet as this for the whole season. For more than a hundred days, from the sixteenth of June until the fourth of October, Darjeeling was closed down. All the workers in the district were on strike, and all the estates were forced to stop production."

"Why did they go on strike?" I asked.

"I won't go into the politics, but basically, the workers here are all of Nepalese origin and want their own state, Gorkhaland. They don't want to be part of West Bengal. The movement is over a hundred years old, but things came to a head last year when the authorities made it mandatory for everyone in West Bengal to learn Bengali. Nepali is the language most used here."

"And did they achieve anything?"

"Nothing whatsoever. It was a complete waste of time!"

When we got back to the bungalow, I assumed that we were done and thanked him for his tour, and for his time and all the tea. But Narendra waved aside my thanks, sat down again at the small table outside and invited me to sit with him.

"Can you bring out more tea for us?" he called, and almost instantly, a servant appeared with a fresh pot.

On my last night in Darjeeling, I splashed out on a room at the Windamere Hotel, the epitome of colonial nostalgia. The hotel was opened in 1880 as a boarding house for unmarried British tea planters and official envoys from the British central administration in Calcutta and was later turned into a high-class hotel. A uniformed porter showed me to my room, which had big flowery curtains and an equally flowery bedspread, and in addition a sofa, a fireplace and an old-fashioned bathtub. But I had no time to sit down and enjoy the room, as afternoon tea was being served. And even though I already felt like an overfull, walking teapot, I could not miss afternoon tea at the Windamere, which is an institution.

In another beautiful room, there were silver platters piled high with home-made scones, shortbread and small sandwiches, and a large pot of perfectly brewed tea. I loaded a plate and moved into Daisy's Music Room, where these delights could be enjoyed in deep, soft armchairs while conversing with the other guests. But the two Indian couples sitting in the room were totally engrossed in their mobile phones.

I could hear all the tea sloshing around inside me as I walked back to my room, which I was now going to fully enjoy. But no sooner had I closed the door than there was a knock on it. The manager informed me that I had been invited to the birthday celebrations for the tour guide of a British group that had booked all the other rooms. The elderly Brits had gathered in the TV lounge and were already singing "Happy Birthday". We were then led into the dining room, which reminded me of a grand, private drawing room. The uniformed waiters ran in and out of the kitchen carrying the day's fare under silver cloches. Feeling wonderfully replete after all the good food and wine and far too many cups of the world's best tea, I waddled back to my room, where a fire was now burning in the fireplace. Overstimulated and giddy, I crawled into the double bed and discovered that someone had been kind enough to put a hot-water bottle at the bottom of the bed in my absence.

I lay awake for a while thinking about who else might have slept in this bed. The author and explorer Alexandra David-Néel stayed at the Windamere when she was in Darjeeling, as did Prince Peter of Denmark and Greece, and Palden Thondup Namgyal, the last king of Sikkim. It was here at the Windamere that he first met the American student Hope Cooke. She was nineteen at the time, almost half the age of the 36-year-old widower and father of three. But, against all odds, they hit it off. Some years later they became husband and wife, and Hope was then Queen of Sikkim.

Both the marriage and kingdom were now history, but their youngest daughter, Hope Leezum, had moved back to Sikkim as an adult. I was travelling there the next day in the hope that I might meet her, but how do you get in touch with a former princess?

The Princess without a Kingdom

Hidden behind a wall of thick mist to the west, Kanchenjunga, the third highest mountain in the world, rose up into the sky. Colourful concrete apartment blocks clung on to the overgrown mountainside. The traffic in the Sikkimese capital was, as always, chaotic, but remarkably quiet. *No-one* was honking their horn.

"Why aren't you hooting anymore?" I asked the driver. On the way out of Darjeeling, he had used the horn frequently, but since we had crossed the state line, he had not used it once.

"There's a five hundred rupee fine here if you hoot all the time," he said, glumly.

1650 MSL   All the hotels in **Gangtok** were fully booked because of the harvest festival, but I had managed to find a room in a small guest house run by a local Bhutia family. Bhutia is one of the names for the tribes who came to Sikkim from Tibet in the ninth century, and the dining room was done out in Tibetan style, with low tables and brightly coloured walls. The proprietor's son brought me some steaming dumplings and local beer.

"There's no tax on alcohol in Sikkim, so people drink all the time," he grinned. "People drink to forget that they're ruled by India!"

"Talking of which, do you know how I can get in touch with Hope Leezum, the princess?" I said.

"You mean Semla?" He went over to the window and pointed into the night. "She lives down the road. Everyone knows her house, so just ask."

"Wouldn't it be best if I called and fixed a meeting with her first? Do you have her telephone number? Or an email address?"

"No, I don't, but you don't need it. Just go to her house and knock on the door."

I spent most of the next morning mustering my courage to do just that. In the meantime, I thought I would answer some emails, and while I was at it, I answered pretty much everything I had been neglecting for the past few weeks. Until there was nothing left to answer.

I told myself that the worst scenario was that the princess was not at home, or *was* at home, but did not want to talk to me.

Even though the hotel proprietor had described the house to me in detail, I carried on walking down the street for a few hundred metres just to be certain that it could not be confused with any of the other houses. It could not. There was a gate to the driveway and I hoped for a moment that it would be locked, but it opened easily without so much as a creak. I hesitated as I walked up towards the brick house. It was not every day you sneaked into the property of an ex-royal. Two women in domestic uniforms looked down at me from the veranda and exchanged glances, but said nothing. There was a large garden up by the house, which was full of exotic plants. A woman in shorts and a T-shirt was on her knees working in one of the beds. When she noticed me, she stood up and sent me a questioning look. It was the princess.

"Hello, can I help you?" She spoke English with a New York accent. "This is private property."

"I'm so sorry just to turn up without an appointment, but I didn't have your telephone number," I stammered, after I had introduced myself. "I'm sorry to bother you, but I wondered if you perhaps had time to talk to me one day?"

"Let's go and have a cup of tea," she said, showing me into the garden.

We sat down on a couple of garden chairs in front of the house. Her husband, a Sikkimese man with a thin beard and narrow face full of smile lines, sat bent over a flower pot a couple of metres away. A servant came out with three large cups of tea.

"Call me Semla," Hope Leezum said. "That's what everyone calls me here. It means daughter."

The fifty-year-old former princess had a deep voice and an easy laugh. She still had flecks of earth on her legs from the gardening, her shoulder-length hair hung loose and she was wearing no make-up.

"I'll show you the monastery and residence tomorrow, because then you'll understand the context better, but for now let's just have a nice cup of tea and a chat." She smiled. "Does that sound like a good plan?"

Semla gave me lots of advice about what to see in Gangtok, and before I left, she showed me round the garden.

"Everything grows here in Sikkim," she said, as we wandered past rose bushes, aloe vera plants and rhododendron bushes. "We're on the same latitude as Miami, but as we're surrounded by high mountains, alpine plants and lowland plants all grow here."

Later in the afternoon, I took Semla's advice and went to drink more tea. The luxurious Elgin Hotel, with its elegant garden and lavish lobby, had served as the royal family's private guest house until 1975. When the 39-year-old crown prince of Sikkim, Palden Thondup Namgyal, married 22-year-old Hope Cooke in 1963, many of the wedding guests stayed there. The couple had been engaged for two years, because according to the local astrologists 1962 was a black year, so a wedding was not possible. Many people in Sikkim would no doubt have been happy if the marriage to a Christian American student had not gone ahead at all. And the astrologists were right, 1962 was a black year, certainly in geopolitical terms: in October, Chinese soldiers launched a two-pronged attack in the Himalayas, sending their forces over the Indian border in the Aksai-Chin region to the west, and Arunachal Pradesh to the east. However, they left Sikkim in peace as the Chinese, interestingly enough, regarded Sikkim as an independent country and not part of India.

When the black year had passed, it was not possible to delay the wedding any longer, and the astrologers eventually found an auspicious date: March 20, 1963. The American media went into a frenzy, describing the romance between the orphaned young American girl and the crown prince of a tiny Buddhist kingdom in the Himalayas. Hope Cooke was perhaps not as glamorous and beautiful as Grace Kelly, but Sikkim was far more magical and mystical than Monaco. Unlike Princess Grace of Monaco, Cooke had to give up her American citizenship when she married into the Sikkimese royal family. The plan was to become Sikkimese herself and live happily ever after with her prince.

Their conjugal bliss was short-lived, however.

I, on the other hand, was utterly content, sitting there in the plush red, Tibetan-inspired bar at the Elgin Hotel. On the low table in front of me was a fresh pot of Darjeeling tea, a plate of piping hot pakora and another with British biscuits.

The following morning, Semla met me outside the guest house, as agreed. Her gardening clothes had been swapped for a more formal blouse and knee-length skirt, and she was just as friendly and smiley as the day before.

"Let's go up to the monastery first," she said. "It's not far, I go there every day."

A few minutes later we were standing outside the main temple. Semla greeted all the little boys we met on the way with a smile. They smiled bashfully in return.

"The monastery is part of the Tsuklakhang Trust, which I manage on behalf of my brother, the 13th chogyal of Sikkim," she said. "My brother spends most of the year in deep meditation in caves and monasteries in Nepal and Bhutan, and has given away more or less all the family's wealth. Who knows, perhaps deep down he's glad that he didn't need to be king. It was actually his older brother who should have been the chogyal, but he died in a car accident in 1978. It's the curse of our family. For the past three generations, the oldest son has died young in some kind of accident."

Semla's father, Palden Thondup Namgyal, was not brought up to be the king, either. But his older brother died in a plane crash during the Second World War, and Thondup had to give up his plans to study at Cambridge and instead take on the duties of a crown prince. Semla's grandfather never got over the loss of his eldest son and retired early from politics in order to dedicate his time to religious activities. He, too, had not been born heir to the throne. His elder brother had been crowned chogyal in 1914, to become the shortest reigning king in Sikkim's history: he died after only ten months on the throne, at the age of thirty-five.

When Semla's grandfather, Tashi Namgyal, died in the winter of 1963, not long after her parents' wedding, her father had in effect been ruling Sikkim for more than two decades. Thondup and Hope were officially crowned chogyal and gyalmo in 1965, when the year of mourning for the old king was over.

"My brother is not interested in politics. None of my family are," Semla said. "After we became part of India in 1975, the chogyal lost all his political power, but my brother is still the religious leader of Sikkim, and he takes the role very seriously. Our culture is threatened by all the people who have moved here, so he has taken it upon himself to save all the monasteries in Sikkim. He invested three quarters of the family wealth in a fund that is used to pay for the upkeep of this monastery, among other things. The boys who live here are given free tuition in Buddhism, of course, but also maths and English and anything else they might need. When they have finished school, they can decide themselves whether they want to be ordained, or if they want to go on to further education and live a normal life."

On the deep beat of a drum, the boy monks came running across the courtyard towards us. They rushed past us and ran up the stairs, out of breath.

"End of the break. They have to go back to their prayers," Semla said, with a smile. We followed the boys up to the first floor. The prayers had already started. The boys blew into long horns, banged cymbals and drums and chanted their mantras.

"It's amazing how much noise little boys can make!" Semla laughed. "They look so innocent in their monk's habits, but they're actually quite naughty!"

Workers were busy laying a new floor in the main temple room, so we kept our shoes on. Frightening statues with sharp canines and red eyes, armed with swords, guarded the temple and the peaceful golden Buddha statues in glass cabinets at the back of the room.

"When I started the restoration work here, all the walls were black because of the smoke from the butter lamps," Semla said. "It was impossible to see the paintings. We have slowly managed to bring the originals back to life. I knew nothing about restoration work and was impatient to begin with, but now I've learned that it's a long, time-consuming process!"

She proudly showed me the section of the wall that she had restored herself, and told me in detail about the various techniques and the invaluable help she had had from German experts.

"But I'm getting carried away now!" she said, with a smile. "I could talk about the restoration for hours on end, but I promised to show you the palace."

We left the temple and crossed the football pitch to get to the small, yellow building with a red metal roof.

"This is really the crown prince's residence," Semla said. "We never managed to have a proper palace built. My grandfather built an extension so there was enough room for everyone. But as no-one lives here anymore, the building has started to deteriorate, and my brother had all the worst-affected parts demolished. So it's even smaller than it ever was, not much more than a cabin, really. And there's nothing inside, I'm afraid, so not much to see. A maharaja came to visit me a few weeks ago, and he asked to see the palace. He showed me a photograph of his own, and boasted about having more than five hundred rooms. I have six!"

An old gentleman opened the gate so we could go right up to the house.

"How are you?" Semla asked, and gave him some money. "He uses all his money to buy food for the dogs up here," she said, as we walked towards the building. We stopped in front of a rather modest front door, and Semla made an open gesture with her hands.

"This is my childhood home. I had a good childhood. I went to the local school, and my friends would often come here after class. We'd play cops and robbers, or bang, bang, as we called it. I hated wearing dresses, so I generally wore shorts and followed my brothers everywhere and did the kind of things that children do. My mother tried to introduce American traditions like April Fool and Halloween, but no-one really understood what it meant. They thought the queen had gone mad."

There was a beautiful garden along one side of the building.

"This is the small family garden. There's a photograph of it in my mother's autobiography," Semla said. "On sunny winter days, my father would take the telephone out and work in the garden. Not that what you write is any of my business, but I just want to say that my mother's autobiography is very one-sided. She tells the story from her point of view, and is rather harsh on my father, I think. As I said, he was the second son, so not raised to be king. He was a reincarnated monk and spent many of his formative years in a monastery. I remember him as being careful and shy. When we got back from school, we would often find him repairing a record player or radio, or something like that."

The marriage between Hope and Thondup was doomed from the start. The king drank too much, and it was a challenge for Hope to be accepted by Sikkim society. She was also convinced that her husband had a mistress. She first took Valium on their wedding day, to calm her nerves, but it quickly became a habit. She and the chogyal had a son and a daughter together. Hope was also close to Thondup's three children from his first marriage, and tried to be a mother to them. They both loved the children dearly, but their marriage went from bad to worse.

As did the fate of the kingdom. When the British withdrew from India, Sikkim went from being a British protectorate to being an Indian one. In 1950, the two states signed an agreement that gave India control of the small kingdom's foreign policy. Prime Minister Jawaharlal Nehru, who was himself from Kashmir, had a deep love of the Himalayas, and during his rule Sikkim was relatively safe. However, when his daughter Indira Gandhi became prime minister, the chogyal was stripped of what little political power he still had and Sikkim was formally subsumed by India.

One of the reasons that things happened as they did was that the composition of Sikkim's population had changed more in the previous hundred years than the chogyal would acknowledge. Two ethnic groups had dominated in Sikkim: the Lepcha people, the original inhabitants of Sikkim, and the Bhutia people, who are of Tibetan ancestry. The royal family were from the latter group and had ruled almost continuously since 1642, with the exception of short periods in the eighteenth century when Sikkim was ruled by its neighbours Bhutan and Nepal. During the struggles with Nepal, large numbers of Nepalese migrated to Sikkim, and by the time that Semla's father was crowned king, the largely Hindu Nepalese accounted for three-quarters of the population. Many of them were strongly opposed to the royal dynasty, who they accused of favouring the Buddhists, and not without reason. But instead of trying to increase their popularity at home, Thondup and Hope did what they could to raise awareness of Sikkim abroad. Thondup had a dream of a seat in the United Nations and of making Sikkim a paradise on earth. But these dreams were never realised, as Indira Gandhi had other plans.

In 1973, thousands of angry protesters gathered outside the royal palace in Gangtok. The demonstrations became more and more violent, and eventually the hard-pressed chogyal had no choice but to ask Dehli for help to regain control of the situation. In return, the Indian government forced the chogyal to accept an agreement that in effect reduced him to a constitutional cipher.

"I didn't understand much of what was going on," Semla said. "I was only five at the time, and the adults did what they could to protect us. Everyone spoke in whispers and was very tense, and we spent a lot of time indoors. The only time I felt that something was seriously wrong was when my brother and I went down to the kiosk by the main gate to buy some sweets. A furious crowd had gathered and were screaming: "Death to the king! Death to the king." The kiosk owner shouted to us to run, and my brother grabbed me by the arm and we ran back to the gate. The guards rushed to help us and I lost a shoe in the chaos. My mother had had the shoes sent from the West, and as it was so difficult to get hold of them, she always bought them two sizes too big, so it would take me a while to grow out of them. That was the only thing I cared about, that I had lost a shoe and would no doubt be told off."

A few months later, Hope fled to New York with the youngest children, while the chogyal and crown prince stayed in the palace. Hope never returned to Sikkim. Thondup still hoped at that point that Sikkim and the monarchy would survive, but the battle was already lost. In 1974, the Indian parliament passed a law that in effect made Sikkim a part of India. The world responded with silent astonishment, but the fate of a small, secluded kingdom in the Himalayas was not a high priority for anyone, particularly not the Americans, who had more than enough on their plate with Vietnam.

In early April 1975, trucks and jeeps full of Indian soldiers poured into Gangtok. Thondup was worried by the increased military presence, but was led to believe it was only an exercise. In the late afternoon of April 9, the palace was surrounded by soldiers. The royal guard were not able to prevent the attack, but one of them lifted his rifle towards the Indian soldiers and was immediately shot and killed. Another was hit in the arm. A few minutes later, the Indians had full control of the palace. All the weapons were confiscated and the 12th chogyal of Sikkim was, to all intents and purposes, under house arrest.

The following day, Dehli announced that the chogyal had been deposed and that Sikkim would henceforth be deemed Indian territory. Four days after the annexation became fact, a referendum on whether the royal family should be abolished and Sikkim should become part of India was rushed through. The voters, many of them illiterate, had to choose whether to put the pink voting card in the pink box marked FOR or the white box marked AGAINST. No consideration was taken of the fact that a ballot should be secret, and in some voting stations the white box was placed at the opposite end of the room from the entrance. Ninety-seven percent of the votes went into the pink boxes, thus giving India's annexation a veneer of democracy. Sikkim is the least populous state in India and the second smallest in terms of area.

On the other side of the world, Hope and Thondup's children were struggling to adjust to American city life.

"My mother had not had an ordinary childhood," Semla said. "Her father was an Irish flight instructor and her mother was the daughter of a rich American. Her grandparents – my great-grandparents –

never accepted the Irish Catholic, and offered him a princely sum of money to leave their daughter. Which he did. But he had already taught my grandmother to fly, and not long after he left, my grandmother died in a plane crash. My mother was still only a baby. Many, including my mother, believe it was suicide, as the plane had almost no petrol in the tank. My mother was raised by governesses and never had a proper family life. Perhaps that was why she had such unorthodox ideas about raising children. I remember once, for example, that she thought I was too shy. I was about eight at the time. She took me to the West Side in New York, gave me two coins and left me there to find my own way home. I missed my father and Sikkim, and was only able to visit him twice, in summer 1975 and again in summer 1980. It was wonderful! We mostly stayed indoors with Father, reading. Soon after, in 1982, he died of cancer. I'm so glad that I at least had those two summers with him."

We were now back down by the main road, and Semla smiled and called hello to right and left. She seemed to know everyone in Gangtok.

"I went to school with him. He is a very intelligent man, a great man," she said. "That's the kiosk I told you about. It's still here. Goodness, that car is about to mow us down!" She grabbed my arm and pulled me to the side. "There are far too many cars here now. When I was growing up, there were only eight thousand inhabitants in Gangtok, so it was like living in a village. Now there's more than a hundred thousand – the same as the entire population of Sikkim only a few decades ago! There are now more than six hundred thousand people living here. The change is enormous."

"How did your father react to the annexation?" I asked.

"It was a huge shock for him. I think he felt betrayed, because we had had a good relationship with India. I've been told that the general who disarmed the palace guards and put my father under house arrest had twice refused to follow the orders. In the end, he was told that if *he* didn't do it, someone who didn't know the family would. They say he cried when he told my father that they'd fired at the guards. Lots of people felt guilty afterwards. What happened was both morally and politically wrong – a huge betrayal. It was definitely not what Indira Gandhi's father, Jawaharlal Nehru, would have wanted, because he was a close friend of the family and loved the Himalayas."

We walked down some steps that were a short cut to the main street, a pedestrian one, which was something of a rarity in these parts. Noisy groups of Indian tourists livened up the place, and a couple of them wanted to take selfies with me. None of them seemed even to notice the princess.

Two bespectacled old men were sitting on a nearby bench, deep in conversation. Semla greeted them warmly.

"Talk to them, they are true Sikkimese nationalists," she said. "I'll be back shortly!"

I sat down on the bench beside the two old men.

"I have never voted," the older one said. "I love the king and hate having to call myself Indian. The whole state is being Hinduised now, and we're in danger of losing our culture. Everything is Hinduised. Education, language, people's thoughts. Everything."

"What was life like in Sikkim before, when it was independent, compared with now?" I asked.

"As different as heaven and hell," the younger of the two said resolutely.

"Heaven and hell," the older man echoed. "That's right."

Semla came back, a bit out of breath, and handed me a bag of beautifully wrapped books.

"Sorry, I met someone I knew, so it took longer than expected," she said. "Read these books, they will help you to understand what's happened in Sikkim."

"Do you think Sikkim will ever be independent again?" I asked.

"No, it's too late," Semla said. "The demographics have changed so much that it wouldn't make sense any longer. Sikkim is a completely difference place from what it was in 1975."

We went into a café and ordered lunch.

"I've dreamed about coming back to Sikkim ever since I was a child," Semla said. "For me, Sikkim has always been home. We had an apartment just by the East River in New York, and I was convinced that if I tried hard enough, I could see over the river and over the Atlantic Ocean, all the way across Europe and Asia to Sikkim. I've always known that I would come back."

"And how was it to come back?"

"The first few years were not easy," she said. "I had been raised and educated in the West, and was suddenly back here, in the Third World, as the king's daughter. People here expected me to behave in a certain way, so it wasn't easy for them either. "Oh god, she's down at the river again, fishing in shorts!"" She laughed. "I love hiking in the mountains and often went for long walks, as I had done with my father when I was a girl. And on those walks I'd bump into groups of tourists, and I noticed that what the guides told them was a load of nonsense. We're talking about people who were genuinely interested in Sikkim and had travelled a long way to come here, only to be fed utter rubbish! I needed a job, so I decided to set up my own travel agency. Even though Sikkim is no longer a country, it's important for me that people are told that Sikkim was once an independent kingdom, and that at least some people out there know how things could have been."

"And how could things have been?" I asked.

"You'll find out when you go to Bhutan," Semla said, quietly. "It's so indescribably beautiful there! I love visiting my relatives in Bhutan, but my heart always aches when I come home again to Sikkim."

*

Far from the concrete apartment blocks of Gangtok, one can find a glimpse of what Sikkim might once have been. Semla had organised my transport and I shared the jeep with a young couple from Kolkata, who were going the same way. Even though we climbed higher and higher, it was like driving through a tropical jungle. The sides of the road were thick with flowers and bushes, and the twittering birds competed with the song of the cicadas.

By the Rongyoung River, in a secluded valley that I needed special permission to visit, the environmentalist Gyatso Lepcha runs a tiny family hotel. He welcomed us enthusiastically and immediately offered us tongba, a Sikkimese alcoholic drink made from fermented millet served in a large wooden mug, with boiling water poured over it several times. It tasted slightly yeasty and slipped down without any problem.

"Let me show you something," said the eager Gyatso, and took me over to the terrace where four other tourists, all Indians, were sitting drinking tongba. "Do you recognise them?"

Over the door was a photograph of him standing with Crown Prince Haakon and Crown Princess Mette-Marit.

"They came here in 2010," he said, proudly. "They had made their booking in the normal way, so we had no idea that they were royals! One day the police suddenly turned up and asked why the Norwegian crown prince and his wife were coming to stay with me. I had to tell them the truth: I have no idea! They stayed for some time, so I think they liked it here."

It was easy to like the place. Three dogs wandered around freely and were always happy to be cuddled. We were served home-made food for dinner, prepared with ingredients from the garden. The family grew everything from broccoli, beans, radishes, pumpkin, spinach and tomatoes to papaya, grapefruit and guava, and were pretty much self-sufficient. The simple guest rooms all had open windows that faced the river. I fell asleep to the calming, steady sound of flowing water.

"I was born in this house and have heard the water of the Rong-young River since I was in my mother's womb," Gyatso said the next morning. He spoke in complete, often poetic sentences, without any hesitation, never having to look for words or facts. "Every time I am away, I miss the river. It's as though it's been recorded in my genes. When I heard about the authorities' ambitious plans to build a dam here, I knew immediately that the plans would be catastrophic for the ecology and rivers around here. So instead of working as a lawyer, which is my training, I became a grassroots activist. People had no idea what the dams would mean, they didn't even know what hydroelectricity was. We started to travel around to isolated villages to educate people, and then we increased our activism with a relay hunger strike in Gangtok."

The relay hunger strike started in 2007 and lasted for two and a half years, one of the longest relay hunger strikes in the world. Every day, every hour, the Lepchas sat in a tent on the Tibet Road in Gangtok, on hunger strike. Some did it for four or five days or a fortnight, but the most dogged hunger striker went for ninety-six days without food.

900 MSL   "The authorities had planned to build seven dams here in **Dzongu**, and we at least managed to stop four of them with the hunger strike," Gyatso said. "The Dzongu Valley and Rongyoung River are sacred to the Lepchas. When Sikkim became a Buddhist kingdom in the seventeenth century, we converted to Buddhism, but also continued to worship nature. The Rongyoung River is as sacred to us as the Ganges is to the Hindus. We believe that we come from Kanchen-junga, and when we die, our soul returns to the holy mountain caves and is reunited with our ancestors. The Rongyoung River springs from Kanchenjunga, which is why it is so important to us: it shows our souls the way home. The Lepchas still live in harmony with nature, we are born environmentalists!"

"Are you afraid that the Lepchas may one day disappear?" I asked.

"The fact is that we have already more or less disappeared. We are the indigenous people, we were here first, but now we make up only eight per cent of the population. We're like the tigers, an endangered species. On the red list!"

"Is it true that you went to prison?"

"Yes, I was arrested shortly before we ended the hunger strike," Gyatso said. "It's part and parcel of being an activist. I was in prison for a month. And I learned a lot from it, but the food was terrible, and it was bitterly cold, and I had just got married, only five days before, so the timing wasn't great."

The Indian government has already built fourteen dams in Sikkim, and recently opened Teesta Stage III, one of the largest dams in India.

"Sikkim is only seven thousand square kilometres, so I am deeply worried," Gyatso said. "India has an enormous, almost insatiable need for energy, but the solution is not to tamper with the fragile ecology of the Himalayas. The Indian authorities have plans to build dams in all the rivers in the Himalayas, and the Chinese authorities are doing exactly the same. We protest loudly when the Chinese take our water, but then do the same to Pakistan and Bangladesh."

"What are the local consequences of the dams?" I asked.

"We've had frequent earthquakes in recent years," Gyatso said. "Some people believe that the earthquakes are linked to the dams. I personally don't think so, but the fact is that the consequences of the earthquakes are far worse. We have had more major earthquakes since the large dams have been built. And there is more rain than ever before as a result of global warming. In the monsoon season, the rivers carry enormous amounts of biomass that then sink to the bottom of the reservoirs by the dams and are transformed into methane, which is a far more potent greenhouse gas than carbon dioxide. When you walk past the reservoirs, you can see the methane bubbling up from the bottom. We now have no more than thirty or so free-flowing rivers left in Sikkim. I only hope that we can keep the few free rivers that we have, not only here in Sikkim, but in the world. Rivers don't complain, they don't protest; they can't ask for help, they just give and give. How long can we continue to abuse their silence?"

Of the many small kingdoms that once existed in the Himalayas, which in many ways *were* the Himalayas, only one remains. All the others have been swallowed up by their big, powerful neighbours in the course of the last century of change. Throughout the mountain region, from Hunza in the west to Sikkim in the east, there are empty palaces. Some have been made into museums, others are slowly crumbling. The inhabitants of these small kingdoms no longer have kings, but they do now have roads and hydroelectricity and a centralised school system. And in the process, something invaluable has been lost. Not only the local kings but small, isolated worlds, complete with sacred rivers and holy mountains, have been slowly erased from the map.

Perhaps this is inevitable. Some of the world's major nuclear powers meet in the Himalayas. And the world's two most populous nations are divided here by a thin, dotted line. The small kingdoms never stood a chance in the great geopolitical game.

But one has survived, against all odds.

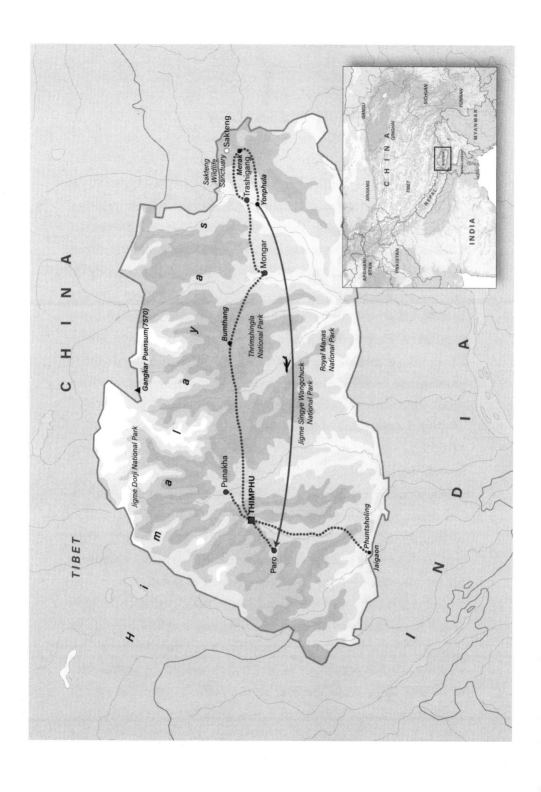

Naked Treasures

The border between India and Bhutan must be one of the strangest in the world. The gateway to Bhutan lies halfway between the Indian town of Jaigaon and the Bhutanese town of **Phuntsholing**, only the two border towns have grown together so one scarcely notices that one has moved from the world's second most populous country to a Buddhist kingdom with fewer than one million inhabitants. In addition, most of the roads in the two towns are one-way, so one has to take a considerable detour to get there, which often entails crossing the invisible border between the towns several times en route, which only amplifies the labyrinthine feeling.

With the exception of Indians, Bangladeshis and, for some reason, Maldivians, all foreign tourists who visit Bhutan must pay a fixed amount per day, equivalent to around USD 250, for an all-inclusive package that covers the guide, car, driver, accommodation and food. The driver and guide met me at the hotel on the Indian side in order to help me navigate my way through the border formalities. They were both wearing traditional Bhutanese clothes, which is obligatory for anyone working in the public sector and tourist industry.

Sonam, the driver, was dressed in the male costume: the gho, which is a kind of woven, knee-length dress that is held together by a thick, tight belt, so that the material creates a voluminous pouch over the stomach which can be used to hold everything from babies to wallets. Knee socks are part of the outfit, but for the sake of comfort, anything goes when it comes to footwear, including trainers. Dechen, the guide, was dressed in a kira, which is the traditional woman's costume. The modern variant consists of a woven, wrap-around skirt that is held up by a belt, but in the past the kira was normally draped over the shoulders and fastened with a brooch, like a dress. The costume includes a long-sleeved blouse and short silk jacket, often in different, but matching colours. The first time I visited Bhutan, I was utterly taken with these exotic outfits and really felt that I had come somewhere different, a special and unique place on earth. But they no longer had the same impact on me, they were already everyday garments. The first impressions of a place and people are priceless, you are open and receptive, and soak up all the unfamiliar details. But the second impression allows you to go deeper, to see beyond the surface.

At the Indian border office in the centre of Jaigaon there were four windows, but nobody at any of them. Dechen managed to find a bespectacled bureaucrat on the next floor, who in turn found another bureaucrat to help us, who another thirty minutes later had managed to turn on the computer and get the system moving. He wearily stamped me out of India.

We drove out of the gigantic republic and into the tiny kingdom. I am not sure when we actually crossed the border itself, but when the shop signs started to be written in Tibetan, I realised we were in Bhutan. No-one knows exactly where the name Bhutan comes from, though it may be an adaptation of the Sanskrit word *Bhota-anta*: "end of Tibet". The Bhutanese themselves call their country Druk Yul: Land of the the Thunder Dragon. The thunder dragon is also the national symbol and has a prominent place on the flag. In the next street, all the signs were written in the Indian Devanagari alphabet, so we were presumably back in India, only to return to the Thunder Dragon's land minutes later. After we had driven up and down and back and forth, following all the one-way streets for some time, we arrived at the tiny immigration office by the Bhutan Gate. The man at the computer was also dressed in a gho. He took my passport from me and started to register me with great respect. With a smile, he adorned an empty page with a triangular stamp and welcomed me to Bhutan.

2334 MSL   **Thimpu**, the capital, lay some two thousand metres higher than Phuntsholing. The road twisted and turned steadily upwards, with green, subtropical vegetation and forest on either side. Bhutan is something of a rarity in that it absorbs more CO_2 than it emits, and one of the reasons for this is that the government has decided that at least sixty per cent of the land mass should be forested. More than seventy per cent of the small kingdom is now covered in trees. Monkeys sat by the side of the road picking each other's fleas as they waited for cars, in the hope that they might be thrown a titbit.

In terms of capitals, Thimpu is not big, with about one hundred and fifteen thousand inhabitants, or about fifteen per cent of the total population. The chances of being born in Bhutan are minuscule. As the capital sprawls over a large area, it actually feels bigger than it is. All the buildings are in the traditional style, with painted wooden details and low sloping roofs, which gives the city a more attractive and holistic feel than Indian cities, where concrete dominates. A policeman stood on a beautifully decorated column in the middle of the city's only major intersection, directing the traffic with soft, fluid movements. We floated by, and soon after reached the hotel. Thimpu is quite probably the only capital in the world without traffic lights.

As I was about to go up to my room, Dechen coughed discreetly behind me.

"I have to tell you something." She looked at me, mortified. "I've been thinking about this all night and day, and I just have to tell you the truth. I can't keep it to myself any longer." She cleared her throat again, and took the plunge. "I've only been to Merak in eastern Bhutan once before, when I was a child, so I'm not sure that I will be a good enough guide for you there. I'm so sorry, but at least now you know."

I assured Dechen that it was not a problem for me and that I was certain we would have an interesting time in Merak.

Dechen's worries were replaced by a relieved smile.

"I had to tell you, I couldn't deceive you," she beamed. "And it's such a relief to have said it."

Later in the evening, Dechen took me for a traditional hot stone bath. The bathing house lay in a field beyond the city centre, below a simple bar where young men in leather jackets and jeans were drinking beer, chewing on chillis and laughing raucously. I was given my own cubicle in the long bathing house. The cubicle was divided in two by a curtain. There was a small bench in the changing room part, where you could leave your clothes, and on the other side of the curtain was a narrow wooden bathtub. A bare bulb on the ceiling provided minimal lighting. The bathtub itself was divided into two chambers, and the outer one had a hatch low down in the wall so the bath attendant could add more hot stones and water without direct contact with the bather. The stones were heated in a fire outside and hissed furiously as they sank into the water. Various herbs floated in the water, mixed with spruce and pine needles and many other plants that I was not able to identify.

Slowly, bit by bit, I lowered myself into the hot, hot water. My heart was thumping in my chest, my skin was burning and prickling, and I was sweating as though I was in a sauna. Hundreds of hours of dust and bumpy roads fell from my limbs and dissolved in the steam. Then, just when I had finally managed to submerge my whole body, the bath attendant put more hot stones in the water. The water bubbled and hissed and I shot up out of the bath and sat on the edge, watching.

"Are you cold?" the bath assistant called. "Do you need more stones?"

"No thank you, not for the moment," I said.

When the water had stopped hissing, I slowly lowered myself back in and allowed myself to relax in the heat. It was completely dark outside by the time I got out of the bath again. My body felt heavy and my head felt light, so I sat on the edge of the bath for a couple of minutes to cool down.

"What are you doing in there? Why are you taking so long?" Dechen asked through the door, clearly concerned. "You mustn't catch cold."

The next morning I got a message that Dechen could not travel with me after all, as her daughter was not well. It was nothing serious – the little girl had a slight temperature and would not sleep – but Dechen's mother did not want to look after a crotchety, sick one-year-old alone. Dechen met me on a street corner to pick up her luggage.

"I'm so sorry," she said, almost in tears.

"Please, don't worry about it," I said. "How is your daughter? Has the doctor seen her yet?"

"We're going to the hospital later on today, but first I have to take her to the temple. I work so much that I haven't had time to take her to the temple often enough. I think that's why she's fallen ill."

Sangye, an energetic, brash man of my age, came east with me instead. The journey to Bumthang was long. There were roadworks everywhere, and the labourers were all skinny Indians in dusty, tattered clothes. There were times when we had to wait for thirty minutes or even an hour before we could move on through the rhododendron forests and over steep mountain passes where thousands of colourful prayer flags hung next to one another. We also drove past litters with fluttering white flags – prayers for the dead. Often only worn tatters remained.

2800 MSL It was dark by the time we arrived in **Bumthang**, which lies more or less in the middle of Bhutan. Bumthang normally has a population of about five thousand people, but that number had tripled for the festival. There were cars and people everywhere, but, unlike in India, there was no hooting. The drivers waited patiently for the traffic jam to unknot itself.

The small square in front of the temple was thronged with people. Muscular monks in saffron silk skirts and grotesque wooden masks danced slowly in a ring round a fire. Four poles stood crossed over the fire, holding up a picture of a goddess. A lone monk sat inside the temple slowing banging his cymbals: *Cling! . . . Cling! . . . Cling!* Thousands of tourists and locals had gathered, and it was hard to find space. A tall Dutch man positioned himself directly behind me and used my shoulder for his camera instead of a tripod. When the goddess went up in flames, he started to adjust the angle of my shoulder to get the best possible pictures.

"It's very good for women to see this ritual," Sangye whispered. "Especially women who can't have children," he added, nonchalantly.

As though they had been given some secret signal, most of the audience suddenly ran towards the open ground behind the temple. There was a door-like structure in the middle: two upright poles with a long pole laid across. It was decorated with spruce branches. A handful of monks approached with burning torches and set the spruce alight. Seconds later, the whole installation was in flames, and people started to run through the burning portal. Round and round and round they ran, again and again, several thousand people shouting and cheering, with their jackets over their head so their hair would not catch fire, old women, young men, children – everyone was running. The minutes ticked by, the flames grew higher and higher, and burning spruce branches fell to the ground, but no-one stopped running until the fire was almost out.

"This ritual is very good for women," Sangye said thoughtfully. "Especially women who can't have children."

The high point of the evening would take place later, but no-one knew exactly when.

"The dancers will come out when they're ready," Sangye said. "They have to drink for courage first."

In the meantime, more people arrived in cars and taxis from outlying valleys. Songs and commotion could be heard inside the temple.

"The dance that will be performed soon was created by the great tantric master, Dorje Lingpa, in the fourteenth century," Sangye said. "He came here to help the locals build a temple, but a swarm of evil spirits played havoc with the work. The master created the dance to distract the spirits, and while they were held mesmerised, the temple was completed. The dance has been performed here in Bumthang every year since, and it is very holy. When the dancers show their treasure, they frighten off evil spirits and bless the audience. All sentient beings come into this world thanks to the treasure."

Sixteen visibly intoxicated men came staggering out of the temple. They had wound long strips of cotton cloth around their heads, so only their eyes were visible. But other than that, they were stark naked. The tantric temple dances are normally performed by young monks, but this particular dance is performed by selected men from the surrounding valleys.

Bumthang lies at close to three thousand metres above sea level, and the night was cold and clear. This had an obvious effect on the "jewels", which shrank and almost disappeared. The dancers gathered around the fire, then stood there tugging and pulling at their penises while jumping up and down to keep warm. Every so often they would loosen up and make indecent, sexual moves against each other. The audience whooped and laughed; they wanted more. The keenest had got there hours before to guarantee a place at the front, and watched the spectacle in reverential silence. Sangye and I had not been fast enough, and had to be thankful for a place much further back. We did not have a great view of the treasure until the sixteen naked men suddenly paraded right past us on their way to one of the other temples. Several of the dancers held their hands protectively over their treasure as they snaked through the crowd.

"Move your hands! Show us your jewels!" people shouted with indignation. Some even hunkered down to get the best possible view.

"It is important to watch the dance with your family," Sangye said. "During the dance, you have to concentrate and focus on the treasure. It will absolve your sins and bless you. It is particularly beneficial for women who can't have children," he said, meaningfully.

When the dancers returned from their round of the other temples, they huddled side by side by the fire to get warm again. Someone in the audience shouted something and moments later the naked men launched themselves furiously at the crowd and started to thrash a young man. People shouted, roared and pushed.

"It's best we go now." Sangye took me by the arm and led me away from the crowd. "I think someone tried to take photographs."

And it turned out that someone had indeed pulled out their phone, but only to check the time. Not that it mattered – the holy dance was definitely over for the night.

The daytime rituals were not as popular. With the exception of some interested older people who had settled themselves on blankets and cushions at the front, with picnic baskets and thermos flasks, the audience consisted of tourists and guides. Like the evening before, one monk played the cymbals while four men in wide, yellow skirts rotated slowly around the square, with theatrical, ritualistic movements. In front of their faces they held heavy, red wooden masks with sharp teeth and bulging eyes.

"This dance was introduced by Padmasambhava in the eighth century," Sangye told me.

The cymbals were still for a moment, then started up again, slow and monotonous: *Cling!* . . . *Cling!* . . . *Cling!*

"This dance was also introduced by Padmasambhava in the eighth century," Sangye said. "The monks have to conquer the evil spirits and capture them in the triangular box that's there on the ground."

Quarter of an hour later, when the evil spirits had been caught and conquered, the dancers disappeared into the temple and a new group came out into the square, also wearing wooden masks and wide, yellow skirts.

"Padmasambhava introduced this dance in the eighth century," Sangye said.

As the dances progressed, the masks became ever more terrifying, culminating in the death dance, where the monks danced with long swords that they dragged along the ground. The black wooden masks had white skulls painted on them. A kind of clown, in a bright red mask and black clothes, raced and leaped around with a huge, red, wooden phallus in his hands. He hit people on the head with it and made vulgar movements in front of the audience, who laughed and threw him money.

"If he touches you with his organ, it will bring you good luck," Sangye said. "Especially women who can't have children." He gave me a meaningful nod.

"Where is everyone?" I asked. "The square was packed yesterday, and now there's only tourists."

"Most people don't spend their time up here," he grinned. "As locals, we have to wear our formal, traditional clothes to get into the temple area. I'll show you later on where they go. Right now, most of them are probably still asleep."

It was surprisingly warm in the afternoon sun, and the tourists retired to the shadows or went back to their hotels. Only the core of old-timers remained, sitting at the front with their thermos flasks watching dance after dance.

Sangye took me over to the temple that the drunk, naked monks had danced around the evening before. The building had been lime-washed, with a red stripe painted just below the yellow roof. The roof itself had an even smaller structure on top, which looked a bit like a treasure chest. The walls were so thick that there was not much room inside, from where large, gilded statues of the Buddha and Padmasambhava gazed at the horizon with narrow, oval eyes.

"This is one of the oldest temples in Bhutan," Sangye said. "In the seventh century, a terrible demon wreaked havoc throughout Tibet and Bhutan. In order to calm her, King Songtsen Gampo, the Tibetan regent, had one hundred and eight temples built in one day, in the year 647. This is one of those temples."

As the sun was setting, and a purplish-blue light settled over the valley, Sangye decided it was time to show me where the rest of the people were. We left the temple compound and went down to the open space behind the car park, where carousels had been set up for the children alongside a number of food tents and stalls that sold everything from water pistols to cheap Indian clothes. Beyond these, I could see people crushed in between the gambling stands. They all offered the same games, with minor variations: you put a 100-ngultrum note or two on a symbol or number, then the dartboard was spun round so quickly that it was impossible to differentiate the symbols from the numbers. One of the players would throw a dart, and if you were lucky he would hit your number. Bands of cheering men had gathered by the booths. Sangye was the only one wearing traditional dress; all the others were in jeans or tracksuit bottoms.

"Strictly speaking, gambling is banned in Bhutan. It's only permitted at festivals such as this," Sangye explained, and put one hundred ngultrum on his lucky number. He lost every single bet. And so did I.

"I should have won today," he said. "It's my birthday. I'm thirty-four. But we don't celebrate birthdays in Bhutan anyway, so it doesn't really matter."

Even though they do not celebrate birthdays in Bhutan, his mobile phone pinged merrily with birthday wishes and greetings. Soon we had almost run out of cash, but had enough to buy a Bhutanese whisky each. It tasted strong and sweet in the evening chill.

We walked back up to the square in plenty of time for the evening's display of the treasure, and were rewarded with excellent places at the front. We could already hear loud singing, nervous laughter and talking from inside the temple. Tourists, grandparents, teenagers and children gathered. After about an hour, the naked dancers had the courage to come out of the temple. They seemed to have warmed up more this evening, though they had absolutely nothing on to warm them, and it did not take long before they were leaping round the square, energetically swinging their treasures up and down, quite literally in front of everyone's noses. One of the dancers had brought a torch and he shone the beam over his comrades' jewels so nothing was left to the imagination. When they returned from the obligatory round of the temples, they seemed to be even wilder, straddling each other and humping away. At regular intervals they went over to the fire and tugged at their treasures to counteract the effects of the cold. Then they turned back to the audience, wiggling, waving, rotating, fully illuminated by the torch beam.

"You should fold your hands and pray for something," Sangye said. "Women without children normally pray to get pregnant," he added helpfully.

The sky was dark and clear, and the waxing moon shone over the temple and the sixteen dancing men. When the last of them had rocked back into the temple, we followed the hordes out to the car park, where we found the car but not the driver. Sangye rang him, and not long after Sonam came running up from the marketplace.

"Did you win or lose?" I asked, but I could already tell from his face what the answer was.

Fairgrounds in every country are suspiciously alike.

The Secretive Forest Ranger

We stopped in **Mongar** on our way east to Merak. The only reason 1600 MSL that tourists occasionally visit this little town is that it is a transit stop between the east and west of Bhutan, and a stopping place on the way to the Indian border in the south-east. But there was nothing to see there. The streets were empty and the houses spread out. A group of men in traditional clothes were playing darts on an open piece of ground by the new hospital, which was also used as a helicopter landing pad. The board they were aiming for was small and about forty metres away, on the other side of the grass.

"The winners go on to the national championships," Sangye said. "Good darts players need enormous mental strength. They need to be able to focus when others are watching."

Most of the darts missed the board, but now and then there was a bullseye, and half the people burst into dance and song.

We carried on to the vegetable market, where chillies were being sold in enormous quantities, as well as guavas, large cucumbers, coriander, aubergines, carrots and other vegetables that thrive at high altitudes – but primarily chillies, which were sold in bags that must have weighed at least a kilo. The Bhutanese love chilli and use it in everything they eat; an average family uses at least a kilo per day. Chillies are laid out to dry everywhere: on roofs, by the roadside, on cars, in the fields. Tourists are generally served blander, tourist-friendly buffet food, without the capsaicin, while the guides and drivers fill their bellies with rice and chilli in the next room. The Bhutanese diaspora often complain about how difficult it is to get good strong chillies abroad, and many of them rely on regular supplies from the homeland. Even children who are still breastfed eat chillies with the same delight that children in other countries eat chocolate.

There was a small monastery at the top of the hill. The houses we passed on the way up were modest, made with any material that was available: corrugated iron, wooden planks, and plastic. A pack of dogs barked in welcome as we entered the monastery grounds. Burgandy capes flapped on the washing line in the afternoon breeze, but there were no monks to be seen. A wrinkled woman with hardly any teeth appeared and offered to show us the temple. She was called Sangye, like my guide. In Bhutan and Tibet, the same first name can be used for boys and girls, and the second name rarely has anything to do with the parents – shared surnames are not usual. And to further complicate things, the Bhutanese have a limited number of first names, about fifty in all.

The monastery complex was only thirty-six years old and one of the most recent in Bhutan. Old Sangye was twice that age. She had lost her husband five years before and started to dress as a nun. She now visited the monastery every day to sweep, change light bulbs, clean and make sure it was kept in good order.

"Soon it will be my turn," she said in a high squeaky voice. "Soon I will die. It's all I think about now. My children – I have seven daughters and one son – have invited me to come and live with them in the capital, but I want to be here. I want to die here."

She sat down on the monastery steps and squinted up at the sun.

"Before, there was no electricity here." She spoke in short sentences, as though the knowledge that she did not have much time left had permeated even her syntax. "No schools either. Or roads. We had to walk everywhere. I have never gone to school. Nor have my children. But *their* children do now. Their lives are easier than ours. But I don't like TV. I grew up without it. I never watch TV. The only thing I think about is that soon I will die."

Kezang, the village astrologer, lived about half an hour's drive from Mongar. He was standing by the side of the road waiting for us, to show us the way up to his simple house on the ridge. It was not a great distance, but it was steep and I could not keep up with him, even though he was at least twice my age.

We entered his dark little house through a well-tended, prolific garden. We came straight into the kitchen, which had open shelving and a couple of electric hotplates. In the living room, which doubled up as the bedroom, Sangye and I were invited to sit down on thin mattresses on the floor. The walls were decorated with calendars from the past ten years, all with pictures of the Buddha and official photographs of the king and queen of Bhutan, and newspaper cuttings about the royal family. There was no glass in the small windows, and the roof, which was made from thin boards, was lined with plastic on the inside for insulation. A large fridge was the most striking piece of furniture in the living room, and there was an old radio on a narrow windowsill. There was no television set.

"People come to me with newborn babies, and when they are ill," Kezang said, unrolling the orange cloth that was wrapped around his astrology book. He sat down gracefully on the floor and put the thick piles of paper down on the table in front of him with great care. His face was wrinkled and weathered, and his eyes were big and kind. When he smiled, he looked like a little boy and an old man at the same time.

"I have no formal education," he said. "I never went to school, but I was a village monk and studied at the monastery."

"That's to say that he lived in the village, but went to the monastery to study every day," Sangye said, who translated everything Kezang said into English. Dzongkha, which is closely related to Tibetan, is the official language of Bhutan, but a total of nineteen different languages and dialects are spoken in the country, which has fewer than eight hundred thousand inhabitants. As Sangye himself was from a village in the east, he and Kezang spoke the same language.

"When I was ready, I went up into the mountains to meditate and pray for three years, as is the tradition," Kezang said. "Only when you've meditated for three years are you qualified to be an astrologist, and only then if the lama gives his consent. The lama set me a test: if I could help three people, I would be allowed to work as an astrologist."

His wife came in from the kitchen and poured warm milk into large cups for us.

"Astrology is complicated," Kezang said. "When sick people come to me, I first have to find out what is making them sick. Is it caused by an evil spirit? And if so, where does it come from? Are they ill because they haven't visited the temple where the protective deity lives? Everything has to be considered. When the cause has been found, one then has to establish which rituals should be performed, and which herbs the patient should take, if there's a need for herbal medicine. In the past, it was the only available treatment, but now we also have to consider whether rituals are enough in themselves, or if the patient also needs Western medicine. The villagers always come to me before they go to the hospital. If your child is possessed by an evil spirit, it can be dangerous to go to a hospital."

"Do you have any children yourself?"

"No." Kezang looked at his wife, who looked at the floor. "It's not because I'm infertile, as my wife has conceived three times. But all the children died when they were tiny. So now we've given up. My wife did everything right when she was pregnant, so it wasn't that. She went to hospital and got checked, and we went to an astrologer as well, and to the temple, and still the children died."

Kezang coughed, and bent over the Tibetan texts.

"When were you born?" he asked. Sangye told him my date of

birth and Kezang sat there and looked things up and read for a long time.

"You won't have any children for a while," he said eventually, even though I had not asked about the possibility of that. "You will not have children until you are around forty-one or forty-two. But you should visit the fertility temple in Punakha and ask the monk to bless you. When you're there, you can pray for a son or a daughter. If you don't go, there's less chance of you having children, so it's crucial that you visit the fertility temple in Punakha. You will meet distractions on the way, but don't be led astray, it is very important that you go there. Otherwise, you're on the right path. You are protected by the gods. You ask them for a lot, but they protect you."

He looked at me earnestly.

"I'm not making this up, you mustn't believe that, everything is here, in the books," he said and pointed at the reams of text on the small table in front of him. "It says here that you will be happy when you see the monks in the temple. The sight of the statues, altars and monks will make you feel happy inside. Perhaps you were a monk or a nun in your former life."

Then he started to mumble. Sangye explained that he was saying a closing prayer to the master and protective deities to protect me and all living beings.

"Do you sometimes have to give people upsetting news?" I asked, when he was finished.

"Yes, now and then, when parents come here with their newborn child and I can see that the child will bring them misfortune, as will the parents to the child," Kezang said. "In situations like that, the child cannot grow up with its parents, but has to be sent to relatives. Fortunately, that doesn't happen very often."

When we had said our goodbyes, Kezang and his wife followed us out of the little house. They filled our pockets with berries from the garden as a farewell gift, and stood watching us as we scrambled down the steep path to the car. They were still standing there when we got in and drove off. The sky over the green mountains was lilac-pink and by the time we got back to Mongar it was dark.

When the sun sets, Bhutan goes to the dogs. Packs of aggressive strays patrolled the centre, and the streets of Mongar felt unsafe, so Sonam drove the short distance from the hotel to the only karaoke bar in town. In a small room at the end of a corridor, three young men in leather jackets sat drinking the local beer. Long red strip lights were the only source of light in the room, and Led Zeppelin had been immortalised on one of the walls by a local graffiti artist. On the far wall was a small TV screen, which was plugged into a karaoke machine. The three young men sang one sad song after another together. It was all "true love" and "broken heart" and "I will never forget you". All the songs were dedicated to named women who sadly were not there to witness the young men's romantic gestures.

After a couple of strong beers and a dozen or so ballads, the young men put down the microphone and wandered home through the dark. The stray dogs continued the night-time concert until day started to dawn.

The next morning, we travelled on through evergreen forests. The further east we went, the more nostalgic Sangye became. He was the youngest of seven children and the only one who had gone to school.

"The school came to the village when I was a boy, but I didn't see the point in sitting still and being hit by the teachers every day," he said with a smile. Sangye smiled almost all the time. He was never serious for more than a moment. "My friends and I used to escape and hide until school was over. It was much more fun being outside and playing."

But one day his game was up: the teacher came to their door and wondered why Sangye had not been to school for a whole week.

"So it was back to school for me. But then my mother died. I was only six or seven. She always had a cough, but no-one knew it was tuberculosis. There was no healthcare to speak of at the time. After she died, things went to pieces. My father remarried and his new wife treated me badly. We had very little money, and we often didn't have enough food or clothes. When the school uniform that I'd been given by the authorities was completely in rags, I stopped going to school again. I had nothing to wear. My sister eventually took me with her to Paro, and I continued my schooling there. My sister didn't have any money either, so after school I would sell betel leaves to get money for shoes and clothes." He smiled, almost apologetically. "I had what you might call a difficult childhood."

The road was so bad for the last few miles that the car barely moved. The unsurfaced road up to Merak was only a few years old, so the fact that it even existed must be seen as progress, but there was plenty of scope for improvement. While Sonam carefully manoeuvred his way along the forest road, Sangye recalled more and more details from his childhood. It was like listening to an old relative talk about the old days, but Sangye was only a year younger than me.

"We didn't have electricity or a toilet," he said. "We lived on the floor above the animals. As children, we would do our business in a corner where there was a hole down to the animals, haha! My parents drank moonshine from morning to evening, everyone in the village did. Us kids too, sometimes. Children are so quiet and easy to look after when they've had a bit to drink! We didn't have shoes, no-one had shoes." He laughed again. "No-one had underwear either, that only came in the mid-1990s. And that's to say, in the capital, not here!"

We were surrounded by pine forest, and there was still no sign of habitation. The speedometer registered nine kilometres an hour.

"When I think about it, though, I actually had a very happy childhood," Sangye concluded. "I miss that time. We had so much freedom as children, we ran around in the village and were always being invited into people's houses. We often had only rice porridge and chilli powder for breakfast, but everyone in the village was poor, so we didn't think anything of it. At school, we wrote with chalk on the blackboard, as we didn't have pens and paper. The teacher hit us if we couldn't remember what we were supposed to have learned, our parents hit us, my sister hit me. I was hit a lot. That's how things were when I was little. Those days are gone now, forever . . ."

Neither Sonam nor Sangye had ever been to Merak, so we kept thinking we were almost there, that Merak was just around the corner, that we would "soon" be there. But "soon" extended into hours, and when we did eventually come to some houses and people, dark was falling.

The east of Bhutan is deemed to be so remote and out of the way that the government gives any tourists who travel here a discount 3215 MSL on the fixed day rate, and **Merak** is one of the most inaccessible villages in the whole of east Bhutan. The local people here are the Brokpa, a tribe that crossed the border from Tibet some four or five hundred years ago. According to legend, they killed their king before migrating south. The king had been so demanding and merciless that he ordered his subjects to grind down a mountain that cast a shadow so he could have sunshine through the palace windows.

We made our way to the only guest house in the village and were invited to sit around the small burner that was in the living room.

"Would you like a little ara to warm you up?" asked the tall young man who welcomed us. The pot of rice spirit was already standing on the burner. He added a couple of spoonfuls of newly churned butter, stirred it around and poured the drink into large mugs. The taste reminded me of sake, except for the melted butter. There was also a pot of boiling water on the small stove, and the lid lifted every now and then to release the steam.

"We always have a pot of water on the stove so the fire doesn't dry out our bodies when we sit around it," Sangye explained. "The fire takes the water from the pot instead."

In other words, the small pot was like a humidifier. A woman in her forties, the proprietor of the guest house, came in with supper, which consisted of red rice and chilli with cheese, dried chilli and salted chilli. She was wearing a traditional black woollen dress and had a wide embroidered belt around her waist. A square of felted wool hung down to cover her behind and the back of her thighs. Around her neck she wore a chunky, colourful necklace and she had pulled short lengths of thread through the holes in her ears. Her hat was flat and round, with six felted-wool plaits that looked like cats' tails sticking out from the black felted-wool edge.

Sangye and Sonam filled their plates with rice, stirred through the chilli and ate with gusto. Outside, the local strays barked and howled like mad dogs.

"It's a good thing they're barking," Sangye remarked as he poured us more ara. "The baying of dogs keeps evil spirits away. Dog is the final incarnation before one is born as a human, so we always treat dogs well. They might be close relatives. If a dog follows you, it's probably a deceased relative."

The young man heated another pot of ara and butter. When I crawled into my sleeping bag later that evening the room was spinning. The bed was rocking. And in the next room, Sonam and Sangye giggled and chatted until late into the night. Outside, under the clear starry sky, the dogs barked as if for dear life.

No evil spirits would dare approach Merak, that was certain.

For breakfast we were given more rice and chilli, served with butter tea, which is black tea mixed with butter and salt. The tea is so nutritious that one needs almost nothing else, but Sonam and Sangye once again filled their plates with rice and ate heartily.

"Do you never tire of rice and chilli?" I asked.

Sangye stopped for a moment, as though the thought had never occurred to him.

"No," he said. "I never feel full if I don't eat rice. And without chilli, it tastes of nothing."

After breakfast we went to the forest ranger's office so I could register. Merak lies in Sakteng Wildlife Sanctuary, and all tourists need special permission to visit the park. I was shown into the head ranger's office, where a middle-aged man in a green uniform noted down all the necessary information and filed it in a ringbinder.

"If I have understood correctly, this is the most easterly wildlife reserve in Bhutan, and one of the newest national parks," I said, and got out my notebook. "Perhaps you could tell me a little more about the reserve?"

"Do you have special permission from the central government to interview me?" the forest ranger asked, with suspicion.

"No, I don't have special permission to interview you in particular," I confessed. "I didn't realise that I needed special permission to talk to you."

"Well, you do, so I'm afraid I can't answer any of your questions," the forest ranger said. He folded his hands on the desk.

"I just wondered what kind of plants grow here, and which animals live here," I said. "Things like that. Basic questions."

"I am not allowed to answer such basic questions without special permission from the central government."

"Why not?"

"It could lead to people coming here for the wrong reasons." He closed his mouth tight as a clam.

"Well, I guess I can look it up on the internet," I said, tetchily, and put my notebook back in my bag.

"Yes," the forest ranger said. He got up from his desk and followed me to the door. Before we left, he said something to Sangye, who nodded seriously.

"What did he say?" I asked.

"Nothing," Sangye said.

We walked aimlessly around the uneven dirt streets, looking for people to talk to. Hammering and sawing could be heard everywhere. Houses were being built, extended, and all from stone and wood, in accordance with traditional methods. Concrete was banned in Merak. The small village was surrounded by forest and gentle slopes, a grey stone wilderness wrapped in green and blue. Other than the construction workers, who were hired in from elsewhere, the streets were empty.

But there was life in the shop. It was a small wonder in itself: a gossip exchange, a bar, an off-licence, a betel-leaf dealer and grocery store. The packed shelves offered everything from sacks of rice and confectionery to Bhutanese whisky. Even though the shop was not very big, there were some benches and a small table so you could take a rest or drink a beer before you went home again. A woman in worn, traditional Brokpa clothes sat spinning wool on a spindle. Her name was Dema and she was forty-six.

"Oh, a lot has changed here since I was young!" she said, without stopping her spinning. "Everything is much easier now. In the old days, the family had to send a messenger if anyone was ill or about to give birth, whereas now we can just call on the telephone. If there's a need for a helicopter, all you have to do is ring! Before, we sometimes had to carry women in labour down to Trashigang. The babies were often born on the way. I had no problems giving birth, but I only have three children. I gave birth to them all here. There was no family planning in the old days, and some families had seventeen children, others twenty. But my husband went in for family planning – he tied his tubes, hahaha!"

The wool was spun and the thread was finished, and Dema was about to leave, but Sangye persuaded her to stay by buying a Druk 11000, the local 8% vol. beer. It was not yet ten in the morning, but she accepted it with a smile and opened the can immediately.

"Have many children do you have?" she asked Sangye.

"One," he said. "A daughter."

"Just one?" Dema looked at him in disbelief. "That's not enough. You have to have more. I got married when I was sixteen. Most people here get married young, but my brother has an education. He was a candidate for DNT, the party that just won the election, and is now an MP!"

She took a large slug of beer and beamed. Her big teeth were red from the betel juice.

"We hope he'll get the road here asphalted, because the one we've got is terrible," she said. "Most of the young people have gone to the town to study, but I like it best here. Where else would I go?"

Dema tilted her head back and drank the rest of the beer.

"My children and my husband are here," she said. "I would never leave my husband. I'd freeze in winter without him!" She laughed loudly, put the beer can down on the table and got up from the low stool. Her shoulders were still shaking with laughter when she went out the door.

As Sangye and I were leaving, we were stopped by an ample young woman with a baby on her back. Unlike most of the other women in Merak, she was wearing Western clothes: jeans and a jacket. Three children of about four or five followed behind her like a tail.

"Would you like to come home with me and talk?" she asked, and to tempt us, added: "I have ara."

We followed her to the small house that she and her husband rented. They were both from Trashigang, the nearest village, but her husband worked for a government food programme and they had now lived in Merak for two years. The young woman put the children on the double bed in the corner, then squatted down by the stove in the middle of the room. Two of the children were her own, and she was looking after the other two for a friend. There were hand-made shelves on the wall laden with cooking oil, rice and pots. The small family only had one room, where they had to do everything.

"Be on your guard," the young woman mumbled as she poured the ara into a pot. I never found out what she was called. "The people round here are dangerous. They poison each other."

"Yes," Sangye said. "I have to admit I was a little nervous as I walked through the village today. The man at the forest ranger's office warned us too."

"Why didn't you say anything?" I asked, thunderstruck.

"I didn't want to worry you," Sangye said.

"A friend of my husband was paralysed after drinking ara with someone here in Merak," the young woman said. "He's still not fully recovered. You mustn't take anything from people here, do you understand? They don't mean to poison you, but they can't help it. The poison is passed from father to son and inhabits them."

"How do you get by here, then?" I asked. "You're not even from here. Do you never accept anything from people?"

"Only from those I know well," the young woman said, gravely. "There's also the risk of physical assault, there's even been deaths. The people here are uneducated, they have lived in the mountains in isolation for hundreds of years, so you have to be careful. The people who live here are not like other people."

She cracked an egg into the pot of ara, and added a goodly amount of butter. Then she poured the mixture into two large mugs. Sangye insisted that she should drink as well, and poured her a large mug. The woman protested, the ara was for us, we were guests, after all, she did not need any, but in the end she was persuaded and accepted the mug.

"It's the custom here," Sangye explained. "I have to serve her, even though she says she doesn't want any."

We had barely tasted the ara before the young woman topped up our mugs with steaming homebrew. I said that I had had more than enough, but she just smiled and gave me even more, until it was in danger of spilling over the edge. As soon as I had taken another sip, she topped me up.

"It's the tradition," Sangye said. "She has to give us at least two refills, otherwise she's a bad host."

The children laughed and sang, and jumped up and down on the bed behind us. The ara relaxed my body, and my head became heavy and warm. Even though I protested, the young woman started to heat another pot.

"Don't worry, the effect wears off as soon as you're out in the cold again. *Pfff*, gone!" Her smile gave way to a more thoughtful expression. "I always wanted to be a singer," she said. "I signed up for *Idol* and even had an audition, but then I got pregnant. I was only sixteen." She poured more ara into our mugs. "My parents were furious, but luckily the father married me. And now here I am . . ."

Before we left, we managed to get her to sing for us. Her voice filled the small room. I had no idea what the song was about, only that it was sad. The children stopped jumping on the bed and sat in silence, listening.

"Before we go, you have to give her some money," Sangye told me.

"Do I have to pay for the ara?" I asked, bewildered.

"No, or yes, I guess. It's the custom here. We always give money when we've had something. She invited us to her home and gave us ara, so we need to give her money. It's expected, not only from tourists, but everyone. Me as well."

I did as he told me, and gave her three hundred ngultrum, around four pounds. At first the young woman refused to accept it, but was soon persuaded.

"Remember to be careful," she said again, as we left. "Don't accept anything to eat or drink from people you don't know!"

The bright afternoon sun hurt my eyes when we emerged. The mountains were moving like waves. We went back to the guest house and ate more rice and chilli. Fortunately, we were given butter tea with it, not ara. We were poisoned enough as it was.

The rest of the afternoon passed in a bit of haze. Sangye and I walked over to the neighbouring village, which was a kilometre away. Burly yaks grazed peacefully in the sunny fields.

A couple of old women were sitting laughing on the grass outside a small house. Their faces were broad and round, their teeth red from betel juice, and their eyes were narrowed into two straight lines, surrounded by a mass of deep wrinkles. They waved to us and called us to join them. When we sat down on the grass, they got up and tottered into the house on unsteady legs. Soon after, they returned with a large bottle of ara and three bowls: one for me, one for Sangye and one for them to share.

"We're sisters, so we can drink from the same bowl," they said, with a smile. The elder sister was called Tsesum and was seventy-seven, and Deng Wangmo, the younger, had just turned seventy.

Cold, and without any egg or butter, the ara was not so easy to drink, despite the sisters' enthusiastic encouragement. No sooner had I taken a sip than they poured me more.

"A lot of tourists have come here recently," Tsesum said. "Maybe ten or so. We serve them ara and some of them give us money, but not all of them. We didn't have money here before, we traded cheese and butter for maize and rice. And rice wasn't so usual either; we used to eat cornbread. We had few kitchen utensils, and no electricity. We only got that seven or eight years ago. Change is needed. Life is easier now!"

Tsesum had had seven children, and six had survived. They all still lived in the village. Her sister had no children, so Tsesum had given her one of her daughters so she would not be alone.

"Now that we've got electricity, we've got TV as well," Tsesum said, and poured some more ara. "Our favourite programme will be starting soon."

Deng Wangmo had already disappeared into the house to watch it. We assumed it was a hint and stood up to leave.

"No, no, you mustn't go. Come and watch the show with us!" Tsesum said. "You will need to warm yourselves up again anyway before you go."

Deng Wangmo had lit the fire in the stove and it was already warm and toasty in the small room. Two puppies and a black cat were lying on a blanket by the stove. Both sisters watched the small television, which stood on a chest of drawers, with reverence. It was flanked by pictures of the royal family. On the screen, a young man in traditional clothes was standing alone on a stage singing against a blue background.

"Is it *Idol?*" I asked.

Sangye shook his head. "We do have *Idol*, but this is not a competition," he said. "This is a programme where young people with problems – who are unemployed, say – can sing on television. The idea is that the experience will give them more confidence to look for a job, for example."

Tsesum put out a plate of dried yak cheese and the village's famous fermented cheese, and insisted that we try them both. The fermented cheese tasted a bit like a cross between sour milk and Roquefort, and was actually not bad at all. We were given more ara to wash it down. One singer appeared after the other on the television screen, and I soon struggled to distinguish between them. With their eyes glued to their favourite song show, Tsesum and Deng Wangmo twisted wicks for the butter lamps they would use the next day.

"Tomorrow is a big day," Sangye said. "It's the Day of the Buddha's Descent and Mother's Day." He took a good sip of the cold ara. "I can't remember what my mother looked like. I have no photos of her. After she died, my sister contacted an astrologer. He told us that our mother would be reborn as a cow. I've heard that the cow – my mother – is still alive, but in a village that's far away."

Before we left, I gave the two sisters two hundred ngultrum each. They accepted the money with a big smile and stuffed the banknotes in their pockets.

Sangye and I headed back to Merak. The sky was golden-pink and it would soon be dark. The wind stung my cheeks and I shivered. As soon as the sun went down, the mountain air was raw and cold. The ground undulated and the mountainside danced. There were double the number of yaks in the field.

Lam Ramchen, the mayor of Merak, had business in Trashigang, so got a lift with us the following morning. He was fifty-two, with a broad, furrowed face, and he wore a camouflage-patterned winter coat. His teeth were stained red from the betel leaves he constantly chewed and spat out.

"Life in Merak has changed dramatically," he said. "Everything is much easier now, but people are less fit as a result, as they don't walk anywhere now. And some suffer from diabetes. No-one was ever ill here before."

Such are the blessings of modern life. Roads and electricity have made life easier and more comfortable; the whole world is available on a screen; and young people are no longer restricted to village life but have the possibility to seek happiness elsewhere, which many do. Journalists and experts expressed their concern about what might happen to the unique Brokpa culture when the road was built, but no culture is a museum. Who would want to swap an ambulance helicopter, education, working lights and well-stocked shops for heavy physical work, potentially life-threatening births in the forest, miles from the nearest hospital, and dark, smoky living quarters?

But in the same way that culture is not a museum, it is not a fragile flower. It does not wither and die simply because it is exposed to exhaust and electricity.

The mayor wound down the car window and spat out the old betel leaves and popped a new portion in his mouth.

"Have you heard about the poison?" he asked, in a hushed voice. "Three or four families in the village have it. Sometimes people even poison their own spouse or children without meaning to. Those who carry the poison can do nothing about it. Whether you fall ill or not from food offered by those who carry the poison depends on how strong you are. I've never got ill, even though I've eaten and drunk with the families, but lots of people try to avoid them."

"What do you do if you fall ill?" I asked.

"If you get a bad tummy after eating something from someone who has the poison, a shaman has to make a small cut in the skin on your belly and suck out the poisoned blood. But it doesn't always help. So many strange things happen in these parts. It's because it's so untouched, so isolated. For example, at the moment I'm writing a research paper about yetis . . ."

"Yetis?" I echoed.

"Yes, there are lots of yetis around here," Lam Ranchen said. "Only last year a young health worker disappeared without trace from the village. They found his clothes neatly folded, but they never found his body. The police searched for weeks on end. He had no doubt been abducted by a yeti woman who wanted him as her husband."

"Have you ever seen a yeti yourself?" I asked.

"No, but I have seen traces of them. Their footprints are enormous. They have long toes and a short heel. Sometimes they change their footprints to look like horse or cow hooves. Lots of people in the villages around here have seen yetis, and every now and then they burn down large areas of forest to drive them out. Not that long ago, a yeti was killed by some villagers. They buried it and told the local authorities what had happened. The authorities asked them to bring the body in, but when they dug up the grave, the yeti had gone . . ."

1500 MSL   The car journey back to **Trashigang** was so slow that it might have been faster to walk, but I did learn something new about yetis for each kilometre we descended. Yetis have a largely vegetarian diet, but they like to drink blood – from time to time the villagers found dead yaks that were completely shrivelled up, their flesh white and bloodless. If you are unlucky, or lucky, enough to meet a yeti, you first have to establish what sex it is. If it is a male, you have to run uphill, because male yetis have long hair and will trip on it. If it is a female, you have to run downhill, because female yetis have such big breasts that it is hard for them to run downhill without falling.

No-one has yet found irrefutable evidence that yetis exist, but there is no shortage of anecdotes and observations.

For example, on one of his many Everest expeditions, Eric Shipton, the British consul general who discovered the arch outside Kashgar, came across some mysterious footprints at about six thousand metres. The photograph of these footprints is still reckoned by many to be the best proof to date that yetis exist.

In spring 2019, there was something of a sensation when the Indian army posted a photograph on Twitter of some mysterious footprints that the company had come across during an expedition in the Himalayas. The soldiers concluded that they must be yeti footprints. They were both mocked and criticised in the harshest terms for spreading such stories.

"It is so arrogant of people to believe that we know everything," said Tshering Tashi, an author I met some weeks later, shortly before I left Bhutan. "The takin, our national animal, was considered to be a mythological animal for a long time. But then it was proved that it did exist, it just looks rather odd. Scientists also thought that the blue poppy was a mythological flower until 1932!* We have more

---

* Tshering Tashi was not entirely correct here, and not without reason, as information does vary. However, it seems that the Himalayan blue poppy was first described by a French missionary in 1886, and was formally named *Meconopsis betonicifolia* in 1912.

than seven hundred different bird species here in Bhutan, and ornithologists are constantly discovering new species. Our ornithologists are lazy; they wander off into the forest for a walk, and when they come home they've discovered a new bird. If the yeti exists, it will be here in Bhutan. Yetis are shy, but there is so much untouched nature here. They're moving slowly north-east, to where there is the most real wilderness."

It started to dawn on me why the forest ranger in Merak had been so unhelpful. However, it turned out that the national tourist council was not as secretive. "The sanctuary is home to people of isolated nomadic tribes," it said on the website. "The reserve is characterised by thick carpets of rhododendrons, and in its habitat roam snow leopards, red pandas, Himalayan black bears, barking deer, Himalayan red fox, the hoary-bellied Himalayan squirrel and even the mythical Yeti (or Abominable Snowman)."

I had seen neither hide nor hair of a yeti, male or female, during my stay in the sanctuary, but nor had I seen a single snow leopard, red panda, black bear, barking deer, Himalayan red fox or hoary-bellied squirrel.

Gross National Happiness

The airport in **Yonphula** was so small that it took a while before I spotted it. The modest square building housed offices, a check-in hall and waiting area, and a superstructure on the first floor that served as the control tower. A woman weighed my luggage, stuck on a label that said *Security Checked* and made a quick inspection of my hand luggage.

"Drink up your water before you board," she said. "Have a nice flight."

I said goodbye to Sangye and Sonam, and went up the stairs into the small aircraft. The pilot, a tall, fair European in his sixties, stood and chatted with the passengers out on the runway before taking his place behind the controls.

The sun shone down from a cloudless sky, and from the oval airplane window, I had a clear view of the forested slopes and snow-covered peaks. Bhutan is about the same size as Switzerland, but has a far more varied topography: in the lowlands to the south by the border with India it is warm and humid, whereas the central belt is full of green hills and low mountains. The flora and fauna are remarkably rich – everything from the rhinoceros to the snow leopard can be found within its borders, and botanists have identified more than five and a half thousand plant species, including more than four hundred different orchids and forty-six varieties of rhododendron. The northern border with the Tibetan plateau is dominated by the ice-capped Himalayas. Gangkhar Puensum is the highest mountain in Bhutan, and at 7,570 metres it is also the highest mountain in the world that has never been conquered. The Bhutanese government has issued a ban on climbing any mountain higher than six thousand metres, in order not to disturb the gods and spirits that live at high altitudes.

The flight attendant handed out snacks and the day's edition of *Kuensel*, which is Bhutan's oldest and, until recently, only newspaper. The front page carried a large picture of the king surrounded by soldiers from the Royal Bhutan Army. The newspaper was celebrating the eleventh anniversary of the coronation of His Majesty Druk Gyalpo Jigme Khesar Namgyel Wangchuck, popularly known as the People's King. In the editorial, the newspaper took the opportunity to reprint parts of his coronation speech:

"Throughout my reign I will never rule you as a king. I will protect you as a parent, care for you as a brother and serve you as a son. I shall give you everything and keep nothing . . ."[6]

Druk Gyalpo means "dragon king" and Jigme Khesar Namgyel Wangchuck is the fifth dragon king in the Wangchuck dynasty, which came to power in 1907.

Little is known about Bhutan's early history, as nearly all the state archives were destroyed in a fire at the start of the nineteenth century. What is known is that Bhutan was united as one kingdom in about 1630, under the rule of the Tibetan lama Ngawang Namgyal, often simply called The Unifier. He ran into problems in his home country, so settled in western Bhutan, quickly gaining control over the most important and populated valleys. Many of the *dzongs* – combined fort, administrative building and monastery – that are to be found in Bhutan were established in this period. Ngawang Namgyal died in 1651, but in order to avoid a return to the lawless conditions that prevailed prior to unification, the local governors agreed to keep his death a secret. And they did so successfully, for fifty-four years.

The eighteenth and nineteenth centuries were dominated by border conflicts and internal power struggles. In 1865, after the Duar

War with British India, Bhutan was forced to cede some of its territories in the south. During the internal power struggles and civil wars that followed, Ugyen Wangchuck, the governor of Trongsa in central Bhutan, became a powerful man. In 1907, the leading lamas and other governors voted unanimously to make him a hereditary king. Ugyen Wangchuck worked closely with the British and in 1910 signed a treaty which gave them control of Bhutan's foreign policy in return for military protection. In 1949, India formally took over this role: if a foreign power attacks Bhutan, it will be seen as an attack on India. Unlike Sikkim, Bhutan has maintained a good and fruitful working relationship with India without having to compromise its independence, and in 1971 the country became a member of the UN.

Bhutan is in many ways an oddity, almost an anachronism. Despite the close working relationship with Great Britain and then with India, the country has never been a colony and is today the only remaining kingdom in the Himalayas. The first two kings in the Wangchuck dynasty were absolute monarchs, and Bhutan was almost entirely isolated from the outside world. About ninety per cent of the population were farmers, and the multitude of monasteries held considerable power and influence. Public health was generally poor, and there were no schools, hospitals or judiciary, nor was there any form of constitution. The written language was classical Tibetan, and only a few monks could read and write; the rest of the population was basically illiterate. There was no monetary economy and all trade was based on bartering.

The third dragon king, Jigme Dorji Wangchuck, was only twenty-two when he ascended the throne in 1952. He had attended a British school in India and visited several European countries, and was determined to modernise Bhutan. Starting almost from scratch, the young king built schools, hospitals and roads with the support of the Indian government, which was glad to have an ally on the border with China. He established the country's first national assembly, as a first step towards limiting the absolute power of the king, and abolished slavery, which had been widespread in Bhutan. In 1968, the country's first bank opened and six years later, the national currency, the ngultrum, was introduced. The ngultrum is pegged to the Indian rupee at parity – a clear indication of the close economic cooperation between India and Bhutan. The rupee is also legal tender in Bhutan and India is still Bhutan's most important trading partner: close to eighty per cent of foreign trade is with its big brother in the south.

In 1972, King Jigme Dorji Wangchuck died in a British hospital in Nairobi. He was only forty-three, but had suffered from heart problems for many years. His eldest son, Jigme Singye Wangchuck, was crowned king two years later, at the tender age of eighteen. In 1979, the fourth king married four sisters in a private ceremony, as advised by astrologists. His wives together gave him ten children.

Jigme Singye Wangchuck carried on his father's work, and continued to modernise and democratise the country. The modernisation of Bhutan has been a gradual and controlled process, unlike that of many other Asian countries. The authorities have tried to balance the need for progress and change with the preservation of Bhutanese culture. For example, television and the internet were not introduced in the country until 1999, and there are severe restrictions on architecture and building styles. It is extremely difficult for foreigners to be granted citizenship – one has first to have lived in the country for at least fifteen years, be fluent in spoken and written Dzongkha, and have a good knowledge of Bhutan's history and culture. A child will only automatically be given a Bhutanese passport if both parents are Bhutanese citizens.

This policy of cultural preservation has been particularly detrimental to the Nepalese-speaking population in the south of Bhutan. The country's population can be divided into three main groups: the Sharcops, the Ngalops and the Nepalese. The Sharcops are an Indo-Mongoloid people who migrated to Bhutan from neighbouring areas in India and Burma around three thousand years ago, and they primarily live in the east of Bhutan. The Ngalops mostly live in the west and migrated from Tibet in the ninth century – in Sikkim, they are known as the Bhutia. The Ngalops and Sharcops, who are predominantly Buddhists, together account for about half the population and dominate in politics and culture. Approximately a third of the population are Hindus and have Nepalese as their mother tongue. They are known as Lhotshampa, which means "people from the south" in Dzongkha.

In Sikkim, the Buddhist Tibetan population was outnumbered by the Hindu Nepalese, which in the end resulted in the small kingdom being swallowed by India. The Bhutanese authorities presumably feared that something similar might happen to them, and in the 1980s implemented the "One Nation, One People" policy. Nepalese was dropped as a classroom language in state schools and all citizens were forced to adopt the traditional national dress, the gho and kira, as daily attire. Many of the Lhotshampa have lived in Bhutan for generations, but not all of them had papers to prove that. Families that could not prove formal ownership of the ground where they lived, or prove that they had paid their taxes as far back as the 1950s, were refused citizenship. At the start of the 1990s more than a hundred thousand Nepalese-speaking Lhotshampa were driven from Bhutan and ended up in refugee camps in eastern Nepal. Nepal does not give citizenship to refugees, so they were stateless. Most of the refugees have now been given a home in a third country, the majority in the USA, but some seven thousand Bhutanese refugees still live in camps in Nepal.

In 2006, after thirty-two years on the throne, Jigme Singye Wangchuck abdicated in favour of his eldest son, the 26-year-old Jigme Khesar Namgyel Wangchuck. At the same time that he left the throne to his son, he stripped him of much of his power: the retiring monarch had decided that the country would switch from being an absolute monarchy to a constitutional monarchy. The first election in Bhutan's history was held on New Year's Eve 2007, giving the country its first democratically elected government. Since then, a further two elections have been held and a new government has been voted in each time.

The national newspaper, the *Kuensel*, reported: "The special bonding between the monarch and the people is ever strong. It is our good fortune to have our People's King to lead, inspire, and serve us. The unprecedented peace, harmony and progress achieved in the last decade can be attributed to His Majesty's unwavering resolution to serve His people. During the past decade, His Majesty steered the nation with steadfast attention and brilliance as the democratisation process began to unfold unprecedented experiences in the country with changes in the polity, economy and Bhutanese behaviour. With a smooth transition to democratic constitutional monarchy form of government and the three successful general elections, democracy is deepening and the future looks more promising. On this auspicious Coronation Day, the nation offers prayers for His Majesty's good health and long life. May Drukyul continue to enjoy peace and tranquillity, security and sovereignty, happiness and prosperity for ever."[7]

In among the green far below, I spotted an enormous, golden statue of the Buddha. The pilot slowed down and started the descent. We were told to fasten our seat belts and straighten our seats. The runway at Paro is surrounded by high mountains and is considered so technically challenging that only seventeen pilots have permission to land there. I caught a glimpse of the long strip, then the airplane banked and all I could see was the sky and mountain tops. A few seconds later, the wheels hit the ground.

3120 MSL   A trip to Bhutan is not complete without a visit to the **Tiger's Nest**, the monastery that clings to a cliff above Paro. Dechen, the guide who had come to meet me at the Indian border, followed me up the steep, sandy path. The visit to the temple had worked, and her daughter was her usual sunny self once again.

It took us an hour and a half to get to the monastery. Along the way, we passed countless prayer flags, fluttering piously in the wind among the evergreen pines.

"How many times have you climbed this hill?" I asked, out of breath.

"Hundreds!" Dechen smiled. "But it's just as magical every time." And she sounded like she meant it. It was only when we reached the same height as the monastery that we could see it, and it truly was a magical sight: the white, red and yellow buildings seemed to grow out of the sheer rock face – they seemed almost to be floating. Legend has it that the monastery was carried up on the backs of dakinis, sacred female spirits, and is tied to the cliff with their hair.

"In the eighth century, Padmasambhava flew here from Tibet on the back of a she-tiger," Dechen told me. "He meditated in a cave here for three years, three months and three days, and managed to tame all the evil spirits that were preventing Buddhism from spreading in the Himalayas. A thousand years later, in 1692, a monastery was built near the cave where he meditated."

The Pakistani archaeologist whom I met in Swat Valley had been right: I came across Padmasambhava, also known as Guru Rinpoche, everywhere in the Buddhist Himalayas. The tantric master is particularly revered in Bhutan: Padmasambhava is the country's spiritual father, the most significant deity and, without a doubt, the most important historical figure.

The stories of Padmasambhava's life are so interwoven with fantastical legend that it is difficult to separate the man from the myth. The master was supposedly born on a lotus flower in the kingdom of Oddiyana, in what is now the Swat Valley in Pakistan, and grew up as the foster son of King Indrabodhi, who had no children of his own. As a young man, he left the kingdom and wandered as an ascetic through India, where he experimented with different tantric traditions and black magic, studied sciences and was a disciple to several different gurus. It soon became apparent that he had special powers and could subdue and tame frightening demons where other masters had failed. King Trisong Detsen of Tibet heard about Padmasambhava's merits and invited him to come north of the Himalayas. The king hoped that the mighty master would be able to tame the spirits and demons that made it impossible to establish Buddhist monasteries in Tibet. Every time he tried to build a monastery, it burned down or was destroyed in some other way. Padmasambhava did manage to do what no-one else had done before: subdue the bothersome demons. In 779, the Samye Monastery, the first Buddhist monastery in Tibet, was finally consecrated.

Padmasambhava is also recognised as the founder of the Nyingma School, the oldest of the four schools of Tibetan Buddhism, but no matter which school they follow, Buddhists throughout Bhutan see Padmasambhava as the most important master and spiritual leader. They recognise him as a reincarnation of the Buddha, and he is therefore often called the Second Buddha. Padmasambhava visited every nook and cranny in Bhutan, and has left his mark everywhere: mystic footprints in stone, the dances and mantras that he taught, caves where he meditated, temples he had built or that were built to praise him. Of all the temples built in his honour, Paro Taktsang, the Tiger's Nest, is the most famous and is regarded as one of the holiest places of pilgrimage in the Himalayas.

We had to climb a long, steep staircase to get to the monastery itself. We took off our shoes and stepped into the sacred space. Dechen stopped in front of a large stone that was leaning against the red-painted monastery wall.

"Close your eyes and walk forwards with your thumb stretched out in front of you," she said. "If you hit the black point on the stone, you have good karma and are close to your parents."

I missed by a good margin.

Outside the cave where Padmasambhava had meditated for more than three years, Dechen prostrated herself three times as she mumbled mantras with great concentration. The cave itself is only open one day a year. There were three dice beside the altar.

"Lift them to your forehead, wish for something and throw," Dechen said. I did as she told me, and got fourteen. Neither of us knew whether this was good or bad, but we hoped for the best and carried on to the next temple, which was dedicated to an enormous, golden statue of Padmasambhava. The master is generally easy to recognise thanks to his thin moustache – unless he is appearing in one of his eight other manifestations. Here Dechen prostrated herself six times with her hands pressed together over her head, first to the lama's empty throne and then to Padmasambhava, as she continued to say mantras under her breath.

A monk was sitting partially hidden by a curtain, fiddling with his mobile phone. Dechen grabbed her chance. "She threw the three dice and got fourteen," she said. "Is that a good number?"

"It's a perfectly good number, but ten or eleven would have been even better," the monk said. "Try again! Everyone has three tries."

"What if I get an even worse number next time?" I objected.

"Doesn't matter," the monk assured me. "It's the best number that counts."

The various chapels were separated by steep, wide steps that were sheltered by simple corrugated-iron roofs. The monastery was in fact a labyrinth, and every staircase led to another altar where hundreds of butter lamps cast flickering shadows. A steep, rickety ladder led from a narrow crevice in the rock down to a small, low cave. We negotiated our way down and wriggled through the cave to an outside platform, from where we had a view up to the temple, which floated above our heads, and down the vertical mountainside. A black cat slipped round a corner and disappeared.

The monastery was built in 1692, but the temples we visited and the statues we admired were new. In 1998, a fire ripped through most of the monastery, and only the main temple, by Padmasambhava's meditation cave, survived. The fire was in all likelihood caused by a butter lamp or an electrical fault, but no-one knows for certain. The monastery was rebuilt and consecrated in 2005 by the new king.

Before we put our shoes back on and started on the downward trek, we went back to Padmasambhava's cave. I touched the dice to my forehead, made the same wish as before and threw them.

This time I got ten.

2559 MSL   In the evening, we went to a *drayang*, a kind of dance bar, in **Paro**. It was in a cellar and the clientele was for the most part young men in black leather jackets and jeans. There was a young woman on the stage dressed in a traditional kira. She moved her arms in time to the music as she wandered back and forth across the stage, smiling. The music was loud and felt both familiar and unfamiliar at the same time; modern, digitised pop music sounds more or less the same throughout the world, even when it's performed in Dzongkha. Dechen and I found a vacant sofa and ordered a beer each.

"*Drayangs* were introduced by the fourth king so that girls who couldn't work anywhere else had the opportunity to earn money." Dechen had to shout to be heard over the music. Soon after, a young girl in a green kira came over to our table and asked if we had any requests.

"Dance for Erika and Dechen!" Dechen said, and gave the girl two hundred ngultrum, which is about two pounds sterling. She wrote our names down in her notebook. Meanwhile, another girl had got up on stage and was dancing as innocently and modestly as the first. I could not distinguish one song from the next: they all sounded the same to me. When the applause had stopped, it was the girl in the green kira's turn. She announced that the next song was dedicated to Erika and Dechen, and started to walk back and forth across the stage, moving her arms.

All the dancers were young and sweet, and looked alike. Only one of them stood out. She had long, straight hair, regular, doll-like features, and full lips. But unlike the other girls, she wore practically no make-up. She was wearing a traditional kira, but the jacket was made from a thin, transparent material so you could see her singlet underneath.

She was called Dechen, like my guide, and she invited us to her house the next day.

She lived just outside the centre of town, in a big house that she rented alone. Even though she had plenty of rooms to choose from, she only used one. She had everything she needed in there: a mattress, a small television, an electric kettle, cups and plates, a heater, a furry kitten and a few framed pictures of herself. There was a large photograph of the fifth king beside a Buddhist altar by the entrance.

We sat down on the floor and Dechen served us coffee that she had made before we arrived. She was wearing tracksuit bottoms and a yellow T-shirt with *Good things take time* on it. Her shoulder-length hair was loose. She was twenty-eight, but looked about ten years younger.

"I have six brothers and sisters, but my little brother is the only one who has gone to school," Dechen said in Dzongkha. She spoke no English, so Dechen the Guide had to interpret for her. "My parents couldn't afford to send the rest of us to school. When I was fifteen, I did one year at college and learned the alphabet, but I didn't manage to do more. My mother was only twelve or thirteen when she married my father, who worked for the army. When he retired, we moved into a small house that we rented from the army."

She spoke quietly, in almost a whisper, and smiled all the time, even though her story was far from happy.

"My parents never told us about when they were young, but I don't think they had good childhoods. I don't remember much from my own either. We stuck together as children, but it was never really much of a home. Our parents argued all the time and they drank. We only had two rooms: my parents slept in the altar room, and the children in the other. Sometimes we had good food, other times not. My father beat us when he was drunk."

"Do you have any good memories from your childhood?" I asked.

Dechen thought about it for some time.

"I played with my friends. That's a good memory. But otherwise, I'm not sure there were many. I was sent to Thimpu when I was nine. My parents couldn't afford to have me at home, so they sent me to someone else."

"Relatives?" I asked.

"No, to strangers, to families where I could work as a childminder. In addition to looking after the children, I did the washing up, tended the animals and did anything else that needed doing. I lived with different families for six years. I lived with so many that I can't separate them all out in my mind. If I did anything wrong, I was beaten, so I'd run home to my parents every time I broke a cup or didn't manage to stop the animals from getting onto the neighbour's land. The father in one of the families made advances to me when his wife was out. I screamed so loudly that he got scared, but I couldn't complain, so I left instead. I got five hundred a month for my work, but never saw any of it. It all went towards my little brother's education."

When Dechen was fifteen, she moved back in with her parents and started going to college. There she met and fell in love with a boy who was seven years older.

"I thought it would be better to marry him than to stay at home," she said, quietly. "Maybe I could build a better life with him, I thought. We moved in together, and I got pregnant almost straight away. When I was five months pregnant, he said he would go to Thimpu to look for a job. He never came back, and eventually I went to look for him. That was when I discovered that he already had a wife in Thimpu."

"What did you do?" Dechen asked, upset on behalf of her name-sake.

"Nothing," Dechen whispered, and shrugged. "I had no family to support me, I was alone. I blamed myself and assumed I deserved it. It was my karma. If he was happy in Thimpu, that was good for him, and it would be best if he was allowed to get on with his life in peace. That's what I thought. But I was in a very difficult situation. When I realised I was pregnant, my father suggested that I go to India and have an abortion, but that was never an option for me."

Dechen had no choice other than to move back to her parents, even though she still had a bad relationship with them.

"When the baby was born, the situation got even worse," she said. "I couldn't work, because I couldn't leave the baby, and we often didn't have enough to eat. My brothers and sisters had all moved out, so I was alone with my parents and the baby. After a year, I started to go into town to sell the vegetables we grew on our tiny patch. And with the money I earned, I finally managed to rent a tiny place of my own. But then, after a year in the city, where I made a living selling vegetables, my mother asked me to come home again. So I did."

"What?" Dechen the Guide was horrified. "Why did you go back to your parents when you were managing fine on your own?"

"Because my parents asked me to," the other Dechen said calmly. "The situation was a bit easier as my son was older, so I could work in the fields again. One day, I heard on the radio that there were jobs available for dancers at a *drayang* in Thimpu. I was tempted, but didn't do anything about it. A year later, when the situation at home had become almost unbearable, I mustered my courage and applied for a job as a dancer at Kalapinka, the famous *drayang* in Thimpu. And I've worked as a dancer for ten years now. I like dancing and I love my job."

She poured us more coffee, and with downcast eyes continued her story.

"Of course people talk about us, and we sometimes have to deal with drunk men who ask things of us, but what I choose to do is up to me. I always say no. Even though I don't have an education, I earn more than many who have studied at university for years, and I only work for four or five hours a night."

As she worked in the evening, her son, who was twelve, went to boarding school. She only saw him at the weekend. Her father, who was now about seventy, had stopped drinking when his new wife died from alcoholism. Her little brother had graduated from the prestigious state university.

"Seven years ago, I met a man," Dechen said. "We were together for six years, but seven months ago he left me. His parents wouldn't have me as their daughter-in-law."

"Are you angry with him?" Dechen no. 1 asked, indignant on behalf of the young woman.

"No," Dechen no. 2 said, with a bashful smile. "I blame myself. This is my fate, my karma. That's what I think."

"Do you have any plans to do anything with your life other than dance?" I asked.

"I might open my own shop one day, that's always been a dream. But for the moment I'm happy as a dancer. It's important to build a good relationship with the clients over time so they keep coming back and paying for requests, because I get sixty per cent of what I earn from requests."

"Have any of the clients fallen in love with you?" I asked.

"It happens all the time," Dechen said. "But I don't believe that they mean what they say. I've lost all trust in men."

Was Dechen happy? I never asked. It seemed too personal, almost rude, and how does one measure one's happiness anyway?

In Bhutan, the measure of happiness has been developed into a science and a national philosophy. In 1972, Jigme Singye Wangchuck, the fourth king, who was still a teenager at the time, declared that gross national happiness was more important than gross domestic product. Since then, the idea has been developed, and when Bhutan's first constitution was drawn up in 2008, it was incorporated in Article 9, paragraph 2: "The State shall strive to promote those conditions that will enable the pursuit of Gross National Happiness." Every new law that is passed must first be approved by the Committee for Gross National Happiness in order to ensure that it is in line with prioritising happiness over economic growth.

But how does one measure national happiness?

"Gross national happiness is something entirely different from what people in the West think of as happiness," explained Karma Wangi, from the Centre for Bhutan Studies and GNH Research in **Thimpu**. "The simplest explanation is that we prioritise things 2334 MSL that are of essential importance to people's well-being and happiness. We have divided gross national happiness into four pillars: fair and sustainable socio-economic development; good governance; environmental conservation; and the preservation and promotion of culture. This does not mean that we're not concerned about economic growth, only that it's not our primary concern. In fact, Bhutan's economy has recorded impressive growth in the past four decades, with an annual growth rate of more than seven per cent."

"Gross domestic product is relatively easy to measure, but how do you measure gross national happiness, in practice?" I asked.

"We measure a total of nine different domains," Karma replied and rattled them off quickly. "Living standards, education, health, environment, community vitality, time use, psychological well-being, good governance, and cultural diversity and resilience. And in order to measure these nine domains, we have developed one hundred and twenty-four variables which are integrated into thirty-three indicators, then divided between the nine domains. Finally, once we have measured all the variables, we end up with a single score."

"That sounds complicated," I said.

"It's detailed, but not complicated," Karma said. "One of the variables, for example, is access to clean water. And for psychological well-being, we have a variable for karmic consequences. Everything we do has consequences for the people around us, doesn't it? We ask people to bear this in mind when they make decisions. We also ask about emotions. We've identified five positive emotions and ask if people have experienced any of these feelings in the past thirty days. Time is also important, so we ask people how they use their time. If people work a lot and are always stressed, it impacts their quality of life. Our definition of happiness is broad."

"Bhutan has become richer in purely financial terms in recent years, but have people also become happier?"

"We've seen developments in fields such as health and material wealth. Medicine and healthcare are free for everyone, and we have managed to increase life expectancy from around fifty to over seventy in the past thirty to forty years. But in the softer, more personal fields, things are not going so well. The feeling of psychological well-being has fallen. Local community doesn't play the same role as before and people interact with people far less, in the towns in particular. People are more stressed than before. The difference between life in the country and life in towns is too great, as is the difference between men and women. According to our surveys, women spend twice as much time on housework as men. Unemployment is another problem. There is only two per cent unemployment over the population as a whole, but among young people it's as high as eight per cent. That's not necessarily because there aren't enough jobs, but rather because a lot of young people now have a higher level of education and therefore are not interested in heavy manual labour. So, even though youth unemployment is high, we're dependent on guest workers from India to make the wheels go round."

"Bhutan is pretty low on the list for global happiness surveys, far behind most European and many Asian countries," I said.

In the 2019 annual UN happiness index, Bhutan is ranked 95, behind Pakistan at 75 and China at 86.

"Only around nine per cent of the people in Bhutan have said that they are *not* happy," Karma said. "That is a very low proportion, in my opinion."

*

Ngawang, who had a different name at the time, was deeply unhappy growing up. When she was twenty-one, she became psychotic. In her dreams, she saw places she had never been to; all she could think about was the past and these places, though she had no idea where they even were. She fell into a trance and lost all consciousness, and later could not explain what had happened. People laughed at her and said she was making it all up. Her family were desperate and took her to various hospitals, but none of the doctors could help her. In the end, they took her to a lama, who told them that she was the reincarnation of a *dakini*, a female deity. The lama gave her a new name, Ngawang, and asked her to forget her past. From that day on, the family stopped taking her to doctors and instead started taking her to lamas. The chief abbot of Bhutan gave her a nun's habit, even though she still lives at home with her family, rather than in a convent. Nonetheless, Ngawang lives as a nun and will never marry. Instead, she dedicates her time to helping others and people travel from all over the country to see her. They no longer laugh at her, and she is no longer unhappy.

On my way to the fertility temple, which all the men from the travel agency were very keen that I visit, we stopped in the village where Ngawang lived. I had a new driver and a new guide, Rinchen, a tall, quietly spoken man in his thirties. A sign outside the house said in English that all visitors had to purify themselves with the incense that was burning in a pot by the door before going in. The driver went straight up the steps without noticing the sign, and we had to call him back. Once we were all sufficiently purified with smoke, we took off our shoes and went up to the reception room, a large, almost completely bare altar room, with only a small sofa and table in one corner. On the walls there were drawings of the Buddha and photographs of the royal family, and on the floor as many as fifteen carrier bags of juice, biscuits, milk and other offerings, as well as a dish with banknotes in it. Another sign informed us that the use of electronic equipment such as recorders and cameras was strictly forbidden.

We sat down on the floor and waited for Ngawang. Ten to fifteen minutes later she swept in through the door and sat down on the sofa with a smile. She was about my age, small and slight, with an odd, crooked smile. We stayed where we were on the floor and Rinchen explained that I had no concrete questions but wanted to hear what she had to say, and whether there was anything in particular that she saw.

Ngawang looked straight ahead in silence for a short while. Then she started to talk in a deep, urgent voice, almost like a chant. Her eyes were distant and she spoke in sustained bursts. It was no longer she who was speaking, but the *dakini* who inhabited her.

"You have a job now, but are considering changing jobs and per-haps moving somewhere else," Rinchen translated, though Ngawang had clearly said much more. "Is that right?"

"No, not really," I said. "I'm happy with my job."

Rinchen translated my answer and explained to the oracle that I was an author and was working on a book about the Himalayas.

Ngawang started to speak again, in the same monotone, urgent voice. This time she had even more to say.

"The book you are writing will take time, but you will become world famous," Rinchen translated. "You should gather stories about the past. Not all stories, not all myths, only those that capture your interest. If you do this, you will become known throughout the world. If you continue to do what you are doing now, if you continue to write books, you will have a long life. You will be offered another job, and if you say yes, it will be too much for you. There will be too much pressure. Don't say yes to the other job, continue to write. What does your husband do?"

"He's a writer as well," I said.

"You will write a book together," Ngawang said. "He will do most of the work, but it will be you who becomes famous. You will be far more famous than your husband."

I thanked her for her predictions, the best so far, and put some money in the donation dish. Perhaps the rule that had applied to the dice was true for horoscopes and predictions as well: you can try up to three times, or until you are happy with the results. Ngawang smiled and said that she would pray for me to become even more famous than she had predicted. Rinchen and I stood up to leave, but the driver remained seated.

"My wife lost a child in May," he said. "She was several months pregnant. Should we try to have another child, or should we leave it?"

"You should try to have another child," Ngawang said. "But only if you visit the fertility temple in Punakha and pray there. If you do that, you will have another child."

We thanked her and left her sitting cross-legged on the sofa. At the bottom of the steps we met three women, each with a child in one hand and a plastic bag of juice, milk and biscuits in the other hand, awaiting their turn.

The driver beamed for the rest of the day.

*

The fertility temple is actually called Chimi Lhakhang and was founded in 1499 in honour of Drukpa Kunley, better known as the Divine Madman, who is almost as popular in Bhutan as Padmasambhava. Drukpa Kunley lived from 1455 to 1529 and originally came from Tibet. When his father died, he decided to become a monk, but he soon tired of the rigid and boring monastery life, and started to travel around as a free beggar instead. Drukpa Kunley was well read and a good poet himself, but is best known for his tantric methods, which included having sex with women, singing obscene songs and drinking large amounts of alcohol – all as catalysts to accelerate the enlightenment process. He also urinated on sacred *thangkas* and derobed in front of lamas to show that one did not need to be sanctimonious to be a good Buddhist. Drukpa Kunley did not build temples himself or establish any schools, but the fertility temple in **Punakha** was built on the spot where he tamed a demon, and the monastery houses the large wooden phallus that he had brought with him from Tibet.

1242 MSL

"The hill where the monastery is, do you see what it resembles?" Rinchen asked and looked at me full of expectation. I shook my head. All I could see was a small hill.

"You really can't see it?" he asked, astounded.

"No," I confessed. "What does it look like?"

"A woman's breast," Rinchen said with a chuckle.

We walked up to the monastery which sat atop the hill like a nipple. I was sweating in the afternoon heat. The houses we passed were decorated with paintings of erect penises wantonly exploding with semen on the walls. Tourist shops outdid each other in their choice of phalluses in every possible colour and size.

The temple was full of people – for the most part Westerners well over the age of reproduction.

"Look," Rinchen said, and opened a photograph album that was lying on display on a table. "Couples from all over the world have had children after coming here!"

The album was full of photographs of babies and smiling parents.

Rinchen coughed and looked at me a little uncomfortably.

"The village astrologer said that it was very important that you were blessed by a monk," he said. Sangye must have told him about it. "But I'm afraid that's not enough . . ." He coughed again and pointed to a large, life-like wooden phallus. It was almost a metre high. "You have to walk around the temple three times carrying that in your hands."

"You're joking?" I looked at him in disbelief.

"No, of course I'm not joking," Rinchen said, affronted. "And I do have friends who were only blessed and still had children," he added quickly.

I could not bring myself to walk around the temple three times with a great wooden willy in my hands. And what was more, I had no burning desire to have children, whatever the male guides from the travel agency seemed to think, so I settled for a blessing from the young monk who looked after the temple. He held up a considerably smaller double phallus that he then lowered to my forehead as he chanted a mantra.

"I'm afraid it may not be enough just to be blessed . . ." Rinchen gave me an imploring look.

"Oh . . ." My fear was that he would insist on my carrying the enormous phallus around the temple.

"You must sit down and meditate deeply on your desire."

I obediently did as he said, glad that he had not mentioned the wooden phallus again. When I had meditated enough, Rinchen was standing ready with the three dice.

"Throw them," he said. When I did, and got thirteen again, Rinchen visibly grew with pride and joy. "Thirteen is very good!" he beamed. "It's the monastery's special number!"

The young monk came over to us with a pile of cards in his hand. A piece of string hung down from each card. I was asked to pull one out.

"What does it say?" Rinchen asked, full of anticipation.

"Kinley Wangchuck."

Rinchen grinned from ear to ear.

"That means you will have a son and he should be called Kinley Wangchuck," he said. "Wangchuck is the king's last name. This is very, very good!"

I said the name a few times: Kinley Wangchuck Fatland Hansen. It would certainly take a bit of getting used to, but it was not a name to be ashamed of.

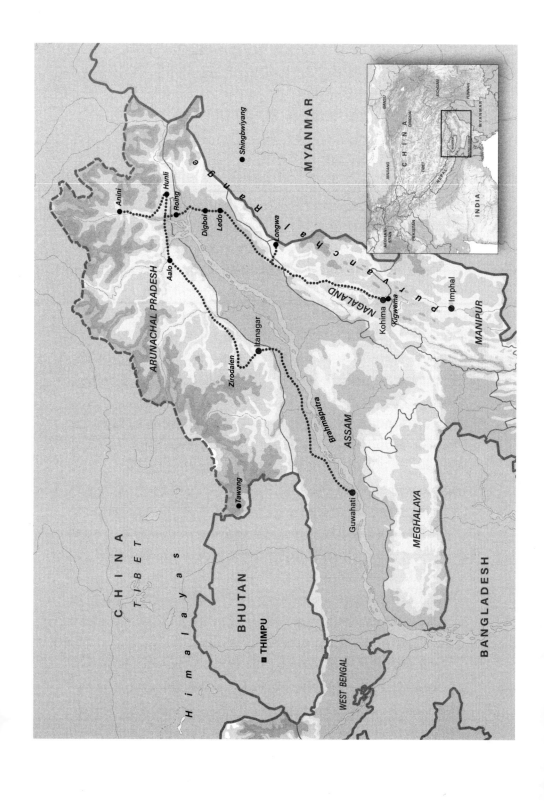

India's Wild East

The passport officer waved me away from the counter. I had to fill in an entry form first and could only do that at the table that was used for filling out entry forms. I hurried over to the prescribed table and filled out the form as quickly as I could. But in the meantime half the plane had got ahead of me in the queue and even more were trying to elbow their way forwards. When there was no-one else left in the passport hall, it was finally my turn.

"Stand there," the border guard snapped at me, impatiently. "Thumb there ... index finger there ... like this ..." he sighed heavily. "Not there, *here!*"

In less than an hour, I had travelled from one of the least populated countries in the world, to the second most populous. Travelling this way, the culture shock was brutal; I already missed the gentle, humorous Bhutanese.

Chaos reigned by the baggage carousel. Half the luggage came out on carousel 1, and the other half appeared on carousel 2, so the passengers ran back and forth in a panic between the carousels, trying to find their suitcases.

"It's not like this in your country, is it?" said a besuited traveller in his thirties. It was as though he had read my thoughts. "Infrastructure is the biggest problem here in India."

I had ordered a taxi in advance and was met by a driver who looked no more than fifteen. The boy strode off energetically towards the car, and I had to jog along behind him with my luggage in order to keep up. The car was hot and stuffy as it had been standing in the sun all day.

"Could you open the windows, please?" I panted, already soaked in sweat.

The driver gave a firm shake of the head.

"But I can turn on the air conditioning, if you like," he said. "It does cost a little extra, though."

As we approached the centre of **Guwahati**, which has one million   240 MSL inhabitants, the traffic ground to a halt. The drivers hooted their horns as though that might help. The air was grey with smog, and half-finished concrete buildings bared their reinforced steel bars to the street. Lean cows and scabby dogs chewed on plastic and rotten food by the sides of the road. Heavily loaded buses and trucks drove off the road in an attempt to bypass the honking, static traffic. At the busiest junctions, the traffic was controlled by policemen, as in Bhutan, but they were not dancing; they marched with a deadly scorn between the cars and ordered them here and there with aggressive arm movements.

Had I already stopped noticing all of this before I went to the land of the dragon king, all the rubbish, the emaciated cows, the miserable dogs, the dirty, hungry children who wandered between the cars, washing windscreens and selling flowers for small change?

It is hard enough to do justice to a small country like Bhutan – but to give an adequate picture of India is simply an impossible task. India is home to more than a sixth of the world's population – there are more people in India than in Europe and North America combined, and over the next few years, India is likely to overtake China as the world's most populous country. India is so vast and diverse that no sooner have you said one thing about the country than you could argue the opposite was true; India is not so much a country as a universe that embraces more than two thousand different ethnic groups, twenty-eight states and twenty-three official languages.

One of the least populous and most inaccessible states is Arunachal Pradesh, which is shaped like a bow pressed up to the Himalayas in the north-eastern corner of India, between the borders with Bhutan, Tibet and Myanmar. The literal meaning of Arunachal Pradesh is "Land of Dawn-Lit Mountains". The state is the same size as Portugal, with one and a half million inhabitants – and twenty-six different ethnic groups.

Foreign tourists who want to visit Arunachal Pradesh need a Protected Area Permit and have to travel with an authorised guide. In addition, all foreigners have to travel in a group of at least three people, but that is not always possible in practice, nor is it necessarily what the clients themselves want. The local travel agents therefore save copies of previous clients' passports and use them as fillers. So, on my entry permit it said that I was travelling together with Meena from the USA and Martin from the Czech Republic, whereas in fact my only travel companions were Tasang, a quietly spoken man from the Apatani tribe, who was in his thirties, and Danthi, a tall, thin Assamese man – my guide and my driver, respectively, for the trip. We navigated our way through the chaotic streets of Guwahati and out onto the motorway. The traffic immediately eased and we sped off down the straight flat road at an almost intoxicating speed.

Later in the evening we came to the state boundary between Assam and Arunachal Pradesh, and Tasang and Danthi got out of the car to sort out the paperwork. I stayed where I was and dozed. Suddenly there was a rap at the window. I started and looked straight into the eyes of a fierce border guard.

"Where are your two friends?" he asked.

"They went in to register," I said, and pretended that I thought he was talking about the guide and driver, not Meena and Martin. With a friendly smile. The border guard gave a deep sigh and marched on.

320 MSL   We spent the night in **Itanagar**, the capital of Arunachal Pradesh, an anonymous provincial city which was small enough that the traffic flowed freely and harmoniously without even a hint of a snarl-up. The next morning we continued to head north-east, towards

Ziro Valley, home to the Apatani tribe. The road itself was in reasonably good condition, but often disappeared either partially or fully under the detritus of landslides, which had been only been cleared sufficiently for a vehicle to pass. The landscape was green and misty, with palm trees and deciduous trees. The contours of low, blue mountains were discernible through the mist. This too is the Himalayas, the Lesser Himalayas: the sub-tropical, lush mountains at the southern foot of the range – a gentle build-up to the steep, snow-capped record breakers of the Great Himalayas to the north.

We reached our destination in the afternoon. The villages of **Ziro Valley** were remarkably similar. The houses stood so close 1500 MSL to one another that they were almost a wall, surrounded by bright-green rice paddies. Most were built in the traditional style, on stilts, with woven bamboo walls, but the traditional bamboo or straw roofs had been replaced by rusty corrugated iron.

"In the past, the Apatani had to defend themselves against the Nyishi tribe, which is why the houses are so close together," Tasang said. "Whenever there's a fire, fifteen to twenty houses are burned down in one go."

Scholars are unable to agree on where the tribes in Arunachal Pradesh are originally from, but some geneticists believe that they came from Mongolia, from the same people who spread to North America and the Amazon many thousands of years ago. The older women all had tattooed faces, with a green line that ran down their forehead and nose, then divided into five thick lines that fanned out over the chin. Many of them also had a round black plug in each nostril. The large plugs pressed together and flattened the nose, which gave the women a rather unusual appearance.

"I've been told that in the old days the women made themselves ugly so they wouldn't be abducted by the Nyishi," Tasang said, but I was not convinced. Body modifications in all cultures are about aesthetics and beauty; I have never heard of any ethnic group or place where women put time and effort into making themselves permanently ugly.

Tasang took me to visit one of his many cousins, Tage Yadii, the first woman in the village to go to school. She was now fifty-three and a teacher to the youngest children in the village. The remains of an old tattoo were barely visible on her forehead, nothing more than a short, faded, green line. Tage lived in a big, traditional house, with walls of woven bamboo. There was a fireplace in the middle of the large, rectangular main room. The furnishing was simple, with chairs along the walls and a single bed in one corner. There were calendars with pictures of Jesus and Mary hanging on the walls. The room had no windows and a couple of bare bulbs were the only source of light.

"When I was young, life was hard," Tage said, like so many others I had met. She spoke clear and articulate English in a loud, resonant voice, and was clearly used to being in the classroom. "We had to work in the paddy fields from a very young age. And those who didn't work starved. Girls didn't go to school. The village school was new and everyone thought that the Indian teachers would tell us improper things and that it would make us too lazy to work in the paddy fields. But I went to school anyway. I told my mother I was going to the fields, but, in secret, I went to school instead."

Tage's father had died when she was little, so she grew up alone with her mother. Her older siblings were already married and had their own homes.

"At the time, girls were married off when they were between twelve and fifteen," she said. "All marriages were arranged, and girls were often promised as babies. The local shaman would come by, kill a chicken, and from the chicken's liver could see in which village the girl's betrothed lived. The parents then later found a suitable candidate from the village in question. I was six or seven when the shaman came to perform this ritual. I was so furious that they were going to marry me off that I picked up the tiny liver and threw it as far away as I could."

Her mother accepted that the planned engagement would not go ahead, but got very angry when she discovered that her daughter had been going to school in secret.

"She didn't beat me, she never did, but she gave me a real telling off. I declared that if I wasn't allowed to go to school, I would run away. And run away I did. I went to my brother, who was married and had a family, and he sent me to a school in Assam. I was there for four years. The first years were hard. I was like a blank page when I got there, as I had only had two years at the village school and couldn't speak either Assamese or Hindi. And like all girls in Ziro at the time, I also had a tattoo on my face. I was maybe four when I got tattooed, I can't really remember, I only remember that it was very painful. All the other pupils stared at me and pointed; it was upsetting. I wanted to be like everyone else, so eventually I had the tattoo removed."

A thin, dark-skinned woman in a sari came over with a tray of tea. When we had helped ourselves, she withdrew to the furthest corner of the room and started to sweep the floor.

"My husband died a few months ago, and my children work in Itanagar, so now I live on my own with my house help." Tage nodded at the woman. "When I finished school, I got a job as a teacher here in the village. My mother was so proud that I was working for the government, and other people in the village realised that it might be a good thing to send their children to school. I became a role model. And now it's mainly girls who go on to higher education here. Times have changed!"

Tage was also the first in her family to become a Catholic. "The school in Assam was Catholic, and I converted while I was there. Thanks to me, lots of people in the family have become Catholics." She smiled happily.

"Are you not afraid that the Apatani culture will disappear, now that so many have converted to Christianity?" I asked.

"No, not at all, our culture won't disappear. Our festivals will keep it alive," Tage replied. "But, as I said, times are changing. A few years ago, I helped to establish the Apatani Women's Society. We have introduced a number of rules to make life easier for people. For example, we've introduced limits on how much should be sacrificed and served for different celebrations, such as when a child is born. Before, you had to invite the whole clan for big celebrations, and that could be as many as seven hundred people. It was incredibly expensive! People had to offer pigs, chickens, cattle, rice wine, wine and food. We've also decided that fizzy drinks and foreign spirits should not be served at festivals and celebrations. We're only allowed to serve rice wine, water and tea."

"What do you do if anyone breaks the rules?" I asked.

"Anyone who breaks the rules is fined up to thirty thousand rupees, which is around four hundred dollars, as punishment. We recently discovered that a man in the village had a big party. And in the next couple of days we'll go to see him and issue a fine. In the past, men played cards during the festivals, but that's forbidden now. Weddings have also been downsized. Two to three hundred guests is fine, but if there are more than five hundred, the bride and groom are fined. We have informants and spies everywhere and always find out if someone breaks the rules."

Tage stood up and went to get a small rule book issued by the Women's Society that gave detailed rules for every kind of celebration held in the valley, village by village, and the fines that could be expected by those who broke these rules.

"In the past, poor families had to take out loans in order to have big celebrations," Tage said. "Many of them used everything they had and struggled to pay the high interest rates. We want rich and poor to be equal. And apart from a few of the richest people, no-one has complained about the new rules."

*

A small square flag with a red circle on a white background fluttered outside more or less every second house in Ziro Valley. The flag was to show that the inhabitants had not converted to Christianity, but were believers of *donyi-polo*, the Sun-Moon religion which is the original faith of the people of Arunachal Pradesh. Although that could be disputed. Unlike Christianity and Hinduism, this belief system was not organised or written down. The myths and beliefs were a part of everyday life and not something people thought about before missionaries from South India started to spread Christianity here in the 1950s. At the time, many feared that the indigenous culture would be eroded, and the old faith with it. The issue was first discussed at a meeting of Adi intellectuals, and eighteen years later, after many long meetings, the Sun-Moon religion was established as an official religion among the indigenous peoples of Arunachal Pradesh, with all that that entails: places of worship, written prayers, prescribed rituals and a Donyi-Polo Day, which, rather practically, coincides with New Year's Eve.

Hage Tado and Hage Tado Naiya, both now in their sixties, brought the Sun-Moon religion to Ziro Valley at the end of the 1990s. The husband and wife lived in a traditional longhouse in the centre of the village, and kept hens and pigs in the garden. There was a fire burning in the hearth, and a thin layer of smoke hung over the room.

"The Apatanis have believed in the sun and the moon since time immemorial," Naiya said, in Apatani. True to tradition, she had also taken her husband's full name.

"But the religion was not officially registered by Talom Rukbo until the 1980s," her husband said.

"We had the first Sun-Moon temple built here in 2000," Naiya said. "We taught people that they could pray for the sick, and that it was not necessary to sacrifice animals. We encouraged them not to make rice wine or kill animals, not even chickens, for festivals, as these sacrifices were very expensive, and most people could not afford them. We tell people that they can celebrate the religious festivals with tea and biscuits, which is far cheaper. Every Sunday, we gather to pray together in the temple."

"We have also written down the shamans' prayers and songs," her husband said. "Our shamans are dying out, as young people don't want to become shamans. We have documented everything for posterity, so that it will not be lost when the old shamans are no longer with us. Now that we've collected the songs in a book, people can sing them themselves."

"We don't worship idols, just the sun and the moon," Naiya said. "Without the sun, there would be no earth. The sun gives us daylight and the capacity to grow rice. The moon gives us light in the evening and night, so the darkness is not complete, and it also helps us to keep track of time. After death, we follow the path trodden by our ancestors down to Nely, which is basically the same as the Christian heaven, and we stay there for ever. But if you are unfortunate enough to die in an accident, or commit suicide, you end up in Tailey, or hell."

"Lots of people have tried to convert us to Christianity, but we don't want to forsake our original faith," Hage Tado said. "Christianity comes from outside, from other people and other countries. The Apatanis believe in the sun and the moon."

"But the younger generation no longer wear traditional clothes," Naiya lamented. "Not even for our festivals. I used to wear traditional clothes every day, but in the end I got fed up with people asking me if I was on my way to a festival. There are now ten Sun-Moon temples in Ziro Valley. We have grown and have lots of followers. Tomorrow is Sunday, and there will be a ceremony in all the temples. They start at half past nine and are open to everyone, so just come along."

At half past nine the next morning, we were standing outside the closed gates of the largest Sun-Moon temple in Ziro Valley. Tasang, myself and three Dutch tourists with their guide were the only people there. At about ten o'clock, a woman came and opened the gates and started to sweep and clean the courtyard outside the temple. After another thirty minutes some ten wrinkled women with tattooed faces and plugs in each nostril appeared.

The temple was a simple concrete building, without chairs or benches or any other kind of furniture. Some low stools and a pile of cushions were lined up against the walls. Two women laid a black plastic covering over the floor and people sat down on the cushions and stools. More believers came through the gates and into the temple. There were about thirty of them, all getting on in years. I sat down at the back, on what I discovered too late was the men's side.

A woman and a man led the ceremony. They sat on the floor facing each other, on a small platform up by the plain altar, with a big painting of the sun as a backdrop. The man read from a book and the congregation mechanically repeated everything he said. The language was so archaic that Tasang, who had grown up in Ziro Valley and had Apatani as his mother tongue, could not understand what was being said. Then everyone sang: monotonous, endless songs sung in soft, meek voices. At one point the woman got out a silver carafe decorated with feathers, came down onto the floor and splashed water on everyone who was there – we all got a generous splash. The congregation then stood up and sang another long, monotonous song before the man carried on reading, without any expression in his voice. The concrete floor was cold and hard and the ceremony seemed to go in circles. It was as though the people who had formalised the religion had copied the most boring elements from a Christian church service and multiplied them. Stiff and aching from sitting for so long on a hard floor, I got up and crept out.

The Christian revival church was far livelier. More than a hundred believers were there, mostly young people and families with young children, and there were, thankfully, enough plastic chairs for everyone. Other than a plain white cross on the pulpit, there were no images or symbols in the airy church. A young man in a suit went up to the pulpit and started to tell us about how naughty and disobedient he had been as a child. In tenth grade he had already started to drink and had had frequent nightmares about the devil, but then he found God and started to go to church. He was a new and better person now, and the terrible nightmares were a thing of the past. *Hallelujah!*

"*Hallelujah!*" the congregation responded enthusiastically.

A young woman from Nagaland then spoke in a mixture of Hindi, English and the local language: "Praised be the Lord, I lay my life in your hands, I am your tool, use me, Lord. Praised be the Lord!"

"Praised be the Lord!" the congregation repeated and broke out into ecstatic song, accompanied by drums and cymbals.

Once again, Tasang and I crept out of the service and went on to the Baptists, who had the biggest church of all. There was not an empty seat in the house; women and children sat squeezed together. An austere cross was the only decoration here too.

We arrived just in time to hear the sermon. A thin man in a grey suit ascended the pulpit and looked out over the congregation in grave silence. Then he started. He talked and talked, about how important it was for the Baptists to stick together, and how important it was that they keep away from the Sun-Moon worshippers, and to distance themselves as much as possible from their festivals in particular, for just as the sun and the moon cannot be in the sky together, Christians and heathens cannot be together, the minister preached, and he exhorted the congregation to stay away from Hindu temples as well; as believers they must keep their path pure and spotless.

When the minister finally ran out of words, a group of women stood up and made their way to the altar. Some knelt down, the others remained standing. And then, as though prompted by some invisible signal, a cacophony of heartfelt prayers rose up to the heavens. The women who were standing stretched their arms out to those who were kneeling, as though they wanted physically to draw the evil out of them. The voices got louder and louder, and more and more ecstatic. And then all of a sudden, as though in response to another invisible signal, they fell silent. Those who were kneeling stood up, and they all went back to their places. The service was over. On the way out, we were all given a sweet to chew.

Not everyone who lived in Ziro Valley went to a church service on Sundays. Mudang Pai, the 75-year-old who normally won the local shaman competitions, had no plans for converting.

"The so-called priests in the Sun-Moon religion have no value whatsoever," he said. "A religion without a *nyibo*, a shaman, is an utterly useless religion. A *nyibo* knows all the spirits by name and knows what each of them wants, be it a chicken or an egg, or something bigger. The spirits are hungry for meat. Offering them sweet things just doesn't work."

Mudang had a wrinkled, almost rubbery face and was missing a fair number of teeth, but his long hair was still jet black. It was pulled into a topknot over his forehead and held in place with a long stick. We were sitting on his veranda with a view to the garden, where he had made a small altar from bamboo branches and impaled eggs. There was a chill in the afternoon air, but Mudang, who was wearing sandals, shorts and a hoody, did not seem to feel it. Tasang had enlisted an elderly relative to help with the translation. Like so many of the young people, he struggled to understand traditional Apatani, especially when the conversation was about religion and rituals. His relative translated from Apatani to Hindi, and Tasang then translated into English.

"Our ancestor, Tani, got his strength from the sun," Mudang told me, via Tasang's relative and Tasang. "To begin with, people believed in Tani, and then they started to worship the sun and the moon. Now, Tani was a wily man, whereas Robo, his younger brother, was capricious. One day, Tani decided to kill Robo and lured him out of the village. He took Robo to a place where there was lots of honey and let the bees attack him. Robo fell off a cliff and died."

Fratricide must be one of the oldest and most widespread religious myths in the world. According to the Old Testament, the history of humanity starts with fratricide: Cain, the first human to be born, kills his younger brother Abel in a fit of jealousy. In the Hindu epic, the Mahabharata, Arjuna kills his older brother, Karna, without, to be fair, being aware of their relationship, and Romulus, the mythical founder of Rome, kills his brother, Remus, after an argument about where the boundaries of the future city should lie. Some scholars believe that fratricide alludes to the extinction of the Neanderthals: *homo sapiens* originally had a brother, but killed him.

"When I grew up, there was no Christianity here," Mudang said. "I was in my thirties when the elders in the village decided that I should be a *nyibo*. I found it very easy to learn the shaman songs, which was why they thought I was well suited."

"How do you treat people who are ill?" I asked. Tasang's Hindi-speaking relative did not translate my question for Mudang, but instead asked Tasang a whole raft of questions. Tasang asked me to elaborate.

"What kind of illness do you mean? Every illness must be treated differently."

"What if the patient has pains in their chest, for example?" It was the first thing that came to mind.

This time, my question was relayed to Mudang and prompted a longer exchange.

"Chest pains are caused by a spirit that lives outside the village," he said. "When you leave the village, you can be attacked. I first have to sing outside the house of the person who is sick, then I boil an egg and cut it in two with one of my hairs in order to know whether the rest of the ritual should take place in the village, or outside."

"What about severe headaches?"

"Headaches can be caused by two spirits," Mudang said. "One is *danyi*, the sun, and the other is a jungle spirit. When there is doubt, I take two eggs, one for each spirit. While the eggs are boiling, I say my prayers, and when they are ready, I cut them in two with a hair to decide which of the spirits is responsible. If it is the sun, I have to sacrifice three hens and four eggs. The sick person cannot leave the house for three days. So that people from the village know that they have to keep away, I leave an egg symbol outside the door of the sick person."

Mudang sighed.

"Almost no-one knows these things any longer, because none of the young people want to be *nyibos*. If someone doesn't appear soon, there will be no *nyibos* left when I die. And if that is the case, the young people will lose their identity, their heritage and traditions. When someone comes and asks them about their culture, as you're doing now, they won't be able to answer."

"Your wife became a Baptist a few years ago now," Tasang's relative said. "How do you feel about a *nyibo*'s wife going to church?"

"Even though I know all the spirits, I also believe that there's only one god," Mudang replied, unperturbed. "There is a monstrously evil spirit that dwells among the Apatani, a hungry spirit that demands a lot of blood. I tried to control it and to get it not to follow my wife, but I didn't manage. I had heard that the Christians were good at exorcising evil spirits, so I sent her to church. It worked! I believe that, in principle, all religions are good, and I respect them all."

*

The main highway in Arunachal Pradesh follows the state boundary from west to east, with only a few, lonely side roads north. Even though we crossed the boundary into Assam several times on the way east, it was not difficult to discern which state we were in: the number of places that sold alcohol was always a giveaway as to whether we were in liberal Arunachal Pradesh or the far more puritanical Assam. Later that afternoon, we turned onto one of the side roads and drove north through green rolling hills, past dozens of liquor shops, free churches and small villages with large, straw-roofed, bamboo houses on poles. We had left the Apatanis and were now in the homelands of the Galo tribe.

619 MSL   We reached **Aalo** in the evening. When we booked into a guest house, we were invited in to meet the family in the main house. They had a large room with a high roof, and an open fireplace in the middle. The floor was covered with bamboo mats and one of the walls was full of gayal horns and skulls – the large bovine is extremely popular in this corner of Asia. Gayals have big, blunt and rounded horns and a short black coat and are used as dowry by many tribes in Arunachal Pradesh.

"These are all the gayals that the man in the family had to sacrifice when he got married," Tasang explained. "The more jewellery the bride has, the more gayals he has to offer. I still owe my parents-in-law five gayals." He gave a heavy sigh. "Gayals are hugely expensive, so I have no idea how I'm going to afford it. Apatanis don't sacrifice gayals when we get married, but my wife is from another ethnic group, so her parents expected gayals."

The local women's association was having a meeting out on the veranda. I was invited to join them, and they made space for me in the semicircle of women.

"The association was established on the thirtieth of January this year to support a woman in the Ori clan who was going through a divorce," Kirken Ori, the secretary, told me in Hindi. "And afterwards, we carried on collecting a small sum from our members to help women in the clan who are in dire straits."

Gyi Ori, the owner of the guest house, a slender, friendly man in his forties, sat down with us and took over the conversation.

"It's hard to be a woman," he said. "You have to do all the heavy work: give birth, harvest the vegetables, carry the wood."

"Who looks after the animals?" I asked.

"The women," Gyi said.

"Who looks after the children?"

"The women."

"Who cleans and tidies the house?"

"The women."

"Who washes the clothes?"

"The women."

"Who makes the food?"

"The women."

"Who picks the rice?"

"The women."

"What do the men do then?"

Everyone laughed.

"Nothing, they just drink all day," Gyi said.

"They must do something?"

"Yes, they hunt in the jungle and fish, and it's their job to build fences around properties and things like that," said Santi, the only woman in the association other than the secretary who spoke good Hindi. "Many of them also work for the authorities and earn money so that we can give our children a good education."

"Do any of you have a job other than harvesting rice?" I asked.

They all shook their heads.

"But we still have it a lot easier than the women in India," Santi said. We *were* in India, but India was clearly another place for them. "We don't need to ask for permission to go anywhere. We do what we want. Our men don't control us."

"Who keeps the children in the event of a divorce?" I asked.

"The man, always the man," Kirken, the secretary, said. "Men can also marry several women without asking their wife. If the wife doesn't produce children, or hasn't given her husband a son after four children, he has the right to take another wife."

"You're lucky to be able to travel to so many places," Santi said. "We can't even go to Itanagar. If we did that, our husbands would refuse to take us back."

"But you just said you could go wherever you like," I said.

"In the village and local area, yes, but we can't go far, and certainly not alone! That would get people's tongues wagging. But the men, they can go anywhere. They can disappear for months on end without any repercussions."

"Where would you go if you could go wherever you liked?"

"To Darjeeling!" she said, with a smile.

Meanwhile, the men were getting ready to rehearse the war dance in an extension to the side of the building. They had on headdresses tipped with swaying white feathers, but otherwise were wearing T-shirts, shorts and grubby jackets. In their hands they held long swords that they banged hard on the ground as they danced. They did the first dance well, but had clearly not mastered the second yet. They were supposed to move sideways in a semicircle with slightly bent knees, swinging the sword from side to side, while two men leaped into the middle and pretended to fight with their swords. A sinewy, grey-haired man in his sixties let out a deep sigh. "Not like that!" he said, shaking his head. "You have to dance in time and with softer movements."

The choreographer demonstrated with the lightest of movements and knee bends, and tried to get the troupe of older men to dance as one. They were going to a festival in Delhi in a few weeks' time and had to know the dance before then.

The next day, we went on an excursion to the neighbouring village. A group of men had gathered outside one of the houses. Two old men were sitting on the grass singing the same notes over and over again in reedy old men's voices.

"A couple of days ago, there was a small fire in the house," the owner of the unlucky house told me. "We managed to put it out, and no-one was injured. And the house has not been damaged. But we see it as a warning that the fire spirit is not happy with us and thinks we should perform more rituals. Presumably there's a bad spirit in the house as well. So we asked two *nyibos* to come and make the fire spirit happy and drive out the bad spirit, so there won't be any more fires. We're going to sacrifice two hens at three o'clock this afternoon. We're just making the altars now."

He nodded in the direction of two men who were plaiting bamboo. The two old *nyibos* sang on valiantly, the same few notes over and over again.

When Tasang and I returned at three on the dot, the two *nyibos* got up from the grass and started to walk down towards the road as they continued to repeat the same short sentence and same few notes. They had been singing all morning and afternoon, and one could almost hear the effort required for every additional repetition. A tail of men followed behind. One of them was carrying the altars that were now ready and looked like fans, and another was carrying two hens in a cage and some logs. The others held bamboo spears threaded with pieces of banana tree bark.

Tasang and I followed at the back. After a short distance, we left the road and followed a steep, muddy path down to the river. A man took the two hens out of the cage as the shamans sang. The hens clucked and squawked furiously in the sun for a minute or two, but very soon there was only one left squawking. The man held the dying chicken over the altar, which was sprayed with blood, and then swiftly cut the throat of the second one. The clucking stopped. The two chickens were then tied to the altars. The owner of the unlucky house took an altar in each hand and waded out into the water. The other men stood on the bank and threw the bits of banana tree bark after him – in this way casting evil spirits from the house, both symbolically and physically. When the owner reached the middle of the river, he dived under each of the altars. Then he sent them down-river on the current and swam back to shore. Before getting out, he took the opportunity to wash his body, hair and clothes with soap.

The two old *nyibos* could finally give their larynxes a rest and they walked slowly back to the village for some rice wine.

*

The following morning we drove north-east to Anini, one of the remotest villages in Arunachal Pradesh. The higher we climbed, the narrower and more potholed the road became. A new road is being built, and when it is ready the travel time to Anini will be halved. But until then it takes longer than ever because of all the roadworks.

1240 MSL   We came to **Hunli** in the late afternoon. The village was unforget-table, surrounded as it was by deep-blue, snow-capped mountains. We were going to spend the night in a simple state-owned guest house, hidden away behind a rusty gate at the end of a road. A woman came towards us with a towel wrapped around her head and a toothbrush sticking out of her mouth.

"You can't stay here," she said, without removing the toothbrush. "The state representative is away."

"But we booked in, we have nowhere else to stay," Tasang said.

"Sorry," the woman said, with an apologetic shrug, and continued to brush her teeth. "You have to be registered to stay here, and as the representative isn't here today, it's not possible to register, so you can't stay. I've already turned away two other tourists today."

"But a friend of mine," Tasang mentioned a name, "is a relative of yours. Are you sure you can't make an exception?"

That changed everything. With the toothbrush still in her mouth, the woman padded across the courtyard and opened the rooms we could stay in. They were simple, but relatively clean and with a kind of toilet. The woman removed her half-chewed toothbrush and spat out the toothpaste.

"You'll have to park the car behind the house, so the tourists I've just turned away don't see that we have guests," she said.

When the sun went down, before the electricity came on, our hostess invited us over to the kitchen where she was chopping vegetables by the fire. We sat down with three silent local men and a PhD student from Assam who was studying the flying squirrels.

"Arunachal Pradesh is the only state in India that is home to the tiger, the leopard, the clouded leopard and the snow leopard," he said, happily. "The wildlife here is so rich and diverse. They even have the king cobra! It often hides in the houses in winter."

"But there are no king cobras in Anini, are there?" I said, with wavering optimism. "I mean, after all, it's more than two thousand metres above sea level."

"Oh yes, there are king cobras in Anini," the PhD student said enthusiastically. "If you're bitten, it's important not to panic, because then the poison spreads faster."

After we had eaten, he put on his rucksack, which was standing ready, turned on his headtorch, and set off to spend the night with the flying squirrels.

At daybreak, we were up. A stretch of road higher up was going to be closed for the greater part of the afternoon, due to roadworks, and we had to get through while it was still open. However, we had not been driving for more than an hour before we had to stop: a tree had fallen across the road. Luckily, a road worker soon appeared with a bulldozer and pushed the tree over the edge of the road. Danthi put his foot on the pedal, but then, half an hour later, we were stopped in our tracks by nature again. This time it was a landslide. Three bulldozers worked hard to scoop up the rocks and mud, but it still took almost three hours before the road was passable. Danthi had only just managed to pick up some speed when we got a puncture and had to change the wheel. When we finally got to the critical stretch, the road had been closed for some time already, and we had no option but to wait until the working day was over.

A crowd of men sat on the slope below us drinking.

"Come on down!" they roared. "Come and have a drink with us!"

When they got no response, one of them scrambled up to the car. He was fifty plus, and dressed in a short loincloth, woollen tanktop and dirty jacket. He had a big, traditional knife over his left shoulder, and the sheath was embellished with fake animal jaws. He had a stick in his right hand, which proved to be a good thing, as he could barely stay upright.

"Do you undershtand?" he slurred in a thick Indian accent. "Undershtand? S'important that you undershtand!"

Tasang rescued me, and we escaped down to the local shop, which had benches along the wall that caught the sun. An official document on the information board stated that thirty-eight voters lived in the village. We had scarcely sat down before a middle-aged man joined us. He was well dressed in a blue shirt and shorts, his hair was well cut, and his gentle face would have evoked confidence and trust had he not been drunk.

"Where are you from?" he asked in his almost non-existent English. "London?" he asked, expectantly.

"No, she's from Norway," Tasang said in Hindi, waving off the local flies that were thirsty for his blood.

"But where *are* you from?" the man insisted.

"Norway," I said.

"Yes, but where *are* you from?" he said again. The conversation was going in circles. "Maybe you'd like to try the local wine?" he said with a grin.

We politely declined and fled back to the car to escape him. There we were met by drunkard no. 1 who was now equipped with a newly purchased bottle of spirits and a packet of cigarettes. He grabbed my hand and wouldn't let it go. "You undershtand?" he asked, peering at me. Then drunkard no. 2 came shambling along. "Where *are* you from?" he asked, his eyes swimming when he looked at me. "Are you from London?"

After sixty-eight long minutes in this nameless but memorable village, the barrier was raised and we could drive on. It felt like a small miracle. The well-dressed drunk jogged along behind the car for a short distance.

"But where *are* you from?" he shouted in desperation. "Where ARE you from?"

It was only much later that it struck me that Norway could be misheard as *no way* or *nowhere*.

It had been dark for a while by the time we reached **Anini**. Vadra, 1968 MSL a friend of Tasang, lived in the biggest house in Anini, a colourful brute of a thing painted in pink, green and blue, a modern concrete palace among all the traditional bamboo longhouses. Vadra was the perfect host. When he heard us approaching, he got up from the dining table and came to greet us and show us the way. He was a retired army man, with a distinguished, square face, a slightly jutting jaw and short, thick hair that stood straight up. He spoke in a loud, nasal and vaguely jarring voice. When his English failed, he continued in Hindi.

A tall, slim man in a long, white tunic and a shorter, more anonymous-looking man dressed in ordinary trousers and a checked shirt were sitting by the fire.

"I am Pastor Paul," said the man in the tunic. He was a Pentecostalist like our host. There was nothing remarkable about that, in itself, even though only about ten per cent of people from the Idu Mishmi tribe living in Anini have converted to Christianity. What was remarkable, though, was that Paul belonged to the highest caste.

"I was passionately against Christianity when I was young, after all, I was a Brahmin," the pastor said, in a clear, strong, preacher's voice. Amos, the more anonymous-looking man who was his local assistant, translated from Hindi to English.

"As a young man, I lived a sinful life and drank a lot. My mother died when I was little, and my father used to give me a spoonful or two of alcohol to help me sleep. When I started school, the servant would send me off with a quarter bottle of whisky in my bag. By tenth grade, I was drinking three or four quarter bottles a day! In the end, it made me ill. My liver, kidneys, lungs, everything was damaged, and the doctors said I only had six months left to live. One day, a Christian missionary came to the house to talk to my cousin. I sat there drinking whisky and listening to what the missionary had to say, and then he suddenly quoted something from the Bible that made an enormous impression on me, something like: 'Do you not know that your body is a temple of the Holy Spirit, who is in you, whom you have received from God?' He went on: 'Why then do you destroy it?' That sentence changed my life. At first I was very angry with the missionary and went to his house with my father's pistol in my pocket, determined to shoot him. I was going to die soon anyway. But the missionary welcomed me so warmly that I forgot my rage. All my life I had only ever thought about one thing: alcohol. But because of all the alcohol, I slept badly at night. Often for only eight to ten minutes at a time. Sleeping pills didn't help. My greatest desire was to sleep the whole night through, and I challenged the missionary: 'If your Jesus is a true god, then ask him to help me sleep. If I have a good night's sleep, I will become a disciple of Jesus.'"

"Let me guess, you slept well that night?" I said.

"Yes." Pastor Paul smiled. "To cut a long story short, I slept well that night. And when I woke up, I felt like a human for the first time. I stopped drinking that very day. I was terribly ill to begin with, I almost died, but the missionary and his wife were doctors and they looked after me. I stayed with them for several months. Nineteen pastors in several countries fasted and prayed for me for forty days, and slowly, after four months and sixteen days, I started to recover. After five months, I was able to sit up in bed and drink some water. After six months, I could stand up and was baptised in the Ganges."

"What is your real name?" I asked.

"Nirmal Kuma Dubey."

"Very high caste," Amos said. "*Very* high caste!"

"How did your family react when you were baptised?" I asked.

"They were furious," he said. "My brothers and my father beat me senseless, broke my skull and left me in a storeroom to die. Once again, the missionary saved me, and he and his wife cared for me again for many weeks. After many trials, I became a pastor. I came here to Anini for the first time in 2003. There were no Christians here then. Some of the villagers welcomed me, and others were extremely rude. Some youngsters threatened me with a knife, and the church I had built was pulled down. Progress was slow to begin with, but now I have baptised close to a hundred people here."

"My own brother was one of those who pulled the church down," Amos said. "Not long after, he was diagnosed with leukaemia. None of the doctors could help him, so he tried to commit suicide, but ended up in a coma. When he woke up, I told him that the church was his only option. He converted, was given a marrow transplant and recovered. As a result, I converted too. Before, I used to smoke more than a hundred cigarettes a day. My wife was always nagging me to stop, and I used to say I would rather give up her than the cigarettes. When I became a Christian, I stopped smoking and drinking!"

"And you are a respectable and decent man now," Pastor Paul said.

A very dark woman with a baby strapped to her back served us rice, curry and water. The courtyard outside was milling with children and adults in tattered clothes, all much darker than the Idu Mishmi, the indigenous people of Anini.

"We never used to have so many helpers," Vandra said. "But one day one of them came here with a woman who then had twins, and we had to get another woman to help out, and now there are many more of them."

"Very costly, I'm sure," I said.

"Oh, we don't pay them, we give them food and accommodation, and in return they help in the house," Vadra said. "As there is not much to do, they can get a day job and earn their own money. In the old days, it was quite usual for people around here to have slaves. The slaves were Idu Mishmi, like us, but they were often orphans or very poor for some reason. Their children also became slaves. But slavery was abolished a generation or two ago."

A thin pubescent girl cleared the table and started washing up. Then she made my room ready. I slept like a log, right through the night, with or without divine intervention.

Sipa Melo was the most powerful shaman, or *igu* as they were called here, in the district. He lived in the small village of Alinye, a few kilometres north of Anini, where he ran a small hotel and an even smaller restaurant. He came striding up the driveway just after we had arrived, closely followed by an elderly German psychiatrist and social anthropologist.

"I have visited Sipa regularly for the past sixteen years, and I still learn something new every time," the German said. "My goal is to document all the rituals and songs, so they are not lost."

He had written a socio-anthropological paper on shamans in Nepal many years before, and there were no longer any shamans in the villages he had visited back then. They had all converted to Christianity.

"To find a real shaman these days, you have to go to villages with no road connection," the German said. "Anini, too, has changed dramatically since the road came. Young people no longer want to live here."

The German retired to his room to rest. Sipa invited Vadra, Tasang and me into the television lounge, and called for some fresh tea. He had a straight fringe and his long, black hair was pulled back into a ponytail, as is the custom among the Idu Mishmi. He was fifty-eight years old, much smaller than me, and was so gentle by nature that it was hard to imagine that he ever got angry.

"He is the most powerful shaman in these parts," Vadra said, and sat down at one end of the sofa. Sipa spoke in a quiet, calm voice, while the corners of his mouth twitched in a smile, even though he was constantly interrupted by Vadra, who finished off his sentences.

"I didn't go to school. Instead, I spent a lot of my time with the shamans, and listened to their songs," Sipa said. "I started as an apprentice when I was twelve or thereabouts, but it took about ten years to learn all the songs and what I needed to know about the spirits. When I sing, I wear special clothes made from bearskin, tiger's teeth and lion's teeth. The clothes make me bolder. Many of the spirits are angry with the shaman, because he is the only one who can control them. The spirits are often temperamental, and sometimes they fight. But the *igu*'s soul can rise higher than any of the other spirits, and it gathers special powers there. When I sing, my body is here, but my soul is in the mountains, in the clouds, far, far away . . ."

He handed me a twig and asked me to taste the leaves. They were sour and bitter, with a hint of aniseed.

"Some illnesses allow themselves to be treated with medicine from wild plants," he said. "That plant, for example, is good for stomach pains. Only the shaman knows where the plants grow. If someone is ill, I sing my way from generation to generation to find out if anyone in the sick person's family has done something to anger the spirits. I then mediate between the spirit and the person: I say to the spirit that the person wants to make amends, and ask it to spare the sick person. I often suck the pain out of the patient and spit it on the ground. In more complex cases, I send the patients to hospital or visit them there. I also assist when people die. Sometimes the soul is so attached to life on earth that it won't leave the house, and then I have to explain to the deceased that they need to move on. The souls of people who have died a natural death go to Asuko, our heaven. We believe that our journey, the journey of life, starts in the east with the sunrise, and ends in the west with the sunset. Asuko lies to the west."

"In the west, yes," Vadra said, nodding. "Asuko lies in the west, that's right!"

"Anyone who dies an unnatural death goes to Yomuko, our hell, but they don't have to stay there for eternity," Sipa continued, patiently, unperturbed by Vadra's enthusiastic interruptions. "For example, if someone has hanged themselves they have to study every single aspect of the rope when they are dead. Where did it come from? Why did it come to them? Someone who has drowned in a river has to find out all there is to know about the river. How many fish swim in it, where its mouth is, where its source is. Someone killed by a knife must climb the steepest mountains in the world because the mountainsides are like the edge of a knife. It can often take two or three thousand years. When these studies are completed the soul will naturally travel to Asuko."

"Yes, it will go to Asuko by itself, yes," Vadra echoed.

"The climate is changing all over the world, and here in the Himalayas in particular," I said. "Daily life here in Anini has changed so much in the past decade or so, and they're building a new road. How have the spirits reacted to all these changes?"

"The spirits are angry," Sipa said. "They want us to apologise to them first before we build a house, or chop down a tree, so we won't disturb them. They are indignant about the roads and the dams, which is why there are so many accidents and landslides at the moment. We humans should at least show that we are sorry for the changes we inflict on nature, and ask for forgiveness before we start anything."

We went out into the garden and drank peppermint tea in the sun. Sipa looked around with a smile.

"Isn't it beautiful here?" he said, opening his arms to the mountains all around. "It feels as though I'm living in the centre of a lotus flower."

Back in Anini, we collected the punctured tyre that had now been repaired, and started to look for somewhere to get diesel. There were no petrol stations in Anini, but Vadra knew a shop owner who also sold fuel. The man brought a plastic jerrycan out from his store and his thin daughter poured the fuel into the tank.

There were masses of shoes outside Vadra's neighbour's house, about a dozen people were sitting tightly packed round the fire in the narrow, dimly lit living room. A small, rotund man sitting by the door was singing songs in a strangely touching, androgynous voice. A thin old man lay on the floor to the left of the singing shaman. He was wrapped in a thick blanket and looked ill and exhausted.

"Whatever he has done wrong, forgive him," the shaman sang. "Give him another chance, protect him, let him walk outside in the sun again."

The others were all relatives of the old man. The mood was relaxed, people chatted and laughed as the shaman sang, and everyone drank lots of tea. A group of youngsters sat in the corner closest to the door, slightly detached from everyone else, boys with too much gel in their hair and girls with pink lips, the screens on their mobile phones illuminated by their restless scrolling.

Pastor Paul and Amos were eating dinner when we got back to Vadra's house.

"What a wonderful day!" The pastor beamed from ear to ear. "We baptised four sisters in the river this afternoon. They are only in their teens, but were determined to be baptised, even though their parents are not Christians. It has been a truly wonderful day!"

The pastor insisted on praying for us first thing the next morning before we headed south again to Roing. He closed his eyes and prayed sincerely that we would be protected on our journey and arrive safely. He himself was going to travel by helicopter.

The pastor's prayers were of little help. It turned out that the diesel we had bought in Anini the day before had been diluted with water and paraffin and the engine started to play up as the morning wore on. In the end, it stopped altogether. Fortunately, there were plenty of car mechanics on the road, and one of them helped us to drain the water from the fuel filter and managed to get the engine going again. By the time we reached **Roing**, Danthi had had to stop and pump life into the engine another five times, at shorter and shorter intervals.

390 MSL

"I've heard there are a lot of opium users around here," I said to Tasang the next morning. "Would it perhaps be possible to talk to someone who smokes opium?"

"Not a problem," he said. "I'll take you to see my neighbour. We're going in that direction anyway."

Danthi had spent the morning at a garage and the car was now fixed and filled with pure diesel. For the next couple of hours, we sped along the hard, even asphalt. It was like driving on silk. We reached Tasang's home in the early afternoon, a peaceful Idu Mishmi village on the Assamese plains at the foot of the Himalayas.

Tasang explained why we were there and his neighbour chuckled, let us into the traditional bamboo house and gladly showed us his equipment. We all sat down by the fire, where everything had its place, from the spoon he used to heat the opium, to the pipe he smoked it in.

"I smoke three times a day," he said. "If I don't smoke, my body doesn't function as it should, and I get very lethargic. But when I smoke, my body feels light and as soft as cotton wool. It's better than wine. When I'm drunk, I lose control of myself. When I smoke, I am incredibly polite. I have full control."

"How long have you been smoking?" I asked.

"About ten years. It was recreational, to begin with. My friends smoked and I let them persuade me to try."

He spoke slowly and laughed a lot. His voice cracked in the way that is so characteristic of long-term drug users.

"I'm super active when I smoke," he said. "I grow my own opium, as it's cheaper than having to buy it, but sometimes, when there is a while to go before I can harvest, I have to buy. You pay around three hundred rupees for the amount I smoke every day, maybe five when the market is at its peak."

Opium, the scourge of Asia, was originally supplied by the Mishmi tribe on the other side of the Chinese border.

"Until 1962, it was easy to cross the border, but now it's patrolled by the army. People sometimes still sneak over at night, though, because they know where the soldiers stand guard."

"Do you notice any side effects from the opium?" I asked.

"No, and that's why there's no motivation to stop. But I have to smoke every day, or I get a fever."

His wife, a slim woman wearing bright red lipstick and a colourful, long, wraparound skirt, came in and asked if we would like tea.

"I hate the fact that he smokes," she said. "And I've asked him to stop countless times."

"No-one else in the family smokes opium," the man said. "All addictions are bad for the body, and I know I'll have to pay the price. I have tried to stop many times, but my body rebels."

"And is it not a bit risky too?" I asked. "The punishments for drug abuse are harsh, aren't they?"

"The police sometimes come round and seize the opium, but it's the local council that decides what is allowed here, not Indian law, and I sit on the council." He sniggered. "We're generally caught up with land ownership issues and wife abduction. If the husband wants his wife back, the man who has "stolen" her has to pay a fine. If the husband doesn't want to keep the wife, she has to pay back the gayals that he paid for her when they got married."

"Do you have a job?" I asked. It was the middle of the working day, and here he was relaxing at home. And yet the family did not appear to be poor – all three children were studying at university in the nearby town.

He laughed for a long time before he managed to answer.

"Of course I have a job! I work for the Department of Education."

"How often do you go to work?

He started laughing again, his shoulders shaking.

"Before, I went into the office once a month to collect my wages, but now the money is transferred straight to my account, so there's no need. I only have to work when there's an election, and the bosses and other important people come to visit."

As we were about to leave, one of the neighbour's opium chums turned up. The neighbour lit the fire and, with a practised hand, started to dry the strips of banana leaf. Then he boiled some water and put a piece of dried opium in the spoon, which was lying ready, poured on some water and let it boil until the opium had melted into a dark, sticky mass. He poured this over the strips of dried banana leaves, mixed it well, then divided it into two equal portions.

"Some people can do this in five minutes, but I'm not that good," he chuckled.

His friend sat down by the fire and the two men poured water into their home-made bamboo pipes and filled it with the banana-leaf mixture. They inhaled deeply and exhaled blue, sweet-smelling smoke. After each inhale, they rinsed their mouths with tea. The mood by the fire became more and more blissful. And then there was silence.

For Tomorrow

The world is full of war graves. Outside **Digboi**, India's oil capital, 165 MSL there are two hundred gravestones neatly lined up over a meticulously mown lawn. Each grave contains a life story, an entire novel.

A Soldier of the Indian Army 1939–1945 is honoured here. The grave was one of the few without a name. Was there no-one who remembered his name? Or had it not been possible to identify him? He was killed on November 15, 1945, several months after the war had ended. *Morto per la patria*, "Died for his country", it said on the grave of Sergeant A. Respanti from the Esercito Italiano. Respanti died on July 20, 1944. Less than a year earlier, Italy had sided with Japan to fight against the Allies. How then had Respanti ended up on the Allies' side in the jungle in India in such a short space of time? *Treasured memories of a loved husband and daddy sadly missed by wife and baby.* G. Marks lived to be thirty-one. Did he live long enough to know he was a father? The words *Patriae memor*, "With his country in mind", were engraved on the headstone of Bolongo, a soldier from Belgian Congo. How on earth had Bolongo ended up here?

As we were making our way out, two boys and a girl came into the cemetery, laden with camera equipment. I assumed that they were going to take photographs of the graves, for a school project, perhaps, but it was in fact the girl who was going to be immortalised, from every possible angle, with the graves as a backdrop.

Depending on where you are, wars start and end at different points in time. In Europe, for example, the Second World War started on September 1, 1939, when Germany invaded Poland. In Asia, however, it started far earlier, on July 7, 1937, at the latest, when Japan launched an attack on China. But the war may actually have started in 1931, with the Japanese invasion of Manchuria in north China, and the terrible suffering that ensued. The precursor for this aggressive Japanese expansion lies even further back, in 1904, when without warning Japan attacked the Russian fleet anchored in Port Arthur, and, to the surprise of Tsar Nicholas II, won victory over the Russian empire. A new, confident Japan was born.

In 1940, Japan allied itself with Italy and Germany, and Japanese expansionism grew in line with Germany's invasions in Europe. In September, after the German-friendly Vichy government had taken over the administration of the French colonies, Japanese soldiers invaded French Indochina (now Vietnam), Laos and Cambodia. The USA, which accounted for about ninety per cent of Japan's oil imports, responded by imposing a complete oil embargo. Then on December 7, 1941, Japan launched an attack against the US Pacific Fleet in Pearl Harbor in Hawaii, and in the Philippines, as well as against the British colonies of Hong Kong, Malaya (now Malaysia) and Singapore. They also attacked the kingdom of Thailand. As in 1904, the strikes were part of Japan's strategy of surprise – war was only declared once it was a fact. The Japanese continued to invade Pacific islands in quick succession, and in January 1942 they also invaded the British colony of Burma. Within a very short space of time, the Pacific had become a battlefield, and Japan was attacking on all fronts.

The Burma Campaign was the longest campaign fought by the British in the Second World War. As is so often the case, it was the local population who suffered the most, caught as they were in the area between Japan on the one side, and the UK, USA and China on the other. It is estimated that about one million Burmese died in the fighting or from the famine and disease that followed in its wake. And just west of Burma, in Bengal in British India, some two to three million people starved to death while the British were caught up with fighting the Japanese.

The war in Burma was in fact about China. Japan's primary goal was to close the thousand-kilometre Burma Road, which ran from Lashio in North Burma to Kunming in Yunnan, and was the Allies' most important supply route to China. In April 1942, the Japanese took Lashio, and so succeeded in cutting the supply line. The American dream was that Chiang Kai-shek, the leader of the Chinese nationalist party, the Kuomintang, would defeat both the Japanese and the Chinese communists so that they could establish a trade agreement with a free and expanding modern China. They were therefore determined to keep supply lines to the Kuomintang open at all costs.

And it did cost, in terms of both material and lives. When the Japanese closed the Burma Road, the Americans started to build a new road from Ledo in north-east India, right on the border with Burma. The plan was that this road would join the original Burma Road somewhere in north Burma and then continue over the border to Yunnan. The British were not particularly keen, as this could give China the possibility of a direct link to India, but Washington forced it through – and footed the bill. Winston Churchill warned that the project was so extensive and labour-intensive that it would probably not be completed before there was no longer any use for it, and he was right. Even though fifteen thousand American soldiers and thirty-five thousand local labourers were employed, it took the whole of 1943 to construct the stretch from Ledo to Shingbwiyang in Burma, which was no more than 167 kilometres. The road went through dense jungle, and as no surveys had been done in advance, engineers had to guess and hope for the best when it came to ground conditions. The climate was warm and humid, and the jungle was full of all manner of bothersome insects and creepy-crawlies, such as malaria mosquitoes, spiders, scorpions and snakes, as well as bigger beasts such as tigers and leopards. About half the soldiers who died in the Burma Campaign did not die fighting, but rather fell victim to tropical diseases, starvation or wild animals.

And while the road was being slowly carved out, metre by metre, the only way to get supplies to Chiang Kai-shek was to fly over the Himalayas. The roughly 1,000-kilometre route became known as the Hump, but was also given more descriptive names such as the Skyway to Hell, Operation Vomit and the Aluminium Trail. The latter referred to the number of airplane wrecks left strewn on the ground along the route. More than five hundred aircraft crashed or disappeared in the three and a half years that the route was in daily operation, and more than thirteen hundred crew members lost their lives. Pilots regularly had to take off in bad weather conditions in planes that were overloaded. There were no control towers or radars, no reliable maps and the radio connection was poor. Visibility was often close to zero and resulted in frequent mid-air collisions. And the mountains were high. Three powerful airstreams meet in this part of the Himalayas, which resulted in extreme turbulence. Most of the pilots were newly qualified with limited experience, and many of them had to fly the route back and forth three times a day for sustained periods.

The Ledo Road eventually opened in January 1945. In the post-war period it was renamed the Stilwell Road, after the notoriously irascible American general Joseph Stilwell, who was responsible for the construction of the road. Allied pilots continued to fly "over the Hump" in order to supply Chiang Kai-shek with munitions until November of the same year.

*

Ann Poyser, our host in this corner of India, did not think that Tasang and Danthi would be able to find the remains of the Ledo Road by themselves, and so accompanied us as our guide. Ann was in her late seventies and overweight, with limited mobility. But she had devised her own techniques for getting around. Her father, Stuart Poyser, had come to Assam from England in the 1930s to manage one of the many tea plantations in the region. Life on the plantation was lonely, and it was not long before the young Englishman fell in love with Monglee, the niece of his servant. Monglee was only fourteen when she gave birth to their first daughter, Mary. Ann was born five years later.

Stuart Proyser would not, or could not, acknowledge the children as his own, or enter into an official British marriage with their mother, but he did marry Monglee in a traditional ceremony in her village and helped to support the small family as best he could. When war broke out in Europe and in the neighbouring colonies, he signed up and was posted to British Malaya. On February 11, 1942, four days before the fall of Singapore, he was killed in combat. He had left an album and some documents with information about his family in Great Britain for Monglee, but not only could she not read them, they were stolen shortly after he died. Ann grew up without knowing even his first name. Her mother thought he was called Stephen.

When Ann was five and Mary was ten, their mother managed, with the help of a Catholic pastor, to send her daughters to a convent school in Guwahati, far, far away. Mary died of dysentery after only a few months, but Ann survived, completed her schooling and got a job as a secretary to an English couple. Some years later, she in fell in love with a Sikh pilot. They got engaged and moved west to live with his family. Only when she was pregnant did she discover that her fiancé had not yet divorced his first wife. She was furious and returned to the village in Assam, where she started to work as a secretary again. It was not easy to find a landlord who was willing to let a single mother of mixed race live in the house, and matters were not helped by the fact that local men would often turn up uninvited at night. Ann had to keep her door locked all the time. But when her daughter got older, Ann managed to get a promotion and slowly their finances improved.

Ann had tried many times to find out more about her father and his fate over the years, without any success. Then in 1985 she came across an article in the *Daily Telegraph* marking the anniversary of victory over Japan. The person who wrote the article had himself served in Assam during the war and was now a major general. Ann wrote to him and, to her astonishment, she received an answer. The major general could tell her where her father was buried and what his first name was. With this information, Ann managed to find her father's sister, who was still alive and had no idea about her brother's secret Indian family. Since then, Ann has visited her father's family in England once a year. When she turned fifty and her employer retired, she bought a tea plantation with her savings and later built the small guest house where I was staying.

The runway was overgrown with weeds. Teenage girls in green and white school uniforms sat bent over their mobile phones and books. Poorly hidden behind a tree, a group of schoolboys were enjoying watching the girls. There were no signs or information boards telling of the thousands of pilots who had set out on the treacherous journey over the east flank of the Himalayas from here, time and again, during the war.

The Ledo Club, where the flamboyant Lord Mountbatten of Burma had his office following his appointment as Supreme Allied Commander South East Asia Command by Churchill in 1943, had also seen better days. The tennis court was now a car park and the billiard table had been put into storage. But the bar was still there, and what was more, it was open; three smiling staff showed us round the dusty, empty rooms. The bar itself was decorated with artificial flowering pot plants and bathed in a harsh blue light.

"I used to come to the dances here at the weekends," Ann said as she struggled down the steps from the old hotel. "Membership cost eighty rupees. It wasn't easy being half-British, half-Indian here. The whites wouldn't accept me as one of them, and nor would the Indians."

Zero Point, the start of the Ledo Road, was a couple of kilometres away. It was marked with a few memorial plaques and faded information boards.

"It's a long time since there was any road here to speak of," Ann said. "But a bit higher up you can see the remains of a bridge."

Only the foundations were left. The bridge itself had been dismantled stone by stone by the local farmers.

Ann turned round in the passenger seat and looked at us triumphantly.

"You would never have found this without me, would you?" She beamed with satisfaction. "There's a fish market round the next bend. We can buy some provisions there."

Our guided tour finished with a picnic on the banks of the Bhramaputra River. Ann's servants had sent us off with sandwiches and other ingredients for lunch. Tasang and Danthi lit a fire, put the rice on to cook and started to chop vegetables. I sat and watched village life on the riverbank. There was something going on all the time, even if it was not of great note. Men wandered down to bathe, young girls came in pairs to wash clothes, cows waded out into the shallows for a drink, a tractor forded the river and almost went under in the process, a wide river boat pushed out upstream and slipped gently by. The Himalayas watched over us in the distance. Soon there were delicious smells coming from the fire, and when the food was ready, it was served on banana leaves. Ann ate with a good appetite and was full of respect and admiration for Tasang.

"You might not be good at finding your way, but you can certainly make good food," she said. Tasang grinned and filled her banana leaf with more.

As we were packing up, the light slowly shifted from milky blue to purple. Soon the riverbanks were empty.

"I didn't realise it was so late, it's almost five o'clock!" Ann said, obviously concerned. "We have to be away before it gets dark. The rebels stay in the jungle during the day, but after dark, no-one is safe."

The idyll was broken. Separatist groups have been fighting for an independent Assam for more than thirty years. The conflict has cost more than thirty thousand lives and the local people have paid the price – quite literally. Like most landowners in the state, Ann is regularly forced to pay protection money.

"I normally pay around fifty thousand rupees a time," she said. "The alternative is death, which makes it a simple choice. One could of course go to the police, but they would only protect you for a week or two, and then you'd be left on your own again. Everyone pays."

We drove back to Ann's house, past armed military patrols, enclosed military camps and signs warning against elephants on the road. During the night, I was woken several times by deep, trumpeting roars from the jungle nearby.

*

We carried on driving south along the Naga Mountains, which are part of the Purvanchal Range, which in turn is a sidearm of the Himalayas. At regular intervals we passed small clusters of bamboo houses in the green, rolling landscape. At some point, Danthi turned east towards Myanmar.

The border between India and Myanmar goes through the middle
1400 MSL of **the local king's house.** The house was made from brick, with a new corrugated-iron roof, but otherwise was very much the same

as the traditional longhouses. A yellow, green and red Burmese flag
hung to the right of the gate, and an Indian one to the left. From
the parking lot, there was a view to the Indian border post, which
was a little higher up the slope, and to Myanmar's rolling, green
hills, which are remarkably like those in India.

We were told that the king was not at home; he was in church.
We wandered down the steep hill to the church and just managed
to catch the end of the service. The place was packed, and everyone
was dressed up. The women wore bright wraparound skirts, or short
dresses, and the men were in suits and shirts. The minister spoke
for some time from the pulpit. The only thing I understood was
"Christmas", and he said it rather a lot. At one point the congregation
sang "Joy to the World" in high, reedy voices, followed by more talk
about Christmas, which was fast approaching. Suddenly, a crescendo
of voices rose to the ceiling, only to fall silent just as quickly, when
the prayer was over. Everyone then hurried out.

We went back to the king's house. The local guide, who was also
there as an interpreter, introduced me to a short, unassuming man.
He had high cheekbones, dark lips and no wrinkles at all, and was
wearing black sneakers and a brown jacket. His eyes were big and
serious.

"This is the king," the interpreter said.

The only thing that gave away the small man's rank was a discreet
name badge on the collar of his jacket that said: "Towei Phawang.
Chief Angh."

Tasang gave him the gifts we had brought with us: a carrier bag
of tea, sugar and biscuits. The king graciously accepted the gifts and
we all sat down on the stools by the hearth, where a woman was
busy preparing lunch.

"I am forty-three years old and the angh for thirty-eight Konyak
villages in Myanmar and four in India, so more than a hundred
thousand people," the king said in a quiet voice.

As the border ran straight through his house, I realised that the king was sitting in Myanmar and I was sitting in India.

"The borders were drawn up by the Indian government in 1971, when my grandfather was the angh," he said. "My grandfather had no education and when he was young, Christianity had not yet come here. When Christianity came, people stopped chopping off each other's heads, and a border was drawn up between Myanmar and India. My grandfather decided that his house should lie on the top of a hill between the two countries, so he was just as much king in each, and there was also the possibility to keep an eye on his enemies. Before Christianity came, we couldn't pass the village Tangyu, as we were at war with them. Now we're all Baptists and one big family. When my grandfather was young, we were headhunters and worshipped stone, wood and water."

"They practised a form of animism," another guide added. Her group, four German pensioners, had sat down by the fire as well and were listening with interest to the conversation. A man with a white beard, expensive camera and a large piece of green snot hanging from one of his nostrils sat so close to the king that he was almost on his lap. The king's house was open to everyone; the doors were wide open and anyone could come in and take as many photographs as they liked.

"I am the eldest son of my father's first wife," Towei said, without paying any attention to his new audience. Their cameras whirred and clicked. "The king's first wife is the queen. She doesn't need to do anything. I have two wives myself. Number two . . ." he nodded at the woman who was kneeling by the hearth, chopping vegetables, ". . . is more like a house help, a worker. The king can have as many wives as he likes. My grandfather had sixty wives, and my father had fourteen."

"Do you plan to take any more wives?" I asked.

"Possibly," he said, and even gave a smile. "I only have nine children myself, but I have so many brothers and sisters, it's impossible to count. I wish them all well, and want all my children to go to school. I have no education myself, as that wasn't the custom in the past. The crown prince did not go to school."

The bearded German tourist knelt down in front of the king and pushed his telephoto lens so close to his face that it almost hit his nose.

"I am responsible for all the villages and have to make all the important decisions," the king said, unperturbed. "If people are fighting, I have to mediate. And in return, the villagers have to pay tax. When anyone kills a large wild animal, I get the head. When a gayal is sacrificed, I get the right leg. People also give me rice, yams and opium. A lot of opium is grown on the Myanmar side, and almost everyone smokes, though I myself stopped three years ago. When you have opium, everything is fine, but when you don't, you can't face doing anything. At the end of every month, I meet representatives from the Indian and Burmese armies. I have dual nationality and both countries recognise me as the king of the Konyaks. I can move freely back and forth across the border, and I can vote in both countries."

"Who will you vote for in the next election?" I asked.

"Nagaland People's Front."

I raised an eyebrow. "The independence movement?"

"Yes, it would make me so happy if Nagaland were to become independent, but India will never allow it," the king said. "Generally, when there's nothing in particular happening in the villages, like now, I live a very ordinary life. I work in the fields and sometimes I take everyone in the village on a fishing trip."

I was about to ask him about his dreams for his people when a delegation of serious-looking men marched in through the entrance. The king jumped up and went over to them.

"The king may come and go as he pleases," the interpreter said. "It is the king's prerogative."

Towei sat down at the head of a long table in what presumably was the meeting room. Our audience was over. We got up and walked back to India. In one of the smaller rooms on the Myanmar side, four men were smoking opium. Half a dozen elderly Western tourists were busy documenting the scene.

*

A war often ends many times before it is over. And the suffering is often drawn out, as very few warlords have mastered the art of stopping in time. Renya Mutaguchi, the lieutenant general who led the Japanese forces over the border into India in spring 1944, was definitely not one of them.

The plan was daring from the outset and Mataguchi faced considerable opposition. He hoped that an attack on the Indian villages of Imphal and Kohima would cut the supply route to China and prevent a counter-attack by the British from Burma. If the plan had worked, the Indian plains would have been at their mercy.

The first Japanese regiments crossed the Indian border on March 8, 1944. The Battle of Imphal commenced. Four weeks later, the Japanese launched a similar offensive on the village of Kohima, about a hundred kilometres further north. Kohima lay at the end of the narrow pass from Burma over into India, and was therefore of great strategic importance.

The Battle of Kohima has gone down in history as South Asia's Stalingrad. The most intense fighting took place on the tennis courts of the deputy commissioner's bungalow, and it was man to man. There were rotting, fly-infested bodies lying everywhere; there was no water, sanitary conditions were appalling and the wounded were left to die.

To begin with, the Japanese soldiers were in the majority, but as supplies could not get through, they slowly ran out of food and ammunition. Almost half of the sixty-five thousand Japanese soldiers who were sent to the front in Imphal and Kohima died. And more than twenty thousand were wounded, but only six hundred were taken prisoner. As many lives were claimed by disease, starvation, suicide, insect and snake bites, and pure exhaustion as by British bullets, bayonets and bombs.

By April 20, the situation was so dire that Lieutenant General Kotoku Sato, commander of one of the infantry divisions involved, decided to withdraw his men from Kohima. Mutaguchi, who was responsible for the offensive, stopped his retreat and ordered the soldiers to start fighting again. At the end of May, Sato reported that they had run out of food, and had very little ammunition left. He warned that he would pull the soldiers out of Kohima unless the promised supplies materialised. Mutaguchi was furious: "How dare you use such an excuse of difficulty of supply and renounce Kohima!"[8]

Sato defied the order and, as he had warned, withdrew his soldiers from Kohima, with the following parting words: "Our swords are broken and our arrows gone. Shedding bitter tears, I now leave Kohima."[9] On June 22, the British regained control of Kohima, and the remaining Japanese soldiers ceased to obey orders. Even Mutaguchi now realised that the battle was lost. On July 3, the Japanese withdrew from India. Sato was sacked a few days later, and devoted the rest of his life to the surviving soldiers and families of those who had died, determined to visit each and every one of them. Mutaguchi was dishonourably discharged. After the war, the Americans had him arrested and he was sentenced to imprisonment for war crimes by a military tribunal.

The defeat at Imphal and Kohima was a turning point and the beginning of the end for the Japanese expansion in Asia. However, Japan continued its aggressive war in China and the Pacific for another year, and was finally defeated in August 1945.

The only evidence that remains of Japan's defeat is the house where Lieutenant General Sato lived during the campaign. The house is just

1585 MSL outside the small village of **Kigwema**, about twelve kilometres from the centre of Kohima.

A sign at the entrance to the village tells that the Japanese arrived here at 3 p.m. on 4.4.1944. Nearby, four men sat on four stools whittling tea cups.

"General Sato's house is just behind the big building," one of them told us, before we had said a word.

Tasang and I followed the vague direction, but did not manage to find either the big building or General Sato's house. When we had wandered around for a while, we met some old men who were drinking tea together and chatting. The oldest of them, a grey-haired fellow in rainbow jogging trousers, jumped up and introduced himself in Hindi as Siesa Yano, and told us that he was born in 1926.

"Wow, you're nearly a hundred then!" I exclaimed.

"Ninety-two," Siesa said. "Come, I'll show you General Sato's house. I guess that's why you are here. I knew him well."

Siesa nimbly descended the steep stone steps that led to General Sato's house. It was smaller than the other buildings in the village, but had obviously been renovated and upgraded since the Japanese lieutenant general deserted the continent. The entrance was adorned with well-tended planters. The door was open, but there was no-one at home. Two clear plastic bags with flattened beer cans were lined up again the wall, even though alcohol is forbidden in Nagaland. There was a spectacular view over the valley from where we stood.

"General Sato lived in this house, but his soldiers stayed down in the jungle. During the war, the British bombed the Japanese camps, and the Japanese bombed the British camps. We got used to all the planes, but we were scared of the bombs. Every time an airplane flew over, we ran and hid. The neighbouring village was bombed by the British without warning. Nine people died and twenty were injured. Those who survived fled to us for refuge."

A tall, fair tourist dressed in khaki from head to toe came down to the house, took a photograph, then left again.

"That's what most tourists are like," Siesa said, with a sigh. "They just take a picture of the house and leave. But the house doesn't tell you anything about General Sato. He was a good man. The Japanese are a bit like us, there were never any problems with them. They don't eat much meat, and they liked our vegetables from the jungle. The British soldiers didn't know the vegetables, but the Japanese paid good money for them. The British got us to do all their heavy work, to carry things for them. General Sato never did. He was a good person. When the war was over, he left. Nearly all his soldiers were killed and left lying in the jungle. Some time after the war had ended, the Japanese came back to bury their dead. There were only bones left."

Siesa followed us to the end of the village. On the way back up the stone steps, we met a young man on his way down.

"Has he shown you General Sato's house?" the young man asked. "Do you know that he worked for Sato? He loves the Japanese!"

Siesa smiled. "General Sato was a good man."

*

Thinoselie Keyho was dressed in a dark suit, woollen waistcoat, white shirt, polished shoes and a flat cap. The 88-year-old was hard of hearing, but his daughter, who was my age, was there to help. I had hoped to talk to him about the Second World War and his experiences from the weeks of fighting in Kohima, but he had very little to say about the famous battle.

"I saw the flames from a distance," was more or less all he said. The war that he wanted to talk about was more recent, and he had taken part in it himself, for twenty years.

"Nagaland declared its independence on August 14, 1947, one day before India," the old man said, in slow, but correct English. "On March 16, 1951, we had a referendum and more than ninety-nine per cent of the votes were for independence, but the Indians would not give it to us. I am the head of the Naga National Council, the original independence organisation, which was established in 1946."

Nagaland is slightly smaller than Kuwait in area, and is one of the smallest states in India, with about two million inhabitants.

"The different Naga tribes were constantly at war until the American missionaries came and gave us Christianity," the old man said. "The British sowed the political seed. If the transfer of power had been peaceful, we might perhaps have gained our independence, but the British withdrew in haste and left Pakistan and India to their fate. We Nagas saved India in the Second World War, we stopped the Japanese, and yet Nagaland was incorporated into India as an Indian state – even though we have never had anything to do with India. Nagas are not Indian and we never have been."

His daughter poured us fresh tea and urged us to drink while it was still warm. Her father carried on talking.

"For twenty years, I fought against the Indians. In every confrontation, many Indians were wounded and died, but few or none on our side. God is on our side, and we have other friends too. Both China and Pakistan support our cause."

But this fight for freedom came at a price: in 1971, Thinoselie was arrested in Bangladesh and handed over to India.

"I was put in an overcrowded cell and was physically tortured, but I rose above all the humiliations. After five years I was released and continued my work to unite Nagaland. It is a difficult task, as the Indian authorities play with us, they set people up against each other. The independence movement is now divided into nine or ten factions, and seven of them are in negotiations and discussions with the Indian government."

"Do you see any benefits of being part of India?" I asked.

"No," he said, without hesitation.

"So you still hope that Nagaland will be independent one day?"

"Yes." His answer was again unequivocal. "An invisible super-power is on our side. That is why we have held out for so long. Not just physically, but also spiritually."

"You have fought for independence all your life, but Nagaland is still part of India," I said. "Is there anything you regret?"

"No, I regret nothing," the old man said, firmly. "We are not fighting for independence, we are *defending* our independence. We may be divided now, but our hearts are united."

"Have you ever voted in an Indian election?" I asked in closing.

"Never! I have never even been near a polling station."

I thanked him for the tea and his time, and got up to leave.

"You are now a guest in the Indian puppet state of Nagaland!" Thinoselie called after me. "Come back again when we are free!"

His daughter followed me out.

"Do the young people in Nagaland support independence?" I asked her.

"No, only a minority do," she said. "Most of them are happy with their comfortable existence."

"And you, do you support your father's fight?"

"Of course," she said, obediently.

The war cemetery in **Kohima** is on the hill where the deputy 1444 MSL commissioner's tennis courts once lay. The graves were neatly arranged in terraces and planted with flowers in the same meticulous manner as the cemetery outside Digboi. No-one was given preferential treatment in death. On the memorial stone at the top of the cemetery, there was a poster bearing the famous epitaph ascribed to John Maxwell Edmonds: WHEN YOU GO HOME, TELL THEM OF US AND SAY / FOR YOUR TOMORROW WE GAVE OUR TODAY.

Small groups of schoolchildren and students wandered through the cemetery, chatting. Flocks of tourists searched out the best places to take a selfie. And in a shaded corner, two cleaners were taking a rest from scrubbing the gravestones.

More than seventeen thousand soldiers from the British Commonwealth were killed, reported missing or badly wounded in the Battles of Imphal and Kohima. Three years later, India gained its independence, and one year after that, Burma. In 1949, Mao's communist army, assisted by the USSR, defeated Chiang Kai-shek's American-backed troops, and the dream of lucrative trade deals was shattered.

Since then, more than fifty thousand people have given their lives for the dream of a free Kashmir, and more than thirty thousand have been killed in the fight for an independent Assam. The independence movement in Nagaland has claimed at least three thousand lives.

The rivers that run down from the Himalayas are red with blood, but both the water and the mountains continue south, unaffected, all the way to the Bay of Bengal, where they spread out under the surface of the ocean like a deep-sea fan.

SECOND STAGE

April–July 2019

"Despite the geologists' knowledge and craft,
mocking magnets, graphs and maps –
in a split second the dream
piles before us mountains as stony
as real life."
Wisława Szymborska

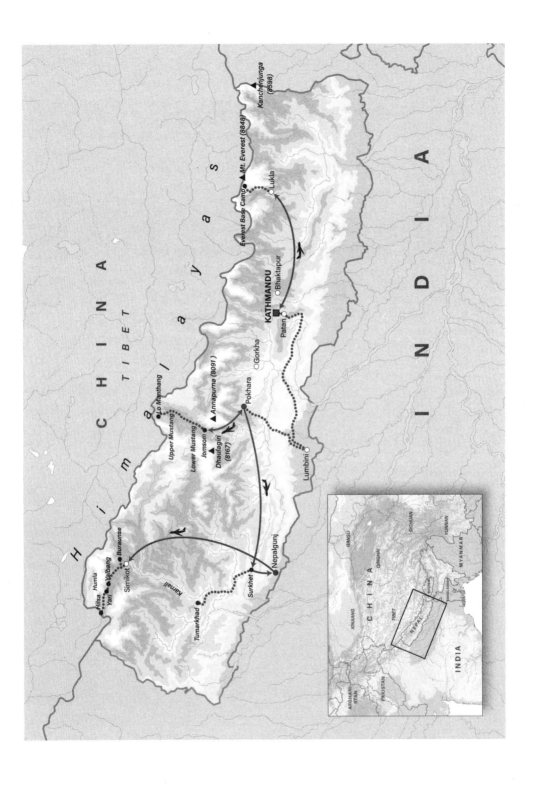

Child Goddesses

When does a journey start and end?

It was sixteen years since I had last been in **Kathmandu**; back 1400 MSL then, I was nineteen and on my first backpacking holiday with my Swedish boyfriend, who now belongs to another life. Kathmandu had changed, and so had I. The city was uglier than I remembered, dirtier, more dilapidated and, above all else, busier. The traffic was hellish, hooting cars and aggressive scooters snaking through the narrowest alleyways. In the tourist district, Thamel, the competition between travel agencies, pashmina shawl shops and sports shops, which were bursting with cheap Chinese copies, was keener than ever. A box of free face masks stood in a prominent position on the hotel reception desk – protection against air pollution.

Still dazed after the long flight, I met my interpreter, Savitri Rajali, an energetic 34-year-old with short hair and a coarse, infectious laugh. She did not waste time on small talk, but instructed me to cover my mouth and nose and get on the pillion of her scooter. She wound her way impatiently past dawdling tourists, around small, crooked temples, through a local vegetable market where men and women sat behind towering piles of carrots and chillies, then out onto the main road where the cars were at a standstill, but not us, and soon we were at one of Kathmandu's many hearts.

The Pashupatinath Temple is the oldest Hindu temple in Kathmandu, and one of the holiest in Asia. The 1,500-year-old temple is built around an ancient lingam, a symbol that represents Shiva. Bare-footed pilgrims from far and near came bearing gifts, often of the edible kind, much to the joy of the local fauna, which included monkeys, birds, dogs, cows and a large selection of rats. Only Hindus are allowed into this holiest of temples, so I had to admire from the doorway the lingam and golden ox that Shiva is riding.

Below the temple complex, a channel of greyish-brown, lethargic water gurgled past in the middle of what once must have been a wide river. Cows were now grazing on patches of grass where the water had previously flowed. White-robed priests were busy preparing pyres. The bodies of the deceased were wrapped in white cloth and placed on a bed of hay and flowers, on top of a pyramid of sturdy logs. Family and friends sat and watched their loved one slowly go up in flames until nothing but ashes remained. The process could take several hours. A scrawny man pushed a simple coffin in front of him through the dirty water, picking up any floating, half-burnt logs that could be reused. Some men in colourful tunics with faces covered in soot and red powder sat on the far bank; one of them was wearing a furry leopard skin. The men shouted to us that they would be happy to pose for photographs, or would I like my fortune told?

"They are charlatans," Savitri said. "They only want money from the tourists."

Up above the river, we found a genuine ascetic in a peaceful square in front of one of the less popular temples. He was thin, humble and draped in faded orange rags. He looked about fifty or so, and was called Birhaspathi Nath Yogi.

"Why did you choose to become a yogi?" I asked.

"Why did you choose to be born a woman?" was his reply. "Everyone makes their own choices in life. Some of my siblings are doctors. I am a yogi."

Birhaspathi lived in a simple shack with no walls outside one of the temples. A half-naked colleague snored peacefully beside him.

"I became a yogi at seventeen," he said. "There is no peace on earth, and the world is an aggressive and violent place. People come here, to me, looking for peace. Some stay, but only a few manage to last long. Our daily routine is too hard for most. I get up at four every day, have a bath and wash my face. Then I drink some tea. After that, I clean the temple square, and eat lunch around eleven. Then I rest for a while, like my colleague here. He is from India, which is why he is not so active. Lots of visitors come here during the day and ask for advice, just like you. In the evening, I play the traditional drums by the river and do *puja*, the traditional prayers."

A colonel came over to give Birhaspathi some money, which he graciously accepted. When he had dispatched the colonel, he turned his attention to me once again.

"There is too much traffic in the centre of town, too much pollution," he said. "It's peaceful here. I am happy with my life. I have found peace."

"I don't understand Hinduism," I said. "It's so confusing with all the gods and reincarnations. How do you keep track of them all?"

"What do you believe in?" Birhaspathi asked.

"I don't have a religion," I said.

"What religion are your parents and grandparents?"

"They are Christian. A couple of them, at least."

"So you are Christian, in other words, because you were born into a Christian family," Birhaspathi said. "I was born into a Hindu family, so I am a Hindu. You Christians have it easy. You only have to believe in Christ. In Hinduism, we have thirty-three million gods and it's impossible to remember them all."

"So how do you keep track of them all?" I asked again.

"At the end of the day, there is only one God," the yogi said. "Inside, we are all the same, and we all hold an invisible power: God. It is He who has made us flesh and blood. God is the same the world over, but His followers have given Him different names. The

Hindus are one group, the Christians another, and the Muslims a third. Of these three, Hinduism is the original, as Hinduism has existed for as long as there have been people on earth."

A bell rang somewhere, and suddenly Birhaspathi was in a rush. It was time for the evening ritual. Down on the riverbank, two more bodies wrapped in white cotton had been laid out on two new pyres. The priests were preparing to light fires, while the families stoically sat and watched.

In another of Kathmandu's hearts there is a living goddess. I had caught a glimpse of her the last time I was here: a little girl dressed in a sumptuous, red dress with red and black make-up on her face, being carried through a sea of people on a litter. The little girl looked out with a blank face at the mass of people who had come to worship her, as though all the fuss made no impression on her whatsoever. I later learned that the girl on the litter was a *kumari devi*, a living goddess, who only leaves her living quarters thirteen times a year, for special events and festivals. As her feet must not touch the ground, she is carried on a litter on these occasions.

The temples in Old Kathmandu had taken a bit of a pounding since I was last there. The powerful earthquake that shook Nepal in 2015 measured 7.8 on the Richter scale. The earthquake killed close to nine thousand people and left more than three million homeless, as well as damaging more than seven hundred historic monuments. Most of the temples in the old town were still closed for restoration work. A number of the old stone buildings had totally collapsed. Men and women wearing masks and gloves sat behind fences and temporary barriers brushing and sorting the stonework. The old temples were being resurrected stone by stone.

By some miracle, the ancient, crooked kumari palace survived without so much as a crack. An open arch led into a square courtyard. There was a low Buddhist stupa in the middle; a large green bush shaded it like a parasol. The building itself was red brick, and the open windows were surrounded by intricately carved, dark-wooden frames. The kumari lives on the second floor. A small sign said that only Hindus were allowed to visit her, even though the kumari herself always came from a Buddhist family.

The Newari people, the historical inhabitants of Kathmandu Valley, have upheld the tradition of living goddesses for centuries. The Newari – who today account for only five per cent of the population of Nepal, but about half the population in the greater Kathmandu area – were originally Buddhist merchants and craftsmen, and were strategically positioned in the fertile valley between India and Tibet, just south of the Himalayas. Kathmandu Valley was at once isolated and an important trade hub: to the north, it was protected by the world's highest mountains, and to the south, by the warm, damp and malaria-ridden plains of Terai, which were impassable for half the year in summer. The Newari language belongs to the Tibeto-Burmese language family, whereas Nepalese, the official language of Nepal, is related to Sanskrit and is therefore an Indo-European language. As merchants and traders, the Newari came into contact with the other ethnic groups in the region, and were naturally influenced by them as well. About half the Newari people are now Hindus, and the Buddhist families have also embraced a number of Hindu traditions, including the caste system.

The Hindu Malla dynasty rose to power in Kathmandu Valley in the fourteenth century. Some hundred years later, the kingdom was divided in three: Kathmandu, Bhaktapur and Patan, the three main cities. Around the same time, the three kings embraced Taleju as their protective deity – Taleju is an incarnation of Durga, goddess of war and one of the most powerful deities in Hinduism – and established the tradition of royal kumaris. The goddess inhabits the body of a young girl, the kumari, and through this young girl the goddess can protect the kings. Once a year, towards the end of the eight-day Indra Jatra Festival, the kumari blesses the king and gives him a red mark on his forehead, a tilak.

In 1769, following a campaign that had lasted for twenty-five years, Prithvi Narayan Shah, the king of Gorkha, managed to sneak into Kathmandu during the Indra Jatra Festival while a huge number of its inhabitants were inebriated. Jaya Prakash Malla, the last Malla, followed the kumari as she was carried in a procession through the streets. Shah's troops forced Malla to flee during the procession, and he was separated from the kumari. So instead of the reigning king, it was Shah who followed the living goddess back to the kumari palace, where he knelt at her feet and was blessed with a red mark on his forehead. Shah's lifelong fight to conquer the powerful and influential Katmandu Valley was crowned by a red mark on his forehead from a little girl. Modern Nepal was born.

Groups of foreign tourists led by guides came into the courtyard and stood looking up at the large second-floor balcony with curiosity and anticipation, as the kumari sometimes came out to greet tourists in the morning. A sweaty man in shorts, canary-yellow T-shirt and baseball cap, with a radio hanging from the pocket of his shorts, jogged in and started to do his stretches in front of the stupa. The Nepalese morning news blared out from his transistor radio.

"I come in here every morning to stretch," he said, in between exercises. "It's so peaceful here."

A jingle proclaimed it was time for the weather forecast; it was expected to be sunny and warm in Kathmandu. The royal priest appeared during the adverts that followed. I had expected a clean-shaven lama in burgundy robes, but the priest was wearing good trousers, a polo shirt, a down jacket and trainers. He also had a smart watch and spectacles. His hair was long enough to be styled with glossy wax.

The most important Newari Buddhist priest started the morning ritual with bureaucratic perfunctoriness. First of all he opened the door to the temple, swept the floor and dusted the five statues of the Buddha. Then he got out the petals, incense and brightly coloured powder that he sprinkled on the statues as he prayed. When he was done he rang a bell decorated with large, white feathers. Before he went up to worship the goddess he arranged some flowers, incense and holy water in the stupa.

"As it is full moon, I have more duties than usual," he said, when he came back out. "Purnima, full moon, is a special day for us. Normally I come straight here, but when it's full moon I have to visit a couple of other temples first."

The royal priest was called Manju Shri Bajracharya and he was fifty-six. We stood in the shade to talk, to one side of the tourists who were waiting below the balcony in case the kumari should appear.

"Kathmandu has eighteen monasteries that belong to the Newari priesthood," he said, and drew up an organisation chart that showed which monasteries fell under which of the four administrative centres. He belonged to a monastery with seven hundred monks, but he only lived as a monk for four days a year.

"For those four days, we're not allowed to sleep in comfortable beds, sing, dance or wear jewellery. The rest of the year, we have to uphold five rules: don't kill, don't lie, don't steal, don't be unfaithful and don't smoke or drink alcohol. Otherwise we live ordinary lives. I am married with two children and am a qualified electrician. My family have been royal priests and have conducted all the rituals in connection with the royal kumari since the tradition was established more than three centuries ago. So my father was the royal priest, and when he died twelve years ago, I took over. I am the only one who can perform important national ceremonies. I carried on doing my normal job until I retired four years ago, as I earn hardly any money as the royal priest. The authorities give me three rupees for the rituals I perform here at the kumari palace every day. It's nothing. I do it out of duty, because I want to preserve our culture."

A gasp rippled through the group of tourists. I looked up and caught a glimpse of a heavily made-up girl in a red dress on the balcony. The tourists all fumbled for their cameras and mobile phones, but no-one managed to hit the shutter button before the living goddess withdrew again.

"The Hindus believe that the kumari is an incarnation of the Hindu goddess Taleju, but the Newari Buddhists think she is an incarnation of Bajra Devi, a tantric Buddhist goddess," the priest told me. "People believe different things, but we don't argue about it. The current kumari is four years old, and was chosen when she was three. The kumari is always selected from the Shakya caste, which is Buddhist. When we need a new kumari, we ask the Shakya families who have daughters of the right age to bring them to meet the selection committee. There are five of us in the committee: myself, the royal Hindu priest, the carer, an astrologist and a government representative. It takes a long time to find the right girl, and there are multiple criteria that have to be met: she cannot have any scars, she cannot have lost any teeth yet, she cannot have any deformities, and she must have a round, beautiful face, long hair and healthy eyes. The first few days are obviously difficult for the children, but they soon adapt to life with the carer's family. We find the next new kumari in good time before she starts to menstruate."

"Why is it so important to find a new kumari before the girl starts to menstruate?" I asked.

"When the girl reaches puberty, she changes and starts to be attracted to the opposite sex," the priest said. "Her thoughts also start to change. As a child, she is innocent."

I did a quick calculation. Manju's father died twelve years ago, in 2007, which meant that his father was the royal priest when the tragedy happened. But as Manju had worked closely with him, he would also have been personally affected.

"How did you react to the news that the royal family had been killed?" I asked.

"It took me an hour to digest the news, but similar things have happened before," Manju said calmly. "A number of our kings have been murdered in the palace. These things happen, it's nothing new. I was of course sad, because we should never kill our own family. We should not kill at all. Yet it happens in politics, all the same."

On June 1, 2001, the Nepalese royal family had gathered for their monthly family meal in an annex at the back of the main palace in the centre of Kathmandu. They were in the billiard room when Dipendra, the 29-year-old crown prince, was accompanied to his room at half past eight. He was so drunk that he could barely stand up, which was not unusual, and the family wanted to avoid a confrontation with King Birendra, who was on his way. Half an hour after he had been sent to bed, Dipendra appeared in the billiard room again, only now he was dressed in camouflage and armed to the hilt. He aimed at the king, who was having a conversation over by the billiard table, fired, then left the room. A short while later he came back and shot his father again. Then he turned the gun on the other family members in the room, and shot and killed his younger sister, two uncles, two aunts and his father's cousin. The queen and Prince Nirajan, the elder of his two younger brothers, fled out into the garden. Dipendra followed them. Nirajan was found badly injured near the garden soon after. He was declared dead on arrival at the hospital. The queen was found by the steps that led up to Dipendra's room; her head had been blown off. Dipendra himself was found unconscious in a small pond in the garden. He had shot himself in the head and was rushed to hospital. On June 4, he was declared dead, having been king for three days. Gyanendra, King Birendra's eldest brother and the third heir to the throne, had not been present at the catastrophic family dinner, and was crowned king.

Many Nepalese people refuse to believe that Crown Prince

Dipendra was responsible for the massacre. To make matters worse, the investigation took no more than a week, and the bodies were quickly cremated and parts of the palace pulled down. The motive for the massacre is still unknown. There are many who think that it was Dipendra's revenge for not being allowed to marry the woman he loved, Devyani Rana, because of caste issues and political alliances, whereas others believe it was the uncle, Gyanendra, who was behind it. There were demonstrations and riots on the streets of Kathmandu in the days immediately after the coronation.

Gyanendra was a remarkably unpopular king. In 1990, his brother had given in to popular pressure and opened the way for political parties and free elections. Gyanendra instead backed the reintroduction of censorship and a state of emergency, so once again the country became an absolute monarchy. The Maoist rebellion had been ongoing since the mid-1990s, but when Gyanendra brought in the army to fight against the rebels, the numbers of deaths on both sides increased dramatically. In 2005, Gyanendra sacked the prime minister and effectively carried out a coup. His autocracy was short-lived, however: after a year of immense pressure from home and abroad, he was forced to reopen the parliament. The government signed a peace accord with the Maoists, and at the same time the king was stripped of all political power. Two years later, in 2008, the monarchy was officially abolished in Nepal.

"Do you think the monarchy will come back?" I asked the royal priest. Like the kumari of Kathmandu, he had retained his title, which was now no more than a linguistic remnant as Nepal no longer has kings.

"No," was his prompt reply. "People no longer support the monarchy. The last king was egocentric, he only thought about himself and not about his people, as a king should. And the kings before him were self-centred as well, only thinking of themselves. The people have been neglected, and still are."

The courtyard noises suddenly stopped. The kumari had come back out onto the balcony and was staring straight at me. Her charcoaled eyes held mine for ten seconds. She had the same sullen, arrogant expression as the girl on the litter sixteen years before. Then she turned on her heel and disappeared again. An enthusiastic chorus of voices rose up from the courtyard.

The old palace where the Malla kings had lived lay close to the kumari residence. The beautiful white building, with a tower crowned by a circular roof that reached up to the sky, had been badly damaged by the earthquake and was now closed to the public. There was scaffolding everywhere and large signs that said that the restoration was subsidised by the Chinese government. The Shah dynasty had in fact moved out long before the earthquake and taken up residence in a bigger and grander building at a more fashionable address.

The more modern edition of the royal palace was completed in 1969 and now serves as a museum. The exterior resembled a sixties pagoda, complete with crematorium chimney. The rooms were impersonal, as palace rooms so often are, but unlike palaces from centuries past, they had surprisingly low ceilings. The furniture and decor were simple, if one ignored the many stuffed and now very dusty wild animals that watched over the staircases from every landing. Everything was frozen in time. Walking through the royal rooms was like visiting a museum of 1970s and 1980s interior design, from the king's Japanese television, which presumably was cutting edge in 1985, to the throne room, which had four decorated, white, pipe-like pillars that rose stiffly towards the ceiling and were the base of the high tower that looked like a crematorium chimney.

A red sign by the exit pointed in the direction of ROYAL MAS-SACRE. A map showed where the various family members had been killed, and the accompanying English text provided the same information, without any mention of a perpetrator.

The billiard room was closed, but it was possible to look in through the windows. The carpets were rolled up, but the billiard table and sofa that many of the family members had used to shield themselves were still there. A sign showed the way to where Queen Aishwarya had been found in the garden, by a building that now stood in ruins. Another macabre sign simply said BULLET HOLES. And there were indeed visible bullet holes in the wall close to where a critically injured Prince Nirajan was found.

There was no sign to show the way to the pond where Crown Prince Dipendra was found, unconscious.

Gautam Ratna Shakya had grown up in the kumari palace and was now in his early fifties. He had initially asked for one hundred dollars to talk to me, which is equivalent to a month's wages for most Nepalese, but Savitri had managed to haggle the price down to thirty.

"My family, who are high caste, have been carers for the royal kumari in Kathmandu since the tradition was established three hundred years ago," Gautam said. "Twelve of us live in the kumari palace. My mother, who is seventy-six, is the main carer, but looking after the kumari is a full-time job for us all. None of us has a second job – we live on the donations that we get from the kumari's followers."

As a foreigner, I was not allowed into the palace itself, so we met at a traditional Newari restaurant nearby. The waitress brought large copper dishes filled with rice, fried boiled egg, spicy potato salad, beans and chatamari, a kind of thick pancake filled with chopped vegetables and egg, cooked in a pan with a lid.

"The kumari gets up at seven or eight," Gautam said. "My mother dresses her and does her make-up, and she is served breakfast at nine. Then the priest arrives, and people come in to worship her between nine and eleven. She has lunch at eleven, and then she has classes in the afternoon. When school is over, she rests for fifteen to twenty minutes, before receiving more worshippers between four and six. In the evening she is free to play, do her homework, watch television or play games on her mobile phone. She has dinner at about half past seven. Her day is a little shorter on Saturdays, but neither she nor we have any holiday."

"How many kumaris have you worked with?" I asked.

"The current kumari is my sixth. They are all sent away at the age of eleven or twelve, before they start to menstruate. And on the same day that one leaves, another little girl takes her place. We teach the new girl the routines, and after a matter of days, really, she is familiar with them. The kumari palace is never empty."

"Have the six girls differed from each other in any way?" I asked.

Gautam looked at me perplexed.

I tried again. "All children are different, so the six kumaris that you've known must have been different in some way, had different personalities?"

"No, they are all the same," Gautam said. "There is no difference between them. To us, the kumaris are not ordinary children, they are goddesses, and we try to fulfil their wishes as best we can. The kumari inherently possesses cosmic powers. When I carry a kumari, I can feel that she is heavier than other children. But that may of course be because she wears such heavy jewellery," he added, as an afterthought.

"What happens if the kumari falls ill?" I asked.

"What happens if the kumari falls ill?" Gautam repeated, again bewildered.

"Yes, do you for example call a doctor or the royal priest, or perhaps both?"

"No, the kumaris are never ill," Gautam said. "It's never happened. They sometimes run a bit of a temperature, but nothing serious enough to call a doctor."

Kathmandu's former royal kumari, Matina Shakya, had returned to her parents' house and an ordinary life two years before. She had been a kumari for most of her life, from the age of three to twelve. She and her family lived in a duplex in the old town that looked out over a large, open square, not far from the kumari palace. Her father, Pratap Man Shakya, gave Savitri and me an effusive welcome. Matina was lounging on a large bed in the living room, her eyes fixed on the television at the other end of the room. She had a narrow, heart-shaped face, framed by two long plaits. The former goddess had pale, almost transparent skin, unusually full lips and large, melancholy eyes. She was wearing black leggings and a black and white blouse. She looked up at us, but said nothing. Her attention was focused alternately on the mobile phone in her hand and the television screen. On the walls there were large, framed photographs of her as a kumari, dressed in red silk dresses, with heavily made-up eyes.

"We have just come back from Moscow," her father said. "Matina is the first kumari in the history of Nepal to have made an official visit abroad."

Pratap told us proudly about everything they had experienced and all the people they had met, and he showed us photographs from their trip on his phone. He spoke a little English, but quickly switched to Nepalese when it became too complicated, or he got excited about something.

"Did you like Moscow, Matina?" I asked.

"Yes," she said, without moving her eyes from the television screen.

"What did you like best?"

She did not answer, but turned to look at the screen on her phone instead.

"We were so well received by everyone and even visited the astronaut training centre," her father said enthusiastically. "They don't normally allow visitors, but they let us in because we were on an official visit. Matina was invited to come and study at the agricultural university there!"

"What is it like to be the father of a kumari?" I asked Pratap.

I realised that I was unlikely to get any more than whispered mono-syllables from the ex-goddess.

"I think I have been extremely fortunate," he said, with a big smile. "I didn't think that Matina could be a kumari, because her mother is not a Shakya like me. Normally both parents have to be from the Shakya caste. But Matina was chosen to be the next kumari, which is a huge honour. I am happy to have been able to help continue the tradition."

"What was Matina like as a child?" I asked.

Matina looked up from her screen and over at her father, but still said nothing.

"She was unbelievably sweet and innocent when she was a baby," her father said. "She was quiet by nature, and loved to learn new things. In many ways, she was more innocent than the other kumaris. Her eyes were enormous, just look at the photographs on the wall. Her eyes were very expressive and strong. I missed having her at home, obviously, but the kumari tradition is part of our culture and we have to uphold it. And I could visit her as often as I liked. I generally went to see her every second day. I always made sure to know what was happening with her and followed things up with the authorities, when necessary. Thanks to my efforts, improvements have been made to the kumari system."

Matina became the kumari in 2008, the same year that the monarchy was abolished and Nepal became a federal republic. The government decided that the tradition of the royal kumari should continue as before, but instead of the king it would now be the president who was blessed by the kumari at the Indra Jatra Festival.

"The country becoming a republic gave rise to a number of practical issues," Pratap said. "I've brought about a change in the system, so the kumari is now registered at the local school. She had a private tutor before, but now the normal teachers come here to give her classes at the end of the school day. I also campaigned successfully for the nation to give financial support to the kumaris. When a girl is a kumari, she receives a wage, and when she's no longer a kumari, she receives a pension. Matina gets 15,500 rupees a month in pension, which is around one hundred and fifty dollars."

He looked fondly at his daughter, who lay there sending text messages to her friends.

"We are so happy to have Matina at home again. The day she came back from the kumari palace, the whole neighbourhood came out to welcome her back and followed her home in a great procession. And the transition to school wasn't too hard as we had made sure that her fellow pupils had met her when she was living in the kumari house."

"I've seen her at school," Savitri said. "And she's completely different there, lively and talkative. It looks like she's happy there. I think perhaps she's just tired now."

"Yes, she's more active at school, and she's also very active during our festivals," her father said. "Now that she's no longer the kumari, she's started to play the flute."

"What was it like being the kumari, Matina?" I asked.

It was a long time before she answered.

"It was good," she eventually whispered.

"Is there anything in particular that you remember?"

"No . . ." Her whisper was barely audible.

"Was there anything that you liked in particular, or maybe something you didn't like at all?"

Again, she was quiet for a long time, then shook her head.

"What was it like to come home again?"

After another long pause, she said: "Good."

"Do you miss being the kumari?"

She stared hard at the TV screen, and did not answer or meet my eyes.

"She often visits the new kumari and has helped her a lot," her father said. "The new kumari loves her and always wants her to stay. To begin with, Matina was there every other day, and often stayed over, but now she has more to do at school, so she doesn't go as often. She doesn't talk much to people she doesn't know," he added. "She doesn't say much to her mother and me either, but she talks to her sister a lot!"

"How was the transition from being a kumari to being an ordinary girl?" I asked Matina.

There was no answer. The former goddess had slipped into a state of absolute silence.

"The parents have to provide guidance, so I'm always with her," Pratap said. "She couldn't find her own way anywhere to begin with, and she wasn't used to being outdoors. So she's generally with us. Lots of press people turned up for her first day at school."

He got up and pulled out a couple of thick files of press cuttings, beautifully filed in plastic envelopes. The name of the newspaper and date were written on a label at the top of each cutting. The files were bulging with articles from both Nepal and abroad.

"I have lots and lots of these files," he said. "We try to help other people understand that a kumari is just an ordinary girl, a child like any other child."

Matina picked up one of the files and started to look at all the cuttings.

"We have just been invited to the USA, but right now school is the priority, so we'll have to see if there is time," her father said. "Whatever the case, it will have to be in the holidays, after her exams."

"What would you like to study when you finish school, Matina?" I asked.

"I don't know," she whispered.

"When she's finished twelfth grade, she will choose herself what she wants to study," her father said. "I want my daughters to be good citizens, and don't want to force them into anything. Matina hasn't yet decided what she wants to study, but she's still so young. She's got plenty of time."

He started to talk about the visit to Moscow again, and showed us more photographs, from the metro stations, the agricultural university, the astronaut centre. Matina watched her father's slide show drowsily from the bed.

Premshova Shakya lived in a small flat on a busy street in the middle of Kathmandu's fortune-telling district. Home-made signs advertised the many different services available, from palm-reading to horoscopes. Premshova used rice to read people's fortunes. She was short and round, dressed in a red sari with a gold border, and had rings on all her fingers, big, solid necklaces and heavy earrings that pulled at her earlobes. Her hair was still dark and thick, even though she was seventy, and she had a large red mark on her forehead. Her lips were painted red, and her many bangles jangled when she spoke. The small living room was full of pictures of the Buddha, Hindu gods and photographs of Premshova when she was the kumari in Bhaktapur, historically the largest of the three Malla kingdoms in the Kathmandu Valley. Various altars and statues of gods were lined up against the long wall, surrounded by half-withered flowers, incense, burning oil lamps and dishes with food offerings. A small insect crawled or buzzed every now and then. And a handful of white mice ran round and round in a glass case beside the small television set. Premshova opened the case and took out the two smallest mice. They were presumably only a few days old, as their eyes had not yet opened and their skin was paper thin.

"They bring good luck," Premshova said, in a deep, hoarse voice and gently stroked the two mice. She indicated that we should sit on the bed in the corner, the only thing to sit on in the room, then she sat down between Savitri and me.

"I've got diarrhoea," she said, "and I don't feel great. I am taking medicine, so it will be fine, but I've still got a sore stomach and feel weaker than usual. Anyway, before we can talk together, you have to make offerings to the gods."

She nodded at a colourful statue of Vishnu, or perhaps it was Shiva, and the offering dish that was beside the statue. We did as she said and each put a banknote down in the dish. Premshova gave a satisfied smile.

"I was selected as kumari when I was one," she said. "At the time, there was a carer family in Bhaktapur as well, and I lived with them in the kumari palace. Women like you, foreigners, came in to see me every day and they used to give me ten dollars as a souvenir."

She gave me a meaningful look.

"What do you remember from your life as a kumari?" I asked.

"When I was nine, I got my first period, and stopped being a kumari," she said. "I was so little when I was selected that I don't remember much, just one or two things. I remember I had lots of toys and teddy bears. Life as a kumari was good. If there was anything I didn't want to do, I didn't have to. My carers would do my hair and colour my feet red. The king came to visit me. I remember that. The neighbours came to worship me. People gave me gifts of gold and silver, and my father, who was a goldsmith, made an ankle chain from those gifts. I remember that. There were five of us who were seen by the selection committee, and I was the only one who didn't cry. I remember that as well."

"Did you understand why people worshipped you when you were a kumari?"

"No, I didn't understand at all, but I could feel the power of the goddess. I could feel that Taleju was in my body. When she was with me, I felt calm and peaceful. It felt good. When I stopped being a kumari, I missed the palace and my carer family. I missed playing with them, but wasn't allowed to go back. I never got any education either. But when I was no longer a kumari, I was allowed to dance.

And that was good. I love dancing. Ten months after I was retired as kumari, another goddess, Kali, entered my body. She is still with me. I didn't get married until I was thirty, because I was scared that my in-laws would force me to touch dirty plates. Kali doesn't like that. My husband understands me, luckily, and always does the washing up."

She turned to Savitri. "How did the photograph you took the last time you were here turn out? Was it good?"

"It was very good," Savitri assured her.

"My photograph is even in America," Premshova said proudly. "When I'm at the temple, people often ask to take photographs of me. They say I look special. My oldest son will be forty this year. Two years after he was born, the fortune-telling goddess entered me, and I started to tell people's fortunes."

"How did you know that the goddess had entered your body?" I asked.

"You just notice it. And others did too. People come here every week so that I can read their fortune in rice. People have lots of problems. They can't have children, or they have children who die. I don't like to give people bad news, so I always make sure to give them a solution as well – I say that they have to donate things, pray to a certain god, go to the temple, and then it will pass."

"Could you read my fortune?" I asked.

"No, Sunday is not a good day," Premshova said, and sadly shook her head. "Monday, Tuesday and Saturday are good days. But not Sunday."

She followed us down the stairs, took our hands and blew on them hard, with deep concentration.

"I have just given you all my energy," she said, and shuffled back up to her living room.

The last of the former kumaris I spoke to came out to meet me on the street.

"Come, follow me," she said firmly, and led me up a narrow

staircase into a reception room. Chanira Bajracharya had been the kumari in **Patan**, the smallest of the Malla kingdoms in Kathmandu   1332 MSL Valley, from the age of five to fifteen. These days Patan has merged into Greater Kathmandu, and it is hard to tell where one city ends and the other begins. The former goddess looked like an ordinary student, dressed in a checked shirt and jeans, with her hair pulled back in a ponytail. She was about a head shorter than me, with an almost perfectly round, moon face.

On the walls of the reception room there were large photographs of Chanira as a living goddess dressed in voluminous, red kumari dresses, with a heavily made-up, expressionless face. She was friendly, but kept a professional distance. She charged two and a half thousand rupees for the interview, a bit more than thirty dollars, which was less than the carer in Kathmandu, but still a considerable amount in a country where a third of the population live on about three dollars a day.

"I do about three or four interviews a week, on average," the 24-year-old said in fluent English. "It takes a lot of time, so it's like a job for me."

When Chanira was selected as kumari at the age of five, her family was in the unique position of having two living goddesses under the same roof.

"My aunt was the official kumari for almost thirty years," Chanira said. "Kumaris are replaced when they start to menstruate, but that never happened for my aunt. When she was thirty, it was decided that she could not take part in religious festivals because of her age, so she was replaced by a new official kumari. But my aunt has continued to perform her duties as a kumari: she still wears red dresses and does not leave the house, and lots of believers come to her to be blessed. When I was a little girl, I was fascinated by my aunt, and I remember vividly the first time I was dressed up as a living goddess. I was five years old and liked it a lot."

Unlike the royal kumari in Kathmandu, who moves into the kumari palace and is raised by a carer family, the kumari in Patan can live at home with her family.

"My family had to follow a lot of special rules," Chanira said. "They could no longer address me as a sister or daughter, only as a goddess. I could still play with my brothers, but they were not allowed to touch me. I always got my food first, and my family did their utmost to fulfil my wishes, so the goddess would not be offended. Financially, it was rather a struggle for my parents, as my father had to close his shop in order to look after me when I was the kumari. My mother managed to find a private tutor for me, but they had to pay for my tuition themselves. The state arrangements are much better now, but at the time it was difficult."

"Did you feel different after you became the kumari?" I asked.

"It did start to dawn on me that I had a special position in society and also a special responsibility, but I didn't exactly feel the goddess within me day and night. When I was being worshipped on my throne or during religious festivals, I might feel that I wasn't a part of society. I didn't feel like smiling at anyone, well, smiling at all . . . It's not easy to explain. But most of the time, I was just an ordinary girl."

"You were a child," I said. "Was it not hard to be indoors all the time? To never go out?"

"No, I didn't miss going out. Perhaps it was the goddess's power, or something else. I don't know why, but I never missed it. My parents took good care of me, and I got everything I wanted. I had video games and YouTube, so I wasn't as isolated as the kumaris once were. As I was a kumari, my parents weren't allowed to scold me, but my mother wrote all the bad things I did in a book, so she could punish me when I was no longer a kumari. It worked – I generally behaved. Many people in the West see the kumari tradition as child abuse, but that wasn't my experience. I loved being a kumari, and still miss it."

Chanira was the last kumari in Patan to meet the royal family.

She was six years old in the summer of 2001 when Crown Prince Dipendra ran amok and killed almost the entire family.

"Before the royal family were killed, I cried for four days," she said. "I was inconsolable. My mother didn't know what to do and sought advice from the royal priest. He said that it was a bad omen and instructed my mother to perform a certain ritual and to ask for forgiveness, because perhaps she had not carried out some of the rituals correctly. My mother started to prepare for the ritual, but then at midnight on the fourth day the phone rang and we were told that the royal family had been killed in a massacre. I laughed and laughed when I heard the news. My mother realised that it was no longer necessary for her to perform the ritual."

"Why did you laugh?" I asked, astonished.

"I don't know. It was the goddess in me who laughed. I only remember that I couldn't stop laughing."

"Was there anything you didn't like about being a kumari?" I asked.

"The tourists," Chanira said, without having to give it any thought. "The Nepalese came to worship me. They came because the kumari meant something to them – the kumari is a part of our tradition. The tourists don't know our culture, they just come to stare. I felt like a monkey in a cage, but as a kumari, I was not allowed to refuse anyone, not even tourists. The kumari in Kathmandu does not receive tourists, but anyone can visit the kumari in Patan. I do think they should introduce some restrictions."

When Chanira got her first period when she was fifteen, she became an ordinary girl again, from one day to the next.

"My parents had tried to prepare me for the fact that one day I would no longer be a goddess," she said. "I was told that my life would change and that people would treat me differently. But it was still a shock. The first few times I went outside, my mother had to hold my hand. I had never walked in the street before, and to begin with

I wanted to be carried all the time. I had no self-confidence in that regard, I felt so helpless, I couldn't find my way anywhere and was overwhelmed by all the traffic. And it was hard at school. I found it difficult to interact with other people, and I wasn't used to talking to people my own age, or being with them. Just wearing normal clothes was a problem to begin with. To make the transition easier for other kumaris, I started a support group for former kumaris. The girls need support during that time."

She glanced at her watch.

"Would you like to meet my aunt?" she said.

I nodded, of course, and was told to wait for ten minutes while the now mature goddess prepared herself. In the meantime, I took some photographs of Chanira, who was clearly used to posing. Ten minutes later, her father appeared in the doorway.

"She's ready to meet you now," Chanira said. "But you must first wash your hands."

I was shown a small basin, then taken into a pink room. In the corner, on a wooden throne that had originally been made for a young girl, sat Dhana, Chanira's aunt, in a red and gold dress, with black eye make-up and her hair pulled back in a bun. The child's throne was surrounded by incense, oil lamps and small bowls of fruit. Dhana was nearly seventy and shrunken, but her oval face was remarkably smooth, almost without wrinkles.

I knelt down in front of her, as instructed, and put some money in the offering dish that had been placed out in front of the throne. Then I leaned forward so the goddess could put a red mark on my forehead. She put a small flower on my head and offered me a banana. She said nothing during the ceremony, and her face was without expression, but her eyes were gentle and patient. When I stood up, the flower fell to the floor. I picked it up and put it back on my head, but it fell off again.

*

The current kumari in Patan did not live at home with her parents, as Chanira had done, but had moved into the kumari palace, an old wooden house a stone's throw away up the street. She lived there with her family. I rang the bell and an old woman opened the door and welcomed me. She indicated that I should take off my shoes and follow her up the stairs.

I was let into a dark and practically bare wooden-walled room. There was a low wooden throne against one of the short walls, but it was empty. A few minutes later, a young woman appeared with a little girl in her arms. The little girl was dressed as she should be in a red dress, her eyes were made up with charcoal and her hair was pulled up in the prescribed bun. The girl smiled at me, but clung to her mother with both arms and legs. The young mother put the girl down on the simple throne, and I knelt down in front of her, put some money in the offering dish and bowed my head. With playful movements, the tiny goddess put a red mark on my forehead.

"Can I take a picture?" I asked, and immediately regretted it. The mother translated for the girl, who very clearly shook her head. The audience was over, so I went back down the stairs and out into the daylight.

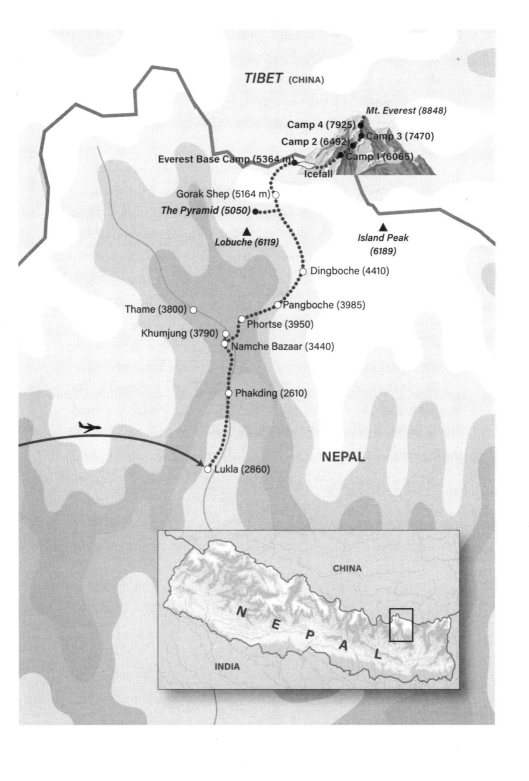

Busy at the Top

I was woken by the chandelier dancing. It only lasted a few seconds, then it was over. I was still half-asleep and was happy to accept that I had dreamed it all, but later in the day I encountered a lot of serious faces. The earthquake had measured 4.8 on the Richter scale, a relatively minor and harmless quake in terms of magnitude, but it had stirred up memories and trauma from the catastrophic earthquake four years earlier.

The Himalaya Range is the highest mountain range in the world, but also one of the youngest at a mere fifty million years. And these two superlatives are connected: ice, snow and rain wear and break down a massif. I still remember the disappointment I felt as a child when I realised that Galdhøpiggen, Norway's pride, was a relatively low mountain in a global context, at 2,469 metres. But once upon a time, around four or five million years ago, there were mountains that towered up to eight thousand metres in Norway. The Caledonian orogeny, which is still to be found in northern Europe, was possibly one of the world's highest mountain ranges at one point. It probably collapsed under its own weight when the compression stress from the continental plates eased. Could the same also happen to the Himalayas? Can a mountain massif collapse under its own weight? No-one knows for sure and geologists continue to argue about this. Mountains grow so slowly that a scientist's lifespan does not suffice.

Everything is moving all the time, including the ground under our feet. Three hundred million years ago, the continents of the world were one super-continent, Pangea. Then, very, very slowly, the super-continent split in two, to become Laurasia, which included North America, Europe and Asia, and Gondwana, which included Australia, India, South America, Africa and Antarctica. India broke loose from Gondwana about one hundred and fifty million years ago, and started to drift north with the continental plate at a comparatively high speed: that is to say, fifteen to twenty centimetres a year. A good hundred million years later, having covered a distance of ten thousand kilometres, the Indian subcontinent bumped into Eurasia. The Tethys Sea, which had separated the two land masses until then, was pushed to one side and the enormous land masses were thrust up by the continental plates: the Himalayas were born. One can still find fossils from the Tethys Sea all over the Himalayas to this day, even on the top of Mount Everest, ammonites in particular, a beautiful, snail-shaped creature that was an early ancestor of the octopus. Ammonites died out sixty-five million years ago, along with the dinosaurs.

The Indian continental plate, which presses up against the Tibetan plateau, is still moving north, but now at a speed of about fifteen centimetres a year. And the far greater and thicker Eurasian plate is moving south, but at an even slower pace. It maintains an average speed of two centimetres a year. In other words, India is shrinking with every year that passes, and the Himalayas are growing higher. The movement in the continental plates not only makes the mountains higher, it also causes enormous subterranean tension, which in turn results in frequent earthquakes.

*

The landscape rolls below us like gentle jade-coloured waves. Every so often one catches a glimpse of some small wooden houses with corrugated roofs that glitter in the sun. One of the warning lights flashes red, but the pilot does not even seem to notice; he remains devastatingly calm. I concentrate on the rice paddies and forests below us: different shades of green, light and dark, fitting into each other like the pieces of a puzzle. The warning light continues to flashes angrily, then suddenly the landscape changes and we fly straight towards a wall of stone and ice.

As the runway in Kathmandu is closed for very necessary improvements, we are taken by helicopter to **Lukla**, the starting point for 2860 MSL all expeditions up Mount Everest from the Nepalese side. I have signed up to a group tour organised by an American expedition company in order to be allowed to stay overnight at Everest Base Camp, which is only open to climbers and expedition members in the high season. Fortunately, it is not a big group: in addition to myself, there are two enthusiastic Americans, Lynn and Jade.

Pasang, our Sherpa guide, meets us at the helipad, and leads us through the muddy, car-free streets of Lukla, past the Thursday market, where farmers sell fruit and vegetables, to a single-storey guest house, where we are served breakfast. At the table next to us, a group of Indians are enjoying sweet milky tea.

"Looks like you're ready for a hike," one of them remarks, a grey-haired man in his fifties, nodding at my pristine, blue rucksack. His own is covered in a layer of brown dust, as are his climbing boots.

"We're going to Base Camp," I say. It is unnecessary really to name our destination, as basically all paths from Lukla lead to Base Camp.

"We've just been there," the Indian says.

"What was it like?" I ask.

"It was . . . marvellous."

"You don't sound very convinced."

"Well . . ." He pauses. "It was hard going, to be honest. Be prepared for it to get really tough. And it's cold. Really cold. Get ready to freeze. And you'll get the famous Khumbu cough. Everyone gets it, it's unavoidable, as hygiene in the guest houses is non-existent. People don't get better again until they're back in Kathmandu."

As though to underline his words, the man beside him breaks into a long, hacking cough.

"We got so ill that we couldn't face the last day, and requested a helicopter. But good luck!" He gives me a forced smile. "I hope you have an excellent trip!"

Moving at altitude is an exercise in slowness. As the body needs time to acclimatise, we walk for short periods, often no more than two or three hours a day. The sun beats down from an azure sky; the temperature is well over twenty degrees centigrade during the day. The path is wide and luxurious, more like a motorway, and winds its way ever upwards through small villages surrounded by pine forests and rhododendrons in full bloom.

Lynn and Jade have both prepared well for the challenges ahead and are equipped with carbon fibre walking poles, breathable sports gear, UV water filters, advanced drinking systems and a first-aid kit that includes cold remedies, altitude sickness tablets, blister plasters, creams, potions and antibiotics enough to last a medium-sized village for a year. Two local porters carry the first aid kits and the rest of our luggage from guest house to guest house. They carry a lighter load than many others, who are weighed down by tins of food, Coca-Cola, beer and noodles as they climb the forested slopes. The porters are in stiff competition with the mules that plod up in long trains, with bells around their necks, laden with gas cylinders and provisions. Only a few days before, a young American trekker had been forced off the path by the animals and fallen to his death – he had been on the wrong side of the path when the caravan approached and did not stand a chance.

On day two, we cross the boundary into Sagarmatha National Park. Sagarmatha, Goddess of the Sky, is the Nepalese name for Mount Everest; the Tibetans know the mountain as Chomolungma, Holy Mother. George Everest, the Briton who was responsible for surveying and mapping India from 1830 to 1843, was never anywhere near the mountain which has been named after him, and nor was he involved in its discovery. In 1856, when George Everest was safely back in England, his successor, Andrew Scott Waugh, and the mathematician Radhanath Sidkar realised that the mountain which they had marked down on the map as Peak B or Peak XV was possibly the highest mountain in the world. The pair concluded that it must be 29,000 feet – 8,839 metres – and added two extra feet to make the calculations more credible. Given that the measurement was made from observation points more than a hundred and fifty kilometres away, the precision is remarkable. Later surveys confirmed that the mountains was twenty-seven feet higher than Waugh and Sidkar had calculated, and was in fact 29,029 feet or 8,848 metres high. In 2005, Chinese surveyors concluded that the last four metres consist of ice, and that the actual elevation is therefore only 8,844 metres, but the authorities in Nepal and China agreed that the established height of 8,848 should remain the official height.

The highest mountain in the world could not have a Roman numeral as its name. Even in Waugh's day it was normal practice to use the local name, but both Nepal and Tibet were closed to foreigners in the nineteenth century and there was considerable confusion as to which name was most widely used among the locals. In the end, Waugh suggested that the mountain should be called after the man who had employed him, George Everest. Everest himself, who must have been a modest man, protested against this and argued that his name could never be written nor pronounced in Hindi, nor, therefore, in Nepalese.* But in 1865, having discussed the matter for close to a decade, the Royal Geographical Society in London decided to follow Waugh's recommendation all the same. George Everest died the following year, but his name remains elevated.

---

* In fact, no-one pronounces his name correctly: Everest himself said "Eve-rest", with the stress on the first syllable.

*

We have to register before we are allowed into the national park. A table of statistics hangs on the wall behind the official. The figures show a twofold increase in trekking tourists over the past twenty years: about forty thousand people now hike to Base Camp every year, in the course of a few months in either spring or autumn. A densely written sign by the entrance to the park lists the rules that apply in the national park: visitors are not allowed to throw rubbish on the ground or pick rare flowers, nor are they allowed to be jealous (!) or consume "excessive amounts" of stimulants, which leaves some scope for personal judgement.

The climb up to Namche Bazaar is very steep. In several places a queue starts to form, and my ears are filled with German prepositions, Italian interjections and thick American nasals as the air thins. Some way up the hill I spot a couple of compatriots. They are easily identifiable, not only because of their blond hair and long legs, but also the unashamed flags sticking up from their rucksacks.

The ascent is harder than it looks. My legs are heavy and clumsy, my heart is thumping so hard that my chest hurts, my lungs are burning. We walk a few steps, stop and gasp for air, then a few steps more, stop, gasp. At sea level, where the atmospheric pressure is 1, the air we breathe in contains 20.9 per cent oxygen. The atmospheric pressure sinks almost exponentially with altitude, so even though the various gas contents in the air remain the same within the earth's atmosphere, the partial pressure of oxygen decreases with altitude. When the atmospheric pressure falls, as it does with altitude, the gas molecules are not as densely packed as at sea level. The higher one is, the fewer oxygen molecules there are in a litre of air. In Namche Bazaar, at three and a half thousand metres, the air contains a third less oxygen than at sea level. At Base Camp, which is 5364 MSL, the oxygen content is half that at sea level, and at the top of Mount Everest, it is only a third.

The heart starts to beat faster to help the body adjust to the low oxygen content, and one's breathing also becomes faster as a result. The body gradually starts to produce more red blood cells to carry and distribute the oxygen from the lungs to the rest of the body – which is precisely the effect that elite athletes seek to achieve when they train at high altitudes. If one ascends too quickly, the body does not have time to adjust to the altitude, and in most cases this results in altitude sickness. The symptoms of mild altitude sickness are a headache, nausea or vomiting, dizziness, fatigue, difficulties sleeping and loss of appetite. These symptoms normally pass if one does not go any higher or, preferably, descends.

How the body copes and adjusts to altitude is entirely individual; some people can start to feel the symptoms of altitude sickness at only two thousand metres. People who have lived at high altitudes for hundreds of generations have adjusted to the conditions and therefore react differently to low air pressure from those who come from the lowlands. The Sherpas, for example, have genes that make them extremely well suited to living at high altitudes. The Sherpas, which means "East People", migrated from eastern Tibet in the sixteenth century and settled in the mountains in eastern Nepal. Scientists have discovered that the Sherpas' mitochondria, which is the part of the cell that produces energy, use less oxygen than the mitochondria of people who have traditionally lived closer to sea level. In other words, the Sherpas need less oxygen than most other people. However, no-one, not even the Sherpas, can acclimatise enough to spend any amount of time at more than eight thousand metres, the so-called death zone, without detrimental effect. The extreme altitude slowly breaks the body down and is deadly.

Severe altitude sickness can cause pulmonary oedema: the lungs fill with fluid due to increased pulmonary arterial and capillary pressure, which makes ventilation less effective. In severe cases, the sufferer can cough up foam. If the climber is not immediately evacuated to lower altitudes, he or she will basically drown. Cerebral oedema is another dangerous form of acute altitude sickness: at extreme altitudes, the body may react to the lack of oxygen by expanding the arteries that lead to the brain. As a result, the brain swells and presses against the skull. The symptoms of HACE (high altitude cerebral oedema) are severe headache, vomiting, confusion, hallucination and coordination difficulties. HACE is recognised as extremely dangerous, as the climber often does not realise that he or she is ill and needs to descend immediately in order to survive.

3440 MSL On the afternoon of the second day, we come to a colourful gateway: the entrance to **Namche Bazaar**. The village is shaped like a funnel; the rows of houses cling to the steep mountainside on terraces. Given that there is no road here, the houses are surprisingly large and modern, often three or four storeys high, with colourful tin roofs. Gasping and sweating, we haul ourselves through the gate, and the first things we see are the lotus fountain, some enormous prayer wheels turned by water, and an Irish pub. If, even for a moment, we had felt like pioneers as we climbed, the illusion is instantly shattered by the sign advertising Guinness and an extended happy hour.

We continue up through the village. The souvenir shops, pharmacies, outdoor shops and supermarkets that appear to specialise in toilet paper and disinfectant jostle for attention. Hand-made signs advertise Thai massage, pedicures, facial treatments and hair removal, and the guest houses have pasta, pizza, beer and wine on their menus – everything is flown into Lukla then transported up by porters and mules. Namche Bazaar's first sushi restaurant recently opened its door, despite being about as far from the coast as it could be, to put it mildly.

The conversation at the table is all about climbing and peak-bagging. Jade and Lynne list one climber after another; they seem to be on first name terms with most of them and follow them all on social media: *Him, yes, oh my God, he's so impressive, love the photographs he posts, what about X and Y and Z, do you follow them too? What, you don't follow Z? He's a badass, completely crazy, you simply* must *follow him!*

I, who have never really been interested in sporting prowess, take an early night. But to be fair, so does everyone else. By eight o'clock the restaurant is empty and the streets are deserted.

Pasang, our Sherpa guide, is from the village of Thame, a few hours' walk from Namche Bazaar. The village was completely destroyed by the earthquake in 2015, and the villagers had to live in tents for months while they rebuilt their houses, stone by stone.

"It was a difficult time," Pasang says. "I don't like talking about it. It brings back bad memories." She shrugs as though to shake them off.

Khumjung, the village closest to Namche Bazaar, was also badly   3790 MSL
damaged. All the houses are therefore brand new, rebuilt in stone to better withstand the next earthquake. The Buddhist monastery that was almost five centuries old was also destroyed, but the main temple building survived. A young man shows me into the dim room. He has just been posted to the village and is the only person living at the monastery. His parents sent him off to become a monk when he was thirteen, but now he's reached the age where those numbers are reversed.

"I didn't know much about Buddhism back then," he says wryly.

A conical skull covered in long, thick dark hair is displayed in a small glass case in the middle of the temple.

"It's terribly old," the monk tells me. "The lama says that it comes from a yeti."

"Have you seen a yeti yourself?" I ask.

The monk smiles, and shakes his head.

"When I was younger and my family used to take the yaks up to the lake, my parents would warn me about going out in the evening, because a yeti might come. I did as they said, and never met a yeti."

In the neighbouring village, **Khunde**, every other man had been   3840 MSL

to Norway. Aurland, Lærdal, Flom, Østerbø, Breidablikk, Preikesto-
len, Finse . . . Relatively obscure place names from the west of
Norway were everyday parlance here. Most Sherpas still live in
villages without any road connection; feet are the most important
mode of transport. Because of the monsoon, they are dependent on
traffic arteries that can cope with enormous amounts of rain, and
so have become experts in building solid paths and steps. Norwegian
cabin owners and trekking associations have known this for a long
time and benefited from the Sherpas' superior dry-walling technique;
colourful prayer flags now hang along the most popular Norwegian
mountain routes, left there by those who built them.

"You have such a beautiful country," says one of the Norwegian
veterans. "Almost as beautiful as here," he generously adds.

On a hill above the busy souvenir streets in Namche Bazaar stands
a statue of the New Zealander Edmund Hillary, who conquered
Mount Everest with the Sherpa Tenzing Norgay on May 29, 1953.
Behind the statue, which for some reason is pink, it is possible to
see a white, triangular peak on clear days.

"This is the only time you will have a view of Mount Everest on
the whole trip, so enjoy it," Pasang says.

I take a couple more pictures before we wander back down to
the souvenir shops and pharmacies.

Mountaineering as a sport and leisure activity is a relatively new
thing. The world's first mountaineering club, the Alpine Club, was
established in London in 1857. Other European countries soon followed suit. The climbers initially focused on European mountains,
but in the twentieth century the number of expeditions to the most
extreme corners of the world rose dramatically; the number of blank,
uncharted spots on the map started to decrease, and it turned into
a race to be the first. It became a matter of national honour, British
honour in particular in the case of Mount Everest, as the British more

or less had a monopoly on the mountain. Even though Nepal and Tibet had extreme isolationist policies in the early 1900s, the British were in a unique position, as they controlled India, the gateway to the Himalayas from the south, and were an important player in the region, even in Tibet, the northern gateway.

The first serious attempt to climb Mount Everest was made on the north face by a British mountaineering club in 1922. The mountaineers were the first in the world to take oxygen tanks with them, and while they did not reach the top, they climbed higher than anyone had managed before: 8,326 metres. The expedition also went down in history for a more tragic record: seven of the porters lost their lives in an avalanche, thereby becoming the first official victims of the mountain.

The British made a second attempt in 1924, again, from the Tibetan side. The mountaineer Edward Norton, who had also been part of the first expedition, this time managed to reach 8,572 metres before he had to turn back. Norton planned to make a third attempt, but suffered from snow blindness and had to be carried off the mountain. This record held for twenty-eight years until 1952. Two of the other expedition members, George Mallory and Andrew Irvine, also attempted to reach the top, but they never came back. In 1933, an ice axe was found at 8,460 metres that must have belonged to one of them. During a search operation in 1999, Mallory's body was found at an altitude of 8,155 metres. Irvine's body has not yet been found. The big question that no-one can answer is whether Mallory and Irvine reached the top or not before they died. Mallory had planned to leave a picture of his wife at the summit, and no photograph was found in his pockets, despite the fact that the body and equipment were remarkably intact. Their camera, which might have solved the mystery once and for all, has never been found.

Even though there is a slight doubt about who actually conquered Everest first, there can be no doubt that Edmund Hillary and Tenzing

Norgay were the first in the world to go both up and down without mishap. (In 1953, Tibet was occupied by the Chinese, so they had to climb from the Nepalese side.) And in the years since, this feat has been repeated more than nine thousand times – from both the north and the south side – by more than five thousand different mountaineers. A peak can only be conquered for the first time once, but there are no limits to how many times one can be the first in some more specific category: for staying longest at the top (21 hours, 1999), first woman to the top (1975), first female amputee to the top (2013), first marriage at the top (2005), first twins to the top (2013), youngest girl to the top (13 years and 11 months, 2014), oldest man to the top (80 years and 224 days, 2013), first cancer patient to the top (2017), first with diabetes type 1 to the top (2006), first colostomy patient to the top (2010), first blind person to the top (2001) and first double amputee to the top (2006).*

3950 MSL **Phortse** lies five hours' walk from Namche Bazaar and is an expedition village above all else. Out in the fields, women bend over to work the soil with simple tools, while other women carry large jugs of water on their heads from the communal water pump. Only women work in the guest houses. Nearly all the men in the village work for expeditions as guides, cooks or porters. The women run the village in their absence and try not to lose their minds with worry.

The Buddhist temple in Phortse is still under renovation following the great earthquake. The external walls are covered in scaffolding, but it is possible to visit the main hall, where a middle-aged woman is busy sweeping the floor. Her face is weathered and wrinkled, but her body is sinuous and strong. Her name is Knachhi Yanjee Sherpa

* In 2017, the Nepalese government banned double amputees and blind people from climbing Mount Everest. The ban was met with loud protests from double amputees and blind mountaineers the world over, and was rescinded six months later by Nepal's Supreme Court, which concluded that it was discriminating to ban people with specific disabilities from Mount Everest.

and she is forty-five years old. Her three children all go to boarding school in Kathmandu, financed by the money her husband earns helping privileged mountaineers climb to the top of Mount Everest and back. The Sherpa guides are left with about three thousand dollars per trip, a fraction of the price mountaineers pay to the expedition companies, plus tips. They are still better off than the majority of Nepal's thirty million inhabitants, but at enormous risk.

"I come here every day to pray for him when he's on an expedition," Kanchhi says. "He's already been to the summit fourteen or fifteen times, but I'm still just as frightened that something might happen to him."

A young woman comes in through the door, followed by a little girl with rosy cheeks. The woman is called Pemba Chhoka Sherpa and is twenty-five. Pemba is from the same village as Pasang, but moved to Phortse when she got married.

"How did you meet your husband?" I ask.

"On Facebook," Pemba said, and laughed. "When we had chatted for some time on Messenger, we went to a café in Namche Bazaar on a date."

As always at this time of year, her husband is at Base Camp. She herself has never been up there.

"I worry about him all the time," Pemba says quietly. "He'll be going to the summit again in a few weeks . . ."

I find myself wondering when the trees disappeared.

We have been walking for a week now and the landscape is no longer green and full of rhododendron bushes and colourful wild flowers, but barren and empty, encircled by bluish-white, terrifying mountains. It is no longer mules we see along the route, but yaks with bells around their necks and hair so long that it almost touches the ground. Overhead, helicopters shuttle back and forth to Base Camp – travel agencies in Kathmandu offer day trips to Base Camp by helicopter; the packages boast a luxury breakfast and quality time in the mountains, before heading back to the capital in time for dinner.

Lynn has started to cough. She is pale and silent and takes tablets every time we stop, but none of the pills from her first aid kit seem to help, and the cough just gets worse.

At four thousand metres above sea level, we order cappuccinos made with Italian coffee machines, just as they should be. The nights are noticeably colder. By half past six, the dining rooms in the guest houses are empty, with people opting for the cosy warmth of a sleeping bag rather than sitting in a draught from the windows. And there really is not much else to do in the evening.

At the top of a steep ascent we come to a plateau that is full of fluttering prayer flags. On the stones and memorial plaques are the names of more than three hundred climbers who have lost their lives trying to conquer the Holy Mother. We trudge on in the thin air 4940 MSL and come to a guest house with an enticing name: **Oxygen Altitude Home.** Our wet woollen clothes steam up the windows in the dining room; the world sits cheek by jowl drinking tea and eating noodles: Japanese, Americans, New Zealanders ... A Spanish woman is doing yoga by the fire, a French couple are giving each other a massage, a German father and his young daughter talk quietly together, three robust Russian ladies laugh loudly. A miniature United Nations.

I am woken early the next morning by the horses fighting in the backyard. They are tied up some distance from each other, but fighting all the same, kicking and biting and snorting and neighing.

A short walk away, hidden among the grey and black stone of 5050 MSL the mountains, is **The Pyramid**, the highest research centre in the world, which was established by the Italian government in 1990. The building lives up to its name: it is a glass pyramid, a small Louvre in the middle of the Himalayas. Just below the pyramid is a basic, stone guest house.

"We monitor air pollution levels and measure the speed at which

Bhutan

Right: During the day, the dances are performed by monks – in clothes. At night, things get wilder.

Universal characters: the Clown . . .   . . . and Death.

Loneliness in ambient lighting: young men in Mongar sing karaoke for absent women.

Darts as an action sport: archery is Bhutan's national sport, but darts is not far behind at number two.

Double hospitality: Two happy sisters in Merak.

The enormous Buddha outside Thimpu welcomes visitors to the city with huge serenity.

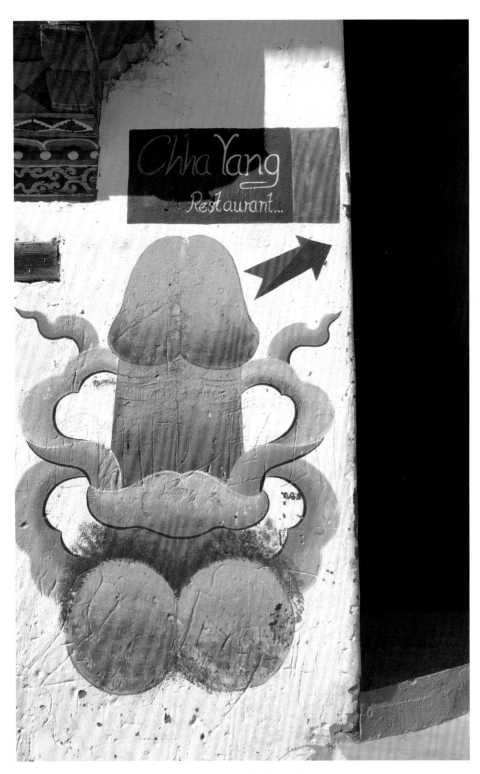

The phallus is a remarkably common symbol in Bhutan.

On the edge between beauty and destruction: the Tiger's Nest, one of the most sacred temples in the Himalayas, clings to the mountainside.

The peculiar takin, Bhutan's national animal, is a goat antelope, or gnu goat. The outside world thought for a long time that it was a mythical beast, like the yeti.

India

Right: King for a new era: Towei Phawang, angh of the Konyak people. His house straddles the India–Myanmar border.

Below: Apatani women from the Ziro Valley, Arunachal Pradesh.

Nepal

Kathmandu Valley: the goddess inhabits them. Matina (*above left*), royal kumari 2008–2017; Chanira (*below*), kumari 2000–2010, and Dhana (*above right*), who never stopped being a living goddess.

Death machine: Everest Base Camp, 5,364 MSL. The treacherous Khumbu Icefall, which climbers have to navigate on their way up to the Holy Mother, can be seen behind the enormous camp on a black glacier.

Everything has to be carried up on tired backs.

Living military legends: the Brigade of Gurkhas. Hopeful aspirants.

More than seven hundred temples and historical monuments were damaged by the earthquake in 2015.

Angel Lama – proud winner of Nepal's first trans beauty contest.

In another world: possessed by the gods, shamans dance for the people of Turmakhad.

Local reformer: Shoudana, the shaman in Simikot, has reduced the number of days that women have to sleep in a menstruation hut from nine to five.

China

The border: Upper Mustang to the left and Tibet to the right of the barbed-wire fence.

Tibet: high-altitude and barren, with one of the driest climates in Asia. The photograph is from the area that was once the Guge kingdom.

Above: Reverent prayer at the journey's end: two Indian pilgrims arrive at Lake Manasarovar, which is so holy that its water can wash away the sins of a hundred lives.

Left: Pilgrims from all over Tibet meet at the holy Mount Kailash to see the flagpole being raised during Saga Dawa.

Opposite: Thousands of pilgrims walk around the holy mountain. Bad weather is no obstacle.

Right: Above the tree line: a few blades of grass among the stones. Mount Everest can be seen in the background.

Below: Lhasa today: a modern, Chinese provincial city on Tibetan soil.

The mighty Potala Palace, which no longer houses the Dalai Lama.

There are prayer flags and butter lamps everywhere, as countless as the prayers and hopes of the devout Tibetans.

Above: Tiger Leaping Gorge: China's mass tourism at home.

Left: In the Kingdom of Women, the maternal grandmother is boss. Kumu welcomes me to her grandmother room. She loves having visitors.

the ice is melting," says fifty-year-old Kaji Bista, the centre manager. "We also measure seismic activity and normal meteorological parameters such as air pressure and moisture. I have a master's degree in economics and history, so I'm no scientist, but I measure and record to the best of my abilities. There are unfortunately no scientists here at the moment. Italy doesn't have the money. So, for the most part, I'm here alone."

He stares up at the white snowcaps, where the ice is melting and billions of microscopic soot particles from India and China swirl around in the clear, low-oxygen air.

"Sometimes the clouds over the mountains are brown with pollution," he says grimly. "All the helicopters cause pollution and frighten the wild animals. Global warming gets worse with every day that passes. For the first time ever, there is almost no water in the Lobujya River, and there was hardly any snow here this winter. Before we would have around fifteen centimetres of snow in winter; last year we had four and this year we had less than two centimetres. It rains more in summer than before, and all the rain accelerates the melting of the glaciers. The glaciers are our reservoirs – and they are disappearing. The rivers are now as good as dry for the greater part of the year, and then they flood in the rainy season."

He lets out a barely audible sigh and waves off a persistent fly.

"When I came here twenty years ago, there were no flies up here. Now they're everywhere. The lakes are drying out and the insects are moving in. Do you see that glacier over there?" He points to a bluish mountainside. "There are avalanches nearly every day now. The glacier is melting fast, soon it will be gone. The average temperature here last year was minus seventeen degrees centigrade. It was the warmest winter ever recorded here."

Kaji looks at his watch. A group of thirty Indian tourists is arriving in a few hours. In the high season, most of his time is spent looking after guests, in a bid to keep the place going.

"It's not easy to be optimistic," he says. "We humans are still making so many mistakes. We're burning the forests and causing pollution with all our plastics. The tourists and porters carry plastic with them all the way up here. We're creating more and more pollution. More and more . . ."

He gives a sad smile and then goes back to the stone building to make up the beds and clean the toilets. I wander back down to Oxygen Altitude Home. A thin, paltry stream runs past the guest house. It is clear to see from the width of the bed that the stream was once a river. Even though the guest house owners do their utmost to capture the water in thin rubber pipes, there is a massive water shortage, and guests are therefore not permitted to wash in any of the accommodation. It is not even possible to rinse your hands. A young man is hunkered down by the stream, scooping up water into a plastic barrel. It is slow work, as it takes time to fill even the bailer.

We sit staring listlessly at the ceiling for the rest of the day, while our bodies work frantically to produce red blood cells.

The next morning we wake up to a white landscape. The mountains have disappeared into a grey fog, and big, heavy snowflakes dance in the air. And it is not just the weather that has turned. I dash to the toilet, then again and yet again, stuff myself with Imodium, put on my rain gear and go out into the fog. The luxuriant rhododendron forests of the lowlands are a thing of the past – here it is stony and uneven, but there are just as many hikers, a whole crowd scrambling up the scree. As before, we have to stop and give way to the porters coming down, carrying loads that are bigger and heavier than themselves. Tinned food, fizzy drinks, cartons of juice and toilet paper are carried up, and the mountaineers' excreta is carried down in large, blue barrels, attached to wide plastic straps across their foreheads. The porters wear thin tracksuits and wet trainers, and some of them look no older then twelve or thirteen, with smooth boyish features and lithe bodies that are still growing.

Gorak Shep is the last station before Base Camp. Only expedition   5164 MSL
members are allowed to stay at Base Camp; everyone else has to spend the night in the overfull hostel at Gorak Shep, a couple of hours' walk further down. We make a brief stop for lunch. The small canteen is crowded and there are big signs saying that there is no water in the taps. Lynn is now chalk white and her cough is deep and chesty. And she is not the only one: people are coughing and clearing their throats everywhere. We eat as quickly as we can, avoid the latrines and hurry back out into the storm. Visibility is down to no more than a few centimetres, we can scarcely see our own feet and the other trekkers are no more than dark shadows. Every step is an effort, the thin air feels like syrup. We stop frequently and stand gasping for air, not that it is of much help. One more stone, one more scree slope, upwards, upwards, the pain in my temples is unbearable. It must be the cold, I think, I want to believe, the headache is probably due to the strain, and the thin straps on my rucksack, it will pass, nothing dangerous.

There is a dull sense of joy when we see some yellow spots through the fog. Cameras and mobile phones click and beep; exhausted, people straighten their backs and pose triumphantly in front of the prayer flags and sign that says **EVEREST BASE CAMP** 5,369 MSL.   5364 MSL
The camp officially lies at 5,364 MSL, but the thin air up here had obviously made the sign-makers a little giddy.

Fortunately, our camp is just by the entrance. Pasang, who knows the place inside out, leads us past small clusters of yellow tents (for some reason, all the tents up here are yellow) to a small hillock by the helipad. The ground is uneven, covered in coarse gravel as the whole of Base Camp lies on a melting glacier. Greg, a tall, smiling American with lots of energy, welcomes us.

"I would normally wish you welcome to a sunny Base Camp,

but today just wishing you welcome to Base Camp will have to suffice!" he says.

We are shown into a large tent. Bowls of American snacks and sweets stand out on a long table. We are each given a mug of warm juice and a plate of tacos. We buy expensive pay-as-you-go cards and log on to the local Wi-Fi. News from home pours in. The signal is perfect.

The camp area is so big that you cannot see from one end to the other, not even in clear weather. Our small designated area has toilets, a shower tent, two kitchen tents, two dining areas, a charging station, a yellow tent for each client, and tents for the Sherpas, kitchen staff and ground staff. A huge amount of logistics is required to get eighteen Westerners to the top of the world's highest mountain. Greg's control tent rules the camp; from here, he and his deputy keep an eye on the weather forecast and the three climbing teams, who climb a little higher with each rotation: first to the top of Lobuche (6,119 MSL), then to Camp 2 (6,492 MSL), and finally to Camp 3 (7,470 MSL). When all the stages are completed, they then have to wait for the perfect weather window to rush to the summit itself. The whole process takes about two months.

Lynn, Jade and I are each given our own yellow tent on a small hill far from the toilet. I unroll my sleeping bag and crawl in. My headache is worse. The paracetamol I took earlier has not helped in the slightest. Lynn coughs and coughs in the neighbouring tent. She has scarcely any voice left. None of us leave our tents until the cook rings the bell for dinner. Three men in their thirties are already sitting in the mess tent when we arrive. They greet us politely, but are preoccupied with their own rotation.

"Jeez, I don't know if I can stand waiting any longer," one of them says.

"If we can't carry on to Camp 3 tonight, I'll go crazy," says Number Two.

"The waiting wears you down," Number Three says. "Lying in your tent all day doing nothing drives you mad."

We get hamburgers for dinner – the cooks clearly do their best to provide a menu suited to Western tastes. I am not hungry and merely pick at my food. As evening entertainment, we follow Greg up to the control tent to look at the oxygen tanks that the climbers use.

"Wow, this is so cool! A dream come true!" Lynn squeaks with what little voice she has left.

Dark has already fallen by the time we go back to our tents. I creep into my sleeping bag with all my clothes on and fall asleep straight away, only to wake up soon after, gasping for air. The water in my water bottle is slowly turning to ice, and it is impossible to find a comfortable position on the thin mattress. The coughing in the next tent is more or less incessant.

The next day, the sun shines down from a cobalt-blue sky, and we can see all the way to Tibet – which is not so far away, to be fair: the border between Nepal and China goes right over the summit of Mount Everest. Base Camp lies like an island of yellow spots surrounded by some of the most majestic mountain tops I have ever seen. Sheer white peaks reach up into the bright sky; from here, they look as though they could break at any moment.

A bad night has left me even weaker, and going to the toilet seems like an insurmountable challenge. In a daze, I watch Jade eat breakfast, but still do not manage to eat even a mouthful. My brain is mush. It takes me half an hour to find my toothbrush in my sponge bag. I lie down on the sleeping bag to muster the strength I need to look for the suncream. It has vanished, I cannot find it anywhere. I eventually give up and open a new tube, put some cream on my face and then collapse, exhausted, on my sleeping bag again. I later find things in the most peculiar places: my telephone charger is hidden in my dirty laundry bag, my reading glasses are in my sponge bag.

My mind turns so slowly that it almost stops; the signals from my nerves swim through treacle and my reasoning gets caught in a mire, then sinks and disappears.

"How are you?" Greg calls brightly from outside the tent.

"Not so good," I say, then, to my dismay, I start to cry. The tears well up and I have no control over them. Greg asks about my symptoms and tells me to take altitude sickness pills. I protest, cannot think rationally, can barely think at all; I argue that it will get better once I have had the time to acclimatise, I just need some time, I hear myself say.

"Do as I tell you," Greg says. "If you get any worse, we have a problem. Helicopters are not always able to land here, and then what would we do? Take the pills. Just do it. Do it for my sake."

I dry my tears, swallow the pills he gives me, and retreat into my yellow cave. When the sun shines, as it does now, the tent warms up like a sauna. I close my eyes. I just want to lie here, with my eyelids coloured golden by the sun. The thought of talking to anyone, asking questions and taking notes, is absurd.

At some point in the afternoon, Pasang forces me out of the tent.

"You need to move," she says. "Get up, jump around."

I crawl out of the tent and somehow manage to get my shoes on my feet. Our final destination is Crampon Point, where the climbers put on their crampons to ascend the dreaded Khumbu Icefall, which everyone has to do in every rotation. The ice mass is full of cracks and crevasses, and is constantly moving; every day, large blocks of ice thunder down the mountainside.

We pass row upon row of yellow tents. I lag behind and have to stop frequently to catch my breath. Even Lynn, despite coughing as though she were in the end stages of tuberculosis, is faster than me.

On the way back to my longed-for sleeping bag, we go to the clinic to talk to the doctor on duty, an energetic Scot in her forties.

"So far this year, we have treated three hundred and fifty-seven patients," she says. "Most of the patients are Sherpas, it's really for them that we're here. Most come in with relatively common complaints, more often than not bronchitis and other respiratory tract infections. Unfortunately, many of the Sherpas are so afraid of missing the climbing season that they don't come to see us, even when they should. We also get a fair number of tourists with altitude sickness. Some ascend too quickly and don't take the time they need to acclimatise. The worst are the ones who ride up. We call them the riders of shame. Anyone who can't walk here should not be here. People don't understand how dangerous altitude is. It can kill."

As we make our way back to the camp, I suddenly fall headlong. The stones slip under my feet, and I manage to put my hands out just in time.

I remember nothing about the rest of the afternoon and evening.

The next morning, brushing my teeth is a joy, and I eat two fried eggs for breakfast. The pills have worked. Lynn, on the other hand, has got worse during the night and does not leave her tent.

A new mountaineer appears in the mess tent. Sam is a British businessman in his fifties. He has just returned from a rotation to Camp 2 and is coughing badly. It sounds like his lungs are turning inside out.

"What is it that drives you?" I ask.

"I want to test my physical limits," Sam croaks, between coughing fits.

"My aim is to climb the Seven Summits, that's to say, the highest mountain on each continent," says José, one of the thirty-year-olds from the evening before. "Mount Everest is the last one."

"But why do you want to climb the highest mountain on each continent?" I ask.

He shrugs. "It's something my brother and I set out to do. My brother has given up already, so now it's just me."

"How long did it take you to get up the icefall this time?" Sam asks him.

"Three hours and twenty minutes."

"Really? It took me six or seven hours. How long did it take you to come down?"

Later that morning as I bound across the glacier to keep up with Pasang, I send the pharmaceutical industry waves of gratitude. We pass Sherpas enjoying the warmth of the sun, climbers chatting on their mobile phones, and eventually stop in front of a large mess tent. Furdiki Sherpa is sitting on a chair in the far corner. Her broad, square face is almost scorched by the sun, the skin is peeling from her cheeks and nose.

"I was nineteen when I got married," she tells me. "My husband, Mingma Sherpa, was an icefall doctor, like my father."

Icefall doctors are responsible for setting the route through the icefall and making it accessible for Western mountaineers using bridges, ladders and ropes.

"My father died a natural death. He was in his sixties when he died at home. My husband died on the job. On April 7, 2013, he fell down a crevasse and died. I was given the news at four o'clock in the afternoon, but refused to believe it was true to begin with. Then the helicopter came, and I knew that it really had happened. I was always worried about him when he was at work, and now my worst fears had been realised."

Together with another widow, Ngima Doma Sherpa, Furdiki plans to climb Mount Everest in honour of her husband and raise awareness of the plight of Sherpa widows.

"About seven days ago, I went to Camp 2," she says. "It was very emotional. As I climbed up the icefall, I thought about my father and my husband, and I cried a lot. I felt completely alone the first few years after Mingma was killed, and I couldn't do anything at all, but three years ago I was invited to join a Sherpa widows' programme in Kathmandu. There were sixty or seventy other widows there. We were asked what the Nepalese authorities had done to support us, but none of us had received any help. I'm doing this so our voices can be heard, but also because I want to understand more about what it was like for my husband and father. They went up alone, they carried ropes and ladders, and had no other aids. We, on the other hand, climb up the ladders and ropes that the Sherpas have already carried up here and prepared for us."

She holds my eyes with a steady gaze.

"I think people should know so they can properly appreciate the Sherpas and the work that they do," she says. "They are the ones who do all the hard work, not the mountaineers. Without the Sherpas, no-one would be able to climb this mountain."

The Sagarmatha Pollution Control Committee has an office tent on the edge of the enormous Base Camp. Here I find a lone officer sitting hunched over a full notebook. Opposite him sits a middle-aged man in military uniform, staring at his mobile phone screen.

"Every climber has to carry eight kilos of rubbish down from the mountain, otherwise they will not get their four thousand-dollar deposit back," the officer tells me, without looking up from his notes. "We have checkpoints at the icefall to make sure that everyone follows the rules. The media make such a fuss about Everest being a rubbish tip, but the photographs they publish are often old."

He gives an irritated sniff.

"This year we started an extraordinary clean-up campaign, which is a joint initiative with the military and the Ministry for Tourism, among others. For the last three weeks, we have been working at Base Camp, and we're about to go up to Camp 2. So far, we've removed more than a ton of rubbish, mostly metal, rope and tents. Next year, we'll go even higher."

The officer stops talking and studies his figures. The man in the military uniform leans towards me and says in a quiet voice: "I'm actually not supposed to say anything, but if you promise not to quote me, I can give you some information."

I promise that I will not use his name, and he searches for a moment or two on his mobile phone, then reads from the screen: "The clean-up operation starts in Lukla on April 14. Two tons of rubbish were collected and sent to Kathmandu for recycling." He scrolls down. "On May 19, the area from Namche Bazaar up to Gorak Shep will be cleaned up, and the rubbish collected will be sent to Kathmandu for recycling. On May 29, the defence minister is coming here for a ceremony." He looks up from his telephone. "I humbly beg you not to say that you have got this information from me. Say that you got it from him." He points at the officer on the other side of the table, who looks up from his notebook.

"You're not a journalist, are you?" His narrow eyes get even narrower. "I don't like journalists."

I assure them that I am not a journalist, but an author.

"Good. Journalists write what they want to write, with no consideration for the truth. The truth is that this is one of the cleanest areas in Nepal, but tourism brings its own problems. Tourists are good for the economy, but bad for the environment. The rubbish comes with them, because foreigners love toilet paper, Pringles and Coca-Cola. But the main problem is actually the porters. They generally have very little schooling and just throw rubbish away anywhere. Here at Base Camp, however, human waste is the biggest problem, if you know what I mean . . ." He leans over to me, gleefully. "Thirteen thousand kilos of crap! That's what we carry down from Base Camp every year. That's how much excrement a thousand people produce over two months."

"I've read that you also carry down bodies that appear now that the ice is melting," I say. "Is that true?"

The officer snorts. "No, it's not true! That's the sort of thing the media love to write about, but it's all lies! And that is the reason that I don't like journalists!"

"I'm sorry, but I had to ask," I say. "After all, it's better that I quote you, who are actually here, than other, unreliable sources."

Later the same evening, the tourism minister announces that four bodies have been brought down from Mount Everest. The news travels around the world within hours.

A spider's web of stars lights up the pitch black sky, and the Milky Way stretches across the universe like a thin veil. The mountains that surround the camp like seating tiers in an amphitheatre can be felt rather than seen. A light shines from every tent in the neighbouring camp. From one of them, meditation mantras and simple drum rhythms stream out into the night. The voices rise and fall, rise and fall. Then they fall silent, and are replaced by the sound of zips being opened and closed. Heavy footsteps. My field of vision is filled with flickering head torches. In the hours that follow until sunrise, the lights rise higher and higher up the icefall; they get smaller and smaller until they eventually resemble slow shooting stars.

As soon as the sun rises over the ridges, the magic is dispersed. Helicopters streak the sky in a continuous throb as long as there is daylight. One of them has been chartered by Lynn, who does not have the energy to walk back down to Lukla, as originally planned.

The mood at the breakfast table is grim. The last team of climbers has still not been given the go-ahead to start their rotation to Camp 3.

"I'm getting desperate," José says, drumming his fingers impatiently on the table.

Climbers from the other teams come back through the morning, having completed their last rotations. One after the other they stumble into the mess tent, exhausted, euphoric and coughing. They look like astronauts in their big, shapeless climbing suits. A month ago, there were eighteen of them, now there are only thirteen left. Five have already given up and gone home.

"I have climbed six of the seven summits, only Everest remains," says Bruce, an American dentist in his fifties. "The greatest challenge with Everest is the rotations. You go up to Camp 3, which is over seven thousand metres high, and then come down again. It takes time. At that altitude, everyone looks like they should be in the intensive care unit in a hospital. They move incredibly slowly. Everything was going fine until I got this damn cough."

With perfect timing, he doubles over in a coughing fit.

"But I'm stubborn," he says, when the worst is over. "The cough won't stop me. I love the feeling of mastering something that is difficult, though I'm not sure if that explains why there are so many doctors and dentists up here. Perhaps it's because we have the money, and because many of us are Type A personalities. The people up here are all driven, they're all Type A personalities."

Type A personalities are described as restless, impatient, ambitious and extremely competitive.

A tall, thin man slumps down on the chair beside me. His name is Avêdis Kalpaklian, Avo for short, and he is from Lebanon, but of Armenian descent. He is forty-seven and a half.

"This is a spiritual journey for me," he says, dramatically throwing out his arms. He looks rudely alert for someone who has just returned from an altitude of seven thousand metres. "I dream of mountains all the time! I climbed twenty-seven mountains last year. Six in one day alone – it only took me twelve hours. I've climbed sixty mountains over four thousand metres. Some people say that I climb mountains to escape, but I don't see it like that. I've found myself."

"Are you married?" I ask.

He holds out his left hand. On the finger where there might be a wedding band he has tattooed a ring, with a mountain in it: Ararat, Armenia's most important national symbol and pride. The mountain also serves as a symbol of all that Armenia has lost: in the 1920s, Ararat ended up on the Turkish side of the border, and is now Turkey's highest mountain at 5,136 MSL.

"I'm married to the mountains, so I have many wives," Avo says with a happy smile. "So far, Denali in Alaska is my favourite, but

I have a feeling that might change now. The mountains here are magical. There are spirits everywhere here, and the colours, oh, green, blue, white ... The colours here are magical, as well."

"What are you going to do when you've climbed Everest?"

"I'll just carry on! I'll set my aims on more mountains, I just want more and more magic!"

On my way out of the tent, overwhelmed by having spoken to so many Type A personalities and polygamists, I bump into Sam, the British businessman. The doctor has given him antibiotics for his respiratory tract infection, and he is now looking for people to share the helicopter ride back down to Kathmandu.

"I don't think I'm going to manage it," he concedes. "With all these rotations up and down, you never get to rest properly. You can't exactly check in to a hotel in the meantime. But I don't see it as a defeat, because I never expected to succeed on the first attempt. And anyway, not many people know that I'm up here."

The 67-year-old New Zealand TV personality Russell Brice is a well-known face in climbing circles: he has climbed all fourteen mountains over eight thousand metres, been to the top of Mount Everest twice, and flown over it twice in a hot air balloon.

"My pitch is the only one that has a view of Everest," he says smugly and points at a rather modest-looking white triangle squeezed in between the jagged peaks. "This is my twenty-sixth Everest expedition. I first came here in 1974. The Sherpas are far better off now than they were then. Their children go to school and they've got better houses. On the other hand, there's more pollution and rubbish here now. Several hundred tourists come to Base Camp every day. They hang up their prayer flags, scribble on the stones and shit everywhere. On my first Everest expedition, there were ten of us in total doing the ascent. That was in 1981. How many are here this year?" Russell takes a dramatic pause, then answers his own question: "Three hundred and eighty-one! And that doesn't include the Sherpas, so you can double the number. It's complete madness."

At no point does it seem to occur to him that his own twenty-six expeditions have contributed to the commercialisation and increased access to Mount Everest.

"Lots of the companies are badly run," he says scornfully. "They bring up climbers who should never be here in the first place; people who don't know how to use crampons or oxygen cylinders. But that's how it is now, a free-for-all. But goodness, here's me blabbering away, and it's not me you should be talking to – you must talk to Phurba! Hey, Phurba, come over here."

A tall, shy man approaches.

"Tell her how many times you've been up Everest," Russell says.

"Twenty-one times," he says, in broken English.

For four years, Phurba Tashi Sherpa was the person who had climbed Everest most times in the world, but in 2018, this changed. The current record is twenty-four times.

"I started out as an expedition cook," Phurba says. "My father was also a cook, and my uncle was a climbing guide, so it seemed only natural that I would join them. I climbed Everest for the first time in 1999. I now have sixty yaks, three sons and two daughters. Two of them are students in Kathmandu, one is a monk and two still live at home."

"Would you like your sons to follow in your footsteps?" I ask.

Phurba hesitates.

"I don't know if I would recommend it," he says, eventually. "But they are free to do as they please."

"Have you lost any friends on the expeditions?"

"Only one. A French friend of mine tried to snowboard down from the summit."

"He may only have lost one friend on an expedition, but he has lost many friends to the mountain!"

"So you miss climbing?" I ask Phurba.

This time he answers without hesitation.

"No. Twenty-one times is too many. My parents and wife begged me to stop . . ." He smiles for the first time. "I like to stay at Base Camp and organise everything from here."

"I can well understand that your family asked you to stop," I say. "It's a very dangerous job."

"The job is fifty per cent dangerous," Phurba says. "Even if you do everything perfectly, you can't control nature. I'm glad I have retired. I already know everything there is to know about climbing Everest that is worth knowing."

I was glad to leave Base Camp. As Pasang and I descended, the air got thicker with every hour that passed, and soon we were surrounded by green, scented pine trees and flowering rhododendron bushes. I bounded down the slopes, my body feeling light. A few days later, I boarded a full morning flight to Kathmandu.

Sam, the British businessman, returned to Kathmandu by helicopter a couple of days after I left Base Camp. The other expedition members that I met up there all made it to the top and back down again in one piece.

Not everyone was so lucky. The 2019 season was to become one of the deadliest in the mountain's history: in the penultimate week of May, the long-awaited weather window opened, and hundreds of climbers all tried to reach the summit at the same time, resulting in hour-long queues in the Death Zone. Eleven climbers in all lost their lives.

Sixty-six years after Edmund Hillary and Tenzing Norgay conquered Mount Everest, the Holy Mother has become a death machine for Type A personalities, thanks to organised, commercial tourism.

And in the year that we write, 2019, there are no longer any blank, white spots left on the map. But there is still a white hell.

Stories from the Capital

"Our house burned down last year and it took us four months to rebuild it," Sharmila Pariyar told me. The 36-year-old had fine features and did not smile once during our conversation. She lived in a 1338 MSL shack by **Kathmandu Airport** together with her husband and their three children. The small, basic room had a corner kitchen and a bed; there were some boxes of clothes along one wall, as well as some thin mattresses and a cheap radio. Savitri, who had come with me as an interpreter, and I both sat down on the bed, which was the only place to sit. Sharmila squatted down in a corner and did the washing up as she spoke. Her voice was deep and commanding.

"The neighbours had lit candles for a Hindu god, that's how the fire started. Their house burned down first, then ours. We managed to rescue about half of our clothes and some rugs, but the house could not be saved. I shouted so loudly for help that I couldn't speak for five days afterwards. When the police came, they got water from the neighbours, but it was not enough to put the fire out. When the fire engine came, it was already too late."

Two boys in sandals, thick jackets and hats appeared in the doorway and stared at me with wide eyes, then ran off.

"Everyone who lives here struggles, but I get no support from my husband and have to fend for the family alone," Sharmila said. "Perhaps you can help me financially? We need help. We can't manage on our own."

"I'm sorry," Savitri said. She was clearly used to this question and had a ready answer: "We meet people like you every day, and many of those we meet are far worse off. We can't help everyone, the only thing we can do is tell your story."

"My husband is from the mountains, and I'm from the lowlands," Sharmila said. If she was disappointed, it did not show. She had finished the washing up and now started to cut the potatoes into small pieces.

"My family has no caste. We were very poor and didn't always have enough to eat. At the time, it was generally thought that girls shouldn't go to school, so my sisters and I have barely any schooling. I went for two years, then stopped. My mother didn't look after my uniform or make sure it was clean, and she couldn't afford pens and books. As I was casteless and wore dirty clothes, the teachers treated me badly. When I was a child, men from higher castes never paid any attention to me, but when I turned thirteen, they suddenly started to touch me everywhere. I was almost raped once, but managed to escape before he thrust it in me. I remember it all, all the attempts, all the times I was felt up. It frightened me, but the men were also scared. They did everything they could not to be seen. The boys of my own age all had girlfriends; the men who wanted me were older, with wives and families."

A woman appeared in the doorway and started to shout at Sharmila, who answered calmly. The woman continued to harangue her for a brief while.

"I was seventeen when I got married." Sharmila continued her story as she got out a bowl, filled it with boiled rice and gave it to her youngest son, who was sitting on the floor following the conversation in silence. "It was an arranged marriage. Love marriages were fairly usual by then, but we were the only casteless family where we lived, so no-one wanted to be my boyfriend. My husband came from a mountain village a four-hour bus ride away. We met for the first time at the ceremony, which was normal then. I remember I was terrified the whole way through the wedding, I was scared about what was going to happen next, and having to have sex with him. We lived with his parents for the first year, but it was hard for me. I had never worked in the fields before, because my parents didn't own any land. My parents-in-law were always shouting at me because they thought I didn't work hard enough. Eventually, we moved out and my husband got a job in my brother's shop."

Prabina, her eldest daughter, came in. She had been washing clothes for the two rich families where Sharmila worked.

"I've just finished tenth grade and think the exams went quite well," she said with a smile. "I want to carry on to twelfth grade, and then I would like to go abroad!"

"Where would you like to go?" I ask.

Prabina shrugged and smiled again. "To a good country! It doesn't matter where."

"My husband drinks far too much," said Sharmila, who was now sweeping the floor. "He still works in the shop, but he gets less pay now because of his drinking. He drinks every day, even when he's ill. But he's a good man, all the same, he doesn't sleep with other women and every now and then he gives me some of the money. He never gives me nothing. When he doesn't drink, he's loving, and when he drinks, he's violent. He often hits me with pots and pans, and one time he even used his scooter. I've had bruises absolutely everywhere on my body. A month ago, Prabina had had enough, she couldn't bear to see him abuse me any longer, and she hit back. Then she went to get the police and they made us come to an agreement: we can fight with words, but not with fists. So now he just shouts. Are you hungry, by the way?"

We both said no, tactfully. Sharmila filled another bowl with rice for herself and ate quickly.

"I work regularly for three families," she said. "And I have to be with the last one at midday."

When she had emptied the bowl, she said a hasty farewell and rushed out the door. With a smile, Prabina sat down on the bed with Savitri and me.

"I want to specialise in journalism when I'm in eleventh grade," she said. "I want to write about people in similar circumstances to us. Life in the slums is hard. There are so many drug addicts here, so many alcoholics. We never talk to the men who hang around on the street, and we never go out after six or seven in the evening. I like school, but it's not easy to concentrate on my homework because my parents argue all the time. I wish I had my own room!"

A room of one's own! It was not hard to understand her wish.

"What other dreams do you have?" I asked.

"I want a better life than my mum's," the seventeen-year-old replied frankly. "I dream of having a stable job and a stable life. A civil service job in the police or army, something with a secure income that will give me a pension when I get old. That's my dream."

*

"I did everything I could to earn money, but the debt just kept growing," Bimala said. "I opened a shop, but none of the customers paid on time, so I had to close it again. I tried to breed cattle, but made losses there too. I had to work for other people in their fields, doing all kinds of odd jobs so I could put food on the table, but I just couldn't earn enough money."

Bimala was thirty-nine, but looked at least ten years older. We met in a seminar room at the Pourakhi Centre; the organisation works to support female migrant workers. There was something subservient about her as she obediently answered all my questions.

The man her parents had married her off to when she was sixteen was of no help whatsoever. He did not beat her, and was good with their three children, but he systematically drank up all the money he earned at the clothes factory (when he still worked there). When their youngest daughter was seven months old, she fell out of bed and sustained a head injury. The doctors said she would die if they did not operate.

"I took out a loan to pay for the operation," Bimala said. Her eyes filled with tears. "I brought her into this world and saw it as my duty to help her, even though we couldn't afford it. In the end, the bank threatened to take our house and the people in the village refused to lend me any more money. They said that as I had two daughters I could let the one die. Everyone else went to work abroad, so I thought I could try too. We needed the money. My six-year-old was begging for food, but I had nothing to give him, not even some rice."

Millions of poor Nepalese travel to other Asian countries every year to earn a living. In an attempt to protect the women from being abused, the government has banned Nepalese citizens from working as housekeepers in the Gulf States, which is where the majority of Nepalese migrant workers go. The ban has made things worse for many desperate women, who are now left at the mercy of illegal agencies and cynical middlemen. For Bimala, her time in Kuwait, one of the richest countries in the world, was a nightmare.

"The wife only gave me food once a day, and the food I got was always a couple of days old. I was only given cold rice, no vegetables and no meat. She didn't even give me salt – I used to lick my arm to get the taste of salt. There were six children in the family, and I was the only housekeeper, so I had to work all the time. I had to wash the clothes by hand, make food and look after the children, and I worked without a break from six in the morning until two in the morning. I was only allowed to go to the toilet once during the day. At night I slept on a thin mattress in the toy cupboard. When the mistress wasn't happy with me, she pinched me hard. She had installed surveillance cameras all over the house, including in the cupboard where I slept, so she could make sure that I was working hard even when she was out. If one of the children cried for more than a few seconds, she told me off. Once when I was doing the washing, I fell and hurt my head. I couldn't work properly for two weeks and kept fainting. When I asked if I could have some time off, just a couple of hours to rest, she refused."

Bimala put up with it for four months. She rang the agent and asked to be given another family, but was told that she could not move families until she had been there for six months. She was worried that she might not survive another two months and decided to run away.

"I left on a Friday. Three of the children were at school, the other three were sleeping. I said to the mistress that I had to go to the loo, that it was urgent. At first, she refused, so I pretended that the need was so acute that I couldn't work, and eventually she let me go. Normally she would send one of the children with me to the toilet, like a guard, but they were asleep. Four housekeepers had run away from there before, so she was super vigilant. If I was on the toilet for more than five minutes, she came and hammered on the door. But I didn't go to the toilet, I went out into the street. I was terrified of what she would do if she discovered that I was running away, but luckily I managed to get a taxi almost straight away. The Indian driver took me to the Nepalese embassy, even though I had no money. There were lots of women in the same situation as me at the embassy, and I was given proper food for the first time in four months. For the first few weeks, I just slept and slept. The mistress reported me to the police for running away, so I had to spend eleven days in prison. Another woman was accused of stealing gold, and she has not come home yet. Thanks to the support of the Pourakhi Centre, I came back home to Nepal in December last year."

The Pourakhi Centre, which is run by women who themselves have been migrant workers, offers emergency accommodation to three hundred women a year, and has its own emergency hotline, which is manned round the clock. For many of the women, the centre is their only hope.

"Since I came home, I have been taught how to make food," Bimala said. "There were five women on the course, and I was the best of them all. Now I hope that the centre will help me to get a food truck, so I can sell street food. Our house is being auctioned, but I can't go back to the village anyway, because I owe so much money there. They know that I've been working abroad, so now they think I'm rich."

Once again the tears welled up.

"If I don't get any help, I'll have to go abroad again. I don't see any other way out."

*

The building looked like a normal house from the street, surrounded by other anonymous-looking apartment complexes. Very few of the neighbours had any idea that the girls who lived there had been saved from a terrible fate and were being hunted down by dangerous traffickers.

Charimaya Tamang, one of the founders of Shakti-Samuha, the world's first organisation run by and for victims of trafficking, was surprisingly small. She was more than a head shorter than me, slight, with light, almost translucent skin. Her voice was quiet but firm. Even though she must have told her story many, many times before, she told it with such feeling that Savitri, who was interpreting, burst into tears as she listened.

"I was born in 1976 near Kathmandu, and come from a humble background. My father was a social worker in the village and always happy to help, as was my brother. The whole village was dependent on my brother, as he sorted out birth certificates, citizenship certificates and other important documents. I was a naughty, restless girl. I was the first child in the village to go to school. It was my brother who sent me. The school was half an hour's walk away, but I had to stop after fifth grade, as the school for the higher grades was too far away. So instead I started to help in the library and with adult education. When the teacher wasn't there, I covered for him.

"Time passed and I turned seventeen. I was out in the woods gathering grass when I was abducted by four men. I normally went to the woods with friends, but that day I was alone. The men surrounded me and took the basket of grass from my back. One of them was from the village, but I didn't know the others. One was tall, the other was fat and the third was just average. I don't know how old they were, but they were all older than me. At first they tried to trick me, they said that they would help me open a shop and that they could offer me an easy life. I didn't believe them and refused to go with them. Then they started to beat me and forced me to eat something, and soon after I lost consciousness.

"When I came to, I was in a large room. I looked out the window, but nothing that I saw outside was familiar. 'Mummy, Mummy, the houses are running away!' I screamed. I had never seen corrugated-iron roofs before. Down in the street, I noticed a sign that said Gorakhpur. Then I realised I was in India.

"There were four beds in the room, and I saw that I was not alone. There was another girl there. I talked to her, but she didn't answer, just imitated everything I did. I was terrified, because I had heard that the towns were full of witches and ghosts. I was convinced that the girl wanted to kill me, but she just continued to do exactly what I did. When I covered my ears, she did the same. I was so frightened! Eventually I took two steps to the side and the girl disappeared. Then it dawned on me that she was a reflection. I had not recognised myself in the mirror, and that wasn't so strange, as someone had dressed me in new clothes and jewellery, cut my hair and made me up. In the village, I always wore a skirt and blouse, but now I was wearing an Indian costume and had lots of bangles around my wrists. How could I have recognised myself? A weaker person than me would no doubt have fainted. I tried to escape, but the door was locked. After a while, the men who had abducted me appeared. I asked them to send me back to Kathmandu, so I could go home.

"'You already know that you're not in Nepal,' they said. 'If we send you back to Nepal alone, bad people will try to catch you, and your brother will report us. So you have to stay with us.'

"They took me with them and we left the house and boarded a train. I had never seen a train and thought it was a moving house. The men gave me food and drink on the train. They ate and drank as well – they were all drinking cold drinks from bottles, but my bottle foamed more than theirs. I asked for another bottle, but they held me down and forced me to drink from the foaming bottle. What happened after that, I don't remember. I don't know if I ate. I don't know how far we travelled. When I came to, we were in Bombay, walking down a street. The men took me to a restaurant that was full of people and left me in a corner, then sat down at another table. One of them went out to make a telephone call, and a waiter put some food down in front of me. As I sat there, I fully regained my senses and started to cry. And I couldn't stop. The plate in front of me had little hollows for the different kinds of curry, and these were filled with my tears. I cried and cried, and none of the guests in the restaurant asked me why I was crying. The people at the next table stared at me, but did nothing. No-one cared.

"After about half an hour, the man who had gone to make a call came back with a Nepalese woman. She introduced herself as my 'auntie'.

"In Gorakhpur, the traffickers had said to me that they were going to take me to Kashmir, and that I would work there for a couple of weeks making shawls. Now they told me that I couldn't work with them, but had to work with other women, so I had to go and stay with the Nepalese woman. When we got to the house where I was going to sleep, I found out that I had been sold.

"The first day I was beaten and left in a pitch-black room. It was so dark in there I couldn't see a thing. When I had been in there for a whole day, I found the door. It was locked, and had bars in front of it like a prison. I tied my shawl to one of the bars and wrapped it around my throat, and made myself as heavy as I could. I didn't want to live in the hell that awaited me, I would rather die. My eyes started to bulge and sound disappeared. Tears and snot ran out of me, I was wet, but I wasn't dead. The shawl ripped and fell to the floor. Had the shawl not ripped, I would have succeeded.

"'Save me,' I remember I begged God in desperation. 'Please, spare me!'

"On the third day, the door opened and I was allowed to leave the dark room. They let me rest the following day. And on the fifth day, I was sent into a room with a client. I hit him and chased him out. As punishment, the brothel owner and the manager beat me so hard that I was badly injured. They threatened to send me to a far worse place if I didn't behave from now on, and they gave me a new name. They called me Onu. On the sixth day, I was put in a room with the other women. Four men came to the door and disappeared into a neighbouring room, where they were served food and drink. I later realised that they worked as security guards for the brothel. The older girls had been there for a long time and exchanged glances, but I didn't understand their coded eye contact. When the men had finished eating and drinking, the room was tidied and I was sent in to them. The door was locked behind me. I cried and cried as they raped me. What happened after that, I don't know. I was as dead.

"When I came to, I tried to get up, but the blood had dried and stuck to the waterproof sheet. I felt like my body had been broken into a thousand pieces. A doctor came in to examine me, followed by the manager and a cleaner. They lifted me onto a stretcher and wheeled me into another room. They made sure I was unconscious while the doctor stitched my wounds. I was given strong medicine in the days that followed. A week went by, and I realised I would never be able to escape.

"Every day for the next twenty-two months, I experienced trauma. I counted the days, and kept track of which days were festivals. I was sad that I was missing them. I understood that no-one could help me where I was, and so devised my own survival strategy and tried to be nice to both the customers and the owner. It was important for me to have a good relationship, as I was never going to get away. The police sometimes carried out raids; the brothel owners in the area always knew in advance when they were coming and made sure we were in hiding before they arrived.

"In February 1996, I was rescued. That year, the Indian government carried out operations all over India to uncover illegal brothels and human trafficking. As the local police weren't involved, the brothel owner was not warned in advance this time. All the police in the state were involved in the operation, and there were policemen everywhere. That day, five hundred girls were rescued. We were taken to a transit home, and it turned out that more than half of us were from Nepal. A new fight started in the transit home: the fight to be allowed to go home. The Nepalese authorities didn't want us and came up with all kinds of excuses: that we had HIV and would spread it in Nepal; that we only *spoke* Nepalese, but weren't *actually* Nepalese. None of us had any papers, none of us could prove where we belonged.

"We were in the transit home for six months. All of us who were there were ill. I don't know what kind of illness it was, but we got no medical treatment, and three of the girls died. Another three married men whom they had met through the brothel. Sixty girls escaped. They were scared they would be sent to another brothel, or would be stigmatised and treated badly when they got back to Nepal. I don't know where they went or what happened to them. And had human rights activists not taken up our cause, we would never have left India. In the end, one hundred and twenty-eight girls went back to Nepal, and we were looked after by various voluntary organisations."

Charimaya handed a tissue to Savitri, who was in floods of tears having heard her story. She comforted her and stroked her back. Savitri sheepishly dried her tears.

"When I think back to that time, I realise I was courageous," Charimaya said. "A week after I got back to Nepal, I told my story anonymously to the press. It made the headlines, as it was the first time a victim of human trafficking had spoken out. Most people had no idea of what went on. No-one had told the truth before, but I did. There was a flame burning inside me, and it got stronger and stronger, I wanted to tell the whole of Nepal about what was going on, and to stop it."

Six months after she came home, Charimaya reported her traffickers to the police. She was the only one of the one hundred and twenty-eight girls who took this step. The law was outdated, no-one had reported human traffickers before, but the four men were each sentenced to ten years in prison all the same. But justice came at a price, not just for Charimaya but also for those who helped her. Her brother, who she lived with while the case was going on, received death threats. A relative in the village had their ear cut off. Someone set light to a neighbour's dried cow dung.

"At the time, I never felt safe," Charimaya said. "The case went through two courts, and went on for eighteen months."

The organisation that helped Charimaya and a number of the other victims offered them a course in basic healthcare. Fifteen of the young women chose to do the course. When it was over, the fifteen girls formed a committee. Shakti-Samuha was born.

"Crying is not a solution," Charimaya said. "We decided to do something. We decided to fight. And we certainly had to fight. It took four years for the Nepalese authorities to let us even register the organisation, but in 2007 we were voted Nepal's best non-governmental organisation."

Five years after she returned to Nepal, Charimaya got married, and has since had two daughters. She is now the president of Shakti-Samuha and has dedicated her life to helping victims of human trafficking.

"There are seventeen girls living in this house. As a rule, we try to reunite them with their families, but in cases where the trafficker lives in the home or is a close neighbour, that is problematic. Some of the girls were sold when they were only four or five and are not able to identify their families. In many ways, the situation is far worse today: there are new routes, the traffickers are better organised, and there are more links and more middlemen involved. Trafficking not only includes sex work, but also other kinds of slavery. We try to help the girls who are rescued to stand on their own two feet one day. The aim is to give them a decent life."

On the way out, I passed a room where the youngest girls were having a dance class. The girls were laughing, and seemed happy and carefree as they moved to the Bollywood music.

It is estimated that more than thirty Nepalese girls are trafficked to India every day. Only a fraction ever come home again.

*

Nahadur Rai was eighty-seven. He came down the stairs from the roof terrace with quick, light steps, and sat down at the end of the sofa in the pink room, ready to answer questions.

"I've just come from physiotherapy," he said, with a smile. "I've got problems with my lower back, you see, from playing too much football."

When Nahadur was twenty, he was recruited to the legendary Brigade of Gurkhas. The tradition of recruiting Nepalese soldiers to the British army dates back to the Anglo-Nepalese War in 1814–16. In the decades leading up to the war, Nepal had conquered substantial areas in the west, south and north. Like Bhutan, Nepal was never colonised, but the country was forced to relinquish many of the newly won territories, about forty per cent of the total area, to British India. However, the courage and stamina of the Nepalese soldiers had made a deep impression on the British, who then started systematically to recruit Gurkhas, as they called them, to their own army. The name Gurkha is a misspelling of Gorkha, Nepal's official name until 1930. More than two hundred thousand Nepalese soldiers fought for the British during the First World War; the number was even higher in the Second World War. The Gurkha Brigade has assisted in most of the armed conflicts in which the UK has been involved in the post-war period, including the Falklands War and Afghanistan. The Far East was their core area until Hong Kong was handed over to China in 1997, when the Gurkhas were moved to the UK.

"The training was hard, but I was young, so everything went well," Nahadur said. "It wasn't easy to meet the required standards, not everyone did, but it's even harder now, as the population of Nepal has increased fourfold, and the quotas have shrunk."

The Brigade currently has about 3,500 soldiers.

Nahadur had been married for four years when he was recruited. It was an arranged marriage, and the couple had their first child after Nahadur had been posted east, first to Singapore, and then to Malaysia.

"I got home leave every three years to visit my family in Nepal, and soon enough my wife and I had three children. If I had met my children outside my house, I would not have recognised them. When I was stationed in Malaysia, I found out that my wife had been unfaithful. She had married another man, and later I also got married again. I had two sons with my second wife."

Nahadur trained to be a field engineer while he was in the army, and helped to build bridges, bunkers and roads in the jungle.

"I like Malaysia and Brunei a lot," he said, "but I found Hong Kong difficult. The winters were very cold and the summers unbearably hot."

A woman in her fifties – his eldest daughter – came into the room and listened to the conversation with crossed arms.

"Were you ever frightened?" I asked Nahadur.

He shrugged. "There were problems with communist rebels in the jungle in Malaysia, but they never bothered us, as we were helping to develop the country. So all was good."

"You used to say that you wouldn't want your children to become Gurkhas," his daughter said. "Why don't you tell her that? And why don't you tell her about when your father died and you weren't given permission to come home and threatened to quit?"

Nahadur gave an inscrutable smile, but did not pick up his daughter's thread.

"What happened when your father died?" I asked.

"He died in 1968," Nahadur said. "The letter from home took a whole month to get to me, so his death was old news by the time I heard about it. I asked for leave, but my superiors refused. So I had no choice other than to stay and do my duty."

"Why wouldn't you want your children to become Gurkhas?" I said.

"Being a Gurkha is a hard life," he said. "If I had known it would be so hard, I would never have signed up. I had more or less no contact with my family in Nepal when I was stationed abroad, but they were safe here, so that was fine. The construction projects we were working on in Hong Kong were top secret, and had to be done at night. We were not allowed to use lights and we were not allowed to talk. It wasn't easy. But the main reason I told my children horror stories was to get them to concentrate on their school work and get a good education."

He glanced over at his daughter, who was standing in a corner, listening intently.

"One of my sons, however, became a Gurkha, like me," Nahadur said. "When I retired, he took my place. I was very proud of him. Sadly, he's dead now. After he retired, he got work on a construction project in Hong Kong and stood on a nail one day. The wound got infected, which then developed into sepsis. He had to have his foot amputated. But that didn't help."

"Is there anything you miss about life with the Gurkhas?" I asked.

He thought about it for a long time.

"No, nothing in particular," he said, eventually. "But I'm grateful that I had the opportunity to travel and experience different countries. I wouldn't have been able to do that otherwise."

When I had said my thank yous and was about to leave, Nahadur pressed his hands together and thanked me for refreshing his memory.

*

The odour of sweat lingered throughout the Salute Training Centre on the outskirts of Kathmandu. Thirty aspiring Gurkhas were already some way into their morning training session: press-ups, running on the spot, leg lifts. All that could be heard were inhalations, groans and the instructor's short, sharp instructions. A group were practising for the interview, which counts for just as much as the physical tests, and later in the afternoon there would be classes in English and maths. The requirements are stringent, but that does not stop thousands of young Nepalese from trying their luck every year; the opportunity to see the world and have a secure British income for twenty years, followed by a secure pension, is naturally an attractive package.

Twenty-year-old Pasang Ngima Sherpa had tried to get in for two years. He was from the Everest region, from a poor, isolated village far from the tourist circuit.

"My parents couldn't afford to send me away to school," he said. He had a chiselled face and spoke English with a thick accent. "There was a school in the village, but they didn't provide for the youngest students."

"Why is it so important for you to become a Gurkha?" I asked.

Pasang gave up trying to speak English and asked Savitri to translate. "To be recruited is my biggest dream," he said, in a quiet voice. "If I can manage the admission tests, I'll be able to earn more money and be able to give the next generation a better education than I got myself. Physically, I'm strong enough. I can pass the physical tests, no problem, but I didn't get in the last time because of my poor education. I've been studying night and day to do better and hope that I'll pass the admissions test later this year. My parents hope I will too. The training costs four hundred dollars for six months, and my parents are farmers – they don't have much money."

"How many times can you try?" I ask.

"Three times. Max."

"And what will you do if you don't get in?"

"I don't know," he said, looking down. "I have no plan B. I've invested everything in this."

The British army recently started to allow girls into the Brigade of Gurkhas. Scores of young women had been training hard for months in the hope of passing the admissions test, but only a couple of weeks before, the Nepalese government, which has the final word, had decided that women would not be recruited that year after all.

"The government talks and talks about equality, but does nothing in practice," said eighteen-year-old Alisha Tamang angrily. She had trained at the centre every day until she heard that women would not be able to take the recruitment test after all. She spoke good English and was tall and athletic. Her brown hair was gathered in a long plait, and she was wearing a black skirt and white lace blouse. She had packed away her gym clothes. Like Pasang, she was originally from eastern Nepal, not far from the Everest region.

"The girls have worked just as hard as the boys, and would easily manage the tests," Alisha said. "I trained for two hours a day, sometimes more, and followed exactly the same programme as the boys. We did tests every Friday, and I set many of the records."

"It's true, she's better than most of us," said Pasang, who had been sitting listening to the conversation. Alisha smiled, showing her braces.

"I love sport, boxing in particular," she said. "I've spent a lot of time and energy on this, and I'm not sure what to do now."

Fifteen girls had trained at Salute Training Centre. All of them had stopped after the Nepalese government's announcement.

"Hopefully they will let girls register for recruitment to the Gurkhas next year," Alisha said optimistically. "And then I'll try again."

*

Angel Lama showed me into her room in the flat she shared not far from the centre of the capital. She wore a short camouflage dress and settled on the bed in the lotus position, leaning back against an enormous red teddy bear. With no make-up, and her shoulder-length hair loose around her smooth face, she looked no more than twelve, but was about to turn twenty.

"Sorry about the mess," she said, with an apologetic sweep of her hands. She spoke English with an American accent. "I was out with some friends last night. We went to see a film, but then one thing led to the next and, whoops, I got drunk." She laughed and rubbed her temples. "And now I'm *sooo* hungover!"

The wall behind her was full of photographs from the beauty

contests she had taken part in. Only a few weeks earlier, she had represented Nepal in an international beauty contest for trans people in Thailand. The long, strappy, purple dress she had worn on stage was on a clothes hanger on the door.

"My life hasn't been easy," Angel said, earnestly. "I have worked hard to get where I am today, but I am still traumatised by things that happened to me when I was a child and I don't sleep well at night. When I was growing up, my parents argued all the time. Sometimes my father got angry and smashed everything we owned. We didn't live in the slums, but we weren't rich either – the whole family lived in one room, so it was impossible to escape the fighting. I was bullied at school because I was so feminine, and I didn't have many friends. Even the teachers called me *hirja*." She pulled a face. "I *hate* that word! It's not part of our culture, it comes from India, but people didn't know much about LGBT issues at the time. It's better now, but we've still got a long way to go."

"When did you know you were trans?" I asked.

"I was always different. I liked wearing lipstick, I liked being with girls and going shopping, and I would take my pink Barbie purse to school. The other boys laughed at me. I thought at first that I was homosexual, but one day I came across a website about trans people and everything fell into place. In a way, I'd always known that I was a woman inside, that I was trapped in the wrong body. Even as a child I would pray to God on my birthday that he would make me into a girl." She smiled. "They say that the wishes you make on your birthday will be fulfilled."

When Angel was sixteen, her parents separated, and her father married another woman. Her mother was diagnosed with cervical cancer and had to have surgery. Angel ran away from home. For a year and a half, she made a living doing odd jobs for Blue Diamond Society, an organisation that works for gay, lesbian and trans rights in Nepal.

"I couldn't tell my mother then that her only child was a trans-sexual," Angel said. "She was fighting for her life. It would have destroyed her. I phoned her now and then, and she said it was good that I was working and earning money. She didn't know that I had already started taking the contraceptive pill and dressing like a woman. We don't have access to hormones here, and there are no Nepalese doctors who specialise in transitioning, so we have to do it ourselves. When I was in Thailand, I was told to stop taking the pill, that it wasn't good for me. I was given advice about what medicines I could take instead, so I bought a whole load that I brought home with me."

"Have you considered surgery?" I asked.

"Of course, but it's very expensive and we have to go to Thailand for that. Even the cheapest operation costs a fortune. If the state paid, I would have done it long ago."

"Have you now managed to tell your mother that you're trans?"

"Yes, some time after I'd run away from home she insisted on meeting me. Fine, I said, come and meet me at the Blue Diamond Society. She was very surprised to see that I'd become a girl. She cried a lot. I had been the only boy, so who would carry on the family now? Now that you're a girl, you'll get married and move in with a man, she said. My mother has such an old-fashioned view of girls! She can't understand that we want to work and earn money and build our own houses. Everything changed after Miss Pink, fortunately. Do you know what Miss Pink is?"

I shook my head.

"Miss Pink is Nepal's first beauty contest for trans people. I'm not really the kind of girl who gets all dolled up, but my friends persuaded me to take part. They said that I should do it to make trans people more visible in society. There were twenty participants from all over Nepal, and I won! It's the best thing that's ever happened to me, I was so happy! And so was my mother. She came over to me with tears in her eyes and we had a real girls' talk, mother and daughter kind of thing. She said she could see that I was my true self now, and she was sorry that I'd had to pretend to be someone else throughout my childhood. If there's something I've learned," Angel said and looked at me with old, wise eyes, "it's that you have to be true to who you are. You must be yourself. Otherwise nothing will go right."

She hugged the big, red teddy bear tight.

"When I ran away from home, I stopped going to school, but I've gone back now. When I've finished school, I want to study law abroad, preferably in the UK. That would be quite something, wouldn't it?" She smiled dreamily. "Afterwards, I would come back to Nepal and help other trans people."

I noticed that she had said nothing about her father's reaction.

"How did your father deal with your change?" I asked.

Angel rolled her eyes.

"We don't talk anymore. I have only met him once since I ran away. He said that if I intended to go around like this, I wasn't allowed to say that I had ever been his son – or daughter, for that matter. I cried and cried and was inconsolable, it was the worst thing that had happened to me in my life. But in the end, I realised that I have to create my own happiness. If people don't accept me as I am, there's no room for them in my life. That's just the way it is. Everyone is responsible for their own happiness."

The Prince who Did Not Want to Be King

As we approached **Lumbini** it started to pour with rain and the
road turned into a smooth, shining river.

"The monsoon is on its way," Raju, the young driver, said and
leaned forward over the steering wheel so he could at least try to see
where the road went. Outside, our surroundings turned into a grey,
wet fog, with all shape and form blurred by the rain and mud. But
at no point did it occur to Raju to slow down. He fumbled around
for a cloth and wiped the condensation from the inside of the
windscreen, which only served to reduce the visibility even more.
The sleeve of his shirt slid back to reveal a tattoo. Even though I could
not read Tibetan, I recognised the mantra that Buddhists the world
over chant when they meditate: *Om mani padme hum*, which literally
translated means "Praise to the Jewel in the Lotus", or, as some translate it, "Oh, Jewel Lotus". Each of the six syllables has so many layers
and meanings that volumes have been written about it.

"Are you a Buddhist?" I said, astonished.

"No, no, I'm a Hindu, but I sometimes pray to the Buddha," Raju
said. "I sometimes pray to Jesus and Allah as well. I believe in all the
gods, they are all equally important."

Just then, the car skidded dangerously, and I sent up a silent prayer
to all the world's gods. Raju turned up his other sleeve, and another
tattoo appeared, a chaotic mass of lines.

"It was supposed to be Shiva," he said, visibly embarrassed, as we
pulled up in front of the hotel. "My friend did it. We smoked way
too much hash at the time."

*

Earlier in the week, the temperature had crept up towards forty-five degrees centigrade, but thanks to the rain it had mercifully dropped a little again. My T-shirt still stuck to my back as I went through the eastern gate in **Kapilvastu**, the very gate that Siddhartha Gautama is supposed to have gone through when he left his carefree, privileged life for good at the age of twenty-nine. Some low, brown ruins surrounded by patchy grass came into view.

According to legend, a prince was born some two and a half thousand years ago in a small kingdom on the border between what is now India and Nepal. He was given the name Siddhartha and was the only son of King Suddhodana and Queen Maya. Scholars dispute whether Suddhodana was really a king, or whether he was a prince or a powerful oligarch, but most agree that he was one of the leaders of the Shakya clan, who at the time were vassals of the king of Kosala.

It is said that when Siddhartha, a much longed-for son, was born, Suddhodana was given an ominous prophecy: if his son chose to follow in his footsteps, he would become a greater ruler than Suddhodana himself, but if his son chose to leave his privileged upper-class life, he would become an even greater leader – a spiritual leader for the world. The king did what he could to shelter his son, so he would not be tempted to leave the protection of the palace walls. Not until he was twenty-nine was the son allowed to go beyond the walls, and then only for short, supervised walks. During those carefully planned excursions, the young prince saw glimpses of the suffering in the world; for the first time in his life he saw sickness, old age and death. These experiences affected him deeply and he understood that suffering is an inescapable part of life. Siddhartha was unable to accept that it *had* to be like that. There had to be a way to free oneself, wholly and completely.

One night, while the guards slept, the prince said a silent farewell to his wife and their young son, and stole out through the eastern

107 MSL

gate. Once outside, he gave away his jewellery and clothes, cut his long hair and lived as an ascetic for six years, until eventually he resembled a living skeleton. He earned great respect from the other ascetics, but was no closer to freeing himself from suffering. He understood that by living such an austere life he was damaging his body and mind, and was unable to think clearly. He decided that there had to be another way, a middle way. When a woman offered him a bowl of milk one day, he accepted, which confounded the other ascetics, and they all left him. Siddhartha Gautama drank the milk, then sat down under a fig tree to meditate. That night, he reached a deep understanding of the nature of things and their interconnection. He understood that nothing is permanent, least of all the human mind, and that the way to freedom from suffering lay in recognising this and letting go. Only then can one achieve enlightenment, the cessation of suffering, Nirvana.

With this insight, Siddhartha Gautama started to travel around north India talking to and teaching others. He earned himself the new name of Shakyamuni, Sage of the Shakyas, referring to his clan, and later the Buddha, the Enlightened One. His following slowly grew, and now, two and a half thousand years later, there are close to half a billion people who practise Buddhism throughout the world.

As with all good stories, the story of the Buddha's life has much in common with fairy tales. It is difficult to separate myth from fact, but like Jesus of Nazareth and the Prophet Muhammed, Siddhartha Gautama was a real person. Nepalese archaeologists believe that he spent the first twenty-nine years of his life right here, on the dry, patchy grass plain outside Lumbini, not far from the border with India. The recently excavated foundations indicate that it was a small town complete with shops, residential areas and temples. However, it would take a good deal of imagination to visualise what the town might have looked like when the future Buddha grew up here, as nearly all the ruins that have been excavated thus far are of houses and walls that were built several hundred years after the young prince walked through the eastern gate and out into the world.

Workers with dark, sunburnt faces were using wooden planks to construct paths and bridges between the ruins, so tourists would not disturb the archaeologists' painstaking work. On a big tree at the edge of the ruined town, thousands of worn prayer flags fluttered in the mild morning breeze. I made my way over to the tree, expecting to find devout pilgrims or Buddhist monks deep in meditation, but there was not a Buddhist to be seen, only elephants. More than a hundred big and small elephant statues stood neatly lined up in rows by the trunk. A small tent had been put up nearby. A bare-footed, dirty young boy saw me, got out a drum and started to play enticing rhythms. A very dressed-up young couple appeared on the path behind me. They did not seem in the slightest bit interested in the ruins of the Buddha's childhood home, but headed straight for the elephants and fell down on their knees.

Siddhartha Gautama was born in Kapilvastu, about twenty kilo-metres from the ruins of the palace where he grew up. As the time approached for her to give birth, his mother Maya set off to return to her parents' home. To this day, many Indian and Nepalese women return to their parents to give birth. Maya was still a long way from her childhood home when she felt the first twinges of labour. She sought refuge in the beautiful gardens of Lumbini, where, leaning against a tree, she gave birth to her only son.

A square, white and remarkably unpoetic temple has been built around the stone that marked where Siddhartha Gautama is thought to have been born, sometime around 400 BCE. Some two hundred years later, the Indian emperor Ashoka visited his birthplace. A pillar still stands there to mark the occasion. The inscription on the pillar reads that the emperor came here to pray at the place of the Buddha's birth, and, as a gesture to the local community, the emperor decided that the village should not have to pay tax. The inscription is the oldest in Nepal.

In the centuries that followed, Lumbini was alternately revered and forgotten, until the place was truly forgotten in the fourteenth century. The Ashoka pillar was not rediscovered until 1896. Close to the square white temple building lie the foundations of 2,000-year-old stupas and monasteries that were built to honour the Buddha and then forgotten and left to the elements.

In order to revitalise the area, the Japanese architect Tange Kenzo was commissioned in the 1970s to design the Lumbini Development Zone, a complex that measures three by two kilometres. The area consists of monasteries and temples built with contributions from Buddhist communities all over the world, set among well-maintained lawns, woods, mosquitoes and twittering birds, making it an attractive tourist destination.

As the distances were considerable and the heat was exhausting, I was not tempted to walk around the complex. Cars are not permitted in the development zone, so cycle rickshaws have a monopoly on sightseeing tours, and an old, sinewy man took me from temple to temple in a very rickety rickshaw. He obviously followed a set route, a kind of whistle-stop tour through the Buddhist world, and pulled up outside every temple, where he would then announce: Cambodian monastery, ma'am, Vietnamese monastery, ma'am, French monastery, ma'am, and so on to the Nepalese, Chinese, German, Singaporean and Thai monasteries – all built in an architectural style that reflected the country's national character and traditions. After twenty temples, I lost the ability to keep them separate in my mind, and they became a gilded jumble.

The development zone has not been a great success in terms of Western visitor numbers. The majority of the tourists were Indian and Nepalese, who hurried from temple to temple, bowed in the entrance, took a selfie, dropped some money in the collection box, then rushed on to the next temple. The Nepalese authorities hope that the number of Western tourists will increase when Gautam Buddha International Airport opens in the near future.

Even though no people are more closely linked to Siddhartha Gautama than the Tibetans, there was no Tibetan temple in the development zone. The Chinese temple was decorated with dragons and fat, gilded Buddha statues, chemically stripped of any detail that might bring to mind the Tibetan Plateau.

But behind the unpoetic Maya Devi Temple was a small, crooked, red and white temple with a flat roof; the style was very Tibetan, and included prayer wheels, tantric demons and Tibetan script. The modest temple was built in the 1960s by the king of Upper Mustang, which once had been a small, Buddhist kingdom on the border between Nepal and Tibet.

And Mustang was my next destination.

The Snow Leopard

Mustang, or the kingdom of Lo, was founded in 1380 and was independent until 1795, when it was incorporated in the Gorkha kingdom, now modern Nepal. The king of Lo was, however, allowed to retain his title and some of his power until 2008, when all Nepalese vassal states and principalities were abolished. Through the centuries, the small kingdom has been more closely linked to Tibet than to Nepal; the population practises Tibetan Buddhism, wears Tibetan clothes and speaks a Tibetan dialect. Thanks to Mustang's geographical and political isolation, much of the old Tibetan architecture and traditional cultural has survived – until 1992, the region was a designated demilitarised zone, and no foreigners were allowed into the kingdom. The substantial entrance fees to visit Upper Mustang are enough to put most tourists off.

Until a road was constructed about a decade ago, one could only get to Lo Manthang, the capital of Upper Mustang, on foot. Even though there is now a road all the way, Savitri insisted that we fly to Jomsom, the nearest airport, to spare us an eight-hour journey on bumpy, dusty roads. So, instead, we had a twenty-minute rollercoaster ride. The small airplane careened towards the black mountainside and the hull shook so much that the curtain in front of the entrance to the cockpit slipped to one side. The two pilots sitting hunched over the controls were unnervingly young.

I had managed to get a seat by the emergency exit, which offered a kind of symbolic security. To my right, I had a view of Annapurna, the most dangerous mountain in the world. Close to forty per cent of those who have tried to reach the summit have died in the attempt. And to my left, I could see the snow on Dhaulagiri, which was believed to be the highest mountain in the world at the start of the nineteenth century, at 8,167 MSL. Then Kanchenjunga was discovered and soon after Peak XV, or Mount Everest. The corridor between the two mountain massifs is narrow, and only navigable for a few hours in the morning – by the afternoon, the strong, unpredictable down winds are too dangerous, so no planes can take off or land in Jomsom after eleven o'clock. The airport at Pokhara had been closed all morning due to fog, and we were several hours delayed. It was already a quarter past eleven, and the hull was shaking so much that I could not hear what Savitri said. She pointed at the black mountainside and made some comment or other, then laughed. I sent another prayer to the gods of the world and was immediately heard: the plane made a sharp turn and a moment later the wheels hit the ground.

Frail old ladies in saris, woollen socks and sandals heaved themselves to their feet and tottered towards the exit. The flight attendants helped them down the narrow steps and out onto the short runway. A bus was already there to take them to Muktinath, one of the most important Vishnu temples in the world. The temple is so holy that it is said that anyone who visits it goes straight to paradise when they die. Muktinath is also a Buddhist pilgrim destination, as Padmasambhava, the tantric master from Swat Valley, is said to have meditated there on his way to Tibet.

I had experienced exactly the same flight, sixteen years earlier, in a cabin full of food, live hens and mountain folk. Back then, there was no road, and the nerve-racking flight had been the only way to reach Jomsom, if one did not want to walk in.

2743 MSL   **Jomsom** was scarcely recognisable. I remembered a windswept, impoverished mountain village, whereas now there were towering apartment blocks; the only thing missing were flashing neon signs.

The local youth sat drinking cappuccinos in modern coffee bars, as they surfed on their mobile phones.

A full, closed jeep transported us on to Upper Mustang. Savitri and I sat pressed together in the front seat, as there were already ten men sitting in the back. The green, rolling hills gradually got barer and soon enough we were covered in a thin layer of light-brown dust, surrounded by countless shades of bluish-brown, greenish-brown, reddish-brown and greyish-brown. The air in the jeep was like a sauna, the road narrow and bumpy – driveable, but not finished.

Six hours later we rolled into the labyrinthine streets of **Lo Manthang.**   3840 MSL

There were one hundred and sixty-seven houses within the red village walls, many of them from around the time that the kingdom of Lo was established in the fourteenth century. The small, crooked houses were whitewashed and low, and the streets between them were so narrow and windy that we got lost all the time. Hairy cattle wandered around between the houses. And in the centre of the labyrinth stood the royal residence, a ramshackle stone building with one hundred and eight rooms (a holy number in Buddhism). The royal family and the local council had long since moved out, and only a few rooms were now in use.

In a sunny corner of the square outside sat a group of old women, all dressed in traditional woollen Tibetan clothes, adorned with colourful, chunky jewellery.

"Can you spare any money for tea?" one of them asked in Nepalese. Savitri handed her a banknote. The woman, who had scarcely any teeth left on top, beamed and bumbled off. A few minutes later she came back with a thermos and a tray of cups. Each of the women got a brimming cup and drank the sweet, milky tea with obvious pleasure.

"The men meet in another place," said a toothless woman in a high-pitched, shaky voice. "The women meet here. To pass the time of day."

She lifted her woollen skirt to show off her black leather boots. The other women all had traditional Tibetan shoes made from felted wool.

"My son sent them to me from America," she said, proudly.

Tenzin, a young monk, showed Savitri and me around Lo Manthang's old monastery. He was the second son in a family of seven children, and, in line with tradition, his parents had sent him to the monastery as a child.

"When I was little, I thought monastery life was boring and I missed my family, but now I am happy being a monk," he said. "It's a good life. Sadly, it's no longer easy to recruit new monks. Times have changed. People now only have two or three children, and they would rather go to the USA than to a monastery. Everyone wants to be rich now."

There were three old monasteries in the village, all dark and dimly lit, decorated with 700-year-old wall paintings so intricate that it would take months, if not years, to study all the details. The Buddha statue in the oldest monastery was on the first floor, so the king could see it from his prayer room across the street and did not have to leave the residence to pray.

I had never interviewed a king before, not even an unofficial king, and was quite nervous and a little breathless as I made my way up the slope to the Royal Mustang Resort. The hotel is the most luxurious in Mustang, and is owned and run by the dethroned royal family, as indicated by the name. The reception rooms were airy and cool, and smelled of fresh paint. Hammering could be heard from the wing where the bedrooms were. The hotel was so new that it was not quite finished, and they were working from dawn until dusk to get it ready in time for the annual spring festival, the highpoint of the year in Lo Manthang.

I was shown to a sofa in a lounge next to the dining room, and served freshly brewed tea. Fifteen minutes later, Zingme Singhe Palbar Bista hurried into the room.

"Why on earth do you want to talk to me?" he said in perfect English, and roared with laughter. He was wearing jeans and a burgundy polo shirt, and plumped down on the sofa opposite me. "I know nothing, I can't even speak proper English! Where is your interpreter?" His shoulders shook with laughter again.

"She's out having a cigarette," I said.

"I'm with her, hahaha! There's no point in talking to me, the monarchy is dead, it doesn't exist anymore! I am not a king, Nepal is a republic, you do realise that?" He laughed even more. "So you, you're from Norway, is that what you said? I was in Norway once. I remember I was terrified when we landed, hahaha! I saw nothing but ice and snow from the window, and I was convinced the airplane would skid on the runway. I didn't know that you had heated runways, hahaha!"

The unofficial king chatted away about his stay in Norway and other trips he had been on, we were given more tea, and he laughed freely. It was not hard to understand why he is so popular with the locals, who still call him king. When the principalities and vassal states were abolished in 1961, the original agreement was that the ruling families would keep their titles for three generations. Jigme Dorje Palbar Bista was crowned the 25th king of Lo in 1964. He was also the last: when the monarchy was abolished in 2008, all royals, big and small, powerful and minor, lost their titles overnight. In 2016, when the 25th king died, his nephew, Zingme Singhe Palbar Bista, was therefore not crowned. (The king left no direct heirs, but when his only son had died at the age of eight, he had adopted his nephew, Zingme Singhe.)

"Yes, people still call me Lo Gyalpo, king of Lo," Zingme said. "Culturally, I'm still the king. I'm present at all our festivals and try to help the people who need it, but I have none of the responsibilities my father had. As king, for example, he was responsible for guarding the border. I have no such power. Fortunately! I think I'm happier the way I am, without a title."

"So you would rather be a hotel director than a king?" I asked cheekily, encouraged by Zingme's jovial, unpretentious manner.

"Life here is hard," he said. His narrow face was suddenly serious. "We only have one harvest, the soil is poor and the climate harsh. Before, people used to go down to the lowlands to work when the harvest was over; now the young people go abroad to work. Many of them go to the USA. At least half have emigrated already, and the population is shrinking. I'm building this hotel to show young people that there are opportunities here as well. My father wanted to open up Mustang, he wanted tourists to come here. I do too. When the road is ready and the border to China finally opens again, Lo Manthang will change for ever."

The half-finished road continued north to the Chinese border, but other than that there were no roads, only narrow tracks. Savitri had arranged for us to get a couple of horses so we could visit the neighbouring village. The small horses were white and hardy, and Lopsang, the horse owner, had leathery, sunburnt skin and narrow eyes. As soon as we had left Lo Manthang and the red village walls behind us, we turned off the road and trekked up the bare mountainside. Other than in a few small green oases down by the rivers, nothing grows here; mountain formations of stone, gravel and sand roll in waves in every direction, as far as the eye can see.

When we reached the top, we dismounted and led the horses down a steep slope that led to a dried-up riverbed at the bottom of the valley. Flanked by steep, orange-brown mountains, we rode along the valley floor, surrounded by silence and thin air. Every so often we passed large herds of yaks moving far up the mountainside, with a herdsman behind them. A black bird with wide, powerful wings sailed overhead then disappeared. All that could be heard was the snorting of our horses and the sound of their hooves on the stone. Time and space merged, the centuries fell away and my thoughts drifted pleasantly here and there.

Suddenly, a large, sandy-coloured feline came racing down the mountainside and crossed the dry riverbed a stone's throw away.

"A leopard!" Savitri gasped. "Oh my god, a *snow* leopard!"

"No, it's probably just a fox," Lopsang said, matter of factly. "I haven't seen a snow leopard up here for ages. I've been taking tourists up here for years in the hope of seeing a snow leopard. We've even camped overnight to increase our chance, but not once have we seen one."

The animal ran up the practically vertical slope on paths that only it could see, then settled on a ledge about a hundred metres above us. It lay there watching us with curiosity. Its spotted orange-brown coat made it hard to differentiate from the dry desert-like mountainside.

"Good grief!" Lobsang looked up at the animal with an open mouth. "You're right, it *is* a snow leopard! It must be ten years or more since I last saw one in these parts."

The snow leopard was still lying on the ledge looking down at us. Lobsang started to call and shout to get it to move, and after a few minutes it stood up lazily, stretched its legs, then wandered up the mountainside, keeping its eyes on us all the while, only to turn round and come back to the ledge, where it once again curled up and looked down at us.

"I think it's a male," our horseman said. "It's so curious and unafraid. Must be young."

I have no idea how long we stood there. Five minutes? Twenty? The horses were not interested and grazed with something akin to boredom. It felt like sacrilege to ride on, but eventually we did. The snow leopard kept its eyes on us for a long time. Then it jumped up from the ledge, padded softly up the steep mountainside and disappeared.

An hour later we spotted some faded prayer flags.

"It used to be green here," Lopsang said, laconically. "Tall, lush grass on both sides of the river. Good farming land."

There was no longer any growth on the right side of the almost dry river, and only some scruffy, scant tussocks pushed up through the poor soil on the left-hand side. Tiny mountain goats that were scarcely bigger than cats were grazing greedily. Two women stood stooped over hoes and spades, and behind them the small, square stone and mud houses of the village climbed up the slope.

Lopsang pointed to a large, rectangular building on the other side of the river.

"That's the school. It's closed now. There are no children left here."

He showed the way to where his friend, Baki Gurung, lived. She was in her sixties and as wrinkled as a raisin, but her long hair was still jet black. Her few remaining teeth were brown and sharp. With a smile, she led us into a tiny courtyard, where small, square pieces of cheese had been hung up to dry – they tasted of very little and were so hard that one could chew on them all day before they eventually softened – and then through a low doorway into the kitchen. In the middle of the small room was a stove that was fired with dried goat dung. The flue disappeared out through a hole in the ceiling. There were no windows in the room, only an opening that was covered with plastic. The floor was stamped earth. Savitri and I sat down on a small rug by the wall, and Baki started to prepare butter tea for us in a *dhongmo*, a long wooden pipe, a kind of churn I had previously only seen in the Sherpa museum in Namche Bazaar. The old woman mixed the butter, salt and tea in the pipe without saying anything, shook it well and filled our wooden cups with a gleaming, greenish liquid. The old woman had lived in the remote village all her life and did not speak Nepalese, only the local language, which was a dialect of Tibetan. Lopsang gave her some money, and grinned when she poured some clear liquid from a metal pot into his cup.

"One for the road," he said. "But first we must visit the museum."

He took us to the edge of the village. The path followed an irrigation canal to a long building, where a woman was waiting with a bunch of keys in her hand. She unlocked the door and let us in. The home-made shelves on the wall held clear plastic bags of bones, sorted and labelled according to the type of bones they contained. There was a yellowed sheet of paper which said how many people the bones came from, if they were from women or men, and from which cave they had been collected. It was still possible to recognise the odd skull, ribcage, finger, pelvis and thigh bone.

An older man wearing a faded blue cap came into the room and opened the shutters. The light flooded in through the window openings. His face was nut brown, with deep furrows. He introduced himself as Topke Gurung, and picked out a bag from a wooden box on the floor. From this he produced a small wooden cup and fragments of Buddhist wall paintings covered in a thin layer of gold, so delicate that they almost crumbled in his hands.

"Everything comes from the caves in the mountains around here," he said, in Nepalese. "The police gathered and sorted the bones. Some of the skeletons are thousands of years old!"

About ten thousand man-made caves have been found in Upper Mustang. The oldest caves are more than three thousand years old and were in all likelihood used as burial chambers. About a thousand years ago, when there was great unrest in the region, many families chose to move into the caves and make them home. A few hundred years later, when the situation was more peaceful again, people moved from the caves into simple houses down by the rivers. The caves were still used, but now as meditation caves, stores and strategic lookout posts.

When we had finished, we sat outside in the sunshine and talked to Topke Gurung. The woman who had opened the museum for us sat and listened in silence.

Topke had been born in the village, and now had four children himself, a son and three daughters. He had sent his second daughter to a convent.

"Life here is hard," he said. "I am poor and didn't have the means to support her. She has more opportunities in the convent and will get a better education. I have no education, I can barely write my own name. I learned Nepalese from the teacher who used to live here, and from my children. I had to learn it so I could fill out forms and documents."

His wife had died two years ago, and he now lived alone in the largely deserted village.

"She had too little blood, my wife, that was the problem," he said, sadly. "I took out a loan so I could take her to hospital in Pokhara and Kathmandu. I borrowed a total of five thousand dollars, but it didn't help. She died. All I have left now is the loan. Practically everyone has left the village. When the water disappeared, we went to the king, Zingme, and told him our problems. He came here to see the situation for himself, and later gave us some land, a few hours' walk from here, by another river. Most people have moved there."

Only a handful of old people had stayed in the village.

"There used to be plenty of water here and we had lots of horses, everything was green," Topke said. "The river was wide and the water reached our knees, and it was easy to farm here. I grew buckwheat, mustard, potatoes and radishes. But the river slowly dried up. It's no longer possible to grow anything here, and for every year that passes, there is less and less water in the river. There's too much sun these days, that's why the groundwater has sunk. When I was a boy, there were always clouds here, during the day and at night. Now the sun is too strong, there's too much wind, and in winter there's too much snow. Last winter, it snowed all the time. For three months, we did nothing but clear the snow. About half a metre fell each day. We ate, drank, slept and cleared snow. I lost twenty-eight goats and two cows. We didn't have enough water or grass for them, and they froze to death. I don't have a building for the animals, we can't afford it. When we dug them out of the snow, they were frozen. Sometimes the snow leopards take them as well. In the past year alone, five of my goats have been eaten by snow leopards. They come into the village and help themselves."

The sun beat down from a cloudless sky. The light was so sharp that I had to shade my eyes in order to see Topke, who was sitting in the lotus position on the ground and did not seem to be bothered by the sun.

"I think the weather is changing because the world is going in the wrong direction," he said. "The world has turned and is going in the opposite direction. There was less sun before, and people were healthier. There was no rubbish here. We didn't have any plastic in the village, but now there's plastic everywhere. The animals eat the plastic and it makes them sick. There's also a lot more wind than before. It comes from all directions and carries bacteria with it. Animals and people are sicker than before. The clouds would keep the ground moist, but they've gone, and the ground is dry, nothing grows here any longer. There's dust everywhere and I have to buy my vegetables and anything else I need in Lo Manthang. I have to buy everything except water. Before, I never had to buy anything."

He sighed.

"I'm fifty-five, I'm an old man now. I am worried about my children's future. So much has changed. Nowadays, everything has to be bought with money, and I don't have any . . . There's too much of everything, too many cars, too much smoke, people wear perfume and other unnatural things. The old god doesn't like it. Perhaps that's why the weather has changed – God is upset?" He looked questioningly at Savitri and myself.

"Are you not Buddhists here?" I asked.

"Yes, yes, we're Buddhists," he said. "As we're Buddhists, we don't sacrifice animals, but offer butter lamps to the gods instead. There are lots of different gods. People in other places have different gods from us. We have our gods and we worship them in our way."

The sun was setting, and there was a cold wind as we rode into Lo Manthang. Ensconced in the guest house dining room, we warmed ourselves with hot soup and raksi, the local spirit. Savitri spent her time chatting on Tinder. A lonely Italian who worked and lived in the jungle in southern Nepal flirted wildly with her. The messages were more and more passionate, but cooled quickly when Savitri politely declined an invitation to travel all the way there to visit him that coming weekend. *Goodbye*, the Italian replied curtly. Savitri ordered more raksi for both of us.

The following morning we swung back into the saddle, even though we were pretty stiff from our long expedition the day before. This time we headed west, to see the nomads. They were staying in four large white tents, about two hours' ride from Lo Manthang.

Lhakpa Gurung, a young woman with long, black hair and healthy, white teeth – a rarity in these parts – invited us into the warmth. She had recently moved home, having studied in Kathmandu for several years, and was now newly married and had had her first baby.

"Everyone is here for the new moon ritual," she said, and gave us a cup of butter tea. Four older women and three men sat spinning their prayer wheels as they mumbled their mantras. Everyone was dressed in traditional Tibetan clothes. At the short end of the tent, there was a framed photograph of the Dalai Lama, and under the picture, the flames of tens of butter lamps flickered. At the other end, there was a small kitchen corner. An entire shelf was filled with more than twenty thermos flasks. A black stove stood in the middle of the tent, emitting a surprising amount of heat. I took off my outer garments, sipped the steaming tea, and felt the sweat trickling.

Lhakpa's four-month-old son lay in a corner on a pile of cushions and stared in fascination at the tent flap.

"I was very happy in Kathmandu, but I plan to live here with my husband for the rest of my life," Lhakpa said. "Unless we move to Lo Manthang, of course. That's what everyone does these days. There are only six families left here. It is more and more difficult to continue living a traditional life. This winter we lost about three hundred animals – there was so much snow that there was no food for them."

Lhakpa was born in Tibet, but grew up in Mustang.

"My mother came here with her husband and extended family when I was small. They crossed the border illegally – I don't know why they left. My father stayed in Tibet. My mother never talks about him."

The hostess sat in a corner on her own, pouring home-made yoghurt into a leather container. When she had done this, she filled a plate with biscuits and chocolates, and was not happy until everyone had helped themselves.

"The new moon ritual lasts all day," Lhakpa said. "Everyone comes with some food, and then we pray together. We meet like this four times a month, on fixed dates, according to the Tibetan calendar."

The mumbling old voices rose and fell, the prayer wheels whirred without stop. Every so often, the old people would help themselves to more butter tea, talk among themselves as the prayer wheels turned, then concentrate once more on the mantras and prayers.

"Have any of you seen a yeti?" I asked, with genuine curiosity.

"Yes," called out a weathered man with a prayer wheel in each hand. "But it was six or seven years ago. There aren't many of them here, but further north, where I come from, there were a lot! They followed our yaks when we were out with them. I never saw them close by, only at a distance. Yetis are twice the size of a yak, their hands and feet are like ours, only they are covered in hair. They have lots of hair on their faces as well! You can't see their faces when they are walking downhill, only when they are walking up. They normally walk on all fours, but sometimes they get up on two legs, like us. They eat yak and grass, and normally run away at the sight of humans. They're scared of us, and we're scared of them, but sometimes they get so angry with a person that they throw them over a precipice!"

Anyone who visited remote communities in Norway a century ago would presumably have heard similar stories, only about hulders and trolls. And presumably these stories were based on a highly subjective reality. Most experts refute the idea that yetis are a zoological reality – but not all.

A middle-aged woman with a round, lively face came into the tent and sat down beside us. She was called Lamo Chhepteng, and was missing her front teeth.

"Both my children are studying in Kathmandu, but I didn't go to school. There was no school here, back then. The only thing I know anything about is yak."

She chuckled, but was soon serious again.

"But these are not good times for yak herders," she said, grimly. "Before, summer was summer and winter was winter, but it's not like that anymore. There is far too much wind now, and too little grass, nearly all our animals have died. My husband and I are building a hotel in Lo Manthang, because we don't know that our yak will provide a livelihood in the future."

"Why do you think the weather has changed?" I asked.

"How would I know?" She chortled and burrowed in her ear with a toothpick.

"Do you think there will be any nomads left in ten years' time?" I asked.

"No, all our animals will be dead in ten years' time," Lamo said. There was no doubt or laughter evident in her voice. "In ten years' time, there will be no-one left here."

*

In ten years' time, the modern road to China will no longer be new and the border controls will be in full operation. A group of business-men from Kathmandu were sitting in the dining room drinking raksi when Savitri and I got back from the nomads' camp. They were going up to inspect the border station first thing the next morning, and we went along with them, even though there was not really enough room for us in their rented car.

On the way, we visited one of the famous man-made caves. It was astonishingly large, built in several storeys; a small community must have lived there. There were narrow ladders leading from one floor to the next, and we climbed up and down, and had to bend over to pass through the low corridors.

We had some fresh chapattis and boiled potatoes in a simple guest house nearby. The potatoes from Upper Mustang are famous throughout Nepal, the businessmen informed me; they had filled the boot with this delicacy. The steaming potatoes had a sweet, buttery taste, and literally melted on the tongue.

How many potatoes have I eaten in my life? Thousands, tens of thousands! And still I did not know that they could taste like this.

The road climbed steeply. The heavy jeep struggled a bit on the gravel and was enveloped in a cloud of light-grey dust. My temples were throbbing from the altitude.

At the **border crossing**, which consisted of a long, half-finished   4660 MSL
white building and a large empty car park, there was a forest of cranes and lots of busy Chinese workers. A barbed-wire fence cut through the landscape. On the other side of the fence, accom-modation tents had been put up for the workers. Brightly coloured clothes fluttered on the barbed wire, where they had been hung out to dry.

Savitri and I went over to the fence to take photographs. Two girls dressed in traditional Tibetan woollen dresses came running towards us from the other side. They had rosy cheeks and long, black hair that danced in the morning breeze. The girls came right up to the fence and reached their hands out to us with a big smile. A greeting from Tibet.

Mustang has for centuries been an important trading station and thoroughfare on the salt trading route between Tibet, Nepal and India. If the border crossing is opened to foreigners when it is finished, Mustang will primarily be a popular route for Indian Hindu pilgrims on their way to Mount Kailash, the home of Shiva. The holy mountain is several days' drive from Lhasa and even more from Kathmandu, but only five hours from the new border station, and pilgrims would also be able to visit the Muktinath Temple.

When the border is opened, *if* it is opened, Lo Manthang and Mustang will change, probably beyond recognition. And the king himself – albeit the unofficial king – is ready to welcome the pilgrims to his luxurious Royal Mustang Resort.

On the way back to Jomsom, we hitched a ride with a lorry, Road King. But on the very first slope, Road King gave in to gravity and had to be pulled up by another truck.

Unlike the jeeps, trucks do not drive on the gravel roads but instead follow the Kali Gandaki River down in the valley. A steep, zigzagging road led down to the river. About halfway down, another truck had got stuck on a bend, and it took half an hour to dig it loose. Then downwards we went again.

The wide gravel bed at the bottom of the valley indicated that the Kali Gandaki had once been a great and mighty river, even up here. Now it was no more than four or five metres at the widest as it snaked back and forth along the valley bed. Earth and sediment coloured the water brown, and we crossed it again and again, forty times, fifty, I lost count. On either side, the bare mountainside reached for the sun. We were always in the shade.

Kali, which literally means "time" or "the fullness of time", is one of the most powerful and terrible goddesses in Hinduism; she is the mother of the universe, the destroyer of evil powers, goddess of power and time. Kali is dark as night and wears a necklace of skulls, and holds a bloody sword in one of her four arms. The river that bears her name forces its way through Mustang before racing on south. At some point it takes a sharp turn and changes direction, heading east, but then turns once again, leaves Nepal and runs on into India, where it joins the Ganges and flows out into the Bay of Bengal. And millions of years ago, the river flowed all the way from Tibet.

Gutta cavat lapidem, non vi, sed saepe cadendo. A drop of water hollows a stone not by force, but by falling often. Water is more powerful than stone, and some rivers are even older than the ancient mountains. Kali Gandaki coursed more or less where it does today long before India collided with Eurasia, forcing the Himalaya Mountains to rise up about fifty million years ago. And while the stone massif has been pushed further and further up, and got higher by the year, the river has bored its way down through the sediment and carved out a course between Dhaulagiri and Annapurna. So, as the mountains grow, Kali Gandaki digs deeper and deeper into the geological deposits, revealing layer upon layer of sedimentary stone from the bed of the Tethys Sea, which once, about two hundred million years ago, covered the greater part of what is now Eurasia, but no longer exists.

The wheels ploughed through the dirty water fifty times, a hundred times, two hundred times. Road King was in fact River King. The river we crossed was never the same, in some places shallow, in others deceptively deep. Later in the afternoon, when we were back on a gravel road and the sun had shrunk to an orange stripe in the west, we got stuck again: the road ahead was blocked by a big rockfall.

The mountains move too. And, like the river, they move towards the ocean.

The Thirsty God

We flew over what seemed like never-ending mountains. From the cockpit, the pilot listed the peaks as we passed them: *Machapuchare. Annapurna I. Annapurna South. Gangapurna.* And then they were gone: the snow, the rock face, all the peaks ending in "a", and we prepared for landing.

No tourists go to Surkhet, but the hotels were fully booked all the same, by representatives of the various aid organisations that throng here to one of the poorest and least-developed districts in Nepal. As the crow flies, it is less than fifty kilometres from Surkhet Airport to Turmakhad, the village where Savitri and I were going to stay the night, but the car journey there took all day. The further we got from the airport, the worse the road became. After about two hours the driver pointed at a cluster of houses up on the hillside on the other side of the valley.

"That's where we're going," he said.

"Oh, so we'll be there soon," I said, relieved.

The driver laughed drily. "There's no bridge here, so we have to drive round."

The road continued over rivers and small bridges, to the left, to the right, up and down. The surroundings became more and more rural and the road and earth were red; every so often we passed roadside shacks that sold noodles and drinks.

We stopped a couple of times to drink some sweet black tea spiced with pepper. It was not until dusk that we arrived at the elusive Turmakhad and got a very simple room made from earth and clay.

The walls were covered with plastic and a coil of wires and two bare light bulbs hung from the ceiling. There was no window, and to close and lock the door you had to put a stick across it.

Early the next morning, Savitri and I walked over the hill to the nearest neighbouring village. The horizon was full of pastures, terraced gardens, gentle hills and large but simple houses made from mud and stone.

We had travelled all this way to talk about menstruation. Among the Hindus in Nepal, women are considered unclean when they are menstruating, and in Kathmandu, many women stay away from the kitchen for the days that they bleed, but nowhere are the traditions as strict as in the Hill Region in the west. Many women here still sleep in small, separate huts when they are menstruating. The tradition is called *chhaupadi*, and is in fact dangerous: every year, an unknown number of Nepalese girls and women die in these menstruation huts as a result of snakebites, scorpion bites, carbon monoxide poisoning or the cold. The practice has been banned and is punishable by three months' imprisonment or a fine of roughly twenty-two dollars. But in the rural areas, where the police only visit sporadically, as good as no-one is punished.

A thin woman in her fifties was washing clothes in a tub outside a large house.

Savitri got straight to the point. "Where does your daughter sleep when she has a period?"

"She sleeps there," the woman said and pointed at a small but clean lean-to by the main house. "When I was younger, I had to sleep in there with the animals." She nodded in the direction of the stall in the cellar of the house. "I used to chase out the animals before I went to sleep. Now we have built a separate place. Do you think it's good enough? If you don't think it's good enough, we will pull it down!"

"She thinks we're from one of the voluntary organisations," Savitri said, as we carried on down the slope. "They've been very active in the villages around here recently, because of all the *chhaupadi*-related deaths."

We came across another woman in her fifties in the neighbouring house. Mana Bayak was dressed in a patterned wraparound skirt and had a pink cotton scarf on her head. A large gold ring hung from her nose. When she smiled, which she did a lot, her face broke into beautiful wrinkles. Her youngest son, who had just turned twelve, hung around while we spoke.

"It was all very strict before," Mana said. "When we were menstruating, we were not allowed to eat proper food, no dairy products, for example. I used to sleep there." She pointed to a little shack, barely one and a half metres in height, made from stone and reddish earth, with logs on the roof. "It's been made into a toilet now," she added.

The door to the shack was open. The floor inside was covered in dry, clean straw.

"I only had a thin blanket over me when I slept in there," Mana said. "I used to make a mattress from banana or maize leaves to keep me warm, but when it rained, that didn't help much. Everything had to be washed afterwards, which is why I didn't sleep on a proper mattress. There was no electricity at the time, and it was pitch black at night. I was always scared, of snakes in particular, but I was also scared of men. Even though the hut was only a few metres from the main house, it felt like sleeping in the jungle."

A small flock of goats came running up the path towards us. Mana quickly stood up and shooed them away.

"What misfortune that we had to go through all that, that we couldn't sleep comfortably in our own home!" she said. "I used to be frightened all the time about what would happen if I didn't follow the rules. I worried that the livestock might die, that my parents-in-law would get angry. When I had a period, I wasn't even allowed to touch my sons, not even when they were babies. We thought it might make them ill. If we were unlucky enough to touch anyone, both of us had to wash ourselves thoroughly."

A man in worn work clothes came over to us, obviously curious.

"Away with you," Savitri said. "We're talking about women's business!"

The man nodded agreeably and wandered off. The twelve-year-old had got a brush and was grooming a goat with long strokes as he listened intently to our conversation.

"My husband is five years younger than me, but I am stronger than him," Mana said. "When he drinks, he gets stupid and says a lot of silly things, but I've got him under control. If my life had been easier, I would no doubt have been even stronger. I gave birth to my first four children in the barn, as was the custom. I lost a lot of blood, and the baby and I had to sleep with the animals for the first few days. When I was about to have my last baby, my mother-in-law said that some people from an organisation had said that nothing would happen if we gave birth in ordinary rooms and it was better for the baby that way. We no longer observe *chhaupadi*, and my last child was born in a room in the house. That was my life, but luckily the customs have now changed."

How much time is needed to change a tradition? A generation, or longer? A group of women approached on the gravel road below the house, carrying enormous baskets of hay. The woman in the neighbouring house was hanging out the washing, and another was sitting on the ground picking small stones out of the corn.

"I've sent all my children to school, but when I was a child, there was no school here," Mana continued. "I can only write my name. When there's an election coming up, lots of people come here and ask for my vote. They show me the party logo and ask me to vote for the plough, for example, because I need a plough, or for the scythe, because I need a scythe to cut the grass. Last time I voted for the tree, because I need shade."

"The Congress Party, that is," Savitri said.

"Yes, possibly."

Mana's eldest son was working in the Gulf States, but she herself had barely left the village.

"We only leave the village if it's absolutely necessary, and we don't go far. I have been to Surkhet and Nepalgunj a couple of times, because some of my siblings live there. You should come back in the autumn," she said. "It's more beautiful then. Everything is brown and dry now, but in autumn the fields are greener and the trees have fruit."

As we were about to move on to the next house, a young woman appeared from the shadows at the back of the house and walked towards us.

"Lots of people still have menstruation huts," she said quietly, when she was beside us. "They're just scared to tell you. Come, I'll show you."

She took us to a house a few hundred metres further up the hill. A woman with long, grey hair, a furrowed face and a big gold ring in her nose greeted us with interest. Her name was Kokila Bayak, and like so many of the old women in the village, she spoke Nepalese that was incomplete and difficult to understand. Savitri struggled to give meaning to the few words she uttered.

"How incredible that you've come all this way to talk to me," the old lady said, and indicated that we should sit down on the ground beside her. "I am old now, older than sixty. I got married when I was five years old. Or maybe it was seven." She pondered for a moment, trying to calculate. "Whatever, I lived with my parents for many years before I moved in with my husband. When I was eighteen or nineteen, I had my first child. I have four daughters and two sons. They are all grown up now. All married."

Beside us was a simple stone and earth hut, about a metre wide and one and a half metres long. It was so low that it would be impossible to stand up in it.

"Does anyone use the menstruation hut?" I asked.

"No." Kokila shook her head. "It was used before, but not any longer."

"Can we have a look?" Savitri asked. Kokila nodded and we opened the low door and looked in. The small hut was immaculate. There was a metal water jug in the corner and a colourful shawl hung from a hook on the wall. Beside the door, there was a small dip in the floor where a fire could be lit.

"It looks like it's still in use," Savitri said.

Kokila ignored the remark.

"I gave birth to all my children in the kitchen," she said. "At the time, we had to sleep with the animals whenever we were bleeding, and had to go far beyond the village to wash. We were afraid of being attacked by tigers, because there were tigers here back then. We were also frightened of snakes. Once, when I went out for a pee, I saw a ghost. It actually wasn't that long ago. We often slept outside under a thin blanket. I always slept badly and would wake up because I was cold or afraid. It was a hard life, but we survived. We didn't die."

She leaned forward and studied my face.

"Is she American?" she asked Savitri, who explained that I was from Europe. Kokila nodded, with a blank expression. It clearly meant nothing to her.

"What are your views on the chhaupadi tradition, that women have to suffer like that?" I asked.

"You have to follow the rules of where you live," Kokila said, with a shrug. "You have to do as everyone else does."

"But menstruation huts are not allowed now," I said. "Are you not afraid of being caught?"

"No, if they come, we just say that we don't practise it any longer. And if they ask what the hut is for, we say that we use it to store wood."

Either she had started to trust us, or had lost the will to lie.

Kokila's daughter-in-law was on the other side of the yard. Nanna had spread corn out over a large mat and hunkered down to pick out the stones.

"I am thirty-five, I think, but I'm not sure, because I've only been to school as a grown-up," she said. "I don't even know exactly how old my children are, but they're all at school now. All of them."

Kokila came over and started to feed the hens behind us. When she had done that, she sat down beside us and listened carefully to the conversation.

"I sleep in the hut for four nights whenever I have a period," her daughter-in-law said. "I prefer sleeping at home, but I follow the rules. If I didn't, I would get the blame if anything went wrong."

Kokila leaned forwards, grabbed hold of Savitri's breasts and weighed them in her hands.

"Good nursing breasts," she said. "My guess is that you have two children."

Savitri had none, but did not contradict the old woman.

"Is it your mother-in-law who has decided that you should sleep in the hut?" I asked Nanna.

"Yes, she says that she did it, so I must do it too."

"Is it not uncomfortable sleeping in such a small hut?" I asked. "Do you get scared? Do you get cold?"

"It's not small," Kokila interrupted. "And it's not cold any longer either. They have thick mattresses now. It was much harder in my time! God was stricter then."

After our morning down in the village, surrounded by goats and barley fields, Turmakhad, with its stalls and alcohol shops, felt almost urban. There was even a bank branch close to the community meeting place by the health centre. The illuminated shiny signs seemed so out of place in the impoverished surroundings. One of the places that sold alcohol also served thali, freshly made chapattis with curry, spicy potatoes and chilli. A family of sparrows lived on the plank over the single bare light bulb. The parents flew back and forth with food to feed their hungry offspring, who cried for food with open beaks.

On the other side of the simple wooden table sat a straight-backed woman in her thirties. Her pink lipstick complemented her mint-green suit, and she had a large briefcase on her lap. Her gaze was firm and she radiated a different kind of self-awareness and confidence from the women we had met earlier in the day.

"*Chhaupadi* is widely practised in the village that I come from," she said in Nepalese to Savitri, when we had finished eating. She had been sitting listening to us for a while and had clearly picked up on the conversation, even though she did not speak much English. She told us that she was called Tara Devi Budha and was the book-keeper for the local road-building projects.

"Almost none of the villagers are educated and they're afraid the gods will punish them if they don't follow the rules," Tara said. "When they get ill, they go to a shaman, not the doctor. The shaman, who says he is talking on behalf of the ancestors, says things like: 'I will throw you over a cliff as punishment if you don't do as I say.'" She sighed. "The shamans also need to be educated, otherwise nothing will change. Would you like to come to my village and see for yourselves? I can show you around. And what's more, I need a lift," she added, with a mischievous smile.

"Tara is a real hero," the vendor said. "She fought with the Maoists for seven years. She was one of the leaders!"

One of the sparrows shat on his shoulder. He was clearly used to it and wiped the mess away with a paper napkin.

"I was only seventeen when I joined the Maoists," Tara said. "Technically, I was already married, even though I was still very young. My parents married me off when I was sixteen, but I moved back home again soon after the marriage. At the time, a lot of Maoist rebels came to our house to eat. Not just men, women as well. The women told me that I should do the same as them, that I should fight for women's rights. I found these encounters inspiring and I wanted to join them, but my parents wouldn't allow it. My mother locked me in to try to stop me, but it wasn't hard to undo the lock. I struggled with it for about half an hour before it slid open, and crept out into the night without waking my parents."

The Maoist rebellion in Nepal lasted for a decade, from 1996 to 2006. The rebellion swiftly developed into a civil war and cost the country close to twenty thousand lives. Hundreds of thousands of people were forced to flee.

"We fought in the jungle without food for days on end, sometimes even a week," Tara said. "We didn't have water, but it often rained all day, so we rarely suffered from thirst. The real disadvantage was that it was full of leeches. We lived in caves and sometimes slept in the trees. Once, when I was eighteen, we were chased through the jungle by the Nepalese army. It was pitch black, and we couldn't use our torches because the soldiers were right behind us. There were sheer rock faces above and below us, and nowhere to hide. Ten comrades were shot and killed in front of me. I still have nightmares about it. When the soldiers eventually left, we buried the dead in the jungle."

Tara bore arms for two years, then became the leader of a group of forty-five Maoists – women and men.

"We were fighting against the monarchy and the Nepalese army. The monarchy didn't provide equal opportunities, especially for poor people. Things are a bit better now, we can stand tall, even if we're poor. After those years as a rebel, I'm not afraid of anything, but I do still have a bad conscience when I see the slogans we used about equal rights for women and men. We never achieved that, and things seem to be going the wrong way ... There isn't equality between the sexes and Nepal is still a patriarchal society. Domestic violence is an enormous problem: women are harassed by men at the market, and the work they do in the home is not recognised."

The Maoists' aim was to get rid of the monarchy and establish a people's republic in Nepal. Two years after the peace accord was signed, the monarchy was abolished and Nepal became a republic, albeit without the prefix of "people". After a decade of short-lived coalition governments, unrest, general strikes, several states of emergency and general political chaos, a new constitution was passed in 2015. A couple of years later, in 2017 and 2018, the country held its first democratic general and local elections. The communists won a clear majority in both elections.

Recently, however, Tara had joined the largest opposition party, the Congress Party.

"I wasn't happy with the way the Communist Party treated us," she said, and folded her arms. "We fought for them, we risked our lives for them, we gave them the best years of our lives, but the party never gave us the support that we asked for afterwards. We haven't been given the respect we deserve. When I think about how much I gave, how much I invested, it makes me sick. I even betrayed my own parents. The sitting communist government is not my government."

It was half an hour's drive to Tara's village. And it turned out that she was not the only one who needed a lift; several more villagers appeared by the jeep and squeezed into the back seats. We were stopped at the edge of the village by a group of children who had built a kind of stone barrier in the middle of the road. The children were barefoot and dressed in torn shorts and T-shirts. Their skin and hair were caked with dirt. They refused to move the small mound of stones and ran off squealing and laughing when the driver brandished a fist at them.

Like so many other times on my journey, I had come to a border. It was very definitely the least official so far, but the symbolic value of it carried weight nonetheless. I sent a nod to the social anthropologist Fredrik Barth and his theory that identity is created by boundaries and encounters with "another". The children's improvised road block was a boundary to the smallest possible community: the village. The small piles of stones created a physical barrier between them and us, theirs and ours. Barth never studied in any depth the psychological mechanisms underlying this, but there is more than sufficient evidence to say that humans are territorial beings at the deepest level. Just think of all the feuds between neighbours that courts around the world have to deal with, not to mention all the meaningless wars that have been fought through the centuries. Most of them have been about borders, big ones and small ones – minuscule, even.

The driver got out and moved the stones, his irritation apparent in his movements. We crossed the now invisible line and drove into the village. Tara took us to a family who had recently built a brand-new menstruation hut. The plain mud hut was clean and tidy, and obviously in use, as there was a small suitcase in the corner. All those who had been in the jeep with us and the other villagers, around thirty to forty people, had followed us and now stood around Tara, Savitri and me, curious to know why we were there.

"A young woman died of monoxide poisoning in the neighbouring village last year. The police forced us to pull down the old hut," said Padam, the owner of the hut, a melancholy man in his forties. "We had spent a lot of time and energy building that hut. A lot of work had been put into it."

"So how did you feel when you found out that you had to pull it down?" I asked.

"We were more than happy to do it," he said.

"But now you've built a new one?"

"Yes, we built it as a wood store first and foremost, but the women can sleep here when they're menstruating, if they so wish. My daughter will sleep here tonight. I have told her that she can sleep inside, but she's afraid that she will bring us misfortune if she does. That's why she's sleeping out here."

"If the women are so worried about it, that's their problem," a man shouted down from the balcony on the first floor. "I've told the women in my house that they can sleep in their normal room when they have a period, as long as they stay away from the kitchen, and otherwise can be indoors – but they just don't listen to me. They're frightened."

"Why do they have to stay away from the kitchen?" I asked.

"Because they're bleeding. The blood is dirty, and the flies are attracted to them."

"A woman who didn't believe in *chhaupadi*, a foreign woman, like you, used the communal water pump once when she was bleeding," Padam said. "She was bitten by a snake. From then on, she started to practise *chhaupadi*. Our village god is called Mate. He's a very powerful god. Puh, we've had so many problems with Mate recently . . . you have no idea."

We found Bimala, the girl who was going to sleep in the menstruation hut that night, out in the fields.

"I sleep in the *chhaupadi* hut whenever I have a period," she said. "I'm always scared, but what can I do? I have to sleep there."

"Why do you have to sleep there?"

She looked down. "Well . . . if I don't sleep there, the god will get angry."

"And what happens then?"

"The god can break your hands and legs, or make you fall over the edge of a cliff. Things like that. My father says that I can sleep inside, but none of the other women in the village do."

"And if the other women in the village slept in the house, you would too?"

She smiled modestly.

"Yes, if everyone else stopped following the rules, I would too, for sure."

Over the course of the afternoon, Turmakhad started to fill up with shamans. They were easily recognisable with their white turbans.

A young shaman was sitting outside one of the alcohol shops, smoking. He was also called Padam, and was twenty-seven.

"The ancestor god entered my body, that's why I had to become a dami, a shaman, that is," he said, in a matter-of-fact tone.

Apart from his white turban, the young shaman looked very ordinary in jeans and a T-shirt. He had several thin gold rings in his ears.

"My grandfather was also a dami," Padam said. "I'm the fifth generation dami in my family."

"What does a dami do?" I asked.

"When the god is in my body, I start to shake," Padam said. "I'm conscious, but because the god is in me, everything feels different. I was about to do an exam in the eleventh grade the first time it happened. I suddenly started shaking and couldn't stop. Someone took me to the temple and they managed to put a white turban on me. And I stopped shaking straightaway."

A novel way of getting out of an exam, I thought. "Why do damis wear white turbans?" I asked.

"White symbolises peace, that must be why, I guess." He thought for a moment. "It's our tradition. People come to me when they are sick. I hold their wrist, around the pulse, and then I start to shake. People get ill because of a ghost or some other spirit. It's usually spirits that are the problem. When I talk to the sick person, it's not me who is talking, it's the god. I don't even always understand what the god is saying, seventy per cent of what the god says is incomprehensible to me. Seventy per cent. The god talks to the spirit or ghost that has made the patient sick. Eighty per cent of my patients get better. Eighty per cent."

"What are your views on *chhaupadi*?" I asked.

"My *personal* opinion is that menstruation is normal and natural," Padam said. "Hygiene is important, obviously, but otherwise I have no problem with menstruation. *The god* sees it differently, though."

He gave an apologetic shrug. "He thinks it's dirty. So a woman who is menstruating must be kept away from the home and temple. It's *the god* that demands that, not me."

"Do you have another job, as well as being a dami?"

"Being a dami is not a job!" He laughed. "I'm a grocer. I've got a small shop higher in the village. But I'm afraid I'm going to have to go now. I've got to get ready for the ritual tomorrow."

As the young shaman stubbed out his cigarette and started to walk up the street, a bird dropping landed on my shoulder.

*

The full moon ritual was going to take place the next day, but no-one knew exactly when. One of the shamans was convinced that it would start at eleven, another was certain that it would begin at one-thirty, and a third was sure they would start at three o'clock *at the earliest*. I was advised not to go up to the temple too early, as there would be no-one there. They would not really get going until five or possibly six, said a fourth shaman. As I had nothing else to do anyway, I followed the narrow path from the village up to the temple after breakfast.

The temple, a simple construction made with stone, earth and timber, was in a clearing in the forest. Three shamans were lying on mats outside, dressed in white tunics with the obligatory white turbans coiled tightly around their heads. All three were puffing on large pipes. A couple of men from the village were busy decorating the temple with small white shells – although we were in the foothills of the Himalayas, only a few days' walk from the Indian borders and hundreds of kilometres from the sea. At the entrance to the inner sanctuary stood a throne made from stone and wood. And inside the sanctuary, I could see some stones and small god statues, decorated with shells and flowers. The light from the candles made the gods' shadows dance; the air was heavy with incense.

One of the men carried out a plastic chair, placed it in the shade and indicated politely that I should sit down. I did as he said. Savitri had to stand beside me – they only had one chair. Then nothing more happened. The minutes and hours ticked by, and the sun rose higher and higher in the milky sky. The men continued to decorate, and the shamans continued to smoke. The oldest of the shamans, a thin, wiry man with leathered skin and a distinguished face, was called Pune and was about sixty-five, we were told. In Nepal, they use the old Hindu calendar, Bikram Sambat, which is fifty-six years, eight months and seventeen days ahead of us, and calculating according to the Gregorian calendar is still a challenge.

"When did you become a dami?" I asked Pune.

He thought about this for a good while.

"A long time ago," he said, in the end.

Slowly but surely other people from the village appeared: a man and his son, a couple of women with babies on their backs, an old man in wellington boots. All had little goat kids in tow. The kids were tied to trees and bushes and stood communicating in thin, tremulous bleats. A man in a worn, black suit jacket registered all the goats and their owners in a big, equally worn notebook; every person and every goat was diligently recorded.

The sun continued its slow journey across the sky and the shade disappeared. The man who had placed me there came over and indicated that I should stand up. He took the plastic chair and carried to it to the other side of the temple, which was now in the shade.

"You are the first foreigner to come here," he said, solemnly. "No white person has ever seen our ritual before."

Another man came over with food for Savitri and me: banana leaves filled with steaming warm sweet curry that stuck to our fingers.

"When will the ritual begin?" I asked him.

He shrugged.

"They're waiting for more goats. We need at least a hundred before we can start. The ritual is called *bisay bog*, which means one hundred and twenty sacrifices. There can be more, but there has to be at least one hundred and twenty."

It was clearly going to be a long afternoon.

A group of women in colourful cotton clothes were sitting on the ground above the temple, chatting away merrily as happy children ran around, spilling juice from plastic bottles. The kids continued their thin, vulnerable bleating. Some drummers tested out their drums a couple of times, and every time I thought, now, now something is going to happen, but then they would stop, and once again the bleating and low hum of voices was all that could be heard.

"Why are the goats so young?" I asked a young woman who was sitting beside me, nursing.

"If it were up to us, they would be older, but we have to make sacrifices so often that we don't have any older goats," she said.

In the meantime, Pune had had a canary-yellow silk cloth draped over his chest and a piece of shiny golden material tied round his turban. A couple of temple servants started to move around to give the members of the audience tilaks, spots of red and yellow powder, on their forehead. The red powder showered down from my forehead onto my clothes. Everything was red. It was now uncomfortably warm, even in the shade, and my clothes were sticking to my skin. How many goats were there now? Fifty?

Later in the afternoon, Pune finally got up and strode into the temple. He stood for a long time looking straight ahead. The drummers tapped tentatively on their drums. Then Pune started to shake. Every part of his long, thin body shook, not violently or in spasms, as I had expected, but quietly and contained. A handful of men rushed towards him and lifted the shaking shaman up onto the throne. He sat in the lotus position, his legs still shaking, and gave tilaks and words of wisdom to the men from the village, who thronged around him. The temple priest, an old man in a long, light-coloured tunic, translated what he was saying for those present.

"He's speaking god language," said the man standing beside me. "It's a mixture of Nepalese, Hindi, English and words that don't exist. Only the priest can understand what he says. You go in too!"

"No, no, there's no need," I said. None of the women were in the temple.

"Yes, yes, go and give him a tilak!" I was pushed into the temple by enthusiastic men. The queue moved to one side and I was encouraged to go right to the front, to the man speaking in tongues.

Pune leaned forward, and I dipped my finger in the red powder, as I had been instructed, and rubbed it on his forehead.

"May all your wishes come true," Pune said, with great ceremony, if I am to believe the priest who translated from god language to Nepalese, and the crowd around us nodded happily.

When all the men present had been blessed, Pune was lifted down from the throne again. He stood up straight, shaking, for a few minutes. The drummers beat out simple, intense rhythms. Slowly he lifted one leg to the side, then the other: he was dancing. Outside the temple, a young shaman prepared himself for another god to enter him. It was explained to me that all the shamans were possessed by different local gods, and the role of shaman to a particular god was passed down through the family. The young shaman had his feet half out of his trainers when he started to shake. He kicked off his shoes as his whole body shook, then started to dance. The drummers played faster and faster rhythms and the two shamans lifted their left leg out, then their right leg. Then more shamans joined them; one danced while the other just jumped up and down on the spot. The lounging villagers watched the active shamans, who now disappeared into the trees to dance around the temple.

While the shamans were gone, one of the audience, an overweight woman in her forties, started to shake violently. She looked straight into my eyes as her body was reduced to spasms. None of the women sitting around her paid the slightest bit of attention, quite the opposite, in fact, they seemed to be ignoring her, and after a few minutes, she stopped shaking and was quiet again.

The shamans appeared between the trees again, and the tiniest kid was carried out. Pune took three long strides, then threw himself over it, gripping it between his teeth, as though he were a wild animal, and ran around the temple with the goat dangling from his mouth. The bleating of the terrified kid was heart-wrenching; its eyes bulged. It was released for a short while as the shamans continued to dance with closed eyes, still shaking. Then the drums stopped. Pune was freed of his cloths and carried up to the throne in only his underwear. His turban also slipped off in the tumult; the shaman sat half-naked under the temple roof with a bare head. This was shaved, leaving a single long thick dreadlock coiled on his crown. His sweat glistened in the dim candlelight.

There was a crush at the entrance to the temple now. Men with bleating kids in their arms pushed their way forward. One of the younger shamans disappeared into the temple with a curved knife in his hands. There was already blood dripping from the blade. I climbed up onto a bench by the entrance to get a better view; the bench wobbled under me. The man with the big notebook carefully noted down each kid, then sent it into the temple.

The temple priest handed Pune a bowl of milk, which he swallowed greedily. Droplets of sweat mixed with the milk. The temple priest then brought him the first kid. Pune pounced on it and slurped and sucked the blood from the holes that had been made in the delicate kid's neck beforehand. The kid was taken back into the sanctuary, where the killing took place, and was immediately replaced by another. The sweaty shaman leaned over the petrified animal, his chin and mouth coloured red, and drank even more warm goat's blood. He stared at me all the time, as though he wanted to see my reaction. Another kid was carried out. And another. And another. The shaman drank the fresh blood of every single struggling kid, faster and faster; it was like a conveyor belt. At no point did he look away from me. More men with kids kept pressing in through the entrance, and headless carcasses were carried out of the back of the temple, the spindly hind legs still twitching. The warm, humid afternoon air was saturated with the sweet, metallic smell of blood.

The slaughter had only just started, the bloodbath would continue for hours to come, but Savitri and I decided to retreat. We wound our way through the crowd and followed the path back down to the village. A faint drumming could be heard from the temples in other villages. Who knows how many kids were beheaded that afternoon, if each family had its own god, its own temple, and all these gods, hundreds of them, demanded the blood of one hundred and twenty kids before the full moon lit up the night sky?

Terra Nullis

Once again, I was enclosed in a shaking aluminium tube thousands of metres above the ground. Turbulence made the hull shake like an old-fashioned spin dryer as the plane slowly ascended through the layers of cloud. I could not understand why we were going so high, until the Himalayas came towards us like a white wall, and in that instant it felt like we were flying too low.

I had taken a seat right at the front, and there was a bundle of seat belts on the floor in front of me. Even though Tara Air was only founded in 2009, the company has already managed to come out top several times in lists of the world's most dangerous airlines. There is no road to **Simikot**, in the north-west corner of Nepal, so 2950 MSL everything and everyone has to be transported by light aircraft. The runway at Simikot is only a little more than six hundred metres long, one of the shortest in the world, so I was already dreading the landing. If we ever got there. We were not even halfway when one of the warning lights on the dashboard started to flash. The youngest pilot called the control tower on the radio and got out a thick manual from one of the seat pockets. It seemed to be the first time he had opened it, because he was obviously flicking through it at random – in the middle, at the front, at the back – until he finally found the right page. He read the entire chapter with deep concentration, and pressed and turned some knobs. Minutes later, the wheels hit the ground, and I thanked all the gods in all the heavens that my last domestic flight in Nepal had ended safely.

A group of Swiss pensioners dressed in bright, dynamic trekking gear were quickly escorted to their waiting guides. Shivering Indian pilgrims, wrapped up well in down jackets and woollen scarves, sat waiting patiently for the helicopter that would take them to Hilsa, by the Chinese border. The flight took less than thirty minutes. At the border, buses were waiting that would take them on to Kailash, the holiest of all mountains for Hindus, Buddhists and followers of Jainism and Bon. If everything went according to plan, they would be at the foot of the mountain by evening.

I was also going to Hilsa and over the border into Tibet, but I was going to walk there. And the journey would take more than a week.

Tsering, the local guide who was supposed to meet me at the airport, was nowhere to be seen. Helicopters landed and took off again, exhausted frozen pilgrims staggered out and others clambered aboard, until, finally, I was all alone on a deserted runway, surrounded by magnificent snow-covered mountains with only some annoying flies for company.

The sun was high above the mountains when a gangly man with a black beard appeared.

"I've been told to look after you until Tsering gets here," he said.

"And when is Tsering coming?" I asked, tetchily.

"In about half an hour," was his vague answer. He took me to a dimly lit café with a hard earthen floor, sat me down at one of the empty tables, then handed me a cup of instant coffee.

An hour later, a man dressed in a high-viz orange jacket came over to me.

"Are you Tsering?" I asked.

"No, I'm from the travel agency," the man said. "I hope the coffee was to your liking."

"When is Tsering going to come?" I asked, even more annoyed.

"He's coming soon," the man in the high-viz jacket said. Then he reversed out of the door and disappeared.

Another hour later, a small man with small eyes appeared in the doorway. He grinned and threw open his arms. "Welcome to Humla!"

"You are hours late!" I snapped.

"Yes, yes, I'm sorry about that, it's a long walk from my sister's village. But now I'm here!"

"Well, you should have left yesterday then," I said.

"Yes, as I said, I'm sorry, but my sister's son had a birthday yesterday, and it was late, and there was a lot to drink . . . But anyway, let's not dwell on it, I'm here now, so welcome to Humla!"

Tsering beamed at me, and threw open his arms again. He had a yellowing front tooth, a bit of a belly, a square face and smelled like the morning after. He was a year younger than me, but looked closer to fifty. To make matters worse, Tsering thought we were going on a trek for twelve days, not eight, and he had no idea where we were going. I already missed Savitri.

"But, irrespective, I have to do the registration and sort out the documentation," he said, still smiling. "If you give me your passport, I'll sort all that out. It won't take long."

While Tsering sorted out all the papers, I wandered around the dusty, car-free streets of Simikot. A little more than ten thousand people live in Simikot, in simple flat houses made from stone, mud and unpainted timber. The village was surrounded by orchards, glossy bushes, flowers in every colour, pine forests and bountiful rye fields, which in turn were framed by blue picture-postcard mountains. When I bumped into Tsering again, he took me to the porter's home further up the street. It was a hut made from stone and mud, with only one room. The porter's young wife dabbed a spot of butter on our crowns, as is the custom here, and gave us some fresh thyme tea. In her arms she had a baby who was no more than a year, and naked from the belly button down.

"I'll just nip home and do my packing," Tsering said. "It won't take long." He pointed to his plastic sandals and chortled. "I can't go in these!"

And so I was left alone in the dark room with the smiling woman and quiet baby. Every time I finished my thyme tea, the woman poured me more, so my cup was never empty.

And then, finally, Tsering was ready to leave. Our first stop was only a few minutes away.

The villages along the Chinese border are largely dominated by Tibetan Buddhists, but in Simikot, Hindus make up the majority. The shaman lived in one of the largest houses in the village. We found him squatting on the terrace, with his wife bent over him, holding a bowl and washing his shoulder-length black hair, after a manner. He had a dreadlock on the top of his head that was so long that he could wrap it round his throat several times like a necklace.

"When the god is in me, I feel drunk and can't take in what is going on around me," the shaman said, once his wife had rinsed out the shampoo. He was called Shoudana and was seventy-one years old. He had a long, horse-like face, with deep wrinkles.

"He is the most powerful shaman in these parts," his wife said, bursting with pride.

"Life here is not easy," Shoudana said. "The road is not finished yet, and it's expensive to fly. The government doesn't do enough for those of us who live in remote areas!" In contrast, the shaman had nothing but praise for their domineering neighbour.

"I've been to China more than thirty times, at least. We used to sell buckwheat and rye to the Chinese, but now it's them who sell it to us. These days, we get everything we need from China. The Chinese are good people, they have good systems, their country is flourishing. Tibet was underdeveloped and poor before, but not anymore, oh no. If the Chinese want us, I would happily become part of China. More than happily."

Shoudana had recently introduced some positive changes in terms of *chhaupadi*: "Previously, women had to sleep outside for nine days, but a while back some people from the government came here to talk to us about it, so I reduced it to five days," he said, with great magnanimity.

The higher up in the village we went, the smaller and simpler the houses became. The Dalits, or Untouchables, lived right at the top of the village. A thin woman was standing in the doorway of an over-full shack. Half-dressed children crawled over her feet and around her. Two of them were her own. She was not yet twenty, but her face was already weathered and angular, and her teeth brown; the only thing that gave away that she was still a teenager was the shy awkwardness with which she spoke.

"I was married when I was twelve," she said. "My husband is four years older than me."

The young mother of two had never been to school. Her parents sent her out into the fields to earn money instead of to school. Neither she nor her husband owned any land; they both worked in other people's fields and got a share of the harvest as pay. There was a simple mud hut on the other side of the fence, outside the neighbour's house. It was so low that to stand up inside it was impossible.

"I don't like sleeping there," the girl said, and looked at the ground. "I'm scared of the snakes and men."

"You do know that *chhaupadi* is forbidden?" I said.

"Yes, but I'm more frightened of the shaman than of the authorities."

One of the children crept up onto her lap, managed to latch on to a breast and started to nurse.

"Do you and your husband practise family planning?" Tsering asked with interest. When he was not working as a guide, he was a social worker and helped to spread information about family planning and the importance of education.

The young woman squirmed with embarrassment, but Tsering persisted.

"Have you heard about family planning? Do you know what it is?"

"Yes, I've heard about it, and know a little, but my husband is against it," the girl said, with a sheepish laugh. "I don't want any more children, it's an enormous responsibility. It's too much."

A group of teenage girls had gathered on the other side of the street. When we passed them, they asked what we had been speaking about.

"*Chhaupadi*," Tsering said.

"Oh, *chhaupadi*!" one of the girls cried. "Even though we don't want to, we have to sleep in the menstruation hut for five days a month! Because the shaman says so!"

She turned to me.

"What do you do where you live when you have a period?"

"We don't do anything special," I said.

"Oh," the girl gave me a sceptical look. "Do you not have shamans?"

I shook my head.

"You're so lucky!"

"Have you ever tried to break the rules?" I asked.

"Yes, I slept inside once," the girl said. "And nothing happened! Nothing at all! But my family forces to me to sleep outside all the same, because of the shaman. Everyone is scared of him."

3200 MSL The majority of inhabitants in the neighbouring village, **Buraunse**, which was only half an hour's walk away, were Buddhists. The traditional single-storey houses were clustered in a labyrinth of steps and ladders that led to narrow passageways which went up and down.

We were going to spend the night with some of Tsering's close relatives, an older married trio. In a region where there is a lack of everything, fraternal polyandry was quite usual, that is to say that two or more brothers married the same woman to avoid having to divide up the farm. We were invited into the kitchen, which was in the middle of the house and without windows. One wall was decorated with dark-blue Tibetan hangings, and there was an old-fashioned television on top of a cupboard. A framed photograph of the Dalai Lama hung in one corner, and the brothers' ancient parents were lying dozing on mattresses by the far wall.

Our hostess gave us each a large bowl of chang, an alcoholic drink made from barley. I was given the milder variant, which tasted like sour beer and had a yeasty aftertaste. Tsering and the husbands were given the strong version, which tasted very much like sake. The younger of the two brothers was the more chatty.

"Our children got married the normal way, with just one spouse each," he said. "We've had our problems through the years, believe me, polyandry is not easy. But life here was hard. I used to go south, to Achham, to get rice. My brother would go north to Tibet to get hold of other necessary things. It was such a benefit that there were two of us. And as we married the same woman, we could keep the house and land – we didn't need to divide the paternal inheritance."

When we had drunk a considerable amount of chang, Tsering took me to meet the neighbours, who were also close relatives, and another married threesome. The younger of the two husbands was in his late sixties and had a white shaman turban on his head.

"I thought they were Buddhists?" I whispered to Tsering, puzzled.

"They are Buddhists, yes, but Buddhists have shamans too," Tsering said.

"As a *Buddhist* shaman I never sacrifice animals, only milk and rice," the younger husband said. His smile lines fanned out over his face. "We don't practise *chhaupadi* either, it's only the Hindus who do that."

With a smile, his wife served us a full mug of chang each. Even though she was more than seventy, she still had long smooth black hair. Before we took a drink, the younger husband blessed the bowls and threw a few drops over his shoulder, in a symbolic offering to the gods. The older husband was very serious and sat silently in a corner. He followed the conversation, dignified and erect, but did not join in. A couple of years before he had been diagnosed with cancer and had had to have a leg amputated.

"You should become a shaman too," the younger husband said to Tsering, and patted the white turban on his head. "As your father was a shaman, it is your duty to carry on the lineage."

Tsering looked embarrassed and emptied his bowl of chang. The wife immediately filled it again.

"I got married when I was fourteen," she said. "Even though I was happy to be married, I tried to run home many times to begin with. I missed my family. But my older husband found me every time and brought me back!"

"How old were you when you got married?" I asked the younger husband, out of curiosity.

"I was only eleven, but she was very beautiful!" he said, with a chuckle.

"Polyandry is the best way," the wife said. "Two husbands are far better than one. When the older brother lost his leg, the younger one could still go to China to work."

"How do you know which is father to which children?" I asked. Tsering, obviously embarrassed, translated my question.

"It's the woman who decides," the younger husband said, very matter of fact. "The women know who is father to which child. But we see them all as our children."

"Have you ever had any problems with jealousy?"

"Yes, of course!" He laughed, and drained his mug of chang. "We just had to deal with it!"

Before we left, the shaman husband put a khata, a white ceremonial scarf, round my neck in parting.

"You must promise me you will carry on the family lineage and
became a shaman like your father," he said again, as he put the white
scarf around Tsering's neck.

"Yes, yes, I promise," Tsering slurred, then stumbled out of the
kitchen, down the ladder to the barn, where a well-nourished, speck-
led brown cow was chewing the cud, and out through the door.

The next morning we set out for Tibet. We followed the new road,
which still lacked a few critical kilometres to the Chinese border,
so there was no traffic. Part way through the morning, we met two
men who were pulling an orange compressor between them. The
tractor they were using for the roadworks had very little air left in its
tyres, they explained. The compressor had just been flown in from
Nepalgunj, the nearest city to the south. The younger of the two had
a round, childish face, with big lips, and his mouth was more often
half-open than closed. He might look like a child, but he already had
two children. His oldest son had just turned five, and he himself
was nineteen.

"Was it an arranged marriage?" I asked.

"Of course," Tsering said. He did not even bother to translate the
question. "All Hindu marriages around here are arranged."

The road sloped down rather than up. The sun burned in a
pale-blue sky. In the late afternoon, we turned off the road and
descended a steep slope to a fast-running river, the Karnali. The greenish glacial water came from a source high up on the Tibetan plateau
and was running south, towards the polluted Indian lowlands.

There was **a large house** on the other side of the river. Our   2300 MSL
porter had already pitched my yellow tent at the back of the house,
but there were so many flies inside that I thought I might as well
sleep outside. But they were outside too; everywhere was thick with

the black, buzzing pests. They were on my arms and shoes, inside my clothes, in the water glasses, they crawled over your face and hands, and waving them away did not help one bit – they just came back seconds later.

A young woman was standing up a ladder slapping pats of mud on the stone wall. Another was mixing the sandy earth with water. And a third sat by a tap, washing herself in the running water, modestly hidden by a yellow, cotton cloth. There were children everywhere: crying babies, toddlers who had just learned to walk, young girls of six or seven, and teenagers.

"They have just opened a school here, but very few people send their children there," Tsering said, with a sigh.

In the evening, the woman who had been up the ladder covering the house with fresh mud earlier in the day served up dinner in the dark, smoke-filled kitchen. There was no netting in front of the door, which was open, so there were flies everywhere in here too. Sarwati was thirty and radiantly beautiful, even with the flies crawling all over her face like restless beauty spots. She had long since given up trying to get rid of them. The food was barely warm. It had clearly been standing there for some time. My stomach was rumbling with hunger. I knew that I would pay for it, that this was not a good idea – if I closed my eyes and concentrated I could see the parasites teeming over the hardened fried eggs. But the alternative was to go hungry for six more days until we got to Tibet. I waved away the flies as best I could, and ate. The whole of me rebelled: the chewy chapattis swelled in my mouth. But I resolutely washed the meal down with hot, milky tea and hoped that a fair percentage of the amoebas would be killed off by the heat. Sarwati nursed her youngest daughter.

"They already have six daughters, but keep trying for a son!" Tsering said with exasperation. Now that we were no longer with the thirsty Buddhists, he had transformed into a responsible and intensely present person. "Her daughters are delightful, why can't they be happy with them? I have two daughters myself, and I can't imagine swapping them for sons! Daughters are the greatest gift."

"I don't want any more children, but my husband wants a son, so we keep trying," Sarwati said.

Tsering tried desperately to convince her not to, but to no avail.

"Would you like one of my daughters?" Sarwati asked him as she put our greasy plates back on the shelf without washing them. "We can't look after them all."

"Children should be with their parents," Tsering said firmly. Sarwati smiled sadly and went out with the baby, who needed to be changed.

That night there was such a thunderstorm that no-one managed to sleep. The lightning lit up the tent like a flashgun; the thunder cracked and bounced between the mountains, the air smelled of burnt rubber. The rain came down like a wall of water and small rivers found their way in through the tent flap. Had there been any internet coverage, I might have googled: can lightning strike a tent?

But at some point I must have fallen asleep all the same, surrounded by puddles.

In the late morning, we met the two road workers again, this time on their way back to Simikot with the compressor. Tsering and I walked on, past more simple mud houses and small barley fields where the harvest was under way. On the other side of the Karnali River, two villages clung to the mountainside. In one, the houses were tightly clustered and the rice paddies down on the riverbank resembled an intricate jigsaw puzzle; in the other, the houses were spread out, and each family had a large plot of land that abutted squarely on the next family's.

"That illustrates the benefit of polyandry," Tsering said. "The Buddhists don't need to divide up their land between sons. The Hindus divide and share between their offspring until the plots of land are so small that no-one can live off them. It's only Buddhists now, from here to the Chinese border," he addd.

The division of land among the next generation is a universal problem in agrarian societies: if each son is to inherit an equal amount, there will eventually be nothing left for anyone. In many countries, as is the case in Norway, this has been resolved by inheritance law: the eldest son – more recently, eldest child – has first right to inherit the farm. What about all the other sons then? In the past, monasteries played an important role in Europe and in the Himalayas. At least one son became a monk. As industrialisation increased, many migrated to the towns, and in the nineteenth century, millions of Europeans crossed the Atlantic Ocean to seek their fortune in America. The demand for land eased. The solution of allowing a family's sons to marry the same woman is a novel but practical solution to what is basically an impossible problem. It has the inherent advantage that population growth is curbed, but there are many disadvantages too.

"What about all the women who don't get married?" I asked.

"They either stay at home with their parents or are sent to a convent," Tsering said. "But nowadays, polyandry is not so popular anymore. My father wanted me to marry my brother's wife, but I refused. It's better to have your own."

The landscape around us reminded me of the Alps. The mountainsides were covered with pine trees, apricot trees, walnut trees, apple trees and colourful wild flowers, and the white peaks towered above the greenery. Bathed in sunlight, it could have been a film set.

"It's like being in Switzerland," I said with delight, and took a couple of pictures.

"I wish we *were* in Switzerland," Tsering said. "Life is a chore here. In winter, we get a metre and a half of snow, and we're cut off for weeks on end. It looks lush here now, but there are not many plants that survive in our poor soil and cold climate. Potatoes, spinach, barley, buckwheat and, in a few places, rice. It's not easy to survive here."

Further on the road was closed and we had to take a long detour. Dusty, lanky labourers, all flown in from the capital, carried heavy boulders, twisted metal wire into fences and dug the soil with worn spades. Most of the work was done by hand. The roadwork had been at a standstill for nearly two years, as they did not have the dynamite needed to blast through the mountainside. What remained now was the most difficult stretch, a kilometre or two, and then at last there would be a road all the way from Simikot to Tibet.

As evening fell, we put up our tents in the garden of two brothers who were married to two sisters. Both were love marriages, they assured us, but it was undeniably practical that the two couples could continue to live together and therefore did not need to carve up the property. They had previously run a small hotel and campsite further down the hill, but a few years before, when construction on the new road started, they had lost everything.

There was a river on the mountainside above the house where the water temperature was forty degrees centigrade. The river came from an underground source and provided the entire local boarding school with hot water. I had a whole **pool** to myself; steaming water 2670 MSL poured down over my back from a small height, and I stood there for half an hour, an hour, as long as I could before it got too dark. The pressure was perfect. Kilos of sweat, dust and flyshit were washed away by the warm water and disappeared down the mountainside.

It was the best shower of my life.

Despite the fact that the road now ran from here all the way to China, most people still travelled on foot, like us. Over the next four days, we saw two trucks and one jeep – that was all. The road was wide and had a gentle incline; the sun was shining and there was not a cloud in the sky. We reached **Yalbang** at midday. A considerable 3020 MSL proportion of the male population sat squeezed together in the tiny village shop, which had a television that showed football and free fighting. The home-made shelves behind the counter were packed with Chinese goods: sweets, potato crisps, noodles, Lhasa beer. Boy monks kept coming to the door with crumpled fifty-rupee notes that they exchanged for sweets, then ran off smiling.

Namkha Khyugn Dzong Monastery is the largest in the Humla district, home to more than three hundred monks. There were clothes hanging out to dry everywhere inside the monastery, which also housed an industrial-sized kitchen, communal toilets and a laundry. And two volleyball courts. It was Saturday, and the monks' day off; those who had finished their laundry wandered around in civilian clothes, accompanied by pop music playing on their mobile phones.

"They have a new school here," Tsering said. "Come, I'll show you." He strode past the volleyball courts, then stopped all of a sudden. "His Holiness, the founder of the monastery, is here! We mustn't disturb him, so it's perhaps better if we come back again tomorrow."

A grey-haired, balding man with a round face was standing watching the volleyball in the playground. Dressed in monk's robes and a purple sweater, he was holding his prayer beads in one hand.

"Goodness, that's good timing! Let's go and talk to him," I said.

Tsering looked at me, horrified. "No, no, no, we can't just walk over to him, we have to make an appointment first!"

I started to walk towards the lama. Tsering ran after me.

"We certainly can't go and speak to him without giving him a white scarf, and I have none left," he said, in desperation.

But it was fine, even without the scarf. The lama spoke broken English and answered all my questions, and though he sometimes stumbled a bit, he was warm and friendly. He was called Pema Rigtsal Rinpoche, and, if I understood him correctly, his grandfather had in his time established a monastery with the same name in the west of Tibet. The monastery was built in honour of Dudjom Lingpa, a wandering monk who had lived in Tibet more than a hundred years ago. It is said that he achieved Nirvana but then chose to come back to earth in order to share his wisdom. The monastery was destroyed during the Chinese invasion in 1959, and his grandfather had been forced to flee to India. A quarter of a century later, in 1985, he, the grandson, had established this monastery on the Nepalese side of the border.

"The people here in Humla have strong faith," the lama said. "I am not worried about the next hundred years, but what happens after that, I don't know."

Before we left, he invited us to come back for morning prayers at dawn the next day.

"That went very well." Tsering beamed as we walked back down to the village. "And I got a blessing, even though I couldn't offer a silk scarf."

We took a seat in the shop and sat watching the free fighting, tennis and football for the rest of the evening. I wondered when I had last felt so relaxed. I was not going anywhere, there was nothing I needed to do, nowhere I needed to be, and because nothing happened here, there was no rush. You can just hum in Humla, I thought, and smiled happily at my own joke.

Early the next morning, we went back up to the monastery. The older monks were bent over thick Tibetan books. And Pema Rinpoche sat on the throne at the back of the room, trying to keep his eyes open. Every now and then he smothered a yawn.

"They are obviously celebrating something very special," Tsering said. He stopped a young monk and asked what the occasion was for the ceremony. The monk just shrugged and hurried on. Tsering did not give up and grabbed another older monk on his way out of the temple room.

"It's the anniversary of the day that Degyal Rinpoche, the monk who established the original monastery in Tibet, achieved Nirvana," the monk said. He then explained that Degyal Rinpoche II, the father of Pema Rinpoche who founded the monastery here in Humla, was the reincarnation of the original Degyal Rinpoche. "The third reincarnation, Degyal Rinpoche III, lives in Kathmandu and is about thirty years old," the monk continued. "He is the son of Pema Rinpoche's brother."

"Ah, that makes it a lot clearer!" Tsering said. "I had no idea, but now I understand how it all fits together."

I was just as confused as before, but I have always had a tendency to get lost when it comes to intricate family relationships. And when reincarnations are introduced to the equation, I simply don't stand a chance.

The courtyard was suddenly full of busy little boys in monks' robes. They hurried down the hill towards the new school building with heavy bags over their shoulders and notebooks clutched to their chests. From inside the temple came the sound of drums and horns and monks chanting.

We continued our trek towards Tibet, but now followed the old trail along the Karnali River. The path was narrow and the slopes were steep; one wrong foot and you risked ending up in the river, far below. But none of us took a wrong step and we arrived safely 3120 MSL at **Muchu**, a picturesque little village of small houses, surrounded by orchards. A tall thin man in a newly ironed uniform was standing outside the largest building in the village.

"Stop!" he ordered. "All foreigners must be registered."

He leafed through a worn notebook and pointed to an empty line. I was the first foreigner of the day, but four Swiss citizens had passed through the day before, and a group of five Dutch people the day before. The policeman's assistant, who was also tall and thin and dressed in a well-pressed uniform, walked restlessly back and forth in front of the police station.

"Is there much criminality here?" I asked. A couple of days earlier I had encountered a guide who was crying: someone had gone into his tent and stolen all the expedition money, which amounted to the equivalent of a year's pay.

The policeman smiled. "No problem!"

"Not even smuggling goods from China?"

"No problem! Don't worry!" The policeman snapped his note-book shut and waved us on.

It was already late in the day and my stomach was rumbling, but none of the cafés along the route were open.

"*No problem, don't worry*," Tsering said, with a smile, then went and knocked on a door. A man in his forties came out, and he and his wife agreed to make food for us for a modest sum. The man was often in China, he said, as it was easier to get work there. Sometimes his work was agricultural, other times in construction. He also bought rugs and blankets that he then sold in Humla, in the even more remote villages.

"Life is easier in China," he said. "Here it's so hard. So very hard. Everything is difficult and we have no money. But we have our free-dom," he said, looking me in the eye, "and they don't have that in China."

I was struck by this straightforward, crystal-clear statement. It could have been taken from Henrik Wergeland's story about Hans Jakobsen's cheese. The labourer Hans Jakobsen was sitting by the roadside eating his plain, brown bread with gusto, when Wergeland walked past. The poet remarked that it was a meagre meal. "Oh," the labourer replied, calmly, "I have some of the finest cheese on my bread." Wergeland could not see any cheese, but the labourer nodded towards some chained convicts who were nearby. "I have the finest cheese on my bread. I have freedom."

Hans Jakobsen's cheese is always and everywhere the best and most precious.

*

3700 MSL   **Yari**, the last village before the border, was no more than fifteen or sixteen basic buildings along the road. Tibet was now no further than three hours' steady walk away, while Simikot was days behind us and Kathmandu so distant that it might as well have been on a different continent. Everyone in Yari made a living from seasonal work in China, and the men were often absent for months at a time. The landscape was no longer green and fertile but brown and dry, and the fruit trees had been replaced by low bushes. We had left the Swiss Alps and were now on the Tibetan plateau, in the Himalayas' rain shadow.

An old woman made spinach dumplings for us in a small, windowless kitchen. Her jet-black hair was gathered in two long plaits extended with green and purple threads and knotted together at the base of her spine. Even the hairstyles were Tibetan here.

By the time the food was ready, the small dining room was full of guides and porters from all over Nepal who were making their way to the border to meet the Indian pilgrims arriving by helicopter. I climbed up the ladder and slipped into my yellow tent, which had been pitched on the roof of one of the empty houses, for want of a better place. The sound of drunken voices and laughter drifted out into the night. When the voices eventually fell silent, the dogs took over.

I was far, far from home, about to enter the strange no-man's-land between two national states, already part of the way into Tibet. The Nepalese mobile phone signal had been lost a while ago, and I was in an electronic terra nullis, alone in a yellow tent on a flat roof under the endless starry sky.

4530 MSL   The **Nara La Pass** lay between us and the Chinese border – a thousand metres up and then down. I gasped for air, but Tsering was on good form and hummed happily to himself. He no doubt relished the thought that he would soon be able to go back home to his daughters, who he missed more and more with every hour.

"How many days will it take on the way back?" I asked.

"Half an hour." He chuckled. "I'm going by helicopter."

There was a constant thrum of helicopters as they passed overhead. At the top of the pass, they were so close they almost grazed our heads. There was still some old snow from the winter on the north side of the pass, and we slid down the slope. Jagged mountains snaked into Tibet and towards Kailash, the last of the Himalayas.

The gravel road that led down to Hilsa was blocked by some major rockfalls. A jeep stood abandoned in the middle of a bend – the driver and passengers had clearly given up and carried on by foot. On the other side of the river, an asphalt road undulated like a shiny, futuristic eel.

Hilsa was a hole. Border towns are rarely charming, but Hilsa 3640 MSL was in a class of its own. The settlement down by the river was surrounded by bare, brown mountains. The low houses, whether they were made from stone and mud, or concrete, all looked as though they had a storey missing. New concrete hotels were mushrooming to cater for the hordes of helicopter pilgrims on their way to the holy Mount Kailash.

Worn-out Indians stumbled around the dusty streets, wrapped in big down jackets, balaclavas, scarves and gloves. It seemed that the down jackets were part of the pilgrim package, as they all wore the same yellow and blue ones. They looked like enormous sweets. Helicopters took off and landed, took off and landed, and out tumbled yet more yellow-and-blue Indians.

The men who hung around outside the bars were dressed in thin clothes and had chiselled faces. They were waiting for the border to open for the Nepalese. Many of them had been waiting for weeks. A Tibetan woman had recently been killed by a couple of Nepalese men on the Chinese side of the border, and somewhere between two and three thousand workers from Humla had immediately been sent back to their homeland. No-one knew when the border would open again for the Nepalese guest workers. There were rumours that it might be the next day, but no-one knew for sure.

I crossed my fingers that the Chinese border guards would at least let a Norwegian private tutor through.

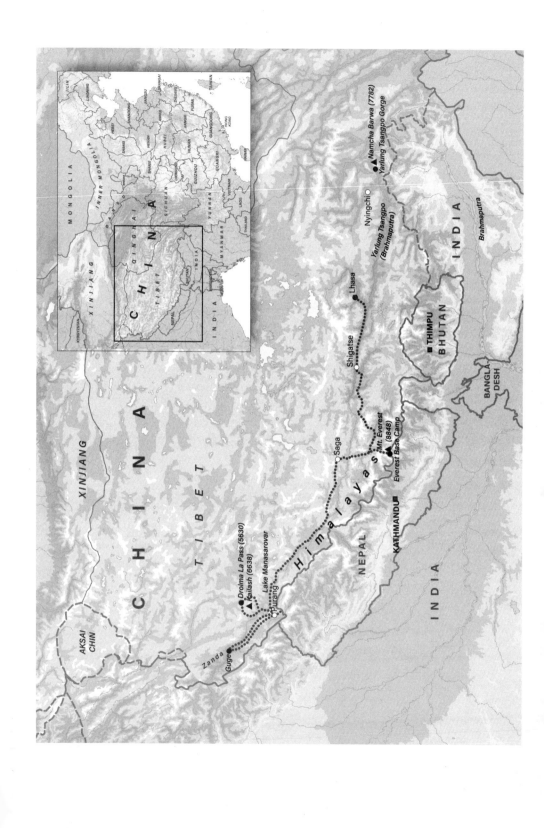

The Lost Congregation

Crossing a border is a rite of passage for the traveller; one leaves a reality that one is perhaps just starting to understand, only to be thrown into the unknown. On the way from one border checkpoint to the next, with an exit stamp but no entry stamp, one is in limbo – what social anthropologists call the liminal phase, the vulnerable stage where one has not yet fully completed the transition, is not yet initiated, and therefore where anything can happen. In some societies, a liminal person is seen as dangerous, sometimes as holy. Those who cross borders are also regarded as suspicious, but never holy: who are you, what is your intention here, and what have you got in your suitcase?

For many years, almost no Norwegians were allowed into Tibet. After the Norwegian Nobel Committee awarded the Nobel Peace Prize to the imprisoned dissident Liu Xiaobo, Norway was famously thrown into the freezer by China. Any political contact between Norway and China was scaled back to the minimum, Norwegian businesses struggled to export their products and Norwegians were denied travel visas to Tibet. After a six-year diplomatic freeze, in 2016 Norway and China signed an agreement to normalise relations. In it the Norwegian government pledged to "attach high importance to China's core interests and major concerns, [and] not to support actions that will undermine them".[10] Since the agreement was signed, China has rapidly become one of the biggest importers of Norwegian farmed salmon, Chinese tourists have poured into Norway and Norwegians have once again been allowed into Tibet. Nearly two years after bilateral relations were normalised, there was news that Liu Xiaobo was dying. When the EU high representative for foreign affairs called for the Chinese government to release the Nobel Prize winner, the Norwegian prime minster, Erna Solberg, refused to comment on the case. Liu died on July 13, 2017, thus going down in history as the second peace laureate to die in custody without having been given permission to travel to Oslo to receive the prize. His crime? He was a co-author of *Charter 08*, a political manifesto that called for fundamental democratic reforms in China.

Journalists are still not allowed into Tibet. On my visa application I had therefore written that I was a tutor, as is my wont.

Before I could be given an entry stamp, I had to be given an exit stamp. Nepal Immigration had its offices in a large stone house with a red roof. Unauthorised persons were not allowed into the building, but were shown to a narrow alley where it was possible to communicate with the bureaucrats during opening hours, through a small window high up on the wall. An ill-tempered woman in her forties studied my papers.

"You need to pay a fine," she said. "Your trekking permit expired yesterday."

"But today's date is on the tourist visa," I said.

The woman was adamant. I had to pay up, but managed to haggle the fine down from fourteen dollars to seven. When I had paid my dues, the woman carefully put all the papers in plastic files; there was no evidence of any computer. Then she ceremoniously got out the stamp, but did not use enough ink, so the print was not satisfactory. She pressed the stamp hard onto a sheet of white paper, once, twice, three times, and each time the print was lighter.

"Come back in half an hour," she snapped.

Three-quarters of an hour later I was given back my passport with an exemplary stamp, all the lines clear, and I walked over the bridge into China.

On the other side of the river, my Tibetan guide and driver were standing waiting by a grey minibus. All foreigners who visit Tibet have to be escorted by authorised guides. Jinpa, my guide, was forty, tall and thin with a narrow face and pronounced smile lines. The driver, Palden, was ten years younger, dressed in a leather jacket and jeans, with generous amounts of gel in his hair.

The Chinese border checkpoint was like a fort: grey, empty and hi-tech. I was the only foreigner there and was given full attention. Two border guards started to look through my luggage with impressive efficiency and soon found the books I had with me. One of the guards had a translation app ready and scanned the titles: *Yeti: Legende und Wirklichkeit* by the Italian Himalayas veteran Reinhold Messner didn't raise suspicion or cause any problems, even though the book basically describes a crime. Messner sneaks into Tibet and wanders around alone for weeks. But for some unknown reason, the trilogy by the Icelandic author Jón Kalman Stefánsson provoked a great deal of scepticism and discussion between the two guards before I was eventually given the thick volume back. To my surprise, they did not ask to see my phone, and I had spent hours deleting all the photographs that might have given away that I was not a tutor. Instead, I was waved on to the automated border control system, which patiently and mechanically guided me through fingerprints and photographs. And hey presto! All the formalities were done, and I was no longer in limbo, but stamped in once again to the People's Republic of China.

4755 MSL   Fifteen minutes later, we arrived in **Purang**, the nearest town. Purang has been an important trading post since the seventh century, but any evidence of its former glory had been erased; everything was brand new, modern and characterless. The town was so new that the roads were not even finished, but bumpy and dusty, with the constant threat of traffic jams. The pavements were crowded with frozen Indians in yellow-and-blue pilgrim puffer jackets, Nepalese construction workers, Chinese police and the odd Tibetan. The sudden modernness was overwhelming.

"There is, quite literally, nothing to see here," Jinpa said.

"What about the old monastery up there?" I pointed to a red and white building that almost merged with the mountainside. It was just possible to see the remains of an old fort behind the monastery.

"Forget it," Jinpa said. "We can't go there."

"But there's a road all the way up," I said.

"The monastery is not on our itinerary."

"But we can still go there, can't we?"

"Not without a special permit, and as the monastery is not on the itinerary, there's no point in even trying."

Later that evening, I logged on to the hotel Wi-Fi via a foreign server to avoid the Chinese internet blocks and googled the monastery. It was called Simbiling and had been one of the most important monasteries in the region, with several hundred monks. The fort, Tegla Kar, dated from the twelfth century, when Purang was the capital of the Guge kingdom. Both the fort and the monastery had been destroyed by bombs during the Cultural Revolution. The monastery had been partially rebuilt at the turn of the century and now was home to a handful of monks.

The rest of the day was taken up with formalities.

"First we have to go to the police and get all the required stamps." Jinpa brandished a thick pile of papers. "And the same will happen in every place we go. The first thing we have to do is go to the police station and get all the necessary stamps."

When the required stamps were duly in place, perfect and clear, we then had to go to customs, which for some reason was in the centre of town, several kilometres from the border checkpoint. The customs house was impressively large and strikingly empty. Jinpa made a quick telephone call and five minutes later, two officers sauntered in. One of them took my suitcase and rucksack out of the building and disinfected both with spray from a large tank that he had on his back. He then put on some rubber gloves, opened the suitcase and immediately found the books. He leafed through them, shook them and checked all the photographs thoroughly. It was almost touching to see how seriously the Chinese authorities took literature. No-one here bothered to check my phone or laptop either; books were clearly far more important.

When the books had been closely checked, the customs officers put them carefully back in my suitcase and closed the zip. Green light. I was the camel that had passed through the eye of a needle.

Although Purang looked impressive, at least in comparison with the impoverished villages on the Nepalese side of the border, it soon became apparent that it was a rather boring provincial town. Jinpa had been right – there was nothing to see here, and nothing to do. Young men played billiards under blue awnings on the pavement. The older generation sat in the tea houses, where they gambled their money as they passed the time drinking cheap spirits. The flies from Humla were still making their presence felt, and I had to spend the evening in close proximity to a toilet, which, given the circumstances, struck me as one of the greatest inventions of modern civilisation.

When the continental plates collided millions of years ago, the land mass that is now Tibet was slowly pushed several kilometres up in the air. The average elevation of the Tibetan plateau is now four and a half thousand metres.

The road was narrow and mercifully straight, without bumps and oncoming traffic. The Himalayas rose up like a pointy white fence to the south that kept the monsoon at bay. On the south side of the mountains, everything was green and full of flowers; here to the north, the landscape was brown and barren. The climate in this part of Tibet is also one of the driest in Asia, and in winter temperatures can drop well below freezing. Our surroundings were now so open that it felt a bit like being in the middle of the ocean, with frozen, ragged waves all around. The canyons had very clear gullies and distinct colour contrasts that looked almost artificial. The snow caps towering over the river valleys were strikingly reminiscent of pagodas. These formations – brown, yellow, rusty red, bronze, silver and gold – twisted and curled in all directions and were seemingly endless.

From time to time, we passed neat rows of single-storey, uniform houses – the central government's unceasing attempt to organise, control and regulate. Red Chinese flags fluttered from the roofs. The houses had been built for the nomads, so they could have a fixed abode for at least some parts of the year. Nomads originally accounted for around a third of Tibet's population, but the lifestyle is now under serious threat. Tens of thousands of nomads have been driven from their traditional grazing grounds and forced to settle in government-built villages. The Chinese authorities have used ecology and the protection of the environment as arguments, but often the real reason is that they want the grazing grounds for mining.

In the afternoon, we drove into a village where the streets were flanked with white, prefabricated houses with glass facades.

"The last time I was in **Zanda** there were only a few houses 3660 MSL here," Jinpa muttered. "The place is unrecognisable."

Even though there were a lot of buildings, the shops and cafés looked like shacks. In the long, dark cafés, there were four or five tables pushed up against the wall. Men in leather jackets, migrant construction workers, slurped up their noodles as they stared intently at their mobile phones.

Behind the concrete buildings, the greyish-brown mountains rose up. A small path twisted up from the rather basic hotel where we were staying to a network of man-made caves.

"Can we go up and look at them?" I asked.

"No." Jinpa shook his head. "We don't have permission."

"Do we really need written permission to go for a short walk from the hotel?"

"We need permission for everything," Jinpa said with a sigh.

So we did not go to see the caves, but fortunately we did have permission to visit the ruins at Tsaparang, the last capital of the once extensive Guge kingdom, which existed for more than six hundred years and once housed Tibet's first church.

Tibet was one of the largest and most powerful kingdoms in Asia up until the tenth century, stretching far beyond its current borders. The cultural and linguistic influence of Tibet is also widespread. Around half of all Tibetans in China live outside the Tibet Autonomous Region, which is abbreviated to TAR and includes only Ü-Tsang from the three regions that made up the original Tibet. Large parts of the two other regions, Kham and Amdo, are now part of the Chinese provinces of Gansu, Sichuan, Qinghai and Yunnan. The cultural influence of Tibet covers a far greater area than the political map might suggest, and tens of thousands of Tibetans now also live south of the Chinese borders in the mountain regions of Nepal and India.

The Tibetan empire was at its greatest at the end of the eighth century, when the Tibetan king ruled over areas far into what are now Afghanistan, Uzbekistan and Kazakhstan, thus controlling the trade routes along the Silk Road. The Tibetan kings were a threat to the Chinese Tang dynasty's weak western border.

The Tibetans themselves see Nyatri Tsenpo (Tsenpo meaning "sky king" or "god king"), who came down to earth on a cord from heaven in 127 BCE, as their first king. When the god king died, he went back up to heaven, and his eldest son, who was also a god king, took his place. The system worked perfectly until the eighth god king taunted his stable boy, who got so angry that he cut the cord that led back up to heaven. The eighth and last Tsenpo was therefore buried on earth in southern Tibet, and mortal kings took his place.

Buddhism reached Tibet in the seventh century, more than a thousand years after the Buddha, Siddhartha Gautama, had died of old age in north India. Believers of the new faith came into conflict with the followers of Bon, the old faith system based on spirits, demons and local gods. However, Bon is still practised to this day, and Buddhism and Bon have existed side by side for so long that Bon has borrowed from Buddhism and Buddhism has borrowed from Bon, making it difficult to know for certain how Bon was practised before Buddhism was introduced. A further complication is that more or less all official records of Tibetan history were written by Buddhist monks. The Tibetans' own name for Tibet is Bod, which may be a remnant from the time when Bon was the dominant faith. It is also the root of the name Bhutan.

The first Buddhist monasteries were built at the end of the eighth century during the rule of King Trisong Detsen, when the Tibetan empire was at its greatest, in terms of both size and power. Trisong Detsen established Buddhism as the state religion and invited teachers and masters from India to propagate the religion. Padmasambhava, the tantric master who has left his mark throughout the Himalayas, was one of those invited. Padmasambhava was given the task of dealing with the powerful and unruly Tibetan gods and spirits so that Buddhism could flourish. According to legend, Padmasambhava succeeded in taming the bothersome spirits, but in doing so made so many enemies at the court that he was then asked to leave Tibet.

The enormous Tibetan empire started to crumble in the ninth century and Buddhism's privileged position as the state religion also started to falter. Langdarma, the last king of the great empire, was a follower of Bon, the old faith, and persecuted Buddhists throughout the empire. Langdarma was killed by a hermit monk in the mid-800s. In modern times the monk is regarded throughout Tibet as a hero, and the cave where he meditated is a popular pilgrimage site.

Following the death of Langdarma, there was a dispute about the order of succession. The oldest queen had not yet produced an heir, whereas the youngest queen had. The family of the oldest queen found a baby for her that she then claimed was her own, and there was an intense fight over which of the two babies should be the next king. This coincided with poor harvests throughout the empire, and old conflicts flared up between the clans again. Years of civil war and power struggles ensued, the once powerful empire collapsed, and the previously expansionist Tibetans withdrew into elevated isolation on the mountain plateau.

At the end of the ninth century, Nyima Gön, one of Langdarma's grandchildren, established a new kingdom in the west. When Nyima Gön died, the kingdom was divided between his three sons. One became the ruler of Ladakh, the second of Zanskar – both of which are now part of India – and the third son became ruler of Guge in north-west Tibet. It is not known which faith Nyima Gön and his sons held, but Yeshe-Ö, the grandchild who eventually inherited the throne in Guge, was a devout Buddhist and was one of the most important driving forces behind the spread of Buddhism in Tibet. Yeshe-Ö sent a number of scholars over the mountains to India, so they could bring back the Buddhist teachings and wisdom. Only two survived the strenuous journey, one of whom was Lochen Rinchen Zangpo, the great Tibetan translator. He translated an enormous number of Buddhist texts from Sanskrit to Tibetan, and his translations are the main reason that Tibetan remains the dominant language in Buddhist monasteries throughout the Himalayas. However, Buddhism was spread not only through the teachings and translations, but also with brute force: Yeshe-Ö banned the practice of Bon and ordered that the Bon teachings should be destroyed. Followers were also persecuted and killed.

Although the Guge kingdom lasted for more than six hundred years, no-one in Europe had heard of it when two Portuguese Jesuit priests crossed the Himalayas from India and more or less by accident ended up in the unknown kingdom, where they were given a warm welcome. The elder of the two Jesuits was the 44-year-old Father António de Andrade, who was already a seasoned missionary. Andrade was accompanied by his younger compatriot, Manuel Marques, a couple of Christian Indian servants and a handful of local porters.

Andrade had first tried to cross the much-feared Mana Pass without Marques, and in one of the two letters from the expedition that have been preserved, he describes how he struggled to breathe. Those with local knowledge believed that the air in the mountains was poisonous, and could tell stories about people who had been in robust health, then suddenly became ill and died within fifteen minutes. But it was not only the mountain air that caused problems for Andrade: it was still early in the year and the snow was thick on the ground; they were caught up in a terrible storm and were forced to turn back.

A month later, when the snow had melted and the weather had improved, Andrade made a second attempt to cross the pass, this time with Marques. The two Jesuits finally managed to cross the 5,632-metre pass to become the first Europeans we know of to have crossed the Himalayas. The Jesuits were in fact searching for the Christian congregation of Prester John. For centuries, stories had circulated about a mighty Christian ruler in the Far East. Many expeditions had been sent out to find his lost congregation, but none had succeeded.

Andrade must have quickly understood that the devout Buddhists he met on the other side of the mountains were not this lost Christian congregation. The Portuguese missionaries were well received by the king and queen of Guge. The royal couple were impressed by the deep faith of the two foreigners, which was not so dissimilar to their own. Andrade, for his part, was touched by the friendliness and hospitality of the Tibetans, but was less taken by the lamas' custom of drinking from skulls. The king appointed Andrade as "chief lama" and gave the foreigners permission to come back the following year to build a church in the capital of Tsaparang. The Portuguese priests did not have to be asked twice and the next summer they once against crossed the challenging Mana Pass, with four other Jesuit brothers, and started to build a mission. The sovereign himself laid the foundation stone of the very first church in Tibet on Easter Sunday, 1626.

When Andrade left Guge some years later, he believed that the church he had built would flourish, despite the fact that he and his missionary brothers had so far not managed to muster more than a few hundred converts in the large kingdom. In 1634, shortly after his return to Goa, Father Andrade died. He was investigating a report of heresy and it is said that he was poisoned by the son of the accused, but this has never been proved.

The fate of his colleague Marques was not much better – rather the opposite, in fact. A few months after Andrade had returned to India, a group of lamas in Tsaparang rose up against the tolerant king and foreign missionaries with the support of Muslim warriors from the neighbouring kingdom of Ladakh. The king was deposed, the town plundered, and the five Jesuit missionaries who were still in Guge, including Marques, were imprisoned and then escorted to the border and thrown out of the kingdom. But Marques was not deterred, and a few years later, in the summer of 1640, he organised a new expedition over the Mana Pass. The aim of the expedition was to reopen the mission in Guge, but before they got there, the party was attacked and Marques was arrested. A year later, the Jesuit headquarters in Agra received a letter from the unfortunate missionary in which he wrote that he had been tortured by the Tibetans and had given up all hope of being rescued. Nothing more was heard from him.

The kingdom of Guge was ruled by Ladakh for a short period,

then, at the end of the seventeenth century, it was conquered by Lhasa under the leadership of the powerful 5th Dalai Lama. Tsaparang, the capital of the once great kingdom, was by then already in ruins and has not been inhabited since.

*

The old capital sits on a porous, pyramid-shaped rock and it is almost impossible to differentiate between the rock and the buildings. At the bottom are the caves and houses where ordinary people lived. Above the caves, but well below the royal palace, are two Buddhist temples, one white and one red, with walls decorated with paintings of hundreds of meditating Buddhas. The paintings are surprisingly well preserved, but all the statues have been destroyed, completely and systematically; only the occasional wooden stand, the skeleton one might say, is still intact. One head is all that was left for posterity, and it sits symbolically above a pile of clay fragments.

The statues survived the sacking of the Muslim mercenaries from Ladakh and the subsequent invasion by Lhasa, but did not stand a chance against the Red Guards, the liberators of the people, in the 1960s.

A labyrinth of underground corridors and ladders leads up to the royal residence at the top, where only the thick walls of the summer palace have survived. From the summer palace, there is a view over the dried-out riverbeds and canyons. The dry, inhos-pitable, brown landscape is so monumental that even the sky is coloured by it.

There is no trace left of the church that was built here with such care by the Jesuit brothers, other than in the history books.

The Middle of the World

A completely different landscape. The lake lay like a pale-blue mirror in front of me, the surrounding mountains reflected in the surface of the water. There was no wind, the sun was starting to warm up. Two women in red saris squatted on the shore, filling plastic bottles with holy water; I later found out that they had scrimped and saved for several years in order to come here. A thin old man sat in the lotus position down by the water in only his underpants. On the beach, a few metres from the water's edge, a long queue of pilgrims – women in colourful clothes and men in white underwear – stood waiting to have buckets of ice-cold water poured over them, quickly and without mercy. *Om Shiva om! Hail, Shiva!* the crowd cried in ecstasy, as the buckets were emptied over the pilgrims, one by one. Previously, pilgrims could submerge themselves in the lake, but a bathing ban had recently been introduced. The buckets seemed to be serving their purpose.

4590 MSL   For Hindus, the water from **Lake Manasarovar** is so holy that it has the power to cleanse you of all your sins, not only those from this life, but the sins accumulated from up to a hundred past lives. *Manas* comes from the Sanskrit and means "thought" or "mind", while *sarovara* means "lake". According to Hindu teachings, the lake first came into existence in Brahma the Creator's mind; in other words, the Manasarovar and Brahma's soul are one and the same. The lake is also holy for Buddhists and followers of Jainism and Bon. Siddhartha Gautama, the Buddha, was conceived here, according to legend, even though Lumbini, the place where he was born, is hundreds of kilometres further south, on the other side of the

Himalayas. He is also supposed to have meditated by the lake on several occasions, as did Padmasambhava, the tantric master from Swat Valley, who managed to meditate all over the Himalayas while he was alive. In the small monastery that sits on the cliff just above the lake, one can see the proof: an enormous footprint, like that of a yeti, preserved for eternity in a claustrophobic cave. Little is known about Padmasambhava's appearance, but he must have had remarkably big feet.

Stooped Tibetan women dressed in long woollen dresses walked along the shore as they chanted the six-syllable mantra, *Om mani padme hum*, over and over, a hundred times, a thousand times, a hundred thousand times. The holy lake has a perimeter of close to ninety kilometres and it would take them several days to walk all the way round.

On the far side of the beach, a slightly leaning, pyramid-shaped peak covered with shining white fresh snow rose up from the lower mountains around it: Kailash, also known as Meru to the Buddhists, is the home of Shiva to the Hindus. In Tibetan the mountain is called Kang Rinpoche, the Precious Snow Mountain, the soul of Tibet, the middle of the world.

There are four holy, life-sustaining rivers that have their sources in the vicinity of the holy mountain: the Indus, the Brahmaputra, the Sutlej and the Karnali, all of which merge with the Ganges down on the Indian plains. It is therefore not surprising that Kailash has been worshipped for as long as there have been people living on the Tibetan plateau, long before the major religions were established, long before the Aryan people migrated from the west.

*

It was early in the morning and the **mountain plain** was already 4750 MSL teeming with joyful Tibetans. Delicate snowflakes pirouetted in the thin air. In the middle of the plain, a long pole, wrapped in yak hide and colourful prayer flags, lay propped at a gentle angle to the ground on a structure of staves. Several thousand people had gathered, many having travelled for days, crossing the mountain range to reach this holiest of holy mountains, in the middle of this holy month, Saga Dawa.

Slowly the pole rose up to the sky, helped by the pole setters and two trucks. When, a few minutes later, the pole had been raised upright, the pilgrims exploded into ecstatic cries: *Ki-ki-so-so!* Paper prayer flags were thrown up into the air with the toasted barley flour known as tsampa. The atmosphere was electric.

I stopped to take one last picture before I went back to Jinpa, who was waiting up at the temple, and managed to capture the flagpole in free fall, for ever.

There was complete silence. The snowflakes seemed to hang suspended in the air; even the police officers stopped their patrolling and stood facing the fallen pole with empty faces. No-one called *Ki-ki-so-so*, no one threw tsampa or prayer flags into the air. Some were weeping. Others stared, paralysed by shock.

I found Jinpa, who had fallen to his knees.

"Come," he said, his eyes wet. "We have to start walking. We have a long way to go."

The long pole lay on the ground, possibly broken, possibly whole; whatever the case, it would take hours before it could be raised again.

And we had a long way to go.

No person has ever climbed Mount Kailash. Not because it is particularly technically challenging or high – it reaches 6,638 metres above sea level – but because it would be sacrilege to disturb the gods who live there. Instead, the pilgrims go *round* the mountain, covering a distance of fifty-four kilometres in total.

The first section of the *kora*, or perambulation, was on a relatively flat, gravel road. Jinpa and I were not alone, by a long way, there were hordes of people both in front of us and behind us. Thousands of pilgrims had started to walk, young women and men in jeans and windproof jackets, grey-haired women in traditional dresses, bearded men in long, thick coats, little children in snowsuits, all with prayer beads in their hands and grave faces. Never before had the flagpole fallen down.

A jeep full of Indians pushed past us through the crowd.

"If you don't walk on your own two feet, you don't get any benefits," Jinpa said. "We Tibetans do it for the next life, we do it so we won't end up in hell."

"I didn't think there was a hell in Buddhism," I said.

"Oh yes," Jinpa said, with a tut. "We don't have just one, we have many hells! We have one where it's hot, one where it's cold, eighteen different levels in all. Everyone is terrified of ending up there."

"I seem to remember reading that, according to the Buddha, hell is more like a state of mind," I said.

"Do you mean to say there really isn't a hell?" Jinpa looked at me, thunderstruck. "Then what's the point in walking all the way round Mount Kailash?"

We reached **Drirapuk**, the world's highest monastery, in the 5210 MSL afternoon. Dizzy and short of breath because of the altitude, I climbed up the steps and entered the red temple, which, to my disappointment, was newly renovated. The Red Guards had even come here, driven by a fanatical need to destroy, a revolutionary zeal and orders from above. They must have marched for a whole day, at least, armed with axes in order to vandalise the monastery.

Tibet had more than six thousand temples and monasteries, and only thirteen were left in 1976, once the crazed destruction had ended.

Some basic hostels had been built below the temple, but there were only a few beds, and countless pilgrims. Many of them had no choice other than to carry on over the capricious Drolma La Pass, even though it was getting dark.

As soon as the sun went down, it was bitterly cold and the wind blew up. I snuggled down into my sleeping bag, took some pain-killers for my headache, which had got worse through the day, and fell asleep.

It was still dark when Jinpa woke me. He had managed to conjure up a bag of longlife buns, which he handed to me proudly. He ate some tsampa mixed with butter that he had brought with him. I tried a mouthful. It was dry and tasted of absolutely nothing, but the steaming mug of butter tea that Jinpa handed me warmed me down to my toes. It was snowing heavily outside. It had presumably snowed all night, as the ground was covered in a thick, white layer. My head still hurt, so I took two more painkillers. We had not been walking for more than ten minutes when I was overcome by nausea and threw up my breakfast.

"I think it's best that we go back," I said, in a feeble voice.

"Let's try just a little bit longer," said Jinpa, who was more con-cerned about the next life than the present. "It would be a shame to give up now when you're so close."

I did not have the energy to argue, so I swallowed another altitude sickness tablet and soldiered on through the snow. The holy moun-tain was shrouded in mist and snow, completely invisible; I could barely see my own feet. In front of me I saw the grey shadows of pilgrims as they bent into the wind. The snow got heavier and heavier, but everyone continued doggedly up the pass, prayer beads and prayer wheels in their hands, Om mani padme hum. The ground was frozen and there was a layer of ice under the fresh snow; people slipped and fell all the time. A group of Indians had to dismount from their horses, which also struggled to stay upright on the ice.

"Riding round Kailaish won't bring you any benefit," Jinpa muttered. "The horses get tired and suffer; riding round Kailash only brings bad karma, there is absolutely no point."

From time to time, we met Bönpo, Bon followers. The mountain is also holy for believers of the old faith, but for some reason they walk in the opposite direction, anticlockwise.

"That's how you can tell the Bönpo from the Buddhists," Jinpa said, without any further explanation. "They walk the other way."

At irregular intervals, we passed frozen pilgrims wearing gloves and aprons, who prostrated themselves on the ground, then got up and walked three or four steps, then prostrated themselves, then got up, as they mumbled mantras with deep concentration. They looked exhausted.

"It takes them about three weeks to get around Mount Kailash," Jinpa said. "Some of them have already walked all the way here from eastern Tibet. They might have taken a year or two, or three, to get here. They do it to win benefit, a lot of benefit."

I lost all sense of time. I was conscious only of my headache and feet, which slowly but steadily transported me up, step by step, on the slippery, deceptive ground. I gasped for air, but could not get enough, could never get enough; my heart hammered painfully in my chest. By the time we got to the top of **Drolma La Pass**, I was unable 5650 MSL to feel anything. I was no longer exhausted or cold, just numb. It was still snowing heavily, and the wind had increased to gale force. The prayer flags, of which there must have been thousands, snapped whenever they were caught by a gust.

The pilgrims, young and old, lit up with happy smiles as they continued to chant the holy mantra, over and over and over again. Some of them fell to their knees.

No-one was able to stay on their feet on the way back down. People tumbled and slipped with loud cries, arms and legs in the air, and often there were chain collisions.

"Take my hand," Jinpa said. I did as he told me, and moments later he fell on his behind with a howl.

Somehow we managed to get down, somehow everyone managed to get down, and we ordered butter tea and noodles in a packed tent to celebrate that the worst was over. Next to us, a young couple sat on either side of an ancient, emaciated, blind man. I have no idea how they got him over the pass, but he had not once considered giving up.

We continued on down, following a gravel road. It was snowing more than ever.

"The more toil and trouble, the more benefit," Jinpa said with a grin, as he filmed the enormous, thick snowflakes that danced around us.

The light was fading and we still had a long way to go.

The sky was blue when we woke up the next morning. All that was left of the storm was a thin layer of fresh snow, which had been dusted over the mountains like powder. Another long journey awaited; five hundred kilometres in a day would be unthinkable in countries like Nepal or Pakistan, but here we sped west on straight, surfaced roads. I sat with my face glued to the window, lost in the changing colours outside. The grass could change from mustard yellow to neon green within minutes. Herds of yak lumbered leisurely around, eating grass here and there; they looked like hairy dots in the distance. The mountains that rose up behind them were brown, red, orange and gold, and were crowned with white peaks against a ridiculously blue sky.

Palden, the driver, and Jinpa were in great spirits and wailed along to Tibetan pop songs. They both sang desperately out of tune.

"He left his pants in the last town," Jinpa giggled.

Palden blushed furiously. "I couldn't find them in the dark!"

"He has a girl in every town in Tibet," Jinpa said, undeterred. "He's mad about the girls!"

"And what about you, what did you do last night?" Palden said.

"I told her I didn't have time." Jinpa lowered his eyes. "I've known her for years, but now she's almost thirty. She should forget me and find herself a husband. I've been married for fifteen years, and in all those years I've only ever had three women other than my wife. That's not so bad, is it?"

At one point, we passed the wreck of a car. The mangled wreckage lay abandoned in the grass, surrounded by dozens of broken eggs. Shortly after, we passed another – the accident was so recent that the police were still at the scene, gathering evidence. More than seven hundred people are killed in traffic accidents in China every day.

Every so often we drove past clusters of small, white tents. The tents were generally empty, but large dogs were there to stand guard. With an average of two persons per square kilometre, Tibet is one of the least inhabited places on earth. Most Tibetans live in the fertile valleys of the south-east; here in the west, one can travel enormous distances without seeing anyone. Later in the afternoon we came across some people: two women out in a field gathering sheep droppings for fuel.

Both women were nomads and had about two hundred sheep each. The previous winter had been harsh, they said, and there had been more snow than usual, so half of the animals died.

"But things like that happen," said the elder of the two, with a shrug. She had wrapped a green woollen shawl round her head to protect it from the wind and looked like she might be in her fifties. "We continue to live as we've always done." She laughed dryly. "What would we do, where else would we go? We're nomads. Being a nomad is the only thing we know."

"You said last winter was particularly bad. Has the weather changed much in the past few years?" I asked.

"Has the weather changed?" The woman laughed again. "The weather is constantly changing, let me tell you. That's the way of weather."

I gave the woman some money as thanks for taking the time to talk. It is seen as good manners, almost obligatory, in Tibet, as in Bhutan, to give a little thanks for any help, no matter how small.

"Why didn't you give some money to the other woman as well?" Jinpa asked me, when we got back to the car. He was clearly annoyed.

"I didn't speak to her," I said.

"That doesn't matter. In Tibet we give something to everyone present. If there's a group of beggars outside a temple, you either give nothing, or something to them all. Have you got more money?"

I shook my head. My wallet was empty. Jinpa sighed and quickly took a bar of chocolate and a packet of biscuits from our food store and hurried back to give the other woman the presents.

"They were frightened, did you notice?" Jinpa asked, as we drove on. "They probably thought you were a spy from Nepal or China. Everyone here is frightened. Why do you always have to talk to people? Can't you just talk to me? I can answer your questions."

It turned out that it was Jinpa who wanted answers to some of life's mysteries. The conversation quickly turned to homosexuality. Jinpa had heard that it existed, he said, and on a couple of occasions, he had even had guests, two men and two women, who shared the same bed.

"But we don't have it here in Tibet," he said with absolute certainty.

"Of course you do," I said. "There are gay people all over the world. People just hide it better."

"No, we do not have homosexuality in Tibet," Jinpa insisted. "It's possible it's normal elsewhere, but not here."

"Surely," I said, and got out my telephone. I googled *homosexual* + *Tibet* and immediately got a number of hits. "Look, there's even an interview with a homosexual Tibetan!" I showed him the website I had just opened and scrolled down.

"Are you trying to get me arrested?" Jinpa screamed. It turned out that the article was illustrated with a photograph of the Dalai Lama. Jinpa pointed silently at the GPS system that was installed on the dashboard. The Chinese authorities had recently decided that the travel agencies in Tibet could no longer use their own cars, but had to use vehicles from state rental companies, for traffic safety reasons, apparently. And all the state cars were equipped with the latest GPS, cameras and microphones, also for traffic safety reasons, apparently.

For the rest of the journey, Jinpa talked only about homosexuality.

"I wonder how two men can have sex with each other?" he said, with a snigger. "Do they stick it in each other's armpits?"

As evening fell and the sun washed the landscape in a golden-pink glow, he was still mulling on the subject.

"I would rather jump in a river than be with a man," he said, as we drove into **Saga**, where we were going to spend the night. Despite the promising name, Saga turned out to be a dull border town, full of Chinese border guards and tourists on their way to or from Mount Kailash, Mount Everest or Nepal. 4640 MSL

Bright and early the next day we drove south towards the Tibetan version of Everest Base Camp. Emerald-green lakes lay like enormous jewels in the dry, brown landscape and every one of them was dutifully photographed by Chinese tourists on coach tours. At regular intervals, we passed through villages with identical white houses, which all had a Chinese flag on the roof. And even more frequently, we passed gigantic red signs with salutary slogans written in yellow in both Chinese and Tibetan.

Together we will build a beautiful Tibet!
Strengthen national unity and build a wonderful Tibet!
Mobilise the masses!

The message that seemed to be repeated most often was a request to people to report dark and criminal forces and to promote social integration. We also drove past men in overalls who were busy putting up brand-new banners and signs with this message by the roadside, on fences and on buildings. Even remote, narrow tea houses had their walls covered with similar posters and stickers. In the bottom corner there were three or four telephone numbers to call if you either knew of or heard of such dark forces.

The ongoing protests in Hongkong, which were getting more violent by the day, must have set alarm bells ringing for the Chinese authorities.

5009 MSL We got to **Rongbuk Monastery** in the afternoon. Once again, the monastery had been renovated, as the zealous Red Guards had been here too. There was no road here then, in the 1970s, so they must have got here on foot.

Now that there is an asphalt road right to the door, anyone can come here. Large tents had been put up to receive all the Chinese tourists and ambitious hotels were under construction. I booked into a simple guest house and got my own room with white sheets, a duvet and pillows – luxury compared with the yellow tents in the Nepalese version of Base Camp. You could even see Mount Everest from here.

The viewpoint was ten minutes' walk from the guest house and cafeteria, on asphalt all the way. A middle-aged Chinese couple trotted along in front of me, warmly wrapped in down jackets, each with their own camera round their neck. At the first bend, the woman had to give up and stood bent double while her dinner and lunch and everything in between came up again. Her husband took the opportunity to snap a picture of the moment and carried on walking, unperturbed.

The sky was unusually clear, and there she was, right in front of us, between two brown peaks: Mount Everest, Sagarmatha, Chomolungma, the Holy Mother. I could see her so well, the mountain ridge that gradually ascended to the peak, the slight kink on the north-east side before the top, the blackish-blue mountainside, the snow whipped up by the wind along the outer ridges, and I could not stop looking at her.

Here, right in front of my eyes at last, towered the world's highest mountain: a massive pyramid of stone.

The Chinese Concubine

Lhasa, the almost mythical Tibetan capital, turned out to be a mini, modern Chinese metropol. Farmers have been moved from the outskirts of the city in recent years to make way for apartment blocks, and there were cranes and scaffolding everywhere. All the buildings looked brand new, with shining glass surfaces and big neon signs. There were plenty of Han Chinese between the buildings, dressed in cheap, mass-produced clothes, and barely a Tibetan to be seen. Had it not been for the Tibetan writing on shop signs – always smaller than the Chinese characters – Lhasa would have been like pretty much any other provincial Chinese city. The uniformity was depressing and a reminder of the government's campaign in the neighbouring province, Xinjiang. Interestingly enough, it is these two remote and sparsely inhabited provinces that have caused the central authorities the biggest headache in recent decades, and it is here, on the periphery, that they have introduced the most draconian controls. Empire builders are always afraid that their work will start to fray at the edges, that they will lose control from the outside in.

I had a few hours to myself before the next part of the sight-seeing programme, so I slipped into the hotel spa. In addition to the usual treatments, such as Chinese sports massage, Indian ayurvedic massage and warm stones, they also offered a Tibetan yak butter and tsampa massage. I opted for this, their speciality, and let myself be lulled into a world of butter and roasted barley flour.

"You mustn't shower for another six hours," the receptionist said as I closed the door behind me.

Tashi, my new guide, was waiting in the lobby. She was tall, with a long, narrow face, full lips and high cheekbones. She had a small rucksack on her back; it is easy to recognise guides the world over, thanks to their small, practical backpacks.

A sickly, slightly rancid smell filled the car; it smelled like the interior kitchens in the houses in labyrinthine Humla.

"What's that smell?" I asked. And immediately realised that I was the source of the smell. I smelled like a yak herder who had not washed since the previous summer.

"It doesn't bother me in the slightest! I like the smell of butter," Tashi said. A few minutes later, she found some credible excuse to ask the driver to open the windows.

The old Lhasa had not entirely disappeared. We stopped in front of the iconic Potala Palace, the Dalai Lama's winter residence and chambers of the Tibetan government until 1959 – the very symbol of Lhasa.

The huge fortified temple rose up in front of us in all its magical glory. The palace, with more than a thousand rooms over thirteen floors, seemed to grow out of the red rock of Marpori Hill. The building continued where the rock stopped – red and white and utterly breathtaking.

Several thousand Chinese tourists, who were all herded by guides with umbrellas, stood stowed together in neat rows outside the entrance. We had all pre-booked our tickets and been given a time slot for our visit.

"It's not too bad today," Tashi said. "Some days we have to stand in the queue for hours before we get in. But we've got plenty of time to go to the new museum before our slot."

The museum building was lavish, and there was no charge to get in. There was a huge portrait of Songtsen Gampo, the thirty-third king and founder of the Tibetan empire, in the entrance hall. It was a highly suitable introduction, as it was Gampo who had the first rooms built in what was to become the Potala Palace. Parts of the original building, including the king's meditation cave, are still intact.

In Chinese history, Songtsen Gampo is first and foremost known as the king who married the Chinese princess, Wencheng, the daughter of Taizong, an emperor in the Tang dynasty. The Tibetan king already had several wives when he sent his prime minister to the Tang dynasty's capital, Chang'an – now known as Xian – to ask for a Chinese princess. Emperor Taizong blankly refused his request: Tibet was a remote and unimportant region at the time, and more powerful men had asked for his daughters' hands in marriage. King Songtsen Gampo was so insulted by this refusal that he sent an army north and conquered the neighbouring region of Amdo. But even though Tibetan soldiers were now at the gateway to the Tang empire, the emperor still refused to give one of his daughters to the king of Tibet. Only when the Tibetan soldiers defeated the emperor's army in battle did Taizong agree to send a princess to Lhasa.

Not much more is known about Princess Wencheng; it is not even certain that her name was Wencheng. All we know is that she did not have any children with the Tibetan king, and that she was widowed in 650, nine years after she came to Tibet, that she lived for another thirty years, was a Buddhist and never went back to China. Despite the fact that so little is known about her, Songtsen Gampo's concubine from Chang'an is given enormous importance in Chinese history. She is credited with bringing Buddhism and civilisation to Tibet, and is held up as evidence that China had already conquered Tibet in the middle of the seventh century. But more than anything, she has become a symbol of the deep historical connection between China and Tibet.

The tone was set, and we passed through the carefully curated rooms relatively quickly. The Tibetans were portrayed as nationalistic and proud, but whenever they were in trouble, such as when the

Gorkhas attacked Tibet at the end the 1700s, the Chinese were there to help them, again and again and again.

When it was nearly time for our slot, we left the museum and walked back to the Potala Palace. There was a stringent security check before we were allowed into the sacred palace. As soon as we were inside the walls, Tashi picked up pace.

"You'll have to keep up!" She ran up the steps in front of me. "We have fifty minutes. If we take longer than that, we'll have to pay a fine. So we have to keep moving, we can't stop until we're out, understood?"

We followed the stream of Chinese tourists through warm, carpeted rooms, and panted through small, intimate temples, past the antique statues, through the reception hall and the Dalai Lama's study, and past the burial stupas of former Dalai Lamas.

The 14th Dalai Lama, who escaped from the Potala Palace and Tibet in 1959, was not mentioned once, and there were no pictures of him anywhere.

The tradition of Dalai Lamas can be traced back to a Mongol ruler in the sixteenth century. The Tibetans had been considerably influenced by their neighbours to the north since the establishment in the thirteenth century of the mighty Mongol empire, of which Tibet became a part. When the vast empire was carved up into several smaller empires, Tibet became part of Kublai Khan's eastern empire in terms of administration. Kublai Khan was interested in Tibetan Buddhism and arranged for a Buddhist teacher to be sent to Beijing. Three hundred years later, long after Kublai Khan's empire had fallen apart, one of his descendants, Altan Khan, renewed the tradition of having a Tibetan spiritual teacher. His teacher was Sonam Gyatso, the abbot of the influential Drepung Monastery in central Tibet and head of the Gelug school, whose practitioners are often known as Yellow Hats, for their headgear. Shortly after the abbot's arrival, Altan Khan established Tibetan Buddhism as the state religion in

Mongolia. The abbot was given the title Dalai, which means "ocean" in Mongolian – a direct translation of *gyatso*, the Tibetan word for ocean. The title was then given posthumously to Sonam Gyatso's predecessors, so the first Dalai Lama was in fact the third.

With support from the Mongols, the Yellow Hats gradually came to dominate the three older schools of Tibetan Buddhism. A few years after Sonam Gyatso died in Mongolia in 1588, a young boy was found who fulfilled all the criteria to be his reincarnation. The boy, who was called Yonten Gyatso, and coincidentally was the great-grandson of Altan Khan, became the 4th Dalai Lama, and was the only one of the fourteen who was not a Tibetan.

It was not until Lobsang Gyatso, the 5th Dalai Lama, often simply called the Great Fifth, that the Dalai Lama became a figure of power in Tibet. With the help of the Mongols, the Great Fifth unified Tibet once again, with Lhasa as the capital. In 1645, some years after he had defeated all his potential rivals, he is said to have climbed Marpori Hill outside Lhasa. There, in the ruins of the palace of Songtsen Gampo, the founder of the first Tibetan empire, he declared that Avalokiteshvara, the Bodhisattva of Compassion, had finally come home. Soon after, work started on the construction of a magnificent palace. Seven thousand men were called in to build the palace, which was named after Mount Potalaka, the mythical abode of Avalokiteshvara, which, according to legend, lies somewhere in the seas south of India. The palace was finished five years later, and Lobsang Gyatso moved in. The belief that the Dalai Lama is the reincarnation of Avalokiteshvara, the Bodhisattva of Compassion, the progenitor and protective deity of Tibet, became firmly established under the Great Fifth.

When the 5th Dalai Lama died in 1782, he left a power vacuum greater than the palace he had built. Incredible though it may seem, the regent, Desi Sangye Gyatso, somehow managed to keep his death secret for fifteen years; the people were told that the Great Fifth was in retreat, and his ceremonial robes were placed on the throne for ceremonies and festivals. It was of particular importance that neither the Manchurian emperor in Beijing nor the Mongolian khan heard about the death. When their representatives came to visit, Desi Sangye Gyatso found old monks who resembled the deceased and then bribed and pressured them to pretend that they were the Dalai Lama. In the meantime, the search to find the 6th Dalai Lama was under way, in secret, close to the border with Bhutan, far from Mongolian and Manchurian eyes and ears. A suitable boy, Tsangyang Gyatso, was eventually found. He was raised and educated in secret. Then in 1697, when he was sixteen, the new Dalai Lama was presented to the people – and to the Mongolian rulers.

The 6th Dalai Lama proved to be more interested in poetry, sport, strong drink and women than in meditation and prayer. He was frequently seen in Lhasa's taverns and often took young women home with him. These worldly pursuits were not reconcilable with a monk's life, and to the dismay of the Tibetan leaders, the young Dalai Lama renounced his monk's vows to live the free life of a lay-man. He moved into a tent north of the Potala Palace, but continued to be the Dalai Lama – one cannot reject a reincarnation just like that. The Bodhisattva of Compassion had clearly chosen an incarna-tion of rest.

In 1703, a new Mongolian khan, Lhabzang Khan, came to power in Tibet. Ever since the 5th Dalai Lama had united Tibet into one king-dom again, a branch of the Mongolian khans had enjoyed the status of royalty in Tibet. His predecessors had been happy to be king in name alone, but Lhabzang Khan, who had killed his own brother to take the throne, had greater ambitions. Having secured the blessing of the powerful Manchurian emperor in Beijing, he set to work: first he killed the regent of Potala Palace, Desi Sangye Gyatso, then he had the boisterous spiritual leader kidnapped. The plan was to take him to the emperor in Beijing, but he died on the journey, at the young age of twenty-four. The poems of Tsangyang Gyatso, the unorthodox 6th Dalai Lama, are still widely read in Tibet.

A new Dalai Lama, presented as "the true 6th Dalai Lama", was installed on the throne by Lhabzang Khan, who now took power in Tibet.

Both Lhabzang Khan and his "true" Dalai Lama were extremely unpopular. In secret, the Yellow Hat monks asked the Dzungars, another nomadic Mongolian people, if they would help them to get rid of both the lama and the khan. The Dzungars did not need to be persuaded and immediately came to the aid of the Yellow Hats. They saw to it that Lhabzang Khan was killed and the new 6th Dalai Lama was deposed. But then their help got out of control: the Dzungars started to kill monks from Buddhist schools other than the Yellow Hats, they destroyed monasteries, and pillaged and ran riot throughout Lhasa.

In the meantime, the seventh reincarnation of the Dalai Lama was found, and the boy was put under the protection of the Manchurian emperor, which complicated matters. The emperor, the mighty Kangxi, China's longest-reigning ruler, sent a large army to Tibet to flush out the Dzungars. To the delight of the Tibetans, they brought the 7th Dalai Lama with them to Lhasa. The Manchurians restored the badly damaged Potala Palace to its former glory and introduced sweeping political reforms in Lhasa.

As a result, Tibet effectively became a protectorate of the Manchurian emperor, and an *amban*, a Chinese high commissioner, was installed in the capital.

Neither the 7th nor the 8th Dalai Lama had the opportunity to show much interest in politics and society during their reign, and generally had to leave that to their officious ministers. The following four Dalai Lamas all died young, in rather mysterious circumstances; the eldest was no more than twenty-one.

The 13th Dalai Lama, Thubten Gyatso, on the other hand, was on the throne for nearly forty years, from when he came of age in 1895 until his death in 1933, and certainly left his mark.

Tibet was, at the time, hermetically sealed to foreigners, other than Chinese and Mongolians. One interesting exception was the Russian Buddhist monk, Agvan Dorzhiev. He came from a village to the east of Lake Baikal in Buryatia, a part of Russia that was dominated by the Mongolian-speaking Buryats. Dorzhiev travelled to Tibet to study Buddhism in the 1870s and eventually became one of the most important advisers to the 13th Dalai Lama.

At the same time that Dorzhiev walked freely in and out of the Potala Palace, another foreigner was wandering the streets of Lhasa in disguise. The Buddhist monk Ekai Kawaguchi was the first Japanese person to successfully sneak into Tibet incognito. Because of his Japanese features, linguistic abilities and profound knowledge of Tibetan Buddhism, he could pass himself off as a Tibetan, Chinese or Mongolian monk, as required. His travelogue has the title *Three Years in Tibet*, even though there is only evidence that he was there for two, from summer 1900 to summer 1902. It provides a fascinating insight into daily life in Tibet at the time. The chapters on hygiene, or, rather, lack thereof, are particularly descriptive. An entire chapter, "A Metropolis of Filth", is dedicated to sanitary conditions in Lhasa: "I have often heard of the filthy condition of the streets in Chinese cities, but I hardly believe they can be as filthy as the streets in Lhasa, where the people live in utter defiance of all rules of hygiene and even decency."[11] He adds that the only reason that people do not drop like flies from the plague must be the healthy cold climate. But it was not just the streets that were filthy, so were the inhabitants, as a Tibetan "never washes his body; many have never been washed since their birth". Many Tibetans believed that they would wipe away their happiness if they washed, and the women as well as the men were often as black as "African negros".[12]

Kawaguchi was shocked by the gender roles, and in particular by the custom of a woman marrying several brothers. According to the Buddhist monk, Tibetan women were every bit as beautiful as their Japanese sisters, but physically much stronger, and he concluded, therefore, that it was only right that they should be paid the same as the men, which they were. In addition, the men had to give their wives everything they earned, and only had pocket money to spend themselves. If the wife thought her husband did not earn enough, he risked a real telling off. The penal system was harsh. According to Kawaguchi, the streets of Lhasa were full of beggars without eyes or who had had their hand or nose chopped off. But he was most shocked by the treatment of those who had been sentenced to death, who were first drowned in the river, then had their heads chopped off. The bodies were cut into pieces and the head was put on public display for a week. In Kawaguchi's eyes, the worst thing was that the heads were thereafter kept in a building with the apt name Perpetual Damnation, so the criminals' souls could not be reborn in this world. A terrible punishment, without any hope for mercy for all eternity.

It was thanks to one of Kawaguchi's letters to an Indian helper and well-wisher in Darjeeling that the British first heard about the Russian monk Dorzhiev's activities in Lhasa. According to Kawaguchi, Dorzhiev had managed to convince the Dalai Lama that the Russian tsar was a Buddhist god, and that Russia was the mystical Buddhist paradise of Shambala, and, furthermore, that the tsar would soon turn the world into an enormous Buddhist empire. Kawaguchi reported that Dorzhiev had evidently returned to Lhasa a rich man after his visit to the Russian capital, laden with gifts, including an entire camel train with American firearms ...

This information naturally was of great concern to the newly appointed viceroy of British India, Lord George Nathaniel Curzon. Ever since Peter the Great's death in 1725, it was rumoured that the tsar had ordered his successors to do everything in their might to achieve Russia's real mission: to become world ruler. This could only be achieved if the Russians conquered Constantinople and India. The suspicious English had their fears confirmed when Napoleon suggested to Tsar Alexander in 1807 that they should unite their armies and together march south to India. The planned unification of the Russian and French armies was never realised, but in the latter half of the nineteenth century, the Russians did conquer great tracts of Central Asia, and were now dangerously close to British India. At the beginning of the century, more than thirty thousand kilometres had separated Russia from British India, but by the time that Lord Curzon became viceroy in 1899, the Russians had recently slipped into Pamir, in what is now Tajikistan, and the distance between the two empires was less than thirty kilometres in some places.

So, thanks to Kawaguchi's letter and other intelligence reports from China, Curzon had good reason to believe that the Russians were planning to take Tibet.

Curzon's initial approach was diplomatic, and he sent a sealed letter addressed to the 13th Dalai Lamai, Potala Palace, Lhasa, in which he expressed his concern about the situation. The letter was returned some weeks later, with the seal unbroken. Curzon then sent another letter, which was less friendly in tone, but this too was returned unopened. The viceroy gave up any attempt at written diplomacy, and decided to send an armed delegation to Lhasa in order to meet the Dalai Lama face to face. The first delegation that he sent over the mountains was ordered to retreat by the Tibetans, with the message that they refused to negotiate with the British on their side of the border. Shortly before Christmas 1903, Curzon responded by sending an even larger delegation over the border – an entire brigade composed of three thousand armed men and seven thousand auxiliary troops. The brigade was headed by Brigadier General James R.L. Macdonald and Lieutenant Colonel Francis Younghusband, who fourteen years earlier had been sent to the mir of Hunza to get him to stop plundering the trade caravans on their way to Kashgar.

The simplest route to Tibet was via Sikkim, but even that meant that the soldiers and porters would have to cross a pass that was four thousand metres high. British soldiers had never before been on a mission to such high terrain, and they would need to go even higher. The locals were friendly to begin with, and offered the soldiers food, but as they got closer to Lhasa, the Tibetans became more hostile. At one point, Macdonald wanted to retreat – the altitude and extreme cold were debilitating and they were running short of food – but Younghusband refused to return without having completed their mission.

By the village of Guru, some way north of Sikkim, but still a considerable distance from Lhasa, the British met with resistance: several thousand Tibetans armed with swords, primitive firearms and crumpled paper images of the Dalai Lama, who refused to let them past. The British soldiers had strict orders not to shoot first, and presumably the same was true for the Tibetans. However, when the British rode towards the Tibetans to disarm them, the Tibetan general did fire a shot, and a massacre ensued. The Tibetans did not stand a chance, but they continued to resist for a long time before they surrendered. Slowly they left the battlefield with bowed heads. Edmund Candler, the *Daily Mail* correspondent, reported that "the impossible had happened. Prayers and charms and mantras, and the holiest of their holy men, had failed them [. . .] They walked with bowed heads, as if they had been disillusioned in their gods."[13]

Hundreds of Tibetans, perhaps even as many as two thousand, were left lying dead and injured on the ground. To the astonishment of the Tibetans, the British set up a field hospital and did what they could to save the wounded, including those from the enemy's side. Then the British set off for Lhasa once again. Four months later they arrived at the legendary Tibetan capital, which so many Western explorers had tried without success to reach before them. The British were suitably impressed by the towering Potala Palace, but as shocked by the sanitary conditions as Kawaguchi had been. "We found the city squalid and filthy beyond description, undrained and unpaved. Not a single house looked clean or cared for," Candler commented.[14]

The Dalai Lama, whom Younghusband had been looking forward to meeting, had vanished without trace. The British later found out that he had fled to Mongolia with the Russian monk. Nor was there any evidence of a secret agreement with Russia, and not a Russian or Russian weapon to be found anywhere. The only weapon forge they did find was so hopelessly primitive that Younghusband decided it would be more effort than it was worth to destroy it.

The British expedition was otherwise a success. Younghusband returned to India with an agreement: the Tibetans promised to pay war reparations to the British (a promise that the poor Tibetans never had the means to fulfil), and to open for trade with the British in three named towns and not to have anything to do with other foreign powers (i.e. Russia). On paper, Tibet was now a British protectorate, but this status was short-lived. Two years later, the British signed an agreement with the Chinese in which they promised not to annex Tibet or interfere in Tibet's affairs, and the Chinese agreed not to allow any other foreign state (again, meaning Russia) to interfere with Tibet's affairs.

Thus, with the stroke of a pen, the British formally gave up their hard-won special rights in Tibet, and recognised the Manchurian Qing dynasty as the guardians of the Roof of the World. Neither party bothered to inform the Tibetans that an agreement had been signed.

Life was never the same again for Younghusband. On the return journey from Lhasa, he went for a solitary ride in the surrounding mountains. As he turned to take a last look at the city he would never see again, he was filled with an intense love for the world and the insight that all people at heart were divine, that nature and humanity were "bathed in a rosy glowing radiancy [. . .] that single hour on leaving Lhasa was worth all the rest of a lifetime."[15] Younghusband had had his epiphany. The British lieutenant colonel, who until then had written bestsellers about his extreme expeditions, now gave more and more time to his spiritual development. At a mature age, he published books such as *Mother World (in Travail for the Christ that is to be)*, *Life in the Stars*, *The Light of Experience* and *The Living Universe*. In his books, lecture tours and own life, he explored and studied topics such as telepathy, extraterrestrials and sexual ecstasy, which he believed was intrinsic to getting in touch with "Nature's Spirit".

The British invasion in 1903–4 had been a wake-up call for the administration in Beijing. They had lost control of Tibet, but they were in no obvious rush. Only six years later, in 1910, did the Chinese send a military expedition to Lhasa to regain control by force. The 13th Dalai Lama, who had recently returned home after five years in exile, once again had to flee, and this time he had no choice but to go south, to India. With two hundred Chinese soldiers at his heels, he rode day and night, often without knowing where he was going, but he eventually found his way to Sikkim, unharmed.

The Manchurian emperor re-established control over Tibet for a short while, but the Qing dynasty had been failing for a long time, and the monarchy collapsed in 1912. The first Chinese republic was declared and the last emperor, still a child, was placed in internal exile in the Inner Court of the Forbidden City in Beijing. Using primitive, home-made weapons, the Tibetans fought for their independence and, in the winter of 1913, drove the last Chinese troops out of Lhasa.

The 13th Dalai Lama returned to the Potala Palace, this time for good. Tibet was safe for the moment, but it was a fragile security. Before his death, Thubten Gyatso, the 13th Dalai Lama, warned that Tibet was in great danger: "If we are not able to protect our own country, then everyone who supports the Buddha's teachings, whether they be commoners or nobility, and the Dalai Lama and Panchen

Lama in particular, will be wiped out so completely that not even their names will remain. The estate and property of the monasteries and monks will be annihilated."[16]

The Great Thirteenth did not live to see his prophecy realised. He died in 1933 at the age of fifty-seven. After a few years, a young boy from a poor family who met all the criteria and passed all the tests was found in north-east Tibet, and in 1940 Tenzin Gyatso was declared the 14th Dalai Lama. Ten years later, soon after the People's Liberation Army had marched into Tibet, he was appointed political leader of Tibet. And not long after that, Tibet's representatives in Beijing were forced to sign a seventeen-point agreement. Point 1 states: "The Tibetan people shall unite and drive out imperialist aggressive forces from Tibet; the Tibetan people shall return to the family of the Motherland the People's Republic of China (PRC)."

Forced family reunions are rarely a good thing, and this was no exception. The Dalai Lama tried initially to negotiate with the Chinese, but the occupiers became more and more brutal. Any resistance or rebellion was stamped out and unpopular agricultural reforms were pushed through. In spring 1959, when the unrest reached Lhasa, the 14th Dalai Lama was also forced to flee over the Himalayas to India.

Close to ninety thousand Tibetans were killed during the 1959 uprising.

The 14th Dalai Lama has not been able to return to Tibet, and the Chinese Communist Party has threatened to assume control of his reincarnation. Traditionally, it is the Panchen Lama, second only to the Dalai Lama, who selects the new Dalai Lama. And the Dalai Lama, in turn, selects the reincarnation of the Panchen Lama. In 1923, the 9th Panchen Lama fled to China because of a tax dispute. When he died in 1937, two parallel searches were set up to find his reincarnation, with the result that two different candidates were found. The Dalai Lama's envoys found a boy in Xikang, to the north-west of the

Tibet Autonomous Region, whereas the Panchen Lama's own people selected a boy named Lobsang Trinley Chökyi Gyaltsen from eastern Tibet. The Chinese authorities supported the candidature of Chökyi Gyaltsen and hoped the boy could help them in the fight against the communists. However, Chökyi Gyaltsen declared his support for the Communist Party and was escorted to Tibet in 1952 by the People's Liberation Army and installed as abbot at the Tashilhunpo Monastery in Shigatse, the traditional position and abode of the Panchen Lama. He championed the communist reforms and remained in Tibet when the Dalai Lama escaped to India. But over time, the 10th Panchen Lama became increasingly critical of China's policies and actions in Tibet and was arrested in 1964. He was detained in prison for thirteen years until 1977, then spent a further five years under house arrest. While he was under house arrest, he married a Chinese woman, and the couple had a daughter together. He died when he was fifty-one in 1989.

Following a long selection process, the Dalai Lama announced in 1995 that six-year-old Gedhun Chökyi Nyima from north-east Tibet was the eleventh reincarnation of Panchen Lama. Not long after, the boy and his family were abducted by the Chinese government and have not been seen in public since. The Chinese authorities then selected one of the other candidates, Gyancain Norbu, as the 11th Panchen Lama. He currently lives in a Buddhist monastery in Beijing and does not often travel to Tibet.

In a rare statement given in spring 2020, the Chinese government said that Gedhun Chökyi Nyima, who was by now thirty-one, had completed his compulsory education, possessed a university degree, lived an ordinary life with a stable job and did not wish to be disturbed.

Tenzin Gyatso, the 14th Dalai Lama, is now an old man. In 2019, when the 83-year-old was hospitalised with a chest infection, a representative of the atheist Chinese Communist Party stated that the reincarnations of "living Buddhas, including the Dalai Lama, must comply with Chinese laws and regulations and follow religious rituals and historical conventions".[17] Twelve years earlier, in 2007, a law had been passed to say that the reincarnation of living Buddhas is "subject to an application for approval".

The current Dalai Lama has said several times that it is quite possible that he may be the last, that there will be no more reincarnations, and that the time for such a feudal system is over. He has also said it would be natural for any reincarnation to be born in the country where he now lives himself, and not in Tibet.

If that is the case, it is highly likely that the Chinese Communist Party will select their own candidate, and that there will be two Dalai Lamas.

It was a relief to get out of the packed museum and into the sun again. Tashi looked at her watch.

"Forty-seven minutes. We just managed to avoid a fine," she said happily, and hurried over to a booth to record our feat.

Then we sauntered down the steps and through a large park. There were stages and loudspeakers set up in several places, and people of all ages danced in a circle to Tibetan pop music.

"People come here every day to dance," Tashi said. "We're quite relaxed here in Lhasa. No-one is ever in a rush."

The atmosphere was perhaps relaxed, but it was in no way free. Within a few decades, Tibet has developed from a backward medieval society, ruled by monks and lamas, with no roads, electricity or schools, to a high-tech surveillance society, controlled remotely from Beijing. As mentioned, any foreign tourists who visit the Tibet Autonomous Region must travel with an approved guide, but in the course of my few days in Lhasa, I was able to move around freely and in secret managed to meet people who were critical of the regime. It was not hard to find them.

"Tibet is an open prison," one of the women I met said with a sigh. "They have forced out all the foreign organisations, and there's now eight Chinese people for every Tibetan in Lhasa. They tempt them here with free housing and healthcare, and Chinese is the main language in schools now. The Chinese have taken over. We're a minority in our own country."

"We can't even talk openly with our friends," one of the men whispered. We were sitting together in a café in the centre of town, surrounded by Chinese teenagers who were all staring at their phones. "They've got even stricter, and we don't know who we can trust. They control our mobile phones as well. Before, we could have a photograph of the Dalai Lama on our phones, but not anymore. There's even more control, and our every move is watched. Several hundred people were killed during the unrest in 2008, and thousands were put in prison and tortured. Those who were released jump every time they see a policeman. It will be a long time until the next uprising . . . And in the meantime, we live here like frogs in a well. We don't even have passports. Tibet is an open prison."

"Tibetans believe in the transient nature of all things," a man in his sixties explained. "Nothing lasts for ever. But we also believe in karma, cause and effect. Maybe that's what this is, the effect of a collective cause? It helps to see it like that. That there's a cause. And that it won't last for ever."

"One of my sons, who was a monk, tried to flee to India a few years ago," said an old woman I met in a flat on the outskirts of Lhasa. "He knew that if he managed, he would never see his family again, but the only thing he wanted was to be a monk in a free country. I gave him some money to help him escape, but he was caught at the border. In a way, it's better for me, because now at least I can see him. He works in a factory. He's not allowed to go back to the monastery."

Dishes of home-made yoghurt, warm milk, sweet, boiled potatoes and soft, freshly baked bread suddenly appeared on the low table in front of me.

"We've got schools and roads and electricity now," the woman said. "We didn't have any of that when I was young. I only went to school for three years, but there's a group of us in the neighbourhood who have tried to educate ourselves. In winter, when we had more time, we would go to the community centre down the street to read Buddhist texts together. That's how we got through the winters. But a few weeks ago we were told by the neighbourhood committee that we can't use the community centre for that, to read religious texts, so now I don't know what we're going to do this winter. When Xi became president, I thought things would get better, because he comes from a Buddhist family. But they've only got worse."

A little girl, one of her grandchildren, jumped up onto the sofa and started to systematically terrorise her grandmother's cat. It patiently accepted everything she did to it without protest.

"I was nineteen when I had my first child," the woman said. "I wanted to wait a bit myself, but my mother advised me to get on with it as my husband was so handsome, and there were plenty of other young girls who had their eye on him . . . Now I've got a flock of grandchildren, but I don't see them that often. Everyone is so busy these days."

"If the border to India had been open, would you have gone there yourself?" I asked, before I left.

She answered without hesitation. "Of course."

There was a calendar hanging by the door, with a large photograph of President Xi. It was a gift from the neighbourhood committee. Not only was it useful, it also served as a symbolic reminder that the Chinese emperors were always addressed as Lord of Ten Thousand Years.

*

In the same way that the Chinese have stories about Xiang Fei, the fragrant concubine, who embodies the mutual love between the

Uighurs and the Chinese, Princess Wencheng, who married the Tibetan king Songtsen Gampo in the seventh century, has been made a symbol of the good and long relationship between Tibet and China. And like Xiang Fei, Wencheng has inspired films, television series and books, and an opera, too: in 2016 *Princess Wencheng* premiered in Lhasa. An outdoor arena has been built especially for the show, with a stage, restaurants, shop and car parks – a massive, extravagant complex on the outskirts of Lhasa.

The stand is far from full, half-full perhaps, and I appear to be the only foreigner. At half past eight, just as the performance begins, almost all the Chinese tourists leap from their places and rush towards the VIP seats in the middle of the stand. The ushers chase them back to their seats, but otherwise are fairly tolerant: the man in front of me has a long video call with his girlfriend during the performance, and the woman beside me films half of the songs on her mobile phone only to play them back while other songs are being sung on stage.

The music is recorded and the singers on stage all mime to play-back, but, other than that, no expense has been spared: more than a thousand actors, dancers and extras appear on stage, all dressed in extravagant costumes. The script, on the other hand, is poor, even for a propaganda musical: a messenger from Tibet visits the Tang emperor in the capital and says that the king of Tibet would like Princess Wencheng's hand in marriage. When the messenger's magic bees are able to identify the princess from among scores of other women (the princess washes her hair with nectar), her father accepts the proposal and sends his daughter to Tibet. The beautiful princess travels for a long time; she crosses mountains and she crosses rivers (brought to life by several hundred extras under long, billowing strips of blue and white material). As she travels she is struck on several occasions by a deep longing for her life in the civilised capital, but she carries on undaunted, all the while dreaming of a future where no-one goes hungry, and no-one suffers from senility, and death comes easily to the dying. At no time is the poor princess informed that the king already has a Nepalese wife and a Tibetan wife.

As the princess approaches the Tibetan plateau and her journey is almost at an end, several dozen horses gallop across the stage. The couple next to me look up from their phones for a moment and make a heroic attempt to film the galloping horses, but are not fast enough, and soon they are both glued to their screens again. Meanwhile, Princess Wencheng continues her journey south. She shivers with cold, and is racked by homesickness, and, goodness me, the snow comes down again, not only on the stage this time, but also on the stand. Soapy foam floats down from the snow machines and leaves wet patches on our clothes. More than half the audience get up and run to shelter under the roof at the back, but the soap opera Princess Wencheng is courageous, and persists, all the way to Lhasa, where she is humbly welcomed by a crowd of Buddhist monks. If one was going to pick holes in the story, one might point out that the first Buddhist monastery in Tibet was not established until a hundred years after the princess came there, but there's no place for pedantry here, and the monks are certainly very visually pleasing, as they bow in the foam in front of the Chinese princess, who, in the very last scene, meets her future husband, the 33rd king of Tibet. The two take each other's hands and are united in the dream that no-one will go hungry, no-one will suffer from senility and that death will come easily to the dying.

And so the eternal bonds between Tibet and China were sealed, according to the Chinese propaganda machine.

If one is to believe the most idealistic Chinese versions of the story, Princess Wencheng introduced useful crops to Tibet and taught the Tibetans how to mill flour and make wine.

However, Chinese and Tibetan historians agree that she brought with her a valuable Buddha statue to Tibet, which is said to be so old that the Buddha himself blessed it while alive on earth. King Songtsen

Gampo built a temple for his foreign wives, the Jokhang Temple, and the statue that Princess Wencheng had with her still stands there and is completely covered in gold. Many of the pilgrims who visit the temple have gold with them, which the monks then melt down and use to gild the statue. The statue apparently portrays the Buddha as a twelve-year-old, but is now so covered in gold that it is barely possible to recognise the outline of a body under all the precious metal.

Anyone who wishes to enter the temple complex has to go through a rigorous security check. Bags, backpacks, jackets – everything is searched. And inside the complex itself there are police and soldiers everywhere, in full uniform, standing upright, looking straight ahead with a fixed gaze. Pilgrims from far and near move around the monastery dressed in colourful woollen costumes, with large, elaborate jewellery. Tashi can easily identify from their clothes and hairstyles where the pilgrims come from in Tibet: Kham, Kailash, Lhasa, Amdo . . . Bent, with sticks, prayer wheels and prayer beads, they walk round and round, from early morning to late afternoon, as they quietly recite the holy mantras.

There are dozens of pilgrims by the entrance. They reverently kneel down in front of the temple, prostrate themselves on the ground with their hands above their head, then stand up with graceful movements and repeat the whole ritual again, fifty times, a thousand times, ten thousand times.

"Many of the pilgrims stay in Lhasa for two or three months in order to complete the number of prostrations the lama has said they should do," Tashi says.

The temple itself is teeming with people A group of women have gathered round a basin and are taking turns to pour water over their heads.

"It's holy water. It's been blessed by the Buddha statue," Tashi says. "Maybe they suffer from headaches."

An old woman is rubbing her knees against a worn stone that is embedded in the floor.

"She must have sore knees," Tashi says.

The pilgrims follow a route that passes through all the chapels on their way to the Buddha statue. They chant mantras continuously with passion, reverence and deep concentration. Three Chinese guards in orange, almost neon, uniforms ensure that none of the pilgrims spend too long in front of the golden statue. Two monks are kneeling by the statue, laying more melted gold on the now unrecognisable body.

Most Tibetans try to visit the statue at Jokhang Temple at least once, as it is seen to be one of the greatest experiences life has to offer. Tashi, who has been there hundreds of times, lays some money in front of the statue and bows her head in deep prayer.

"I took the Five Vows five years ago," she says, as we walk back out into the sunlight. "My mentor advised me to take them. I have vowed not to kill, not to steal, not to lie, not to use intoxicants and not to go with men other than my husband. The vows cannot be broken. Better to die than to break them."

"Not to lie? That doesn't sound easy," I say. "What if a friend asks you what you think of her new dress, and you don't want to upset her?"

"Well, in cases like that it is alright to lie," Tashi says, pragmatically. "If the lie doesn't hurt anyone, it's fine."

"What if you stand on an ant without realising?"

"That's fine too. It was not done on purpose."

"What if you get pregnant and the doctors advise you to have an abortion to save your own life?"

"That is not a good enough reason to kill. Then it is better to take the risk and see what happens."

"What if you're attacked by a bear, and it's a matter of you or the bear?"

"Then it would be better that I was killed," Tashi said. "If you break the vows, there will be terrible consequences, both in this life and the next. I am very glad to have taken the vows. It's given me real peace."

*

On the last day, we visit a temple on the outskirts of Lhasa. About ten monks are performing a ceremony on a hill nearby. A pillar of smoke rises up into the blue sky, the doleful sound of the monks' horns rises and falls in rhythm with the drums. A small, white tent stands beside them.

"They're performing a sky burial," Tashi said. "First they cut up the body and feed the flesh to the birds. Then they crush the bones and mix them with tsampa, so the animals eat them. It's brutal, but there's also something beautiful about it, as one is giving back to nature. The birds get something to eat, you offer your own body, nothing is left, you don't take up any space and there's no pollution. It's a very ecological burial."

"Do you do that with children as well?" I ask.

"No, small children are generally buried under the house," Tashi says. "We believe that their souls will come back in future children. Senior lamas are not buried like that either, they are normally cremated or buried in a stupa. But sky burials are the most usual here."

A monk comes down the path towards us and Tashi exchanges a few words with him.

"I was wrong," she says, when the monk has carried on. "It's not a sky burial. I did wonder about the tent, because normally there's no tent. They're performing a ceremony for rain, for the farmers and wild animals. The rain is delayed. It hasn't rained for a long time. It's so dry everywhere in Tibet. We desperately need rain."

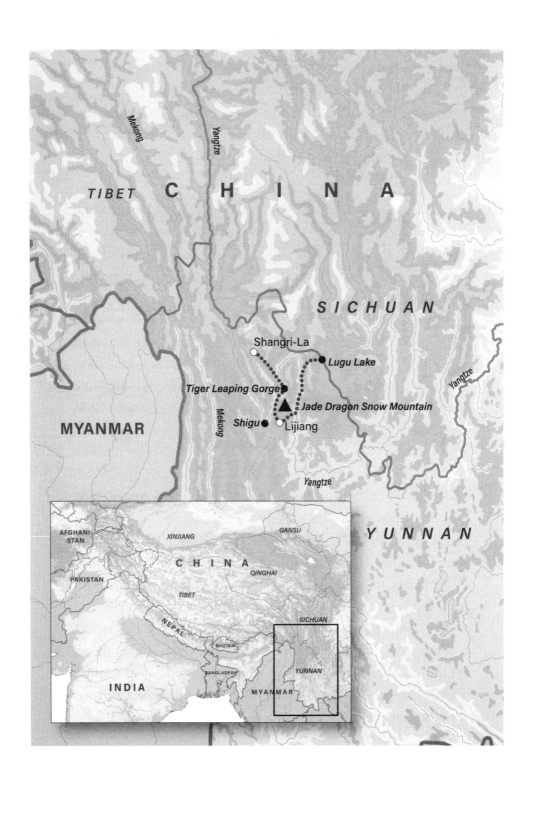

Scheduled Flight to Shangri-La

I found Gate 42, from where the flight to Shangri-La was due to depart, and sat down to wait. Owing to restrictions that no-one could fully explain, foreigners were not allowed to use the main road out of the Tibet Autonomous Region into the neighbouring province of Yunnan, so I had to cross the boundary by air.

There was a Starbucks by the gate. I am always filled with joy when I find a Starbucks in China. Nowhere else, by a long shot, does the sight of the green and white logo have the same effect on me, but China is not like anywhere else. In China I am illiterate and mute, and even the simplest thing, such as ordering a cup of tea, feels insurmountable. I find myself fumbling in a high-tech world that is so like my own, but that I cannot quite understand. But I understand Starbucks. There is something safe and recognisable about the green and white logo and the bitter, watered-down coffee. For the first time since I crossed the border from Nepal, I was on my own, and the first thing I did was to order an Americano. Never has bad coffee tasted so good.

As the plane taxied onto the runway, the flight attendant gave a long speech about everything that was forbidden: opening the emergency exits was not allowed. Opening the emergency exits was not allowed *under any circumstances*. Damaging anything was not allowed, anything at all, not the seat, the lifejacket, the toilet, above all else, not the toilet. Smoking was not allowed. Not anywhere, not in our seats, not in the aisle and not in the toilet. Above all else, not in the toilet. Having a mobile phone switched on was not allowed; it must be switched off or in flight mode. We had to remain seated when we were told to remain seated and not wander down the aisle unless it was strictly necessary. There was then a long list of the punishments and fines that passengers risked if they broke any of the above rules.

In the past few decades, more than two hundred million Chinese have joined the middle classes, and, every day, many of them will take a flight for the first time. Several times a month, flights are delayed or have to make an emergency landing because inexperienced passengers for various reasons, often simply "to get some fresh air", have pulled the red handle. Regulations on who can sit by an emergency exit have recently been tightened.

About an hour later, the wheels hit the ground again. Even the oldest and frailest passengers jumped up from their seats and started to take down their hand luggage, paying no notice to the flight attendants' screamed instructions over the PA system.

3160 MSL   We had arrived in **Shangri-La.**

In May 1931, eight white inhabitants had to be evacuated from Barkul in Afghanistan, where a revolution had started, to Peshawar in British India. Four of them were taken in the maharaja's private plane: Conway, the British consul, Mallinson, the vice-consul, a female missionary and an American crook. The four passengers soon realised that the plane was following a different route from the one planned; they flew north-west, over the icy peaks of Karakoram, and they flew and they flew until the fuel ran out and they crash-landed somewhere on the Tibetan plateau, north of the Himalayas. Conway guessed they were close to the lesser-known Kunlun Mountains.

Before he died, the pilot managed to tell the passengers to seek help at a nearby monastery called Shangri-La. The terrain was difficult and steep, but the four survivors eventually came to a lush valley with an astonishingly mild microclimate. Here they were taken care of by the local monks in a monastery that was surprisingly comfortable and modern, given its remote location, with central heating, bathtubs, a library and a grand piano. They were all happy in the remarkably luxurious monastery except for Mallinson, who was obsessed with finding porters and getting home. Life in the valley was peaceful and harmonious, and no-one lacked for anything.

When they had been in Shangri-La for a while, Conway was given an audience with the head lama, which was a great honour. The lama told him that the monastery had been established at the start of the eighteenth century by a Catholic monk from Luxemburg, Father Perrault. Conway quickly understood that the ancient lama in front of him *was* Father Perrault. Thanks to a diet of local, mildly narcotic berries and a regime of meditation, yoga and moderation, Perrault had discovered the secret to eternal youth. But at the age of two hundred and fifty, he was now dying and wanted Conway to take his place. The world was on the brink of an untold catastrophe, the head lama predicted, humanity would destroy itself and the world, and the destruction would come from above, from airplanes. Only the blessed Shangri-La, with its library and many accumulated treasures from the civilised world based on Christian and Buddhist philosophies, would survive.

Conway himself would have happily stayed in Shangri-La, but Mallinson was having none of it and wanted to escape from the valley with a Manchurian woman who had stolen his heart. Conway had also fallen in love with a charming "young" woman and eventually was persuaded to leave Shangri-La. He spent the rest of his life trying to find the lost paradise.

That, more or less, is the plot of *Lost Horizon*, a book written by the British-American author James Hilton. The novel was published in 1933, when Tibet was still closed to foreigners, and was an immediate hit with its pacifist message of a secret, harmonious paradise in the mystical Asian mountains. This depiction of a modern utopia became a huge bestseller, and a Hollywood film, directed by Frank Capra, was made four years later, at an equally utopian cost of two million dollars

– four times more than the budget. The film was originally six hours long, but was cut to a third of that. The cut version was awarded an Oscar for Best Art Direction and is worth the watch for the modern, Beverly Hills interior design of the monastery in Shangri-La alone.

Franklin D. Roosevelt called the presidential retreat in the hills of Maryland Shangri-La (it is now known as Camp David), thus starting an international trend. There are now Shangri-Las everywhere: the name has come to encapsulate the notion of an unachievable, earthly paradise, a kind of Himalayan equivalent of the Garden of Eden. In 1963, thirty years after Hilton's book was first published, Carl Barks played on the already hackneyed expression when he sent Uncle Scrooge to the hidden valley of Tralla La in the Himalayas.

Ri means "mountain" in Tibetan, and *la* means "mountain pass", and *shang* is the name of the handbells that Buddhist monks use for rituals and ceremonies. The name was made up by Hilton, who may have been inspired by Shambala, the mythical Buddhist kingdom that appears in various Tibetan texts, and which may refer to an actual place on earth, or to a spiritual paradise. While lamas and Tibetologists continue to discuss what Shambala is and where it might be or have been, it is possible to prove that Hilton's Shangri-La is made up. He never visited Asia, and said that he got his inspiration from *National Geographic* and library books. But there still have been heated discussions about where the novel really took place. And the theories have been many. In fact, you can travel all the way through the Himalayas, from the Hunza Valley in north Pakistan, via Ladakh and Sikkim in India, to Bhutan, Nepal and Tibet, and stay only in hotels called Shangri-La.

Then, in 2001, the Chinese government put a stop to all these discussions once and for all by renaming the small town of Zhongdian Shangri-La.*

This PR trick worked beyond expectations, and millions of

* The town is called Gyalthang in Tibetan, meaning Royal Plains, and is recognised as being part of the original Tibetan Kham region.

tourists started to flood to the small mountain town in north-west Yunnan. The town that had been there for more than a thousand years grew uncontrollably, and on January 11, 2014, a fire broke out in the wooden buildings of the old town. More than two hundred and forty buildings were totally destroyed, and more than two and a half thousand people were left homeless, but thanks to an efficient evacuation operation, no-one was killed. However, they were not so efficient in putting the fires out. The fire engines turned up with empty tanks and had to drive to the nearest river to refill them.

The old town was rebuilt at express speed, and it shows. None of the new buildings look any older than they are, even though they have been built in the old style. The pedestrian streets of the pretend old town are full of shops that sell pretend Tibetan souvenirs, *made in India*. At the market place, tourists can dress up as Tibetan princesses and be immortalised riding white yaks.

The new town, with its low concrete buildings, is even further divorced from Hilton's earthly paradise, and so is Ganden Sumtseling Temple, the largest Buddhist temple in the region. The monastery was originally built by the 5th Dalai Lama in the seventeenth century, but was destroyed during the Cultural Revolution. The completely renovated monastery that is there today is little more than thirty years old.

How many Buddhist temples had I visited over the past few weeks? I dutifully walked through all the shrines and halls and admired the newly painted walls and gilded Buddha statues, but I had reached saturation point, the Buddhist temple equivalent of Stendhal's Syndrome. I could no longer differentiate one temple from another in my mind; they had merged. Dizzied by it all, I dragged myself from Buddha to Buddha, from hall to hall, surrounded by swarms of Chinese tourists. The Buddhas flicked past with their mysterious smile.

Exhausted, I took the bus back to Shangri-La's brand-new old town.

*

China's fate is decided slightly further south. The Indo-Australian tectonic plate turns to the south, towards the Bay of Bengal, and the mountains and rivers move in the same direction.

So I ask once again: where does a mountain chain begin and end? Nanga Parbat in Pakistan has traditionally been seen as the western anchor of the Himalayas, and Namcha Barwa in eastern Tibet has the honour of being the mountain chain's eastern anchor. A great river runs round both mountains: the Indus does a ninety-degree turn just north of Nanga Parbat, and the Yarlung Tsangpo has a 180-degree swing, a U-turn, around Namcha Barwa, which is effectively locked in by the river. At the western end of the Himalayas, the Indus changes course and heads south-west towards Arunachal Pradesh in north India, where it is known as Dihang, before ending its journey in the enormous Bengal Delta, under the name Brahmaputra.

The Himalaya mountains are anchored by mighty rivers at each end. The obvious question then is: what came first, the rivers or the mountains?

There is no simple answer, but recent geological studies show that the Yarlung Tsangpo is one of the contributing factors to Namcha Barwa growing so tall as fast as it did. At 7,782 metres, Namcha Barwa is one of the highest mountains in the world, and also one of the youngest. The mountains in the Himalayas have generally taken around fifty million years to reach their current height – which, to be fair, makes them relatively young in geological terms – but Namcha Barwa only took between two to three million years, presumably with good help from the Yarlung Tsangpo River.

The Yarlung Tsangpo is Tibet's longest river, and one of the most turbulent, with a descent of more three thousand metres. Over millions of years it has carved its way through the landscape like a butcher's knife, and at Namcha Barwa, where it turns, the height difference is at its greatest: almost two and a half thousand metres over fifty kilometres. The water has created a canyon that is five kilometres deep, the deepest in the world. Enormous amounts of stone have been carried away by the river, which in turn has lightened the pressure on the earth's crust, which may help to explain why Namcha Barwa has been able to grow so fast. Like all high mountains, the Himalayas have deep roots that pierce through the mantle under the earth's crust. The higher the mountain, the deeper the root, rather like an iceberg. When a river washes away large amounts of stone from the surface, the mountain will rise to redress the balance. Many geologists believe that a similar process has taken place in Nanga Parbat in the west. A combination of uplift and erosion, created by the collision of tectonic plates and millions upon millions of litres of rain and meltwater, may have helped to create the beginning and end of the Himalayas.

In the east of Tibet, by the border with Yunnan, where the fissure between the continental plates points south, the mountains and rivers turn. They all follow the fold loyally towards India and the Bay of Bengal.

All except one.

The Yangtze, the longest river in Asia, has its source in north-eastern Tibet, and to begin with runs a steady course towards the Bay of Bengal, like the other rivers. But by the small town of Shigu, just south of Shangri-La, it makes a sudden about-turn. It turns sharply north in almost a hairpin bend, and crosses the whole of China before running out into the East China Sea by Shanghai.

What would China have been without the Yangtze, also known as Dri Chu (Yak River in Tibetan), Jinsha Jiang (Gold Sands River), Chang Jiang (Long River), or simply Jiang, which means river in Mandarin? Only the Nile and the Amazon are longer than the Yangtze. More than two hundred million people live along the Yangtze River, and more than twice as many are dependent on its water.

One might say that without the Yangtze River there would be no China. And yet very few tourists visit Shigu and the Yunling (Cloudy

Peaks) Mountains, where the Yangtze turns so suddenly. Instead, the tourist buses drive back and forth to Tiger Leaping Gorge, a bit further north, where the Yangtze's waters are turbulent and energetic as it thunders north.

For reasons that no-one could explain, the Yarlung Tsangpo Canyon is closed to foreigners at Namcha Barwa, but everyone is welcome to visit Tiger Leaping Gorge. At 3,790 metres, it is not as deep as the canyon, but notable all the same. It is said that a tiger once leaped across the gorge at its narrowest point to escape a hunter, hence the poetic name.

In the past, tourists had to walk up to the gorge – they had to work hard and sweat in order to earn the magnificent view. But as dams have been built there more recently and power cables installed, there is now a road, which is also suitable for tourists. As it was pouring with rain and the paths were slippery, I chose the most popular way 1800 MSL to visit **Leaping Tiger Gorge**, in other words, to drive all the way to the viewing platform.

Together with fifteen thousand middle-class Chinese, all equipped with rain clothes and umbrellas, I was more or less forced down the steps to the riverbank, where there was a large, kitsch tiger statue, in memory of the tiger that may once have jumped over the river right here. I took a selfie with the brown, frothing water in the background. There were cameras clicking all around me. And it struck me that I was remarkably like everyone else here, apart from not being Chinese. Brief visit to dramatic gorge with tiger: *click*. Forty-five minutes in a centuries-old Buddhist temple: *click*. Market in the old town: *in the same morning, click*. Local delicacy: *eaten before bed*. Evening of local folk dance: *seen so many like it before, didn't bother*. Fridge magnets: *bought*. Visit to tea house: *better in Darjeeling*. What were once unique experiences and ancient, intricate, interwoven traditions and stories have become swiftly served, easily digested public goods; the world is like a playground for the middle classes and the middle classes are growing. Shangri-La? Never existed, but *been there, done that*, me too. "*Auch ich in Arkadien!*" Goethe wrote in *Italienische Reise* two hundred years ago. Me too, me too – key words. I too can see, if only in passing, this world's distant and mystical Shangri-Las and Samarkands, South Pacific atolls and highest peaks. All those unique things that in the past could only be experienced by the privileged and hardy can be mine, and yours.

Why do we travel? Why do I travel? I suddenly felt so tired. But there was still an important part of the itinerary left.

The old town in **Lijiang**, west of Shigu, was intact, unlike the burnt-out old town in Shangri-La. Large parts of the new town had been destroyed by a powerful earthquake in 1996, but the old town, which was built to withstand the earthquakes, had survived more or less without a scratch. So while the new town was even newer, the old town in Lijiang remained one of the most beautiful and picturesque in China, with narrow, cobbled streets, canals, stone bridges and wooden houses with traditional tiled roofs. And behind the town, like a photogenic stage set, is the Jade Dragon Snow Mountain. 2400 MSL

There was not much room between the stalls in the local market, which offered almost everything: fresh and dried mushrooms, vegetables in unfamiliar shapes and colours, frogs' legs, snakeskin, herbs, peaches, figs – a cacophony of sounds and smells.

I had been warned about the huge number of tourists, but wandered alone down empty alleys and seemed to have the old town to myself until I stumbled on one of the main arteries and was engulfed by Chinese tourists from every direction, thousands of them. The street was flanked by food stalls and garish souvenir shops. Lijiang is becoming more and more popular: about two million tourists visited the town in 2007, and just over ten years later, in 2018, that figure had jumped to forty-five million, boosted primarily by Chinese tourists discovering their own country.

Lijiang's main source of income may now come from tourism, but originally it was from trade: the town was an important hub on the old Tea Horse Road, the Himalayas' answer to the Silk Road. Tea from Yunnan was traded for Tibetan horses, and a number of caravan routes linked Lijiang with Sichuan, Burma, Nepal, Tibet and north India.

At a local cultural centre in Lijiang, I met one of the last people alive who had travelled the old caravan routes. My local interpreter, Apple, wrote his name in Chinese characters on my notebook, but refused to transcribe it in Latin letters, as she was of the firm view that the name could not be translated into English, so I never found out what he was called. He was an artist, impeccably dressed in a suit and flat cap, with kind eyes and a warm smile.

"He is from an old Lijiang family," Apple said. "You can read about his father on Wikipedia. He was a very powerful and important man in Lijiang in his time, one of the few with an education, and he played an important role in the tea and horse trade."

I had not crossed any national borders to get here, only a provincial boundary, and yet it was as though I was in another country, another reality. Almost everything was new: the references, the people, the language – once again I had to orient myself in the unknown terrain. China, like India, is not really one country, but many: the province of Yunnan alone is not one country, but many. Twenty-six different ethnic groups live here – no other Chinese province is home to such ethnic diversity – and that is only those that are registered; there are many more sub-groups.

"The trade caravans went from Lijiang to Tibet, Nepal and India," the venerable old gentleman said. "Our old town is a result of the exchange of ideas, styles and materials that came with the caravans. But it wasn't possible to travel the whole route on horseback, even if it is called the Horse Road," he added, in a didactic manner. "From here the merchants rode west on horseback to Sichuan, and from there they used camels. And the journey east to Tibet and Nepal was most often done with yaks. It was a complicated trade route: anyone travelling it needed passes, and it was dangerous and prone to bad weather. There were bandits everywhere. It could take several years to reach the desired destination and many people never came home again. Small caravans could not do it alone, and that was where my father's company came into the picture: he negotiated with the bandits and acted as a protector. By the 1950s, shortly after I was born, the old caravan routes had been replaced by roads and borders were closed. My father was the last person in the family to deal with trade, and I was one of the last to travel the old trade routes."

His smile was gentle.

"Unfortunately, I don't remember much from the journey as I was in my mother's womb. She accompanied my father to Tibet when she was pregnant with me. When I was young, Lijiang was a poor and isolated town," he said. "I was nine when the town got its first light bulb. It was water-powered. My sisters took me to see it, and I remember that everyone was there, everyone talked enthusiastically about the phenomenon. There were rumours that people in the West had them in their toilets."

Xuan Ke is a living legend in Lijiang. He established the town's famous Naxi orchestra and was the conductor until very recently. The Nakhi – Naxi in Mandarin – are one of Yunnan's ethnic minorities. There are about three thousand of them in the province, and they have their own traditional costumes, language and script, as well as a rich musical tradition that goes back centuries.

Apple, my interpreter, had arranged for a friendly man in his seventies to accompany us. He had taught himself Russian, and was a good friend of Xuan Ke.

"In China, you can't just appear at a stranger's house, you have to go via someone, or they won't let you in," she said. "It's all about contacts here. Without good contacts, you don't stand a chance."

Xuan Ke lived in a large house outside the centre of town. He was sitting in an armchair watching a concert by the Vienna Philarmonic when we arrived. There was an ashtray on the small table beside him, and a bucket by his feet where he emptied the ashtray whenever it was full. The walls were full of poems written in beautiful calligraphy, photographs of people who were alive and dead – most of them dead – and diplomas and awards. The shelves were full of books in both English and Chinese. And on one of the speakers beside the television was a cross.

The old conductor was in remarkably good form, given that he was almost ninety. He spoke good English, but often switched to Chinese without even noticing. His hair was still jet black and his face was still very much like the photographs I had seen of him when he was fifty or sixty.

"Harald the Fifth, my good friend!" he exclaimed, when he heard I was Norwegian. He lit another cigarette and turned down the volume on the television. King Harald and Queen Sonja of Norway had come to Lijiang when they were in China on a state visit in 1997, and like all other heads of state and dignitaries who came to Lijiang, they were taken to one of the Naxi Orchestra concerts conducted by Xuan Ke.

Xuan Ke did not have an ordinary background. He was the son of a musician who had converted to Christianity as an adult. When Xuan Ke was a child, he went to a missionary school in Kunming.

"There were lots of pianos at the school," he said. "Maybe twelve. No other school had so many pianos. So that's how I started to play the piano."

Both his faith and music had caused problems over the years. When he was a boy, his father was sent to prison because of his faith, and he himself had been in prison twice.

"In 1948, I was put behind bars by the nationalists, but was released the following year by the communists," he said. "Eight years later, I was arrested again, this time by the communists. And I was in prison for twenty-one years. It's safe to say that I spent my prime years in prison."

When I asked about it, Xuan Ke said that he had not suffered much in prison. Others had had it far worse, he hastened to add. As he could paint, he was asked to paint propaganda pictures all over the country.

"I painted farmers and soldiers, and mixed in Chinese mythology," he said. "I had no personal investment in the paintings, because I did not believe in communism, but they were very popular."

In his autobiography, which I bought later in the day, Xuan Ke describes in detail those first years in prison, before he started painting propaganda pictures. "Those valuable years when your mind is at its peak were in my case spent on hard labour, without Beethoven, Bach, Haydn or the piano, without carpets of spring grass and wild flowers, without Dante's Beatrice. My constant companion was the hideous scraping sound of the ball mill; I had no other music. The way a ball mill works is that several steel balls, which are smaller than a volleyball, are put in a cylinder and the metal is pulverised by the friction between the balls. The bone-shaking banging of the heavy hammers would be enough to finish off someone who was sensitive or had a weak heart. From first thing in the morning until last thing at night, the thumping filled every nook and cranny, there was no way to escape it."

He was almost fifty when he was released from prison.

"Are you bitter that you had your best years taken from you?" I asked.

"No, I'm not bitter," Xuan Ke said, mildly. "I'm not a stubborn person, I go with the flow. When I got out of prison, I met my wife and we started a family."

"I think he's trying to say that what he experienced in that period made him who he is today," Apple said. "Everyone was traumatised at the time."

"You have to take into consideration that it was a very special period in Chinese history," the Russian-speaking friend added.

"Anyone who had any talent or education at that time was a target," Xuan Ke said. "But life is short. Times change. We have to lift our eyes to the future. When I was in prison, I had no freedom. I felt numb, I couldn't think normally. I couldn't have feelings, I couldn't have my own ideas. I had to turn everything off. I had no opinion about what was up or down, left or right, any such assumptions ceased to exist."

When he was a free man again, he got a job as a music teacher at a junior high school in Lijiang.

"I also composed a number of symphonies and established the Naxi Orchestra," he said modestly. "Our music traditions are incredibly old, they go right back to the Tang dynasty. Lijiang is a border region to the east of the Himalayas, we're a long way from anything here. During the Cultural Revolution many traditions died out closer to the centre, but they survived here. When Lijiang opened up again in the 1980s, I wanted to share these rich traditions with the world. I have given the music my own personal touch, of course, but the Naxi Orchestra is primarily about preserving the musical traditions that have survived here. Come and hear for yourself, we still have concerts every evening!"

He lit yet another cigarette and emptied the full ashtray into the bucket.

"But the thing I am most proud of are the twenty-one songs that I composed for the twenty-one schools in Lijiang," he said. "Every school has its own song."

"He should also be proud of the fact that he managed to get Lijiang on the UNESCO World Heritage list," his friend said. "People in Lijiang see Xuan Ke as Lijiang's compass. When the Cultural Revolution was over, he was the only one left with an education and qualifications. What he has given Lijiang is invaluable. He's like Jesus for us, he's built a bridge between Lijiang and the world and made our old town famous! If we hadn't been on UNESCO's World Heritage list, Lijiang would still be a poor, ordinary little town in the mountains."

We had talked for a long time about so many things; the maestro was tired.

"China is a strange and unpredictable nation," he said, as we were about to leave. "Historically, we were ruled by an emperor. If the person at the top is good, the people benefit. Xi Jinping has no faith, but his wife is a Christian. She was my pupil many years ago. She came to Lijiang, and twenty thousand people came to see her kneel down in front of me and acknowledge me as her teacher. My hope is that she can influence her husband with her Christian values. I believe that only then will China move forwards. The alternative is to stagnate."

"What was Xi Jinping's wife like?" I asked, bursting with curiosity.

"It's so long since I was her teacher that I can't really say what she was like," the honourable conductor said with great diplomacy. "She is another person now, she is in a completely different position."

Xuan Ke's Russian-speaking friend joined us for lunch. I never found out what he was called, as, once again, Apple said his name could not be translated and refused to transcribe it in pinyin.

"Please just say if you're too tired to talk," I said, once we had ordered the food.

"Not at all, I'm only seventy-one, I'm still a youth," he said, with a friendly smile. He had a pointed face, with a small mouth and a rasping voice. He reminded me of my grandfather.

While we waited for the food, he showed me a book he had translated, *Rozovye Rozy*, or *Pink Roses*, by the Russian author Viktoriya Tokareva. He had two versions with him, one old and worn and one more recent. The translation had never been published, but he had brought it with him and showed it to us proudly, page by page.

"One day, when I was still repairing bikes in the old town, a young Russian girl, a tourist, came over to me and we became friends," he said. "When she went home to her own country, she sent me *Rozovye Rozy* in the post."

He had also brought with him a copy of the handwritten letter he had sent to President Putin, in which he proposed twinning a town in Russia with Lijiang and told his own story, all in Russian, in beautiful, careful handwriting.

"Tolstoy!" he cried, with great enthusiasm and gesticulation. "Pushkin! Russian literature is the greatest!"

Plates of food were put down on the table in front of us – cabbage, rice, spring onion, tofu, fried meat – and we ate in silence.

"My generation is the generation that Mao sacrificed," he said, when the plates were empty. He had given up speaking Russian, which he hadn't spoken for many years, and let Apple translate.

"When I was eighteen, I was sent to the country, to the area where the airport is now. It wasn't that far away, but life there was hard. People who lived in the town had an easier life. I had to plough the earth with the most basic tools, my hands were covered with blisters all the time. I was there for three years, I worked hard and was always hungry. The farmers had to give nearly all the food to the government, so we never had enough to eat. I never managed to eat enough to be full. At one point, I longed desperately for ham . . . and then there was an opportunity to get five hundred grams of ham as an extra ration. I did everything in my power to get it, even though it meant I had to work even harder. I was obsessed with that ham, and overcame all the problems and challenges. For a week I worked as hard as I possibly could. The ham weighed two kilos, and I got a quarter. I still have nightmares about the ham and how obsessed I was."

He swallowed, and lowered his eyes to the table.

"Many people died of starvation during that time. As a member of the Red Guards, I suffered less than ordinary people. We were like a gateway between the people and the Party. But my soul was wounded. That ham scarred my soul for ever. All that my generation had to go through . . ."

His eyes welled up and he swallowed again.

"I grew up at a time when young people could finally get an education. We could have had a completely different future, but instead we were sent to rural villages to suffer and be tortured. Too many fell by the wayside. I was good at school, top of the class. I always got the best grades, I could have had a very different life. But the schools were in chaos at the time. I completed the first year of senior high school, and intended to go to university, but everything was in turmoil, like boiling water, no-one did what they should. Everyone was mad. I saw teachers being tortured and killed in front of me. If the Cultural Revolution had gone on for ten years, China would no longer exist. Those of us who had gone to school, who could read and write, were easy targets. Nothing was constant in those days, everything was shifting all the time. The rich became poor, the poor became rich, black was white and white was black, guidelines and directions changed constantly depending on who was in power, people no longer knew what was right, no-one understood anything. People informed on each other, reported each other. That's the Cultural Revolution for you!"

He picked up the book he had translated and talked about it again, and about the Russian tourist, and Russian literature, the greatest of them all. Then he pulled himself together and continued to tell us his story.

"My family are not originally from these parts. They came to Lijiang during the Qing dynasty to work for the central government. Most of my family were farmers, but because my great-great-grandmother had inherited a piece of land that we inherited, we were seen as rich. And we weren't rich at all! We didn't have servants and my sisters and I had shoes made of grass. I worked hard from morning until night. We were *not* rich! But because of my great-great-grandmother's land, we were labelled capitalists, like Russian kulaks, which was the same as being a criminal. Our background, our portfolio, if you like, was not clean, so a lot of doors were closed to us. We could forget ever working for the state."

"Were you able to keep the land, or was that taken from you too?" I asked.

Apple looked at me in astonishment.

"*Of course* the authorities took their land!" she said.

"Yes, the land was taken from us as part of the land reform and divided up between other farmers," the old man said. "But the worst of it was that people slandered us. The family got a bad reputation, and so many lies were told about us. Had it not been for my great-great-grandmother, things would have been very different. Then we would have been representatives of the hard-working lower class, we would have got medals and awards."

He let out a heavy sigh.

"I had grey hair after three years in the country. And my health was ruined. I couldn't take any more, my body couldn't take any more. I was broken and decided to become a mechanic. I worked as a mechanic and repaired bicycles in the old town for thirty years. Lots of people thought I should become a teacher, as quite a few members of my family had been teachers, but teaching had a bad reputation in those days. It was better to be a worker. Workers were respected. My life is a result of the irony of fate, and we can't run away from fate . . . On the bright side, the challenges I faced later in life were nothing compared with what I had been through. I developed an iron will."

He looked me in the eye. "To be clear, in my eyes, President Xi is a leader. He has experienced the same as us, he was sent to the country too when he was young. Xi doesn't treat people at the bottom badly. He understands us. I also have great respect for Chairman Mao. I even went to visit his childhood home when I was a youth. But Chairman Mao said two things that changed my life: he said that the educated should go and help the farmers and he said that the educated should lead the fight to eradicate the classes. These two sentences changed my life. What happened after that was out of my control."

"How did you come to learn Russian?" I asked.

He smiled.

"When I was training to become a mechanic, I got books and cassettes sent from Beijing. That's the sort of thing that was offered to workers at the time, so I taught myself Russian."

I stood waiting outside the doors of where Xuan Ke's Naxi Orchestra was going to play in the old town. It was just before eight. To my surprise, the old Russian-speaking man was waiting for me.

"I just wanted to give you this," he said, and handed me two bags full of green tea. "One of the bags is for your interpreter. Could you give it to her for me? She was going to pop by and collect them, but she didn't have time, so I decided to come and give them to you myself. I knew you would be here."

I was deeply touched. The old bicycle repair man touched his hat, nodded a polite goodbye and hurried off.

It is often not evil that breaks you, but people's goodness that makes your heart burst.

I was met by an apologetic box office lady in the dim foyer.

"I'm afraid you are the only one who has bought a ticket for this evening, so the concert has been cancelled," she said. "People are not interested in traditional music any longer. They would rather go to a bar or the shops." She sighed.

The streets outside the concert hall were teeming with tourists, forty-five million of them, but no-one stopped, no-one was interested in hearing twenty old men play centuries-old Naxi music.

Why do we travel? I have no answer, but I do know that I will never regret having travelled all that way, halfway around the world, only for a concert to be cancelled.

Kingdom of Women

Where does a journey end?

My long journey was going to be rounded off with a visit to Lugu Lake and the Mosuo people, the world's largest matrilineal society. The drive from Lijiang took more than four hours. We crossed the Yangtze River and headed north, towards the green mountains. Apple had warned me that the road was bad, but compared with the mountain roads in Pakistan, India, Bhutan and Nepal, it was like a miracle.

Apple was slightly younger than me and had worked as an English teacher for several years before she gave up on the Chinese education system and became a full-time guide and interpreter.

"I was too impatient," she said. "I got angry when the children didn't listen, and there were too many children in each class. The teachers are punished when the children don't do well enough in their tests. I'd had enough.

She had a slight limp and did not use make-up. Her hair was straight, smooth and shoulder-length.

"My parents want me to get married and have children, but I don't want to," she said. "I want to be free. To travel. See the world. There are so many expectations to live up to. I just want to be able to live the way I want. But being a woman in China is better than many other places. I went to India many years ago. The Indian men are terrible! I had never experienced sexual harassment until I got to Kolkata. When I came home, I saw China with new eyes."

"I have never experienced any sexual harassment in China," I said. "It does feel like you have equality here compared with lots of other countries, but I still get the impression that most of the leaders are men. How many of the government ministers are women?"

"Why do you ask when you already know the answer?" Apple said with audible irritation.

"I don't know the answer," I said. "That's why I asked."

"China has resisted Western influence for five hundred years," Apple said. "Why should we change now? Why should China be like the West?"

"I didn't say that China should be like the West," I said, perplexed. "Surely having female bosses and ministers isn't specifically Western?"

In the days that we had spent together in Lijiang, Apple had primarily interpreted for me. Now that we had more time to talk together, I began to understand why her teaching career had not taken off.

"I've always said that the differences between the East and West are insuperable," Apple said with conviction. "You are simply unable to understand how we think. Eastern and Western people will never be able to understand each other, we're too different."

We drove on in a tense silence. Green hills whizzed by. I passed the time reading the news on my phone. The protests in Hong Kong were headline news in all the Western newspapers; hundreds of thousands of protesters had taken to the streets, and the situation was becoming increasingly tense. I took the opportunity to ask Apple what the Chinese media were reporting from Hong Kong.

"I don't know, I never watch the news," she said tersely from the front seat, without turning to look at me. "But I can ask the driver, if you like."

The driver, it seemed, had plenty of things to say on the topic.

"They're saying in the media that the protests were started by the British and the Americans in an attempt to prevent or influence the elections in Taiwan next year, when Taiwan will be returned to China," Apple translated. "He says that he thinks it sounds like a plausible explanation."

"What do the Chinese media say about the situation in Xinjiang and the internment camps?"

Again, Apple asked the driver.

"He hasn't heard about the internment camps, he says, but he thinks it's only natural that there should be more security in Xinjiang after the knife attack at the train station in Kunming a few years ago. The security wasn't good enough and the people have to be protected."

I could feel that Apple was starting to get annoyed, but risked it and asked another question.

"What do you learn about Tibet at school?"

"What do you mean?" Apple asked, on her guard.

"What do you learn about the Chinese annexation of Tibet in 1950?"

"It's a small chapter, very short, so short it didn't really make sense," was her measured reply.

I did not dare ask any more questions and went back to the news on my phone.

All of a sudden, Apple turned around and looked at me.

"Why do you ask about these things?" she said angrily. "It's as though you've made up your mind and just want your opinion confirmed. You know that you're asking about highly political things? The Chinese don't talk about things like that, and then you come along and obviously have your own views, and seem to be judging us. Why are you asking me about all this?"

Her eyes were shiny and her voice quavered.

"I've spent twenty years avoiding things like this and now it's all coming back – *you* are bringing it all back! We live in a communist country, how do you think it works? It doesn't matter what we think about this and that! I thought the agreement was that I would help you talk to other people, not that you would ask me about such personal things!"

"I'm so sorry to have upset you. To be honest, I didn't think it was personal to ask you what the Chinese media are saying about different things," I said, in my defence. "I don't speak Chinese, how else would I find out?"

"You just ask and ask!" Apple shouted. A tear trickled down her cheek. "Stop it, just stop!"

We drove on in silence. That is the way successful dictatorships work: they worm their way into people's heads, then sit there and guard against questions. Daily life is easier that way.

When we stopped to buy tickets at the entrance to **Lugu Lake** – 2685 MSL the Chinese authorities classify Lugu Lake as a scenic spot, so an entrance fee is required – Apple turned to me again.

"I'm sorry, I should not have got angry," she said sheepishly. "I can give you back the money you've paid and help you find someone else to interpret for you, if you like."

"Don't be ridiculous, that won't be necessary," I said. And then to change the subject and perhaps lighten the mood, I started to ask her about the differences between the various ethnic groups that lived in the area, the Yi, Bai, Nakhi and Mosuo, but every now and then I repeated a question, and at other times I revealed my complete ignorance.

"Did you not read up on it before you came?" Apple asked, more surprised than irritated.

We got our tickets and drove into the tourist site, past hotels, simple houses and parked tour buses. The lake lay to the left of the road, glittering and tempting, surrounded by beautiful hazy, blue mountains. Large yellow signs informed us that swimming was strictly forbidden. An hour later, we arrived at the small, family-run hotel where we were going to stay.

"Sadama, a good friend of mine, lives next door," Apple said. "She has invited us for dinner."

"How kind of her," I exclaimed.

"You don't understand," Apple said with exasperation. "Sadama is my friend, like I said. She *has to* invite us for dinner. It's her duty."

On the wall in Sadama's kitchen was a poster featuring the five most recent leaders of the Communist Party, including Xi Jinping, as well as a large poster of Mao. By the Buddhist altar in the living room, there was a framed picture of the 11th Panchen Lama, the reincarnation that the Chinese authorities selected, who now lives in Beijing. It was the first time that I had seen a picture of him in a private home.

Sadama was twenty-nine and eight months pregnant. She served us some delicious vegetarian dishes and asked with a smile if we would like beer or spirits with our meal. Her father, who was visiting, and her husband, a tall and strikingly good-looking Tibetan, did not need to be asked twice.

After we had eaten, we all sat down on plastic chairs in the back garden. Other than the sound of the cicadas and the television that was talking to itself in the living room, it was completely quiet. The evening air was soft and warm. Sadama had lived with an American family in Lijiang for several years, so she spoke good English, despite never having gone to school.

"We were allowed to choose whether we wanted to go to school or not, and for me it was a simple choice," she said and laughed. Unlike Apple, Sadama was patience itself and happy to answer all my questions about Mosuo traditions and life on Lugu Lake. She laughed a lot too.

"It's been said that we live in the kingdom of women," Sadama said with a smile. "I like the name, even if we don't have a king. Here it is the *grandmother* who is boss. She decides what should be done and who should do what; it's the grandmother who arranges all the rituals and ceremonies and looks after the household money. When the grandmother retires, she hands on the responsibility to one of her daughters, normally the eldest. But even though we're a matrilineal society, it doesn't mean that the women decide everything. Uncles are also important! The oldest uncle, generally the grandmother's eldest brother, is number two in the house. Men are strong, but women can do everything a man can and we give birth to children. Men can't do that. That is why we respect women."

The Mosuos do not get married in the usual sense, but practise what is known as "walking marriages".

"The man visits his wife at night and leaves again in the morning," Sadama said. "The children live with their mother and their mother's sisters and brothers. Only people who share the same blood live together. It's simpler like that, there aren't as many problems. You don't need to get on with your in-laws and things like that. And, it's also very easy to get divorced: he can either stop coming or she can lock the door. At the start of the relationship, he will come late at night in order to avoid the girl's brothers. The Mosuo are very private. We never talk to our brothers about love or sex. Never! People say so much nonsense about us, that we have multiple men and are promiscuous, but none of it is true. Some Mosuo women have two men, maybe three, in the course of their life. But three isn't that usual. They also say that we don't know who our fathers are, but of course we do! I have a close relationship with my father, but I have an even closer relationship with my mother and grandmother."

Sadama lived with her mother, who had chosen to move out of *her* mother's house when she was young to live with her husband. Sadama also lived with her husband.

"My husband comes from a village that is far away, so we can't live in the traditional way but have to live together," she said. "And anyway, the authorities have now decided that we need to have marriage certificates. It doesn't mean anything to us, it's just a piece of paper that we need to have. The party is more important! We normally have a big wedding party with friends and family, often with lots of drinking games. I had been looking forward to the party and drinking lots and enjoying myself, but then I discovered that I was pregnant . . . Everyone was happy, of course, because you don't have to have had a wedding party before you have children together, but it meant no drinking games for me at the party."

Sadama tried to find a more comfortable position on her chair, without much success.

"Lots of the Chinese guides who come here tell the tourists that we have a different man every night," she said, with a sigh. "Some of them even encourage the tourists to try our model of marriage! The tourists really want to believe them. Some years ago, some Chinese women came here and dressed up as Mosuo women and worked in the brothels . . . The tourists started coming about twenty years ago, when Lijiang became a UNESCO town, and now that we have an airport here, even more come. The old people think it's good here now, because when they were young, everyone was poor, but we've also lost many of our traditions. When you get something new, you lose something old, that's the way it is."

She smiled sadly and patted her big belly.

"We don't sit around talking together in the evenings any longer, we're either on WeChat or watching television," she said, pensively. "I think our culture will disappear. There are so few of us, only thirty thousand. In recent years, lots of Mosuo women have married Han Chinese men and moved away from the lake. By the way, would you like to visit my grandmother? She loves having visitors!"

Sadama's grandmother, Kumu, lived in a big, traditional Mosuo house five minutes' walk from Sadama. She lived there with three of her seven children, but she was sitting alone by the hearth in the grandmother room when we arrived. When she saw us, she clapped her hands, delighted to have guests.

"All traditional Mosuo houses have a grandmother room," Sadama said. "There is always a small hearth in the grandmother room, where the families can make offerings to the fire spirit, and the grandmother sleeps by the hearth."

The old woman was wearing traditional clothes. She wore a thick, pink belt around her waist, a black blouse, a light-blue, pleated skirt, and a big, black turban on her head. The room was built of wood, and was spacious, with a high ceiling. Kumu had lost nearly all her teeth, but her body was still lithe, and she had good hearing, bright eyes and a lovely, infectious laugh. Sadama prepared some green tea and bowls of fresh, home-made yoghurt for us.

"Does it feel like a big responsibility to be head of the household?" I asked Kumu.

"Oh, it's not so much responsibility anymore." The old woman laughed so hard that her whole body shook. She did not speak Chinese, only Mosuo. Sadama translated for Apple and me. "I'm old now, and there are not as many people living here now."

"What was it like here when you were young?" I asked.

Kumu laughed again. "Oh, let's not talk about the old days. It was terrible here in the old days. We worked a lot and ate very little. Things are much better now! We had to do everything by hand before, we had to mill the corn ourselves, and we didn't have rice. We didn't have roads either, and everything was dirty and dusty. Now it's clean and tidy everywhere and lots of people come to visit. I tell you, it's not possible to compare then and now."

"How old were you when you got married?"

"I don't even know how old I am now, so how can I know how old I was when I got married?" Kumu said and laughed, showing her toothless gums.

"I don't know my date of birth, either," Sadama said. "My parents don't know exactly when I was born."

She tried to help her grandmother work it out, and they decided that her oldest child was born in the year of the monkey, but when was that? None of them knew.

"And I also had more than one man," Kumu said, with a chuckle. "How am I supposed to remember who I had children with and when?"

"How many husbands did you have?" I asked.

"Only two, not a pack, hahaha! My parents found one of them for me, and I found the other. One is dead now, and the other lives somewhere else."

"Have there been many changes since the communists came to power?" I asked.

Kumu gave me a puzzled look.

"She doesn't understand the word 'communist'," Sadama said. "When I talked to her about it before, she said that everyone worked for the authorities and that the authorities interfered with everything. Whenever they slaughtered a pig, they had to give half to the authorities, so people slaughtered their pigs in private and were terrified of being caught. These days everyone has their own plot of land."

"What do you think about all the tourists who come here now?" I asked Kumu.

"Oh, it's good that people come here!" She beamed. "I love having guests, you see. But sometimes it gets too busy. Sometimes there are too many people." She smiled. "But I have no reason to complain. All my grandchildren have grown up and done well for themselves."

"I often think that she's lucky," Sadama said. "I see how happy she is when she has her children and grandchildren around her. Everyone respects her. I worry about how it will be for me, as everything is changing. I once went to visit an old people's home and it was an awful experience. The family didn't care about their old relatives and no-one came to see them. It made me so sad to be there that I started to cry."

"Are you worried that the Mosuo culture might disappear now that everything is changing so fast?" I asked Kumu before we left.

"As long as people are happy, it doesn't matter so much if the

Mosuo culture disappears," she said. "My grandchildren can speak Chinese. I can't speak Chinese, but I'm very glad that they can!"

She started to laugh again. Her entire being shook with laughter.

"You keep asking me about things that happened long ago, my girl! How am I supposed to remember all that?"

The village was going to say farewell to an old woman the next day. Sadama's mother invited Apple and me to go with her. Sadama could not come, as she was pregnant: birth and death should be kept separate.

"*Everyone* will be there," Sadama said. "I would so like to go as well."

"But won't it be very sad?" I said.

"No, it's an old woman who has died. And when that's the case, we're not sad. We see death as a new beginning."

The house where the woman had lived was full of people. Sadama's mother introduced Apple as a friend of Sadama's, and me as a friend of Sadama's friend, and everyone made us feel welcome. On the instructions of Sadama's mother, we had brought cooking oil, cigarettes, a small bottle of spirits and cakes. We left the gifts in the grandmother room where the ceremony took place. The room was small and square, and a small altar had been set up in the corner, with incense, flowers, lit butter lamps, colourful cakes made from tsampa, and bowls of sweets, nuts and peaches. The walls were covered with sacred Buddhist paintings that the monks had brought with them, and there were garlands and banners with Tibetan mantras hanging from the ceiling.

Apple bowed down in front of the altar and gave me strict in-structions to do the same. When we had put down our gifts, we were led out to one of the tables in the back garden and offered food and drink. Big plates of roast meat were put down in front of us. The family had slaughtered a cow the day before so there would be enough food for the guests.

"This is our lunch," Apple said. "There won't be any more lunch today."

"But it's only nine in the morning," I argued.

"As I said, this is our lunch," Apple said again, with obvious irritation.

There was a kind of altar in the back garden as well. Inside the colourful, home-made frame, which looked like a lotus flower, was a photograph of a smiling, grey-haired woman.

When we went back to the grandmother room, the monks were sitting side by side on a bench next to the altar. To my untrained eye, they looked like ordinary Buddhist monks, with their horns and drums and Tibetan prayers, but it turned out that they were Bon monks, the old faith.

"Bon goes back some ten thousand years," one of the monks explained. Rinzhen Dorje was a very serious young man of twenty-four. "By comparison, the Yellow Hats are only six hundred years old. Our texts are different and our ceremonies are also different. Practitioners of Bon believe that the world is influenced by dark and light forces, and we try to balance those forces. Like the Buddhists, we believe in karma, reincarnation and enlightenment, but our traditions are older. As Lugu Lake has been so isolated – there was no road here until the 1980s – the Bon traditions have been preserved better here than in Tibet. For example, we still sacrifice goats and cattle."

He got out his mobile phone and started to search for books that we could read to gain a better understanding. He scrolled quickly down the screen with a furrowed brow.

"Unfortunately, all the books are either in Chinese or Tibetan." He gave an apologetic shrug. "And what I just said, that Bon is still pure here by Lugu Lake, is not strictly true. The Bon traditions are mixed with local traditions here. People still use *dabas*, shamans, for example. And a *daba* will be coming here this afternoon. His role is to open a passage for the deceased's soul so that it can be reunited with the ancestors. Our role is to open the passage to the six different stages the soul has to go through before it understands that it is dead, so that it can gain entrance to paradise or be reborn."

A set of colourful clothes hung on a line by the altar, and on one of the poles that supported the ceiling there was a decoration made of feathers, rope and home-made fabric flowers.

"That's to symbolise the saddle," Rinzhen said. "Tomorrow, they will tie the decoration on a horse and the horse will be sent up into the mountains, as an offering to the mountain god. It's an old Mosuo tradition. The horse will come back, but as Mosuos we believe that the soul must pass through forests and climb a mountain on its way to paradise. The clothes are a gift to the deceased's soul. When Mosuo women get married, they are given new clothes. This is something similar. Death is a new beginning. The body is cremated in the foetal position, a symbol that death is a transition to something new."

The kitchen was full of women. Some were busy cutting meat and preparing food, others were busy eating it. On the walls were the same posters that Sadama had, of Xi Jinping and his predecessors.

"I live in a traditional home," a young woman in a black tracksuit told me. The dress code was fairly informal. Most of the guests were wearing jeans or joggers. "A traditional Mosuo home has four houses. The grandmother's house, the flower building that belongs to the women, the grass house for those who don't have a partner, and the temple."

The young woman was called Bima, and she shared the house, or rather houses, with her grandmother, her uncles, her siblings and her own children.

"It's a good arrangement for the children," she said. "They live with their family, no matter what happens. If the marriage falls apart, they don't need to experience the home being divided. They live with their mother and everything is pretty much the same as always.

If the man behaves badly, the woman just needs to lock the door at night, so he can't get in. But we don't have many separations here," she said. "We don't have tragic marriages, like some other places. Lots of Han Chinese men have mistresses, but that's not so usual here. It's not accepted, the whole clan turns against people who behave badly."

Apple and I went back to the grandmother room and found the monks drinking tea. A lama was lying on the bench, snoring. On the floor in front of the hearth was a man in black trousers, a white shirt and grey rain jacket. He was making small figures out of tsampa dough.

"That's the shaman," Apple whispered.

Some of the figures resembled goats or horses, other were like small pyramids, decorated with tiny, white drops of butter. The figures that were finished were put on a tray covered in sand, rice and maize.

Relatives streamed into the room carrying wide old planks with meat and rice. They placed the planks and offerings in front of the altar, bowed so deeply that their heads touched the floor several times, then left.

"The planks are from their houses," Apple said. "Each relative has to bring a plank. They will burn them tomorrow."

The whole room smelled of the pork that the relatives had given in offering. The monks straightened their backs and started to recite their mantras again; the voices and cymbals rose and fell. Every now and then they took a sip of herbal tea from a can to soothe their throats. A few flies buzzed lazily around the room, landing occasionally on a monk's bald skull, where they wandered around for a moment or two, then flew off again.

"The Mosuos believe that the deceased's soul will possibly return in a grandchild, which is why death is both an end and a beginning," Apple said in a whisper.

*

The *daba* was called La'nji and was forty-six.

"First thing this morning I sang a special song for the deceased, so that she will be reunited with her ancestors," he said. We had gone out into a field behind the house, because he felt it was not appropriate to talk about religious matters in the deceased's family home. The shaman chain-smoked his way through my questions.

"The *daba* plays an important role at all major events in the Mosuo culture," he said, between puffs. "When a child is born, when a girl turns thirteen, when someone dies. The *daba* also has to come when someone builds a house, when the hearth in the grandmother room is blessed, and when two people get married. The lamas and monks chant in Tibetan, and the *dabas* perform their rituals in Mosuo, our own language, so that everyone can understand what is happening."

He stumped out his cigarette and immediately lit a new one.

"People also come to me when they are ill. I can't cure the illness, but I can find out why they are sick, and when I have understood that, I can remove the cause. For example, if they have offended the earth element, I can open a passage to the earth element and correct the invisible imbalance. I have contact with the ancestors and all the other spirits that surround us. We believe that everything in nature has a spirit and that everything has a protector."

"Why did you become a *daba*?" I asked.

"I had a distant relative who was a *daba*, and I learned from him," La'nji replied succinctly.

"Do you need special abilities to be a *daba*?"

"Of course." He dropped his cigarette, ground it into the earth and lit another.

"How are the rituals performed?" I asked.

"I sing and make tsampa figures." He blew out a smoke ring and followed it with his eyes until it dispersed. "A figure can symbolise many different spirits. As *daba*, I look after the whole community here on Lugu Lake. I help anyone who needs me. Later this afternoon

I will perform a ceremony for the deceased outside the village, in nature. You can come and watch."

A few hours later, we followed the road out of the village to the spot where the ceremony would take place. It took no more than five or six minutes to drive there. La'nji was sitting on a piece of canvas on a slope, and seven young men were sitting on the same canvas below him, drinking beer, playing cards and smoking. A small bonfire was burning brightly beside them.

The *daba* chanted and moved the tsampa figures around. He did not seem to be disturbed in the slightest by the chatter from the beer-swigging young men, who were paying no attention to the ceremony and were only interested in themselves. Every so often, a helper would move one of the figures a few metres up the slope and set it in a particular place on the grass.

"I am opening the passage to the ancestors' home," La'nji explained, when he took a break from the chanting. "The tsampa figures represent the different spirits: the mountain spirits, the freshwater spirit, the wind spirit, and so on. We are telling them all that grandmother is on her way, and asking them to welcome her and to help her over and into the ancestors' home tomorrow. According to tradition, at least seven boys or girls must be present when this happens, and they have to be drunk when they go home. That is the tradition."

The cremation was to take place early the next morning, further up the mountainside.

Thick smoke was rising from the small fire. A larger bonfire was standing ready to be lit some distance away. The relatives' offerings had been placed on the wood; each gift was dedicated to a particular ancestor. On the grass beside it lay three long strips of material: one black, one green and one blue. If the deceased had lived a sinful life, the soul had to follow the black path. The green path was for souls who had lived a more average life, whereas the blue strip symbolised the path for souls who had lived a "different" life, whatever that meant.

A light rain fell from the skies and settled like fresh dew on the grass and the tsampa figures and the shaman and his helper and the seven young men and the empty beer cans.

Later the same afternoon, before I left Lugu Lake and the mountains, and flew first west and then home from the new airport, I visited the deceased's house for the last time. The sky was dark blue, and the sun was setting.

The Mosuos' most important lama, an old man with a yellow hat on his head, was standing in front of the altar, surrounded by the monks and kneeling relatives. The lama chanted with deep sincerity. His role was to open the passage that the deceased's soul would pass through to reach paradise or rebirth.

At the same time, on a slope a few kilometres away, the *daba* was opening another passage to the ancestors' home.

Two passages were being opened in parallel, and no-one seemed to find this in the slightest bit strange. The deceased's soul was perhaps already on its way to the ancestors' home or to paradise, or perhaps would soon be reborn, in a new, small body on the shores of Lugu Lake.

Through the oval plane window, I caught a final glimpse of the Himalayas. From up here, the mountains were as blue as the sky, covered in snow, ice and a thin layer of cloud. The people far below were invisible; all that I could see was stone, water and air.

The mountains seemed endless, permanent, unchanging. And yet, I knew, stone by stone, they were on their way to the sea. I knew that, because I had seen the enormous rivers carry with them sand and gravel through deep canyons. From up here, you could not see that the eternal snow was melting, that the glaciers were thawing at an ever-quickening rate. But I had seen it. And down there in the valleys, I had seen new roads twisting like lindworms of black asphalt with modernity riding on their backs. I had seen it. I had seen the migration, and mobile phones light up with the same alluring, harsh glow on dark evenings in Himalayan villages as everywhere else where young people meet. Everything is changing, always.

The small is swallowed by the big; small kingdoms disappear. Cut-off valleys are opened, and the world floods in, here as anywhere else. And in those valleys, the interests of one global empire clash with the interests of another, and what happens then to the people who live along the valley floor? I had seen repression and a desire for freedom, pessimism and optimism, religious oppression and deep devotion, intolerance and enlightenment, exasperation and ecstasy.

The small is swallowed by the big, but the small continues to live as best it can. There are so many ways to live! You could not see from up here, but I knew, because I had seen it. The many, many small lives in among the towering mountains. Nor could you see the slow growth and erosion of the mountains or the endlessly slow movements of the tectonic plates as they collide.

From up here, all that could be seen were the mountains and clouds.

Acknowledgements

This book would never have been written were it not for the help I received during my travels and in the process of writing.

My heartfelt thanks go to all the people I met on my journey who were happy to share their stories with me. I was met everywhere I went with a kindness, openness and curiosity that touched me deeply. This book is the result of all those meetings.

Some of those who shared their stories did so in the knowledge that if the authorities in their country found out that they had spoken to an author, they risked imprisonment. In such cases I have changed their names and any other information that might help to identify them. In other places, I have had to change names and biographical information in order to protect those who spoke to me from repercussions from family members and other people in the local community. A few of the people who appear in the book were never told that I was writing a book, for the sake of their safety and my own. This is particularly true of some of the people I met in Tibet. They have, of course, been anonymised.

My deepest thanks go to Anne Christine Kroepelien; without her help, I might well still be stuck in Kashgar, waiting for a visa to Pakistan. Thank you, also, to Sidsel World, NRK's correspondent in Turkey, for her help with contacts in Pakistan. I would particularly like to express my gratitude to Akhtar Hussain, my helpful guide in Hunza, for all the doors he opened for me in north Pakistan.

In Kashmir, I am indebted to the three mineral water factory owners who showed me a reality other than houseboats and beautiful gardens. And to Anayat Ali Shotopa, who showed me the human consequences of all the wars between Pakistan and India.

A big thank you to the king's daughter, Hope Leezum Namgyal Tobden, better known as Semla, who was generous enough to share her story with me and show me around Gangtok.

In Bhutan, I received invaluable help from the excellent team at Heavenly Bhutan. The owner, Raju Rai, did everything in his power to organise interviews with everyone I wanted to meet.

Tasang Tage also gave me his all in the few weeks we travelled together in Arunachal Pradesh and Nagaland. Without his support I would barely have scratched the surface.

And had it not been for the help of the amazing Savitri Rajali, the chapters about Nepal would not be so varied. There was nothing she could not fix, always with a smile and without complaint, no matter how long our days were. Thank you, thank you!

I would also like to give my sincere thanks to Apple, who helped me to understand more about Yunnan and the workings of a dictatorship.

My eight-month research trip to the Himalayas would not have been possible without the generous financial support of Fritt Ord and the Norwegian Non-Fiction Writers and Translators Association – thank you!

And I am deeply grateful to the Dutch Foundation for Literature, which offered me a writer's residency in Amsterdam. It helped get the writing off to a great start.

There are many people who know a lot more about the Himalayas than I do; I was fortunate to get good help from experts along the way. Thank you to my colleague Mah-rukh Ali, who read the chapters on Pakistan and Kashmir. And to Associate Professor Heidi Fjell for her wise comments on the manuscript as a whole, and Professor Jens Braarvig, who read and commented on the chapters about Buddhism and Tibet. The geologist and writer Reidar Müller also provided useful advice about the geology of the region, and Dr Gunnar Hasle checked all the sections about altitude sickness. My thanks to you both.

Heartfelt thanks also to my English translator, Kari Dickson, who carefully fact-checked the whole manuscript before publication. Any errors that still remain – and there are always some – are my responsibility. I would like to thank, in advance, all my other translators who will no doubt alert me to them. And thank you to my wonderful agent, Anneli Høier, who gives my books wings.

It would be hard to a find a more enthusiastic, well-read and well-travelled person in Norway than Jens A. Riisnæs: I am so grateful for all our valuable conversations during the project and for all the maps, books and films that you so generously lent me. And for your excellent advice on the manuscript.

And thank you, of course, to my attentive and enthusiastic editor, Tuva Ørbeck Sørheim, for her enormous and unwavering help with the manuscript and all other aspects of publication, as well as my publisher, Erling Kagge, for valuable feedback as someone who knows the Himalayas well – and to my mother, my first and only test reader.

But my greatest thanks of all go, as always, to my husband, Erik. He is my ground crew and always there to support me, whether I am travelling or at home. And once again, no-one has read the manuscript more times than he has. I am endlessly grateful for your patience, your well-founded advice on language and content, and for the fact that you are always there for me. You are my Mount Everest, the greatest, and unparalleled.

Amsterdam, Oslo, Moorea, Hiva Oa

2019–2020

Bibliography

I have only referenced my sources when quoting directly, in order to maintain the flow in the text. However, the following books were very useful when planning my journey and writing about it.

Ali, Tariq et al.: *Kashmir. The Case for Freedom.* London: Verso, 2011.

Allen, Charles: *A Mountain in Tibet. The Search for Mount Kailas and the Sources of the Great Rivers of Asia.* London: Abacus, 2013 [1982].

Allen, Charles: *The Search for Shangri-La,* London: Abacus, 1999.

Andrade, António de: *More than the Promised Land: Letters and Relations from Tibet by the Jesuit Missionary António de Andrade (1580–1634).* Translated and presented by Michael J. Sweet. Edited by Leonard Zwilling. Boston: Institute of Jesuit Sources, 2017.

Barth, Fredrik: *Political Leadership Among Swat Pathans.* Oxford: Berg, 2004 [1956].

Bell, Thomas: *Kathmandu.* London: Haus Publishing, 2016.

Bolingbroke-Kent, Antonia: *Land of the Dawn-Lit Mountains. A Journey Across Arunachal Pradesh – India's Forgotten Frontier.* London: Simon & Schuster, 2017.

Brophy, David: *Uyghur Nation. Reform and Revolution on the Russia–China Frontier.* Cambridge: Harvard University Press, 2016.

Choo Waihong: *The Kingdom of Women. Life, Love and Death in China's Hidden Mountains.* London: I.B. Tauris & Co., 2017.

Clark, John: *Hunza. Lost Kingdom of the Himalayas.* London: Hutchinson & Co., 1957.

Conefrey, Mick: *Everest 1953. The Epic Story of the First Ascent*. London: Oneworld Publications, 2012.

Cooke, Hope: *Time Change. An Autobiography*. New York: Simon & Schuster, 1980.

Crossette, Barbara: *So Close to Heaven. The Vanishing Buddhist Kingdoms of the Himalayas*. New York: Vintage Books, 1995.

Dalai Lama: *My Spiritual Journey*. In collaboration with Sophia Stril-Rever. Translated by Charlotte Mandell. New York: HarperCollins, 2009.

Datta-Ray, Sunanda K.: *Smash & Grab. Annexation of Sikkim*. New Delhi: Westland, 2016 [1984].

David-Néel, Alexandra: *Gran Tibet et Vaste Chine*. Paris: Plon, 1994 (collector's edition).

Devasher, Tilak: *Pakistan: At the Helm*. Noida: HarperCollins, 2018.

Duff, Andrew: *Sikkim. Requiem for a Himalayan Kingdom*. Edinburgh: Birlinn, 2015.

French, Patrick: *Younghusband. The Last Great Imperial Adventurer*. London: Penguin Books, 2011 [1994].

Færøvik, Torbjørn: *Kina. En reise på livets elv*. Oslo: Cappelen Damm, 2014 [2003].

Hannigan, Tim: *Murder in the Hindu Kush. George Hayward and the Great Game*. Gloucestershire: The History Press, 2011.

Harrer, Heinrich: *Sieben Jahre in Tibet. Mein Leben am Hofe des Dalai Lama*. Berlin: Ullstein Taschenbuch, 2017 [1952].

Herzog, Maurice: *Annapurna. Premier 8000*. Paris: Arthaud, 1952.

Hillary, Edmund: *High Adventure*. London: Hodder & Stoughton, 1955.

Hilton, James: *Lost Horizon*. London: Vintage Books, 2015 [1933].

Hopkirk, Peter: *Trespassers on the Roof of the World. The Secret Exploration of Tibet*. Los Angeles: Kodansha, 1995 [1982].

Hopkirk, Peter: *The Great Game. On Secret Service in High Asia*. London: John Murray, 2006 [1990].

Kawaguchi, Ekai: *Three Years in Tibet*. Benares and London: Theosophical Publishing Society, 1909 (Kindle edition from 2016).

Keane, Fergal: *Road of Bones. The Siege of Kohima 1944. The Epic Story of the Last Great Stand of Empire*. London: William Collins, 2010.

Keay, John: *The Gilgit Game*. London: John Murray, 1979.

Khan, Yasmin: *The Great Partition. The Making of India and Pakistan*. New Haven and London: Yale University Press, 2017 [2007].

Koehler, Jeff: *Darjeeling. A History of the World's Greatest Tea*. New York: Bloomsbury, 2015.

Krakauer, Jon: *Into Thin Air. A Personal Account of the Mt. Everest Disaster*. New York: Anchor Books, 1999 [1997].

Kumar, Radha: *Paradise at War. A Political History of Kashmir*. New Delhi: Aleph Book Company, 2018.

Lane Fox, Robin: *Alexander the Great*. London: Penguin Books, 2004 [1973].

Lieven, Anatol: *Pakistan. A Hard Country*. New York: Public Affairs, 2011.

Macfarlane, Robert: *Mountains of the Mind. A History of a Fascination*. London: Granta, 2003.

Mallet, Victor: *River of Life. River of Death. The Ganges and India's Future*. Oxford: Oxford University Press, 2017.

Matthiessen, Peter: *The Snow Leopard*. New York: Penguin Books, 2008 [1978].

McLynn, Frank: *The Burma Campaign. Disaster into Triumph 1942–45*. New Haven: Yale University Press, 2011.

Mitchell, David: *Tea, Love and War. Searching for English Roots in Assam*. Leicestershire: Matador, 2011.

Notovitch, Nicolas: *The Unknown Life of Jesus Christ*. Translated by J.H. Connelly and L. Landsberg. New York: R.F. Fenno, 1890.

Palin, Michael: *Himalaya*. London: Weidenfeld & Nicolson, 2009 [2004].

Phuntsho, Karma: *The History of Bhutan*. New Delhi: Penguin Random House India, 2018 [2013].

Pierre, Bernard: *Ils ont conquis l'Himalaya*. Paris: Plon, 1979.

Rampa, T. Lobsang: *The Third Eye. The Autobiography of a Tibetan Lama*. London: Secker & Warburg, 1956.

Salisbury, Richard and Hawley, Elizabeth: *The Himalaya by the Numbers. A Statistical Analysis of Mountaineering in the Nepal Himalaya*. Kathmandu: Vajra Publications, 2011.

Schaik, Sam van: *Tibet. A History*. New Haven and London: Yale University Press, 2011.

Searle, Mike: *Colliding Continents. A Geological Exploration of the Himalaya, Karakoram, & Tibet*. Oxford: Oxford University Press, 2017 [2013].

Shakya, Tsering: *The Dragon in the Land of Snows. A History of Modern Tibet Since 1947*. London: Penguin Compass, 2000 [1999].

Shipton, Diana: *The Antique Land*. Oxford: Oxford University Press, 1987 [1950].

Shipton, Eric: *Mountains of Tartary*. London: Hodder & Stoughton, 1953.

Skrede, Wilfred: *Veien over verdens tak*. Oslo: Gyldendal Norsk Forlag, 1949.

Snelling, John: *Buddhism in Russia. The Story of Agvan Dorzhiev, Lhasa's Emissary to the Tsar*. Dorset: Element Books, 1993.

Spitz, Bob: *The Beatles. The Biography*. New York: Little, Brown and Company, 2005.

Strittmatter, Kai: *We Have Been Harmonized. Life In China's Surveillance State*. Translated by Ruth Martin. Exeter: Old Street Publishing, 2019.

Svensen, Henrik: *Bergtatt. Fjellenes historie og fascinasjonen for det opphøyde*. Oslo: Aschehoug, 2019 [2011].

Sæbø, Sun Heidi: *Kina. Den nye supermakten. Jakten på Xi Jinping og det moderne Kina*. Oslo: Kagge, 2019.

Talbot, Ian: *Pakistan. A New History.* London: Hurst & Company, 2015 [2012].

Theroux, Paul: *The Great Railway Bazaar.* Boston: Mariner Books, 2006 [1975].

Thubron, Colin: *To a Mountain in Tibet.* London: Chatto & Windus, 2011.

Tree, Isabella: *The Living Goddess.* Haryana: Penguin Random House India, 2014.

Ward, Michael: *Everest. A Thousand Years of Exploration.* Cumbria: Hayloft Publishing, 2013 [2003].

Whelpton, John: *A History of Nepal.* Cambridge: Cambridge University Press, 2012 [2005].

Winchester, Simon: *The River at the Centre of the World. A Journey up the Yangtze, and Back in Chinese Time.* London: Penguin Books, 1996.

Woodman, Dorothy: *Himalayan Frontiers. A Political Review of British, Chinese, Indian and Russian Rivalries.* London: Barrie & Rockliff, The Cresset Press, 1969.

Younghusband, Francis: *Kashmir.* London: Adam and Charles Black, 1909.

Younghusband, Francis: *The Heart of a Continent. A Narrative of Travels in Manchuria, across the Gobi Desert, through the Himalayas, the Pamirs, and Chitral 1884–1894.* New Delhi: Rupa Publications, 2013 [1896].

Notes

1   Marco Polo: *The Travels,* Penguin Classics, Penguin Random House UK, 2016, p. 53.

2   *Across the Roof of the World* by Wilfred Skrede.

3   *The Heart of a Continent. A Narrative of Travels in Manchuria, Across the Gobi Desert, through the Himalayas, the Pamirs, and Chitral 1884–1894* by Francis Younghusband, New York: Charles Scribner's Sons, 1896, p. 272.

4   Ibid. p. 286.

5   *The Unknown Life of Jesus Christ,* the original text of Nicolas Notovitch's 1887 discovery, by Nicolas Notovitch, translated by J.H. Connelly and L. Landsberg, New York: R. F. Fenno, 1890.

6   https://kuenselonline.com/coronation-of-the-peoples-king/

7   https://kuenselonline.com/coronation-of-the-peoples-king/

8   *Road of Bones: The Siege of Kohima 1944 – The Epic Story of the Last Great Stand of Empire* by Fergal Keane. London: William Collins, 2010, Chapter 24, p. 390.

9   *The Burma Campaign: Disaster into Triumph 1942–45* by Frank McLynn. New Haven: Yale University Press, 2011, p. 321.

10 https://www.regjeringen.no/globalassets/departementene/ud/vedlegg/statement_kina.pdf

11 *Three Years in Tibet* by Ekai Kawaguchi, Project Guthenberg Ebook, 2016, p. 409.

12 Ibid, p. 265.

13 *Trespassers on the Roof of the World. The Secret Exploration of Tibet* by Peter Hopkirk. New York: Kodansha USA, 1995 [1982], p. 75.

14 Ibid. p. 184.

15 Ibid. p. 193.

16 *Tibet. A History* by Sam van Schaik. New Haven: Yale University Press, 2011.

17 "Dalai Lama's reincarnation must comply with China's laws, Communist Party says." By Ben Westcott. Downloaded on 26 May 2020. https://edition.cnn.com/2019/04/11/asia/dalai-lama-beijing-tibet-china-intl/index.html

ERIKA FATLAND was born in 1983 and studied Social Anthropology at the University of Oslo. Her 2011 book, *The Village of Angels*, was an *in situ* report on the Beslan terror attacks of 2004 and she is also the author of *The Year Without Summer*, describing the harrowing year that followed the massacre on Utøya in 2011. For *Sovietistan* (2019) she was shortlisted for the Edward Stanford/Lonely Planet Debut Travel Writer of the Year, and *The Border* (2020) was shortlisted for the Stanford Dolman Travel Book of the Year. She speaks eight languages and, when not travelling, lives in Oslo.

KARI DICKSON is a translator from Norwegian of literary fiction, crime fiction, children's books, theatre and non-fiction. She is also an occasional tutor in Norwegian language, literature and translation at the University of Edinburgh, and has worked with the British Centre for Literary Translation at the National Centre for Writing in Norwich.

Second stage

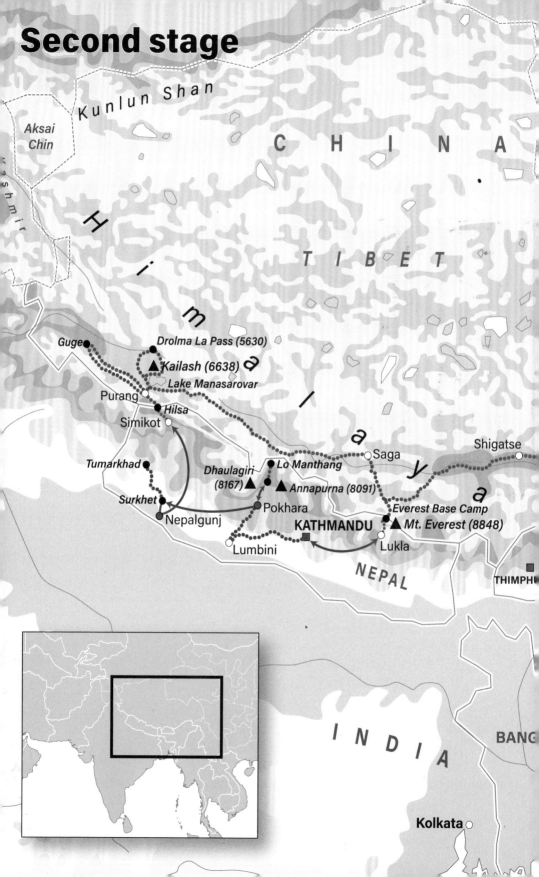